Religion and the American Experience

A Social and Cultural History, 1765-1997

RELIGION

and the

American Experience

Donald C. Swift

M.E. Sharpe
ARMONK, NEW YORK
LONDON, ENGLAND

Library of Congress Cataloging-in-Publication Data

Swift, Donald Charles, 1937–
Religion and the American experience: a social and cultural history,
1765–1997 / Donald C. Swift
p.   cm.
Includes bibliographical references and index.
Illustrations reproduced from the Collections of the Library of Congress.
ISBN 0-7656-0133-8 (hc : alk. paper).   ISBN 0-7656-0134-6 (pbk. : alk. paper)
1. United States—Religion. 2. Religion and culture—United States.
3. Religion and sociology—United States. I. Title.
BL2525.S95   1997
200'.973—dc21
97-25937
CIP

Printed in the United States of America

The paper used in this publication meets the minimum requirements of the
American National Standard for Information Sciences—
Permanence of Paper for Printed Library Materials,
ANSI Z 39.48-1984.

∞

BM (c)   10   9   8   7   6   5   4   3   2   1
BM (p)   10   9   8   7   6   5   4   3   2

To Anne, my partner in life.

Contents

Illustrations

Introduction

It has been said the United States is a nation with the soul of a church. Prominent literary critic Harold Bloom has observed that "The United States of America is a religion-mad country."

There has been a veritable explosion in American studies, and much new ground has been plowed. This recent surge in American religious studies indicates that scholars consider religious history central to understanding the American past. Nevertheless, textbooks at all levels of education do not reflect the growing importance of religion as a means of understanding American culture, politics, and society.

This overview of the impact of religion on American society is intended for the general reader. It is also intended for classes dealing with American social history and as supplemental reading in classes that survey the history of the United States. Substantial knowledge of religious developments is essential to understanding the American experience.

Religious concerns and a worldview rooted in religious concepts contributed to the coming of the American Revolution. Since the 1790s, religion has had a substantial impact upon politics and party affiliation. When considered in conjunction with ethnic identities, religion has been a significant variable used in interpreting political developments throughout much of our history. By the decades preceding the Civil War, it was possible to describe American politics in terms of an ethnocultural interpretation—one in which religious affiliation was a key factor in accounting for whether a person was a Whig or a Republican or a Democrat. Today, the religious right plays a major role in the nation's politics and has contributed greatly to Republican success at the polls.

Disagreements and hostilities between religious groups often reflected important societal changes and divisions. Through much of the nineteenth century, the mutual antagonism of Scots-Irish Presbyterians and Irish Catholics erupted in violence and was an important determinant of political allegiance. Many humble folk joined revivalistic religions and sects as a means of asserting their equality and respectability. For some, the church was a haven. Immigrants who had not practiced their religions in the old country often became devout here as the church sheltered them from hostile nativists and accepted their cultural distinctiveness.

Divisions among religious groups often can be seen as reflections of social stratification, but involved much more. There was a spiritual dimension to these activities—what went on between the individual and her or his maker. This was a major factor but it is beyond the scope of this work.

In the early nineteenth century, some responded to social change by becoming "come-outers," joining new or relatively new churches, such as the Church of Jesus Christ of Latter-day Saints or the Methodist Episcopal Church. Spiritualism appealed to some of these people. Communitarian movements were attractive to those who wanted a sharp break with former modes of thinking and living. Many became involved in revivalistic wings of existing churches.

Frequently, American religions have begun as reactions to prevailing socioeconomic conditions, initially standing outside the pale of respectability, as was often the case with early Methodists and Baptists. Eventually many of them would be accepted, partly through accommodation. This has been the dominant pattern for churches to respond to modernity; they increasingly make peace with the general culture by adopting rational and pragmatic approaches to society. As denominations grew in size and social acceptability, their success eventually conferred respectability upon practices initially seen as odd or eccentric. Some individuals were nonbelievers but wanted to keep the church in their community. They may have seen it as a stabilizing factor in times of change.

In the first half of the nineteenth century, the United States experienced a wave of religious convulsions that greatly influenced American society and culture. Religious principles would underpin the perfervid arguments of abolitionists; other elements of religious thought would be employed by southerners to defend slavery and secession. The upsurge of religious enthusiasm spawned a panoply of social reform movements and served as the basis of subsequent reform efforts.

People use religion to define themselves. In the United States, populated by people of many different origins, religion defined and differentiated groups. For most of American history, people put physical or cultural distance between themselves and others. It was a segmented society, and religion was a way of demonstrating distinctiveness. Theology, the ultimate expression of a people's values, was at least as important as place of origin or language as the basis of subgroup identity. Communities defined themselves and communicated with others through religion. Churches provided society with rites of passage that helped people deal with difficulties associated with birth, adolescence, marriage, and death.

The French observer Alexis de Tocqueville was very much on target in noting that religion was the most important American institution. The religious experience was central to American life and related to all aspects of life. He noted that religion provided cohesion for American society and was used to cloak with legitimacy national goals and interests. In this sense, Tocqueville seemed to be discussing what would be called American civil religion or the religion of the republic. Civil religion is a term used to describe those religious rites and beliefs that relate to nationhood and God's plans for the nation. It could be described as a hybrid of American nationalism and Judeo-Christian values; it tied America's place in history and the individual citizen's role to ultimate questions of meaning and existence. This was more than national self-worship. It encompassed a common set of values that gave coherence to American culture. It emerged during the revolutionary era, stressing providential guidance in the quest for national unity, liberty, and independence. Americans were to be God's agents in proclaiming the gospel of liberty to mankind. It is ironic that deist Thomas Jefferson wrote so much of civil religion's catechism, beginning with the Declaration of Independence. In times of war, it was used to demonize opponents. Civil religion evolved over time, existed in different versions, and was not accepted by all. The African American slave would have had difficulty believing it brought liberty to all. The Roman Catholic, anxious to be a good citizen, would accept much of the myth but not its close identification with Protestantism. Mormons objected to its use in attacking polygamy.

In today's society, characterized by emphasis upon multiculturalism and diversity, civil religion is not the potent force it once was, and many claim it never existed. Though it no longer appears to be a major force in this land of diversity, it certainly did have a key, integrative function prior to contemporary times.

By exploring the religious experience as the taproot of American culture, it is possible to develop a fuller understanding of political, social, economic, and cultural developments. Knowledge of the cultural and social history of American religion greatly facilitates understanding the complexities we call the American people and American culture. The dynamic of American history has involved the interaction of subcultures, and understanding of this process will be of great assistance in dealing with pluralism and multiculturalism today. Study of religious developments facilitates the study of diversity while sometimes revealing integrative themes. Though it reveals many intricacies and contradictions, it exposes more than a small measure of cultural coherence. The social history of American religion is a huge subject. It has been impossible to deal with all of its facets, and it is hoped that the reader will be satisfied with this selection of topics, and that this will contribute in a small way to a deeper understanding of American history.

Bibliography

Bailey, Edward. "The Implicit Religion of Contemporary Society: Some Studies and Reflections." *Social Compass* 37, no. 4 (1990): 483–497.

Berger, Peter L. *The Social Reality of Religion.* London: Faber and Faber, 1969.

Bloom, Harold. *The American Religion: The Emergence of the Post-Christian Nation.* New York: Simon and Schuster, 1992.

Butler, Jon. "Historiographical Heresy: Catholicism as a Model for American Religious History." In *Belief in History: Innovative Approaches to European and American Religion,* ed. Thomas Kselman, pp. 286–309. Notre Dame: University of Notre Dame Press, 1991.

Campbell, Joseph, with Bill Moyers. *The Power of Myth.* Garden City: Doubleday, 1988.

Caplow, Theodore. "Tocqueville and Religion: Introduction." *Social Compass* 38 (September 1991): 211–213.

Dean, William. "Religion and the American Public Philosophy." *Religion and American Culture* 1 (winter 1991): 47–72.

Finke, Roger, and Rodney Stark. *The Churching of America, 1776–1990: Winners and Losers in Our Religious Economy.* New Brunswick: Rutgers University Press, 1992.

Geertz, Clifford. "Religion as a Cultural System." In *Anthropological Approaches to the Study of Religion,* ed. Michael Banton, pp. 1–46. Edinburgh, Scotland: Tavistock Publications, 1966.

Gehrig, Gail. *American Civil Religion: An Assessment.* Storrs, CT: Society for the Scientific Study of Religion, 1981.

Hammond, Philip E., Amanda Porterfield, James G. Moseley, and Jonathan D. Sarna. "Forum: American Civil Religion Revisited." *Religion and American Culture* 4 (winter 1994): 1–23.

Handy, Robert T. *A Christian America: Protestant Hopes and Historical Realities.* New York: Oxford University Press, 1984.

Koritansky, John C. "Civil Religion in Tocqueville's *Democracy in America.*" *Interpretation* 17 (spring 1990): 389–400.

Marsden, George M. "Afterword: Religion, Politics, and the Search for an American Consensus." In *Religion and American Politics: From the Colonial Period to the 1980s,* ed. Mark A. Noll, pp. 380–390. New York: Oxford University Press, 1990.

McGuire, Meredith B. *Religion: The Social Context.* Belmont, CA: Wadsworth, 1992.

Thomas, George M. *Revivalism and Cultural Change: Christianity, Nation Building, and the Market in the Nineteenth-Century United States.* Urbana: University of Illinois Press, 1989.

Tocqueville, Alexis de. *Democracy in America.* Trans. George Lawrence. Ed. J.P. Mayer and Max Lerner. Garden City: Doubleday, 1969.

Wiebe, Robert. *The Segmented Society: An Introduction to the Meaning of America.* New York: Oxford University Press, 1975.

Williams, Peter W. *Popular Religion in America: Symbolic Change and the Modernization Process.* Urbana: University of Illinois Press, 1989.

Religion and the American Experience

One

Religion in the New Republic

Religion played a major role in the revolution, and the revolutionary experience had a great impact upon American religious life. At the least, the revolution led to significant changes in ecclesiastical organizational arrangements. Support for the revolution did not come in equal measure from all the religious communities. The revolution was not only a political struggle, but it had a strong religious dimension. Religious considerations influenced the political views and allegiances of many Americans. Sometimes the relationship between religious affiliations and positions on the revolution reflected socioeconomic and geographical factors. The revolutionary emphasis on liberty and equality fueled the growth of some denominations, such as the Baptists and Methodists, and would also affect theology and the ways people worshiped.

Loyalists charged that the American Revolution was the result of a Calvinist conspiracy to sever the connection with the Mother Country and create a republic. The "conspiracy" existed only in the minds of the revolution's opponents, but the involvement of Congregationalists and Presbyterians in the patriot cause was great. It is possible to question whether the war of independence would have occurred had Calvinists not been present in large numbers in eighteenth-century provincial America. Through annual election sermons, Congregationalists had learned to fear abuses of governmental power, valued natural rights and constitutionalism, and understood the citizen's responsibility to resist tyranny. The revolution was more than a Calvinist uprising, but these heirs to the radical Protestant tradition played a central role in shaping it and winning independence. There were more Calvinists than other Protestants in revolutionary America, and their religious mind-set proved fertile ground for the development of a revolutionary mentality.

Impact of the Great Awakening

Among the American Calvinists, those whose views were shaped by the Great Awakening were often the most fervent supporters of the patriot cause. The Awakening was a great evangelical movement that stressed revivalism, personal religious experience, and orthodox Calvinism, and it crested in the North in the 1730s and 1740s. It became an important force in the South in the latter decade and lost force there in the 1770s. Because it was directed at leading people to orthodox Calvinism, it affected mainly Calvinistic denominations. It led to the fracturing of denominations, with Congregational supporters of the revival being called New Lights, and its Presbyterian adherents being called New Sides. Adherents of the Awakening were called New Lights—a term that will be used here to describe the awakened—because they insisted that the individual must experience a conscious conversion that marked Christ's illumination of the soul of the saved. Frequently finding it necessary to leave settled and tithe-supported congregations, the New Lights were also called Separates. The Separates frequently became Baptists—or Separate Baptists—after they concluded that infant baptism was wrong and that God ordained that a believer's baptism was necessary for the purity of the church. For them, immersion in water fully represented the complete rebirth of the believer.

In the South, there were clear class divisions between the awakened— poor and modestly situated farmers of the backcountry—and planter-led Anglicans who were frequently found in coastal areas. In New England, these socioeconomic divisions are less easily found. There were wealthy people among the New Lights, but to the converted, status was based on religious experience and not wealth and birth.

The awakened supported religious toleration for Protestants. Their advocacy of religious freedom would blossom into a somewhat democratic political philosophy that emphasized both the ability of the individual to make political judgments and God's concern that people live in freedom. Their voluntarism in religion led to the conviction that people should decide for themselves how they should be governed. These evangelicals believed that the saved were guided by the Holy Spirit, and the awakened emphasized the community's general will rather than simply the consent of the governed. Religion was rooted in personal experience rather than in doctrine; similarly their notions of the will, virtue, liberty, equality, and fraternity were founded upon their own experiences rather than reasoning. Their desire for unity and liberty of all believers made it possible for them to overcome a tendency toward religious tribalism and to focus on larger objectives. Through revivalism, the awakened had acquired an aspiration for unity of believers that provided a basis for demanding unity of Americans and separation from sinful Britain.

In the revolution, Old Lights and New Lights would stand together in resisting British tyranny, but the New Lights were inclined to be more radical. Rough treatment at the hands of Old Light civil authorities made New Lights reflect deeply on the rights of minorities. In the ante-revolution years, New England politics centered in the competition between the New Lights and Old Lights. These groups shared the fear that the Crown would establish Anglican bishoprics in America. Dread of this prospect was an important factor in leading to the revolution.

An American Mission

Though liberty and individualism were important in colonial America before the Great Awakening, the Awakening placed more emphasis on these values; individualism, over the long term, would contribute significantly to the decline of deference in American society. No one had given more thought to the rights of minorities than the Separate Baptists who fought many battles with the entrenched Old Lights over tithing and religious freedom.

Some evangelicals saw the revolutionary struggle in terms of millennial theology. Millennialism, the belief in the second coming of Christ and his thousand-year reign, would be a major theme in nineteenth-century American thought. Through the revolution, they believed, God was assisting the United States, an elect nation, in winning Christian liberty. The divinely ordained nation that would be blessed by brotherhood, peace, liberty, and justice would play a major role in battling evil and bringing about the thousand-year reign of Christ and the second coming.

Those influenced by the Awakening thought it necessary to sever the linkage with sinful Great Britain in order to obtain this status. Evangelical laymen were familiar enough with millennial imagery that they could interpret historical events in this way without explicit sermons laying out this scenario. Popular religion and culture were so steeped in this thought that application of these ideas to historical events resulted in a form of prophecy. During the French and Indian War, New England evangelicals had grown accustomed to thinking of themselves being locked in a massive struggle with Satan, whose agent was Catholic France. Now, they saw an acceleration of the struggle, and this time the devil's surrogate was Great Britain. For them there was no question whose side God supported. A popular hymn by William Billings makes it clear that the patriots were certain God was on their side:

> Let tyrants shake their iron rod,
> And slavery clank her galling chains;
> We fear them not, we trust in God—
> New England's God for ever reigns.

When God inspired us for the fight.
Their ranks were broken, their lines were forced;
Their ships were shattered in our sight,
Or swiftly driven from our coast.

What grateful offering shall we bring?
What shall we render to the Lord?
Loud hallelujahs let us sing,
And praise his name on every chord.

New England clergymen most closely in touch with the thought of Jonathan Edwards avoided civil millennialism, spoke about the sinfulness of slavery in America, and argued that a society cannot prosper if its citizens are not virtuous. God governed the world and nations through moral law. However, they saw British rulers as embodying political corruption and sinfulness, the very opposite of government based on divine law. They also insisted that Americans would win the great struggle against degenerate Britain's tyranny because the patriot cause was consistent with God's laws. Anglican efforts to obtain advantages from government and bishops in the colonies led New Englanders to interpret their history in a new manner. New England's founders were cast as men deeply committed to religious and political liberty. They came to the New World when they saw that these liberties were in peril in Great Britain.

During the troubled years prior to the Revolutionary War, writers outside of New England would view the American past in the same way. In the poem *Liberty Song,* John Dickinson wrote that "Our worthy forefathers . . . for freedom . . . came, And, dying, bequeath'd us their freedom and fame." Another Pennsylvanian, Benjamin Rush, proudly claimed that his passionate attachment to liberty had been "Early cultivated by ancestors." Dr. Rush had been a convinced republican since his student days in Edinburgh, Scotland.

In an address to King George III, the Continental Congress expressed its gratitude that God permitted them to be heirs to freedom. A myth of liberty took shape, embodying a people's vision of its origins, highest values, and place in history. In it, Americans traced their devotion to freedom to their ancestors' attachment to liberty of conscience. A symbol of these beliefs was the liberty tree from which effigy figures were often hung. In European folk belief, a tree represented creative and renewing forces; by touching the sky it linked the divine and human realms. In this tree, life forces were identified with liberty, and it sometimes needed to be fertilized with blood. The myth of liberty would become the basis of a civil faith or civil religion that allowed Americans, who lacked a single religious heritage, to explain their past and present in religious terms. A religion located "at the boundaries of the denominations and the state," it was based on the idea that God planned for Americans to lead others in the pursuit of liberty.

The liberty myth possessed great vitality and commanded the allegiance of many Americans, whereas the Loyalists lacked a cogent myth that could explain the American experience and attract similar numbers to their cause. Years later, in his first inaugural address, George Washington offered a classic restatement of American civic religion: "Every step, by which [the people of the United States] have advanced to the character of an independent nation, seems to have been distinguished by some token of providential agency."

Belief in this myth of liberty made it possible for large numbers of Americans to accept the political arguments of the True or Real Whigs, a small group of radicals who believed that the Crown and its supporters were conspiring against constitutional government and the liberties of Englishmen on both sides of the Atlantic. Calvinistic political thought, which emphasized natural law and the idea that rights were conferred by God, prepared Americans for the ideas of the True Whigs. Two of the earliest and most important of these radical Whigs were John Trenchard and Thomas Gordon, authors of *Cato's Letters*. Their political philosophy was rooted in the traditions of the English Civil War and Glorious Revolution, which were shared by English Calvinists in America. These radicals believed that placemen—those enjoying the patronage of holding government positions—were motivated by greed and the desire for more power. Though essentially republicans, they did not call for the abolition of the monarchy.

True Whigs defended individual liberties, called for the curbing of executive power, and often advocated reforms quite radical for Britain but not too far in advance of actual practice in many colonies. They believed that God would support oppressed people who found it necessary to defend their rights against tyrants. Trenchard and Gordon argued that when civil authorities refused to act justly, "we must have recourse to Heaven." The embattled patriots were to echo this theme. The True Whigs' fear of the Church of England and call for toleration of dissenting Protestants appealed to American dissenters, and the political reforms they advocated were often close to American practices. New World Calvinists also heartily endorsed the argument that the people are the ultimate source of political power and, given significant justification, can opt to alter forms of government. Rooted in both their secular and religious outlook was their common belief that men tend to be corrupted by political power and that it was dangerous to give the state too many powers.

The New Lights were particularly inclined to accept the view that there was a massive conspiracy against liberty and that debauchery and sinfulness had weakened England to the point where tyranny could not be resisted.

The argumentative style of the True Whigs was forcefully clear, unadorned, and directed at the common man, very much as was preaching in the tradition of the Awakening. Doubtless the Awakening's rhetorical style made Americans particularly receptive to Thomas Paine's *Common Sense,* which applied radical or True Whig principles to the American situation in 1776 in a manner that especially appealed to the ordinary reader. These radical theories were rooted in both classical republican and Lockean thought. New England clergymen nurtured their congregations on frequent doses of John Locke's Christian liberalism. Locke maintained that it was God's will that each individual study Scripture for himself and make his own judgments about salvation. The English philosopher found this position in St. Paul's Epistles to the Romans. If the individual had the duty of making judgments about salvation, then the free Christian was also obligated to evaluate the performance of government and decide whether or not to obey it. Based on this thinking, New England ministers were to see liberty as God's cause and conclude that free Christians had the obligation to take up arms in defense of liberty.

With the decision for independence, the belief in a providentially guided quest for liberty became the basis for identifying liberty with God-fearing Americans in a republic. Separation from Great Britain and independence were necessary steps toward the realization of a thousand-year reign of Christ. Collective salvation had a political dimension. The republic was identified as the collectivity of God's people in America; patriotism was considered a response to the commands of God; and virtue was defined in terms of both republican ideology and Christian theology. Evangelicals, seeing freedom in a moralistic framework, spoke of the problems growing out of governance by an unconverted king and Parliament. They believed that a good society was one in which all of the saved enjoyed equality and brotherhood and were ruled by men who observed God's ordinances. In their view, George III became the Antichrist and the Tories were the enemies of God. The American patriots emerged as the people of God.

Revolutionary Americans came to see independence and the establishment of a republic as part of God's plan for America. The patriots, likening themselves to God's chosen people in holy scriptures, saw their cause as "a protest of native piety against foreign impiety." New England Calvinist clergy had long focused their congregations' attention upon a covenant between God and his or her people. By the mid-1770s, patriot ministers in that region stretched the covenant to include all Americans. They spoke more frequently about the prospect of the millennium. After independence was declared, they saw the breach with England as a major step in hastening the coming of God's kingdom on earth. There are indications that the Calvinist clergy of the southern and middle regions developed similar concepts in their sermons, but support of the revolution was not confined to Calvinistic and millennialist clergy.

Patriots, Loyalists, and Neutrals

A Hessian soldier wrote home that the revolution was not "an American Rebellion, it is nothing more nor less than an Irish-Scotch Presbyterian Rebellion." Horace Walpole, considering Presbyterians and Congregationalists the same sect, quipped, "America has run off with a Presbyterian parson, and that is the end of it." It was noted in September, 1775, that among Maryland Presbyterians "an itch for independence exists" and "they make no secret of it." The New England Loyalist Peter Oliver claimed that "Mr. Otis's black regiment, the dissenting clergy," played a major role in bringing about the American Revolution. In Pennsylvania, Presbyterians were the most important patriot group. They were joined by most of the English-speaking members of the German Reformed and Lutheran churches. The less assimilated, German-speaking members of those faiths were likely to support the Crown.

Most of Virginia's patriot leaders were wealthy planters affiliated with the Anglican Church. They found it necessary to ally with religious dissenters whom they had harassed and upon whom they had heaped scorn. Back-country Presbyterians had been harassed by the authorities and sought guarantees of religious liberties. By 1758, these people were numerous enough to be able to demand of candidates for election protection of the Presbyterians' civil and religious liberties.

While the Presbyterians had some educated clergymen and country gentlemen, the Baptists did not require their clergymen to be educated, and they appealed to humble folk. Their very presence was seen by the Tidewater aristocracy as a threat and a condemnation of Virginia gentry. Baptists opposed the lifestyle of the country gentry by denouncing dancing, gambling, horse racing, drunkenness, quarrels over property, slander, and violations of the Sabbath. They were a standing rebuke to the traditional, Anglican culture of the South. In 1769, there were seven Separate Baptist congregations in Virginia; five years later there were fifty-four. Rejecting what they saw as a disorderly, sinful society marked by convivial excess, Baptists created among themselves a closed, corporate community that provided acceptance and emotional support for its members. Baptist congregations had mechanisms for policing the lives of their members and ejecting unrepentant, recalcitrant sinners. Their religious practices of foot washing, anointing the sick, the kiss of peace, and the laying on of hands encouraged an equalitarian outlook.

Regular Baptists questioned revivalism and were willing to apply for preaching licenses. In 1770, Baptists began petitioning for complete religious liberties, including exemption from taxation to support the Anglican Church. Six years later, they indicated their willingness to join Tidewater aristocrats in the war for independence if granted religious equality and the disestablishment of the Anglican Church. In 1775, Virginia accorded dissenters in the militia the right to hold their own religious services rather than attend those conducted by Anglican chaplains. The Methodists, who were also evangelicals and considered lacking in social respectability, did not support the revolution and preached pacifism. In England, their founder, John Wesley, called upon them to accept the rule of King George III and Parliament.

Obtaining the allegiance of Protestant dissenters in the backcountry of the South was considered crucial to the success of the patriot cause. The Continental Congress funded a four-month tour of two Presbyterian clergymen to win support in the frontier areas of the Carolinas. Reverend William Tennent and William Henry Dayton, a member of the provincial congress, spoke in the Carolina backcountry in an effort to win support for the patriots. Tennent won the support of some local Presbyterian clergymen, and he also recruited German preachers to work for the revolutionary cause among their people. John Witherspoon, president of the College of New Jersey (Princeton) and a member of Congress, wrote a plea to Scots in the southern backcountry urging their support of the patriot cause. Other clergymen were recruited to send similar pleas to southern dissenters.

Of course, the revolution also attracted the support of non-Calvinists. A majority of Anglican laity in the South and a significant number of those in the North supported the revolution. Two-thirds of the signers of the Declaration of Independence were nominally Anglicans. A majority of Anglican clergy opposed the revolution; about 150 priests were Loyalists, and 123 have been identified as patriots. Anglican priests were Loyalists in proportion to their church's weakness in the colonies in which they resided. Tory Anglican clergymen such as Samuel Seabury and Charles Inglis of New York played important roles in the literary warfare between Loyalists and patriots. Many Tory clergy left the country rather than live outside the jurisdiction of the Crown.

Every denomination had some Loyalist clergy. Among the Dutch Reformed, those clergy and laity who were most assimilated and favored the ordination of clergy in America backed the revolution while traditionalists were usually Tories. Older Lutheran clergy were likely to be Tories, while patriots tended to attract younger and more assimilated Lutherans. Henry M. Muhlenberg remained a supporter of the House of Hanover, while his sons played active roles in the patriot ranks. Quaker patriots were disowned by their meetings as the Society of Friends took a neutral position and refused to support the insurrection. For many this position reflected not only genuine attachment to pacifist principles but fear of Calvinist domination. German pietists also tended to take a neutral position.

The revolutionary years were a difficult time for Quakers. In Pennsylvania, citizens were required to take an oath supporting the revolution and the new constitution of the state. Quakers who refused to take the oath were barred from voting and holding office. Some Quakers encountered additional difficulties because they refused to pay war taxes. Twelve Quaker leaders were arrested and sent into exile in Virginia. Among them were Israel and James Pemberton, Thomas Gilpin, and Henry Drinker. Many Pennsylvanians believed that those who were not with them were against them and saw the Quaker pacifists as Tories or Loyalists.

It is likely that a considerable number of Quakers did hope that Great Britain would win the war, but many Quakers ignored the guidance of their leaders and actively supported the revolution. By the end of the revolution, nine hundred Friends were disowned for supporting the revolution. In 1781, the disowned Friends created their own society, the Free Friends. They denounced the practice of disownment, claiming it was better to reason with an erring fellow Quaker than to disown. They defended defensive warfare and denounced "ecclesiastical tyranny."

Catholics and Jews

Catholics and Jews were overwhelmingly favorable to the patriot cause, although nowhere in the thirteen colonies could they hold high office. Catholics could worship openly in two colonies, but vote in none. Jews could vote and run for municipal office in New York, where there were several anti-Semitic incidents. Jews suffered prejudice everywhere, but they were permitted to worship openly. A minority of Jews backed Britain out of gratitude for the protection Jews enjoyed in the British Empire at a time when the people of Israel were suppressed in many lands. There were about two thousand Jews in the thirteen provinces at the time, and about one hundred were active in the revolution. Some were blockade runners, smuggling goods into the revolutionary American states, and others were contractors seeking to supply the patriot forces with goods produced in America. Several were military officers, including a few lieutenant colonels. Haym Salomon, of New York and Philadelphia, a Polish Jew and a member of the Sons of Liberty, was arrested by the British for helping burn British stores in New York, and subsequently escaped the Old Sugar House prison. He later was assistant to Superintendent of Finance Robert

Morris and the official broker for Congress, trading Continental currency for hard money. He loaned money to the Continental government, never presented a bill for repayment, and played an active role in the Philadelphia Jewish community. Other Jewish merchant patriots were Isaac Moses of Philadelphia, Aaron Lopez of Newport, Simon Nathan of Richmond, and Mordecai Sheftal of Savannah. Sheftal was a leading patriot whom the British arrested and placed on a prison ship.

In New York City, Congregation Shearith Israel was well accepted by its Protestant neighbors, in part because it would not accept as members converts from Christianity. During the revolution, Gresham Mendez Seixas, its cantor, led a number of Jewish patriots into exile from the British-occupied city. In 1787, he was named an incorporator of King's College (Columbia). The situation of Jews in America was not ideal, but American Jews enjoyed rights and acceptance denied Hebrew people in most other places in the world. Some ignorant gentiles blamed the economic problems of the revolutionary era on Jews, assuming that merchants who took advantage of wartime shortages had to be Jews. Denouncing the rights that the Quebec Act conferred upon Catholics, the First Continental Congress told Englishmen that the Roman Church "has deluged your island in blood, and dispersed impiety, bigotry, persecution, murder and rebellion through every part of the world." Despite this statement and the open bigotry of many patriot leaders, the great majority of the twenty thousand Catholics in the colonies supported the revolution. They opposed what they thought was British oppression and hoped that their own situation would improve in the independent states.

Priests played a significant role in supporting the war for American independence. Fathers Robert Harding and Robert Molyneux, who served successively as pastors at Philadelphia's St. Joseph's Church, were patriots. Harding was a member of the American Philosophical Society and had endorsed John Dickinson's *Letters from a Pennsylvania Farmer.* Their backgrounds were those of English Whigs and they learned natural law theories in seminaries, where they read Robert Cardinal Bellarmine and Spanish Jesuit Francişco Suarez. The Italian prelate wrote in opposition to tyranny, and neither writer was hostile to voluntarism in religion. Molyneux and Harding represented what has been called the "Maryland tradition," the somewhat liberalized approach to Catholicism found in America. Molyneux studied for a time at St. Omers, which Tory Daniel Dulany said was "the best seminary in the universe for the champions of civil and religious liberty." Charles Carroll of Carrollton, a signer of the Declaration of Independence, also spent some time at St. Omers, but he was determined not to give ordinary men very much political power.

There were Catholic Loyalists. Some Philadelphia Catholics fought for

Britain, and some Gaelic-speaking Scottish Catholics fought in two regiments that were involved in the efforts of Colonel Barry St. Leger to control parts in New York state in 1777. These Highland Scots had been forced to abandon their Mohawk Valley homes and flee to Canada. The revolution did improve the lot of America's most harassed religious minority, particularly in two states where most of them resided. In 1776, Pennsylvania gave Catholics political rights to match the full religious freedom they already enjoyed there. A year earlier, Maryland began to drop its penal laws against Roman Catholics. In most other places the position of Catholics improved. Even the Catholic Native Americans of Maine now won the consent of Massachusetts to permit a priest to live among them. Charles Carroll of Carrollton, a leading Maryland Catholic, was in sympathy with much of the political thought of the Real or True Whigs in England. Another Maryland Carroll, Daniel Carroll, and Thomas Fitzsimmons, of Pennsylvania, were signers of the Constitution of the United States. Charles Carroll and his distant cousin Father John Carroll accompanied Benjamin Franklin and Samuel Chase on an unsuccessful mission to win Canadian support for the revolution.

Fruits of the Revolution

Following the revolution, America moved closer to accepting fully the ideal of freedom of conscience in religious matters. Complete religious freedom existed in Virginia and Rhode Island, where there were no established churches and no one was deprived of citizenship rights on religious grounds. Great progress was made in all the states, and religious minorities could worship anywhere without harassment, even though New Hampshire and Connecticut carefully refused to guarantee toleration for Jews and Catholics. Catholics and Jews were forbidden to hold office in a number of states. Many states barred non-Christians from holding office, and Catholics were forbidden to vote or hold office everywhere in New England except Rhode Island. In addition, they were barred from public office in New York, New Jersey, North Carolina, and Georgia. For a time Pennsylvania and Tennessee required that public officials believe in life after death. Until 1880, eight states barred atheists from holding office. It was not until 1902 that the word "Protestant" in the New Hampshire constitution was changed to "Christian." In 1912 New Hampshire voters rejected an amendment that would have deleted the word "Christian" in favor of more inclusive language. Still, national sentiment was moving toward the ideal of full religious freedom.

The Northwest Ordinance of 1787 endorsed this principle and the federal Constitution stated that Congress shall require no religious test as a qualification of office. The First Amendment added that "Congress shall make no law respecting an establishment of religion, or prohibiting the free exercise thereof." People were now free to worship as they pleased or not worship at all. The South Carolina Anglican Commissary accurately reported to the Bishop of London that the revolutionaries were united in calling for "liberty, both civil and religious."

Virginia's Act Establishing Religious Freedom (1786) represented the era's most sweeping statement of the principle of religious freedom and disestablishment. Inspired by Thomas Jefferson and pushed through the legislature by James Madison, it was clearly intended to establish the principle of absolute separation of church and state. Madison insisted that religion's ally should not be the state; rather it should be reason. He wanted America to become "an Asylum to the persecuted" and thus be true to the principles of the revolution. Jefferson had also written that religion only needed the protection of reason because "truth is great and will prevail if left to herself . . . she is the proper and sufficient antagonist of error." He and Madison believed that the churches might possess greater moral influence if they were in no way beholden to the state. Yet there can be little doubt that most Americans did not share Jefferson's belief in absolute separation or his willingness to deny that the United States was a Christian state.

The Protestant dissenters who resented paying rates to support other Protestant churches considered the United States a Protestant nation and expected government to favor the Protestant religion without establishing particular sects. The Calvinists thought that if men were given liberty of conscience, they would eventually respond to God's will by becoming Calvinistic Protestants. Many were less than enthusiastic about according religious freedom to some despised minorities. Isaac Backus, the leading New England Baptist, never endorsed toleration of Catholics, Shakers, and Universalists. A "sweet harmony," they thought, should characterize church-state relations, with the state enforcing morality and assisting Protestants whenever possible. There was little objection to laws requiring regular attendance at Protestant services. The Scots-Irish Presbyterians who ruled revolutionary Pennsylvania wanted to establish a Christian commonwealth in which the rights of Catholics and Jews to worship would be curtailed. However, practical considerations prevented them from establishing a commonwealth with only limited freedom of conscience. From their perspective, however, such a commonwealth would have been most pleasing to God.

Public officials were expected to refer to the deity in their pronouncements, and officially proclaimed days of repentance and thanksgiving were the order of the day. New Hampshire retained a day of prayer and fasting until 1991, but in recent years it survived only as a work-free holiday for state employees. It was thought natural that the states assist church-owned or -dominated schools and colleges so long as the institutions were in the hands of major Protestant bodies.

The ideal of religious freedom encompassed more than separation of church and state. In revolutionary America, it meant the right to think for oneself about religious matters, free from restraints imposed by churches or the state. There was a crisis of authority in which all authority was called into question. Two of the dominant and most respectable churches, the Anglican and Congregationalist, would lose power and standing. Presbyterian clergy would also worry about declining ecclesiastical power. Elias Smith, a Massachusetts Baptist minister, reflected the spirit of the times when he ceased wearing clerical dress because it was a badge of respectability and was linked to times when clergy held the people "under mental bondage."

The growth of the Free Will Baptists was another expression of this yearning for freedom of conscience. Among them, Reverend Abner Jones accepted their ordination only if it was unnecessary for him to submit to a doctrinal test. Reverend William Smythe Babcock and his Vermont congregation broke ties with the Free Will Baptist meeting because this connection threatened their independence. This hostility to religious authority was also reflected in the brief popularity of deistic writings by Ethan Allen, Elihu Palmer, and Thomas Paine.

New Divinity Thought

The revolutionary spirit was reflected in the so-called New-Light Stir that marked the last years of the century. Many who were attracted to this movement were concerned that the latitudinarian ethics of a growing marketplace economy would erode traditional communal values and the republican spirit. The New Divinity thought of Reverend Samuel Hopkins is best considered in this context. Leaders of the New-Light Stir such as Hopkins and Sarah Osborn, who frequently spoke on religious subjects to mixed audiences, opposed economic principles rooted in selfishness. Both saw the rum trade and commerce in slaves as frightening symbols of the new economic order. The target of many of Hopkins's sermons and writings was the "ethic of enlightened self-interest." From a spiritual perspective, it was benighted, not enlightened. Hopkins thought that capitalism left few men uncorrupted and pointed to the benevolence and spiritual strength of women. The test of benevolence was the extent to which it did not serve the individual's self-interest or promote self-love. One approached Christian perfection through acts of disinterested benevolence. It was necessary to act consistently with the essential nature of God, which was benevolence. Salvation required looking after the downtrodden and poor—especially slaves. This emphasis on disinterested benevolence was the core of his New Divinity theology, which represented a refashioning of the thought of his mentor, Jonathan Edwards (Figure 1).

New Divinity thought took shape by the 1760s, and its advocates were sometimes called "Hopkinsonians." Samuel Hopkins had lived with and studied under Edwards in Northampton for several years and served in Newport, Rhode Island, from 1770 to 1803. He was committed to a social ethic that emphasized corporate responsibilities, communal harmony, and personal restraint. Hopkins worried that Edwards's acceptance of self-love could be used to promote departure from communal norms and responsibility. Hopkins was concerned that followers of the rational philosophers would find in Edwardsian thought theological grounds for maintaining that if every person pursued self-interest the greatest good for the greatest number would be served. Hopkins's doctrine of disinterested benevolence, which he maintained was rooted in the thought of his teacher, was intended to prevent a shift from communal ethics to individualistic ethics. His thought gave the evangelical movement a social activist thrust. Society, according to God's plan, was to be bound together by self-sacrificing love of God and neighbor. Hopkins lived out this theology in his own life, particularly through his crusade against slavery and the slave trade. Whereas Edwards identified good with an overall benevolence, Hopkins insisted on a theology of evangelical activism. Some of his followers were the first American missionaries to Asia, and others fought the slave trade and slavery, intemperance, and other evils. Some founded orphanages and Bible and educational societies. Social reform was to become a central part of the agenda of American evangelicals.

New Divinity thought would form the foundation for the theology of the Second Great Awakening. Its proponents emphasized that true virtue was disinterested in the sense that the saint followed Christ purely out of love of God. The true saint and patriot would habitually opt for the public good over private interests. A test of whether an individual was truly regenerated was whether one would favor acts of disinterested benevolence even if they might deprive one of eternal bliss.

Salvation depended upon moral perfection. This perfection could not have existed without disinterested benevolence, and perfection only existed to the extent that one was willing to be damned for the glory of God. To Hopkins, God was disinterested benevolence, and man must seek to emulate the nature of the Creator. Holiness, then, was disinterested benevolence.

Sarah Osborn of Newport was a strong advocate of Hopkins's views, and women like her thought that by taking a more active role in the church they could lead men to altruistic principles. Twice widowed, Osborn supported

SAMUEL M. HOPKINS, D. D.

HYDE PROFESSOR OF ECCLESIASTICAL HISTORY AND CHURCH POLITY

Theological Seminary, Auburn, N. Y.

Figure 1. Samuel Hopkins. Samuel Hopkins (1721–1803) was a student of Jonathan Edwards, whose views he restated, and a leader in New Divinity thought. It defined sin as selfishness and emphasized "disinterested benevolence" and had a strong influence on the Second Awakening and American reform thought. (Courtesy the Library of Congress.)

herself by teaching and taking in boarders. Her chief activity was discussing religious subjects with mixed audiences of African Americans and whites of all ages and both sexes. Baptists as well as Congregationalists attended her almost nightly meetings. She always took a humble posture with respect to her gifts for teaching religion. She was initially sponsored by Reverend Joseph Fish, but he eventually withdrew his support. For a time she had no clergyman to sponsor her, but Hopkins became her fast friend when he arrived in Newport. Osborn and Hopkins urged women to form voluntary benevolent associations through which they would work to create the Kingdom of God on earth and lead men toward altruistic attitudes and actions. Historian Hannah Adams of Cambridge, Massachusetts, anticipated this position when she urged female patriots to battle Satan's representative, Great Britain, through spiritual and benevolent activities. These associations sprung up in many places, particularly in New England. Later, during the Second Awakening, men would play leading roles in benevolent enterprises and would work to end the ladies' associations or strictly subordinate them to male-led efforts.

The Churches

As a result of the revolution, the Episcopalians, who had been one of the largest religions, lost membership, property, and status. The church would be disestablished in the South and in the four eastern counties of New York where it had enjoyed public support. The Congregational Church would remain established in New England until the 1830s, but the revolution set in motion forces that would weaken and then end its special position in the land of the Puritans. Roman Catholicism, one of the smallest religions, would reflect revolutionary influences in the desire of the clergy to elect their own bishop and in efforts of laymen to control church property. The revolution also affected other faiths in important ways. Three evangelical religions, Methodism, Baptism, and Presbyterianism, flourished in the early republic and reflected the individualism and equalitarianism of the age.

Christianity was being republicanized, and common folk were finding affirmation and community in two mushrooming denominations—the Baptist and the Methodist.

Ordinary people were concluding that they could decide for themselves what to believe. Radical Baptist Elias Smith claimed people must be free of creeds and catechism so that their decisions are based only on the scriptures. The Baptists benefited greatly from the antiauthoritarian spirit and they proliferated in part because formal education and theological training was not required of their preachers. Baptist ministers were often bivocational, supporting themselves with their own hands. They were multiplying with greatest rapidity in Kentucky and Tennessee.

Methodism had been transplanted from Britain to America on the eve of the revolution, and after the war a separate Methodist Episcopal Church emerged. Like the Baptists, Methodists enjoyed great success in attracting members from the lower orders of society. Like the Baptists, they held love feasts, and their quarterly meetings often were revivals. Though the Methodist Episcopal Church had bishops, it was not perceived as authoritarian. The Methodists were to build a substantial base in New York and Ohio and were active on the southern seaboard and in the Ohio valley and Kentucky. Around 1805, more than half of all American Protestants were Baptists or Methodists. The Baptists experienced the greatest growth in the revolutionary period, becoming the largest denomination by 1800. Before the revolution, there were fewer than 10,000 Baptists, and by the turn of the century they numbered 170,000. In 1780, the Methodists may have had as many as 50 congregations, in contrast to 400 for the Baptists and Episcopalians, about 750 for the Congregationalists, and 500 for the Presbyterians. By 1820, both the Methodists and Baptists claimed to have 2,700 congregations in the United States. By then, the Presbyterians had 1,700 and the Congregationalists 1,000 congregations. Virginia Baptist leaders thought the state would rapidly become "a Goshen for Israel to dwell in."

Evangelicals upheld communal love as opposed to the competitiveness of the market economy, calling one another "Brother" and "Sister." In fraternal manner, they helped one another with problems such as gambling, drinking, dishonesty, slander, and brawling. Baptists cherished a number of New Testament practices that deepened intimacy. Some congregations had public confessions in which members shared hopes and weaknesses with one another. Common Baptist practices were "feasts of charity" or "love feasts," "foot washing," "laying-on of hands," "the kiss of charity," anointing the sick, and exchanging the "right hand of fellowship." They celebrated the Lord's Supper regularly.

Religion and Political Affiliation

Religious affiliation was an important determinant of party affiliation in the early republic. In the so-called first party system, the Democratic-Republican followers of Thomas Jefferson and James Madison vied for power against the Federalists, who supported the Washington and Adams administrations and the economic policies of Alexander Hamilton. In the South, small farmers and producers felt oppressed by creditors and shared Thomas Jefferson's opposition to the "Anglican monarchical aristocratical party."

New Light Congregationalists, New Side Presbyterians, Methodists, and Baptists often shared the Jeffersonians' distrust of lawyers. They thought that lawyers were depraved and greedy, and they opposed the growing complexity of the legal system, which they thought served special interests and not common folk. These people, who found religious authority in the believer's heart and experience rather than in churches or highly educated clergymen, believed that lawyers sought to become a secular elite and were at least as dangerous and authoritarian as elite clergymen. They wanted simplified judicial principles and procedures, the appointment of lay judges, and arbitration tribunals that excluded lawyers. Most of the evangelicals who held these views were rural-minded people who had little exposure to commerce and finance.

In the cities and towns, those whose lives were shaped by market forces resisted these judicial reforms; they were better educated and more prosperous than the rural backers of radical judicial reform. Opponents of reform were often Old Light Congregationalists, Old Side Presbyterians, or Episcopalians who wanted a legal system that protected contracts and private property, reflected the complexities of the business environment, and would provide a stable atmosphere in which to do business.

Religion had its greatest influence upon political affiliation in the northern states. The Old Light Congregationalists tended to lend strong support to the Federalists. Many Congregational clergymen espoused the theory advanced by Reverend Jedidiah Morse that the French Revolution was brought about by conspiratorial free thinkers known as the Illuminati, who plotted to destroy religion and public morality. They saw Jefferson, a deist, and his party as an American extension of the Illuminati. Nevertheless Republicans drew considerable support from New England New Lights, who opposed legislation favoring the Old Lights. In Massachusetts, the Democratic-Republicans avoided taking a clear position in favor of disestablishment, but by degrees worked to respond to the dissenters' grievances. But the New Lights drifted into the Federalist camp once disestablishment was virtually accomplished. In the Bay State, essential disestablishment occurred in 1818, and its last vestiges were removed there in 1833. Baptists thought that separation of church and state was the most important issue in American life and gave solid support to the Republicans.

Presbyterians, many of whom were egalitarian Scots-Irishmen, disliked the British and those who yearned to enjoy the lifestyle of the English aristocracy. These sons of John Knox gave the Republicans strong backing. In the Middle Atlantic states, the Democratic-Republicans could almost be called the Presbyterian party because so many of its leaders were connected with that denomination. In the state of New York, Jefferson's first vice president, Aaron Burr, the Livingstons, and George Clinton were Presbyterians and Democratic-Republican leaders. In New York City, many Democratic-Republican artisans were Presbyterians; others were Baptists, Methodists, and infidels. Americanized German-Lutherans and Dutch Reformed tended to back the Republicans in that state, while the more traditional elements in those faiths were disposed to be Federalists. They feared the political influence of New England Yankee clergy, insisted upon absolute separation of church and state, and opposed governmental involvement in matters of personal morality. They were localists, and thoroughly anti-aristocratic. In the backcountry of the Middle Atlantic states and the South, Catholic, Methodist, Presbyterian, and Baptist congregations were particularly strong in their Republican convictions. These alignments reflected a tendency for those with less social standing to identify with the Jeffersonians, while the Federalists were strongest among those who enjoyed greater wealth and social standing.

It is not surprising that Philadelphia Irish Catholics were strongly Democratic-Republican, and party leaders there included many Presbyterians, Lutherans, and Baptists. Some Democratic-Republican leaders there were Anglicans and Quakers; however, much larger numbers of Anglicans and Quakers were found among the Federalist leadership. In New England, where the Congregationalist Standing Order was dominant and enjoyed the benefits of establishment in some places, the Quakers supported the party of outsiders, the Democratic-Republicans.

Pennsylvania and New Jersey Quakers were usually Federalists, but different social conditions in Delaware led Quakers there to back the Republicans. In Philadelphia, the Universalists were inclined to support the Jeffersonians. Universalist ranks there included radical craftsmen as well as some liberal intellectuals. Israel Israel, a prominent innkeeper, advocate of workers' rights, and a Jeffersonian, was a Universalist. Alexander James Dallas, another prominent Jeffersonian, was also a member of the Philadelphia Universalist Church.

Catholics and Jews generally supported the party of Jefferson. However, Maryland Roman Catholics followed the lead of wealthy coreligionists in supporting the Federalists, and a significant number of Philadelphia Catholics voted for Federalists because Thomas Fitzsimmons was a major leader of that party. Later, some wealthy Catholics and intellectuals supported the Whigs. These facts have misled some in declaring that Catholics largely supported the Federalists and Whigs. In another exception to the normal pattern, the Federalists claimed the support of Presbyterians in western Virginia and the Cape Fear area and the backing of Methodists on the Delmarva Peninsula.

In New York, Jews identified with the Democratic-Republican Party, and one of its leaders was Solomon Simpson. A Federalist paper there suggested that the Democratic-Republican Party was made up of Jews, like Simpson "of the tribe of Shylock; they have that leering . . . and malicious grin that seems to say to the honest man—*approach me not.*" Democratic-Republicans also sometimes exhibited anti-Semitism. A Philadelphia newspaper complained that Alexander Hamilton's funding plan was designed to see that "spies and Jews may ride in coaches." Major Benjamin Nones, who had served in the revolution with George Washington, found it necessary to publish in the Federalist *Gazette of the United States* a response to a Mr. Wayne who had attacked him for being a Jew, a Republican, and poor. He proclaimed, "I am a Jew, and if for no other reason, for that reason I am a Republican. . . . Among the nations of Europe we are inhabitants everywhere, but citizens nowhere unless in a republic." He was implicitly arguing that the Jeffersonians best represented republican principles.

In 1815, a Democratic-Republican secretary of state and future president, James Monroe, recalled Mordecai Noah as consul to Tunis because his religion might be "an obstacle to the exercise of your Consular function." This action prompted Isaac Harby, a Charleston editor, to address a letter to Monroe reminding him that Jews and Catholics had the same citizenship rights as other Americans. By then, American Jews were sufficiently accepted that they felt no compunction against openly defending their rights in public forums. However, they had assimilated to the extent that synagogues no longer enjoyed the cohesiveness that enabled them to demand full community support for a Hebrew school or assistance to their poor. Community sanctions also became increasingly difficult to enforce. There was a tendency toward the development of separate Sephardic and Ashkenazic congregations, which probably reflected more the differences between newly arrived Jews from Germany and central Europe and the older, more established and prosperous American Jewish community.

In the backcountry of Pennsylvania in the early 1790s, evangelical millennialism was associated with opposition to the whiskey tax imposed by the Federalist administration. Farmers there used whiskey as their cash crop because they could not transport large amounts of rye or wheat to market. The first person arrested by federal forces under Alexander Hamilton was Reverend Herman Husband, a Baptist. He had spent some time in jail two decades previously for his involvement in the North Carolina regulators movement. He preached that the New Jerusalem would be established in the West, and believed that the enemies of the coming New Jerusalem were slaveholders, tax gatherers, and ambitious politicians. Arrayed on the side of the Lord were farmers and landless laborers. In the New Jerusalem, ferries, taverns, markets, and mills would belong to the public.

Though many of the whiskey rebels were Scots or Scots-Irish, their Presbyterian clergymen did not support the rebels' activities. Husband's comments on the millennium were matched by those of others who saw in the French Revolution evidence that a millennial age was not far off. This brief surge of Francophilic millennialism reached its zenith in 1794. Samuel Hopkins thought it would materialize in two hundred years and be marked by universal benevolence, spiritual enlightenment, and common property. Many saw in the revolutionaries' attacks on the Roman Catholic Church clear evidence that the revolution was part of God's plan to bring about the millennium. Episcopalian bishop James Madison believed that God was extending the American revolution into France. A southern Baptist anonymously published a pamphlet claiming the millennium would come when democracy had overcome "animal nature" and selfishness.

In Virginia the Baptists backed the Democratic-Republicans, strongly opposed the use of troops against the whiskey rebels, and reacted against George Washington's policy of neutrality in the struggle between France and England. Democratic-Republicans were more interested in books about millennialism than were Federalists, and some of the works on the millennium that appeared were written by people who were clearly sympathetic to the French Revolution and the Democratic-Republican Party. New England Baptists supported the Democratic-Republicans in calling for the disestablishment of Congregationalism. However, they did not oppose the Federalists in upholding laws against gambling, profanity, blasphemy, theatergoing, intemperance, and dancing. Isaac Backus approved of Jefferson's position on religious liberty and the frugality of his administration.

Southern Baptists and Methodists were inclined toward republicanism in part because they opposed state involvement in religion. In 1800 most of them did not hold slaves, but their opposition to governmental interference in their affairs was shared by slaveholders bent on preserving slavery. They equated the Federalists with state-supported religion and also thought that moral suasion was better than legislation in moving people toward godly ways. By the 1830s, many Methodists changed their minds about legislating morality and saw legislative activity as one way of serving the Lord. New Side Presbyterians, Methodists, and Baptists tended to be Democratic-Republicans. There were some exceptions to this generalization. Scotch-Irish Presbyterians in the Cape Fear, North Carolina, area and in western Virginia were likely to be Federalists, as were Methodists of the Delmarva Peninsula.

In the late 1790s, most clergymen worried about social leveling, unchecked popular passions, and the excesses of the French Revolution. Some who had seen the French Revolution as the work of God reversed their positions when they concluded that it represented an attack on religion, order, and property. By 1798, the United States was in an undeclared naval war with France.

Anarchic individualism was found almost everywhere, but it seemed to reign supreme in the West, where secularism and infidelity held sway. To preserve the republic, clergymen called for a great missionary effort to bring God to benighted westerners. In the West, Methodists tended to identify with the Democratic-Republicans; the Jeffersonian party organization in central Ohio seemed to almost parallel Methodist organizational units. Edward Tiffin and Thomas Worthington, both governors and prominent Methodist laymen, were leading Jeffersonians. Tiffin, a lay preacher, assured the Ohio legislature that his heart was always in the right place even though he sometimes made mistakes. He saw society as a vast extended family bound together by Christian brotherhood. His substitution of Christian virtue for the civic virtue of classical republicanism foreshadowed a development that would characterize the revivalism of the first half of the nineteenth century. Some men of the stature of Worthington and Tiffin were found among early Methodists in other states. Not all Methodists were poor, and their egalitarianism was directed against deference, privilege, and pretensions rather than against mere wealth, which could have been accumulated through industriousness and frugality.

Many had come to question the classical republican concept of civic virtue when it seemed to have failed during years the Articles of Confederation were in effect. Popularly based state governments were seen as frequently corrupt and arbitrary. It appeared that man could only be a good citizen if his virtue was inspired by a Christian love for his fellows. In order to promote virtue in the civic arena, chapters of the Tammany Society were founded in Ohio around 1810. These societies and Tammany's central wigwam in Ohio were dominated by Democratic-Republicans.

The War of 1812

The churches played an important role in shaping public opinion during the War of 1812. Most denominations supported the nation's war effort, but the New England Congregationalists, cherishing trade and cultural ties with Britain and suspicious of Republican war aims, denounced the war and claimed it was God's punishment of an apostate people. In election sermons and in pamphlets these clergymen noted that in fighting Great Britain, the United States government was allying itself with Napoleonic France, an infidel nation. A few Presbyterians allied with the Congregationalists in opposing the war, as did some Episcopalians. The ecclesiastical opponents of the war left the impression that they were extremely numerous because they published their sermons and had a number of journals. The following toast reflects the view most Americans had of these clergymen: "The tory-clergy; may they fight more against the devil, and less against their country."

The great majority of clergymen supported the war. Many of them, notably the Baptists and Methodists, did not print their sermons or have numerous publication outlets. Supporters of the war noted that the Antichrist was not Napoleon but the Roman pope and others who opposed religious liberty, particularly the Church of England and the Congregationalist clergy of New England. Theirs was a fight for freedom and the rights of man. Baptists recalled the role of James Madison in bringing religious liberty to Virginia and saw it as suitable that he lead this struggle. In New England, the heart of "tory" country, noted Baptist evangelist John Leland prayed for American troops from the pulpit and supported the war while denouncing its critics. Francis Asbury led Methodists in backing the war.

Roman Catholics demonstrated their loyalty to the nation by joining others in honoring the national fast days requested by President Madison. It was still a common belief that Christians could favorably influence God by fasting. While backing the war, however, they did sing Te Deums when the British freed Pope Pius VII from Napoleon's captivity and when Paris was liberated from the Corsican's grip. To make clear that his animus toward Napoleon did not diminish his American patriotism, Boston's Bishop Jean Cheverus manned a wheelbarrow when it became necessary to quickly fortify the city against possible attack. The bishops' private correspondence indicates that some saw Napoleonic France rather than England as their principal enemy. In New Orleans, the Roman clergy offered public prayers for the success of General Andrew Jackson and his forces in defending their city. Most Episcopalians supported the war and made clear their separation from the English church and the Crown. Nevertheless the war presented them with some internal tensions, and they heartily rejoiced in its end.

The end of the war ushered in a brief period known as the Era of Good Feelings, a time marked by nationalism and the diminution of sectionalism. For Protestant churches, it saw a refinement of the nation's civil religion, or the religion of the republic. A sense of urgency attended the nation's God-given mission to be the torchbearer of liberty for the world. In resisting British aggression, Americans had proven their worthiness for this mission to extend republicanism throughout the world. Radical Republicans thought the mission involved exporting more than republicanism; the gift of democracy was to be taken to others. The nation's mission also included evangelism to the rest of the world. Missionaries were to take evangelical Protestantism to others. They would take with them not just Bibles and tracts but a burning commitment to a variety of humanitarian reforms. The interdenominational American Board of Commissioners for Foreign Missions, founded in 1810, predated the war, but its activities would be vastly accelerated after the cessation of hostilities. It would be joined by numerous similar ventures. Although the Federalist political philosophy of New England lost influence after the war, the New Divinity theology, as preached by Timothy Dwight of Yale, became identified with the religion of the republic.

Bibliography

Albanese, Catherine. *Sons of the Fathers: The Civil Religion of the American Revolution.* Philadelphia: Temple University Press, 1977.

———. "Whither the Sons (and Daughters)? Republican Nature and the Quest for the Ideal." In *The American Revolution: Its Character and Limits,* ed. Jack P. Greene, pp. 362–387. New York: New York University Press, 1987.

Baldwin, Alice M. *The New England Clergy and the American Revolution.* New York: Frederick Ungar, 1958.

Barney, William L. *The Passage of the Republic: An Interdisciplinary History of Nineteenth Century America.* Lexington, MA: D.C. Heath, 1987.

Batinski, Michael. "Quakers in the New Jersey Assembly: 1738–1775: A Roll-Call Analysis." *Historian* 54 (autumn 1991): 65–78.

Bauman, Richard. *For the Reputation of Truth: Politics, Religion, and Conflict Among the Pennsylvania Quakers, 1750–1800.* Baltimore: Johns Hopkins University Press, 1971.

Bloch, Ruth H. "Religion and Ideological Change." In *Religion and American Politics: From the Colonial Period to the 1980s,* ed. Mark A. Noll, pp. 44–61. New York: Oxford University Press, 1990.

———."The Social and Political Base of Millennial Literature in Late Eighteenth-Century America." *American Quarterly* 40 (September 1988): 378–396.

———. *Visionary Republic: Millennial Themes in American Thought, 1756–1800.* Cambridge: Cambridge University Press, 1985.

Bockleman, Wayne L., and Owen S. Ireland. "The Internal Revolution in Pennsylvania: An Ethnic-Religious Interpretation" *Pennsylvania History* 41 (April 1974): 125–159.

Bonomi, Patricia U."Religious Dissent and the Case for American Exceptionalism." In *Religion in a Revolutionary Age,* ed. Ronald Hoffman and Peter J. Albert, pp. 31–51. Charlottesville: University of Virginia Press, 1994.

———. *Under the Cope of Heaven: Religion, Society, and Politics in Colonial America.* New York: Oxford University Press, 1986.

Borman, Ernest G. *The Force of Fantasy: Restoring the American Dream.* Carbondale: Southern Illinois University Press, 1985.

Breitenbach, William. "The Consistent Calvinism of the New Divinity Movement." *William and Mary Quarterly* 3rd Ser., 41 (April 1984): 241–264.

Bridenbaugh, Carl. *Mitre and Sceptre: Transatlantic Faiths, Ideas, Personalities, and Politics, 1689–1775.* New York: Oxford University Press, 1962.

Buckley, Thomas E. "Evangelicals Triumphant: The Baptists' Assault on the Virginia Glebes, 1786–1801." *William and Mary Quarterly* 3rd. Ser., 45 (January 1988): 33–69.

Buel, Joy Daj, and Richard Buel Jr. *The Way of Duty: A Woman and Her Family in Revolutionary America.* New York: Norton, 1984.

Burton, David H. "The Jesuit as American Patriot: Fathers Robert Harding and Robert Molyneux." *Pennsylvania History* 48 (January 1981): 51–61.

Calhoon, Robert M. "The Evangelical Persuasion." In *Religion in a Revolutionary Age,* ed. Ronald Hoffman and Peter J. Albert, pp. 156–183. Charlottesville: University of Virginia Press, 1994.

Carey, Patrick W. "American Catholics and the First Amendment, 1776–1840." *Pennsylvania Magazine of History and Biography* (113 July 1989): 323–346.

Carwardine, Richard. " 'Antinomians' and 'Arminians': Methodists and the Market Revolution." In *The Market Revolution in America: Social, Political, and Religious Expressions, 1800–1880,* ed. Melvyn Stokes and Stephen Conway, pp. 282–307. Charlottesville: University of Virginia Press, 1996.

Chambers, William Nesbet. *Political Parties in a New Nation: The American Experience, 1776–1809.* New York: Oxford University Press, 1961.

Conforti, Joseph. "Samuel Hopkins and the New Divinity: Theology, Ethics, and Social Reform in Eighteenth Century New England." *William and Mary Quarterly* 3rd Ser., 34 (October 1977): 572–589.

Conkin, Paul. "Priestly and Jefferson: Unitarianism as a Religion for a New Revolutionary Age." In *Religion in a Revolutionary Age,* ed. Ronald Hoffman and Peter J. Albert, pp. 290–307. Charlottesville: University of Virginia Press, 1994.

Cooper, James F. "Enthusiasts or Democrats? Separatism, Church Government, and the Great Awakening in Massachusetts." *New England Quarterly* 65 (September 1992): 265–283.

Davidson, James West. *The Logic of Millennial Thought: Eighteenth Century New England.* New Haven: Yale University Press, 1977.

Davis, Richard Beale. *Intellectual Life in Jefferson's Virginia, 1790–1830.* Chapel Hill: University of North Carolina Press, 1964.

Dworetz, Steven M. *The Unvarnished Doctrine: Locke, Liberalism, and the American Revolution.* Durham: Duke University Press, 1990.

Ellis, Richard E. *The Jeffersonian Crisis: Courts and Politics in the Young Republic.* New York: Norton, 1971.

Faber, Eli. *A Time for Planting: The First Migration, 1654–1820,* vol. 1, *The Jewish People in America.* Baltimore: Johns Hopkins University Press, 1992.

Fennell, Dorothy. "Herman Husband's New Jerusalem: Frontier Radicalism and the Millennialist Tradition." In *Autre Temps, Autre Espace: Etudes Sur l'Amerique pre-industrielle,* ed. Elise Marienstras and Barbara Karsky, pp. 67–75. Nancy, France: Universitaires de Nancy, 1986.

Fisher, David Hackett. "Patterns of Partisan Allegiance, 1800." In *After the Constitution: Party Conflict in the New Republic,* ed. Lance Banning, pp. 143–170. Belmont, CA: Wadsworth, 1989.

———. "The Social Basis of Parties in 1800." In *The Early American Party System,* ed. Norman K. Risjord, pp. 94–111. New York: Harper and Row, 1969.

Formisano, Ronald P. *The Transformation of Political Culture: Massachusetts Parties, 1790s–1840s.* New York: Oxford University Press, 1983.

Friedman, Leo M. *Jewish Pioneers and Patriots.* Philadelphia: Jewish Publication Society, 1992.

German, James D. "The Social Utility of Wicked Self-Interest: Calvinism, Capitalism, and Public Policy in Revolutionary New England." *Journal of American History* 82 (December 1995): 965–998.

Glazer, Nathan. *American Judaism.* Chicago: University of Chicago Press, 1972.

Goen, C.C. *Broken Churches, Broken Nation: Denominational Schisms and the Coming of the Civil War.* Macon: Mercer University Press, 1985.

———. *Revivalism and Separatism in New England, 1740–1800: Strict Congregationalists and Separate Baptists in the Great Awakening.* New Haven: Yale University Press, 1962.

Goodman, Paul, ed. *The Federalists vs. the Jeffersonians.* New York: Holt, Rinehart, and Winston, 1967.

Greene, Jack P., and William G. McLoughlin. *Preachers and Politics: Two Essays on the Origins of the American Revolution.* Boston: American Antiquarian Society, 1977.

Hamm, Thomas. *The Transformation of American Quakerism: Orthodox Friends, 1800–1907.* Bloomington: Indiana University Press, 1988.

Handy, Thomas O'Brien. *The American Revolution and Religion: Maryland, 1770–1800.* Washington: Catholic University of America Press, 1971.

Hatch, Nathan O. *The Sacred Cause of Liberty: Republican Thought and the Millennium in Revolutionary New England.* New Haven: Yale University Press, 1977.

Henry, Patrick, et al. "Holy Passion for Liberty," *Christian History* 50, no. 4 (1996): 22–25.

Hertzberg, Arthur. *The Jews in America: Four Centuries of Uneasy Encounter, A History.* New York: Simon and Schuster, 1989.

Holmes, David L. "The Episcopal Church and the American Revolution." *Historical Magazine of the Protestant Episcopal Church* 47 (1978): 283–288.

Isaac, Rhys. *The Transformation of Virginia, 1740–1790.* Chapel Hill: University of North Carolina Press, 1982.

Karp, Abraham J. "In the Early Republic." In *The Jewish Experience in America,* vol. 2, ed. Abraham J. Karp, pp. vii-xix. New York: KTAV Publishing House, 1969.

Kashatus, William C., III. "The Inner Light and Popular Enlightenment: Philadelphia Quakers and Christian Schooling, 1790–1820." *Pennsylvania Magazine of History and Biography* 118 (January/April 1994): 87–116.

Kerber, Linda K. *Women of the Republic: Intellect and Ideology in Revolutionary America.* Chapel Hill: University of North Carolina Press, 1980.

Kelley, Robert. *The Cultural Pattern in American Politics, The First Century.* New York: Knopf, 1979.

Koch, G. Adolf. *Religion of the American Enlightenment.* New York: Crowell, 1966.

Learsi, Rufus. *The Jews in America: A History.* Cleveland: World, 1954.

McLoughlin, William G. "The American Revolution as a Religious Revival: 'The Millennium in One Country.'" *New England Quarterly* 40 (March 1967): 99–110.

———. *New England Dissent, 1630–1833.* Cambridge: Harvard University Press, 1971.

Lovejoy, David S. "Samuel Hopkins: Religion, Slavery, and the Revolution." *New England Quarterly* 40 (June 1967): 227–243.

May, Henry F. *Ideas, Faiths, and Feelings: Essays on American Intellectual and*

Religious History. New York: Oxford University Press, 1982.

Miller, Perry. "The Moral and Psychological Roots of American Resistance." In *The Reinterpretation of the American Revolution,* ed. Jack P. Greene, pp. 251–274. New York: Harper and Row, 1968.

Miller, Richard G. *Philadelphia-The Federalist City: A Study of Urban Politics, 1789–1801.* Port Washington, NY: Kennikat, 1976.

Moore, R. Lawrence. "The End of Religious Establishment and the Beginning of Religious Politics: Church and State in the United States." In *Belief in History: Innovative Approaches to European and American Religion,* ed. Thomas Kselman, pp. 237–266. Notre Dame: University of Notre Dame Press, 1991.

Noll, Mark A. *Christians in the American Revolution.* Grand Rapids: Christian University Press, 1977.

Pfeffer, Leo. *Church, State, and Freedom.* Boston: Beacon, 1967.

Procter-Smith, Marjorie. " 'In the Line of the Female': Shakerism and Feminism." In *Women's Leadership in Marginal Religions: Explorations Outside the Mainstream,* ed. Catherine Wessinger, pp. 23–40. Urbana: University of Illinois Press, 1993.

Radbill, Kenneth A.R. "Quaker Patriots: The Leadership of Owen Biddle and John Lacey, Jr." *Pennsylvania History* 45 (January 1978): 47–60.

Sachar, Howard M. *A History of the Jews in America.* New York: Knopf, 1992.

Schultz, Ronald. "God and Workingmen: Popular Religion and the Formation of Philadelphia's Working Class, 1790–1830." In *Religion in a Revolutionary Age,* ed. Ronald Hoffman and Peter J. Albert, pp. 125–155. Charlottesville: University of Virginia Press, 1994.

Sellers, Charles. *The Market Revolution: Jacksonian America, 1815–1846.* New York: Oxford University Press, 1991.

Stein, Stephen J. *The Shaker Experience in America: A History of the United Society of Believers.* New Haven: Yale University Press, 1992.

Stout, Harry S. "Rhetoric and Reality in the Early Republic: The Case of the Federalist Clergy." In *Religion and American Politics,* ed. Mark Noll, pp. 622–676. New York: Oxford University Press, 1990.

Tuveson, Ernest Lee. *Redeemer Nation: The Idea of America's Millennial Role.* Chicago: University of Chicago Press, 1968.

Valeri, Mark. "The New Divinity and the American Revolution." *William and Mary Quarterly* 3rd Ser., 46 (October 1989): 741–769.

Walters, Kerry S. *The American Deists: Voices of Reason and Dissent in the Early Republic.* Lawrence: University of Kansas Press, 1992.

Warren, Sidney. *American Free Thought, 1860–1914.* New York: Gordian Press, 1966.

Wills, Garry. *Inventing America: Jefferson's Declaration of Independence.* Garden City, NY: Doubleday, 1978.

Wood, Gordon S. *The Creation of the American Republic, 1776–1787.* New York: Norton, 1972.

———. *The Radicalism of the American Revolution.* New York: Knopf, 1992.

Two

Early African American Religion

Christianity did not inspire Americans of the revolutionary era to free all slaves, but it became very important to many African Americans. It would assure them of their equality in the sight of God and hold out the promise that they would experience liberation just as the Hebrews had under the leadership of Moses. African American Christianity would be a major instrument for resisting slavery. Though religion would play a central role in the lives of African Americans, significant numbers of them did not embrace Christianity until well after the American Revolution. Some found in their African religious heritage the strength and worldview that enabled them to endure slavery.

African Americans adapted Christianity to meet their needs and to fashion the Black church, the only institution over which they could exert some control while slaves in a racist society. Through religious observances, they created some space in which they found refuge in a hostile society. Through religion and the singing of spirituals they found a way to speak about their hopes and trials and resist white cultural hegemony. Religion provided a means of self-expression and resistance to the dominant culture. As in the case of medieval European minority groups, African American resistance often took the form of revolutionary millenarianism. Slave leaders often saw themselves and their revolts as the Lord's special instruments in bringing about the Day of Jubilee and the thousand-year reign of Christ.

African Background

Slaves came from a variety of ancient civilizations, most located on the west coast of Africa. They brought with them rich and diverse cultures having many common features. Their religious world was inhabited by many spirits, as well as by a supreme being. The high god was the all-powerful creator; below him were lesser, ancestral gods. When slaves became Christians, their high god was replaced by Jehovah. The African religions did not have a single, very powerful devil, but Africans did believe that spirits could be malevolent.

Africans also had gods that animated nature. It would be wrong to refer to their worship as animism as this term refers to the worship of impersonal deities confined to specific localities. A key element in African religions was reverence for ancestors. It was believed that ancestors could influence the lives of the living. Upon death, one continued to exist as a spirit, and a protracted and elaborate funeral marked this occasion. Ancestors who had been deceased the longest possessed the greatest power. The living offered them food as an expression of respect, fellowship, and solidarity, but this was not ancestor worship. African rulers led their people in communicating with dead ancestors and with other spirits. In America, African American preachers performed the role of priest-king in interpreting Scripture.

Some of the many spirits who inhabited the world dwelled permanently in rivers, pools, animals, or trees. Others lived temporarily in objects, and some inhabited human beings. It was considered necessary to propitiate these spirits through various ceremonies and offerings, which included animal blood. Human sacrifice was sometimes practiced. It was believed possible to persuade spirits to inhabit charms and amulets (inscribed charms), which Africans wore from birth. Sometimes these charms contained feathers, alligator teeth, bits of broken bottles, grave dirt, eggshells, and parrots' beaks. Africans carried these objects in small parcels called "gre-gre-bags" or "hands." The charms, or "obies," were sold by medicine men, or obeah men, to heal illnesses or provide protection and good fortune. W.E.B. Du Bois referred to this religion as "Obe Worship." (It should be noted that Puritan folk religion included the use of man-made objects that were considered to have magical qualities. Amulets were also common in European history.) Africans believed that every person had a personal spirit somewhat akin to the Christian guardian angel. However, the African's personal spirit was not as reliable as the Christian's guardian angel as it had to be induced to perform its functions.

Africans communicated with deities through the use of drums and rattles. They employed ritualistic dances in worship, often performed by priestesses. Religious plays were frequently used in worship, performed by masked dancers or puppets. There were also conjurers employed to cast evil spells on enemies. A slave might need to consult an adept to learn the best way to poison a harsh master. The adept was sometimes forced to leave a village if people associated him with some calamity. In some respects, the African conjurer was practicing theurgy, a form of white magic in which humans are able to cause divine action.

Adepts, conjurers, or priests were particularly important in the voodoo cult of the West Indies, today a great force in Haiti. This corruption of African religion contained some elements borrowed from Roman Catholicism. Voodoo was often brought to the mainland colonies by slaves from the West Indies. As late as 1851, New Orleans authorities found a dozen women gathered to practice voodoo rituals, led by voodoo queens. Slave masters attempted to outlaw the practice of all African religions, believing that these religions could be used to stimulate slave revolts. In the West Indies, this happened after revolting slaves were convinced by their African cult priests of their invulnerability. Elements persisted and were known as "hoodoo" by the nineteenth century.

African slaves were brought first to the English North American colonies in 1619. In the late seventeenth century, their numbers increased enormously as southern planters turned away from reliance on white indentured servants for labor. Christian clergymen joined planters in configuring American slavery; they taught that slaves owed their masters absolute obedience. To some degree, enslavement and Christianity undermined the religious systems Africans brought with them. Moreover, slave owners would not permit the practice of African religions. An "African spiritual holocaust" occurred, but significant elements of their African religious heritage would survive and reappear in African American Christianity. The cultures and identities of Africans were rooted in African religions, and African American Christianity would serve as a vehicle for the preservation of many elements of African culture and reflect the hopes and aspirations of African Americans.

Late-Eighteenth-Century Conversions

The Great Awakening proved to be the occasion for many conversions of African Americans. Prior to this, a relatively small number of slaves were converted by Anglican clergymen. The effects of the Great Awakening were felt in the South in the latter part of the eighteenth century. Presbyterians had some success in winning conversions among both whites and Blacks. Presbyterians often won the support of members of the upper class, previously Anglicans, and a significant number of their slaves became Presbyterians. Baptists won many slave converts in the second half of the eighteenth century. By 1800 there were about 25,000 African American Baptists, a number that would swell to 150,000 half a century later. In Philadelphia, the great itinerant evangelist George Whitefield converted many African Americans, his appearance marking the beginning of Black Christianity there. African Americans heard his general sermons, and he met privately with them for additional preaching and instruction.

Though not part of the Great Awakening, the Methodist missionaries attracted many slaves to this religion of the heart. In the South, significant numbers of slaves were converted in the 1770s, and even larger numbers were converted in the 1780s and 1790s. In 1790 there were already 11,682 Black Methodists, and 18,000 or more Black Baptists by 1793. Black Methodists numbered around 50,000 by 1820, and there were approximately twice that many Black Baptists. House slaves often joined their masters' families in evening prayer, and the mistress of the plantation sometimes taught slaves the Christian precepts. Slaves often attended churches frequented by whites, seated in the back or gallery. If permitted to hold separate meetings, a white led the service or observed the proceedings.

As of the late eighteenth century, the vast majority of slaves remained unconverted to Christianity. Evangelical clergymen actively sought African converts, and their revivalistic techniques were more effective than had been the rationalistic sermons or subdued rituals of nonevangelicals. African Americans noticed that the evangelists encouraged emotionalism in worship, a characteristic of African religion. Evangelicals preached to racially mixed congregations and emphasized the conversion experience over doctrine. They stressed that unlettered slaves could have conversion experiences. In this sense, slaves experienced a form of near equality with whites. Sometimes the whites called them "Brother" and "Sister," and Blacks sometimes spoke to biracial audiences.

Slaves who embraced evangelical Christianity approached it with a different attitude than did whites. The African communal ethos, reinforced by conditions in the slave quarters, militated against a deep sense of individual sin and guilt. Dancing was seen as an important way to express community and would eventually become an important part of Black evangelical worship, though whites avoided it as part of their effort to see that the spirit triumphed over the flesh.

The ceremonies and techniques of revivals were somewhat similar to African religion. Slaves responded to the preachers' message with trembling, shouting, and crying. When the white man did so it was because he had been convicted of sin. However, when the African American trembled, she or he was being elevated and in contact with God; she was a complete person equal to all others. To an extent, evangelical religion substituted distinctions based on morality and piety for those based on class and family. In the late eighteenth century, southern evangelicalism often was such a sociohistorical process. It tore down barriers separating whites and Blacks, lessening distinctions. The two races frequently worshiped together and considered each other brothers and sisters, sometimes hearing Black preachers.

African Americans were more accustomed to ecstatic worship and contributed to the shaping of southern revivalism. They helped whites become open to religious ecstasy and to pass through highly emotional religious experiences. Filled with the Spirit, African Americans sometimes had "visions," traveling backward in time or viewing the terrors and fires of hell. Spirit possession was a major feature of African ecstatic religion, and possession by the Holy Spirit was an important element in the religion of African Americans. Spirit possession was to have an influence on American Christianity, enabling evangelical Protestants to revive this primitive Christian practice. The Africans' religious and cultural background and experiences prepared them to accept and offer criticism when they were full participants in tightly woven evangelical worship communities.

Some white Baptist and Methodist preachers were critical of slavery. The year 1780 was the high-water-mark of Methodist opposition to slavery. Printed Methodist catechetical material made plain their "disapprobation" of those who held slaves. Some itinerant preachers talked about the equality of all men and criticized slavery. Some were accused of fomenting slave revolts. There was a brief antislavery movement among Virginia Baptists in the 1780s when clergy spoke against slavery, but the Baptists soon found acceptance of slavery was a precondition for function in the white community. David Barrow, who preached in Virginia and Kentucky, freed his slaves and spoke forcefully for emancipation. In Kentucky, his association expelled him for taking this position but later revoked its action. Barrow refused to have anything more to do with the association.

In general, revivalists spoke against abusive masters but avoided a condemnation of slavery. Their approach was similar to that of Methodist bishop Francis Asbury, who thought more could be done to help slaves by working to ameliorate their condition than by denouncing the institution and demanding emancipation. In time, the practice of itinerancy declined, and ministers were more likely to work only within the boundaries of one conference, making it more difficult to be outspoken about slavery.

African American Christianity

Despite great obstacles, African Americans created their own approach to evangelical Christianity. Where whites looked to the second coming, African Americans focused on the end of bondage and the advent of freedom. The story of Exodus was very important to them as they looked for their own deliverance into the promised land. They knew that Christ had suffered mightily and had sanctified endurance. In their suffering, the African American Christians saw themselves as God's chosen people; a few thought that white people were not admitted to heaven. The Day of Jubilee, they believed, would mark their liberation from slavery, based on the Hebrew usage of freeing bond servants every fiftieth year. African American Christians were premillennialists in that they believed that Christ's second coming would occur before the thousand-year reign of Christ. They believed that human agency was necessary to help bring about liberation and the millennium.

The greatness of African American Christianity has always been related to its ability to inspire hope in the face of bitter adversity. African religion did not include the concept of original sin, and it called for a joyful approach to life. The absence of the notion of original sin deprived white Christians of a means of convincing slaves that they deserved subjugation, and the African American inclination to celebrate life assisted them in reshaping Christianity to meet their needs.

The theology of the late-eighteenth-century evangelists seemed to dissolve the barrier between the sacred and the profane, corresponding to holistic African spirituality. African Americans found remarkable similarities between the ways they could worship the new God and the ways they did homage to their old deities. The high god of African religion was replaced by Jehovah. Christ and the saints took the places previously held by lesser African gods. The African heritage eased acceptance of death because it meant finding fulfillment and union with ancestors. As Christians, the African Americans helped whites see death as something other than an event to be feared. Southern whites also learned from African Americans the importance of family, and attached great importance to preserving close family.

Opportunities were found to incorporate African musical and liturgical motifs into the worship. The Baptist insistence on full immersion in water reminded slaves of their native religions in which initiation was accomplished by full immersion. There were a number of river cults in West Africa whose priests dealt with powerful water spirits. The river cult priests resisted the spread of the Kingdom of Dahomey (centered in today's Benin) and were frequently sold into slavery. Despite the Methodists' disapproval of dancing, an important element in African culture and religion, the slaves were attracted to Methodism. The fact that the Baptists and Methodists were the first to demonstrate a great interest in converting slaves was as important as the appeal of their style of worship.

The initiation rites for African mediums included the idea that the initiate died and was born anew. This often occurred in rites marking the coming of people to womanhood and manhood. This background made it easy for African Americans to deal with the concept of being born again; indeed they were able to help whites understand it. During revivals, people often fell down as though dead during an exhortation. This marked their rebirth in Christ. African Americans were more comfortable with ecstatic religion and helped whites be more open to this. Christians from the first century onward have experienced visions; these had also been an important element in the African heritage, as a person traveled to other times and places. This experience was carried over into evangelical Protestantism. The African belief that deities communicated through dreams and visions was particularly consistent with Methodist belief. Some African American Christians refrained from dancing, as a sign of their commitment to Christianity, but others continued to employ the dance as a means of spiritual expression.

The appeal of clergymen of the Methodist and Baptist denominations to the downtrodden and dispossessed was particularly relevant to slaves. The thought of an afterlife in which Blacks as well as whites were rewarded or punished offered the slaves the justice they were denied in this life. Belief in a glorious afterlife offered an escape from their pain and suffering. Slaves identified with the story of the captivities of the people of Israel and noted that the God of the Old Testament eventually liberated them. Many white clergy attempted to counterbalance these beliefs by preaching the need for the slaves to serve God by accepting their lot, working hard, and obeying their masters.

The "Invisible Church"

By the late eighteenth century, a folk religion or "invisible church" had emerged among the slaves and proved to be more meaningful to them than white Christianity. Religious meetings took place beyond the scrutiny of whites and were presided over by African Americans; these places were sometimes called "hush harbors." Sometimes, free African Americans preached to the slaves. By the nineteenth century, it was often illegal for free Blacks to preach, but they did so anyhow, often risking severe punishments. Efforts to limit the activities of free Black preachers were especially pronounced in the decades after Nat Turner's rebellion in 1831.

Members of the invisible church heard a fellow slave preach. Many of these preachers were unlettered, but dedicated to their tasks. Often they had memorized many passages of scriptures and the liturgy of some services. These people found it necessary to avoid calling for resistance to slavery, but emphasized the dignity and personal worth of all. They preached applied Christianity, summarized as "Let us do as Christ has commanded us: let us do as he wishes, let us love one another." Sometimes, they spoke about the Lord separating sheep and goats, the latter meaning whites in slave folklore. Whites worried that Black preachers would preach insurrection, but they usually tolerated the slave preaching because the slaves preferred it. During the Civil War, Blacks who were assigned to work for southern armies were permitted to have their own preachers.

Meetings were marked by emotional fervor, ecstatic worship, song, and active involvement in a call-and-response dialogue with the preacher. As the preacher-storyteller made telling points, members of the assembly would inter-ject shouts of "Praise God," "Hallelujah," and "Amen"; the preacher also inter-jected grunts and shouts for added emphasis. This interactive form of preaching can be traced to African storytelling practices. Shouting, or the frenzy, indi-cated that the devotee was full of supernatural joy.

Many African Americans believed that one could not enjoy communion with God without physical manifestations of frenzy. It was a religion of solace and joy, not of guilt or shame. The slaves were not judgmental about one another, and Christianity reinforced their deep sense of community. They would not tell the master about one another's conduct. They believed in resurrection and a return to Africa, and for a time in some places bodies were buried facing east. Some equated heaven with their African homeland. What had emerged was a syncretic African American Christianity. It em-phasized faith, love, deliverance from evil, and the promise of a better life in heaven. In prayer, song, and sermon African Americans made clear their desire for freedom in this life as well. In the invisible church or "invisible institution," African Americans learned that the essence of Christianity was love of one's neighbor. This is illustrated in the encounter of a planter and his slave who had run away thirty years before. The master asked if he had been forgiven for a severe beating and the African American replied, "I love you as though you never hit me a lick, for the God I serve is a God of love, and I can't go to his kingdom with hate in my heart."

The development of a distinctive messianic Christianity was part of a strategy for surviving slavery. Christianity did not represent for slaves a means of escape but became a vehicle for resisting slavery. The African Americans were in touch with a Christianity that promised liberation to all who were oppressed. Slaves rejected their masters' approach to Christianity, which stressed obedience and acceptance of suffering in this life. Instead, they saw themselves as a chosen people whose bondage and suffering were destined by God to be brought to an end and replaced by freedom. The story of Lazarus, to African American Christians, prefigured the emergence of their people from slavery, which was social death.

The appearance of many nuclear families and kinship networks facili-tated the emergence of an African American subculture after 1760. Above all, it would be rooted in the invisible church, as well as in the African heritage and formal Christianity. The development of this culture could not have occurred at an earlier time, when there was a relative absence of families, when most of the slave population was made up of young men who had recently experienced the trauma of the middle passage—the voyage from the west coast of Africa to the West Indies—when reproduction was limited, or when the slave population was made up of new arrivals from different African peoples unable to communicate with one another. While the emergence of an African American culture points to the strength and resilience of these African Americans and the survival of many significant elements of their native cultures, it is to be noted that the highly developed religious systems of the Ashanti, Ibo, Akan, Dahoman, and Yoruba societies did not survive as single systems. The uprooting, physical abuse, and oppression of African American slaves represented a cultural holocaust in which these rich religious and cultural systems could not survive as such. However, where African Americans greatly outnumbered whites, such as in the Charleston, South Carolina, area, significant elements of these cultures have survived.

Within the framework of their folk religion, Blacks developed their spirituals, an original form of singing that dwelt upon Christian themes but always conveyed the slaves' desire for liberation, freedom, and equality. Through the spirituals, figures like Moses or Jesus became significant in their lives. Christ was seen as a second Moses who would lead them to freedom. Through this music slaves sensed immediate contact with God. Many whites, however, saw the spirituals as songs of defiance and escape clothed in religious expressions. The spirituals emerged in the invisible church, where music preceded preaching, and the preacher's sermon took on musical qualities.

African American Christians understood sin to be primarily a broken relationship with God rather than an offense by an individual in violation of a code of conduct. While their values stressed that individuals should act responsibly, their emphasis was on corporate or community responsibility. Black preachers stressed the importance of accepting the literal words of the Bible but thought that responding to the promptings of the Holy Spirit was even more important, a more reliable guide to conduct than a Bible that condoned slavery. Their gatherings reflected a blending of African religious practices and attitudes with Christianity, which gave slaves a taste of spiritual freedom. The blending of African cultural elements with Christianity continued well into the nineteenth century. By 1860, Black Christianity contained more African elements than it had in 1760.

By the eve of the Civil War, more than a third of slaves had attended meetings of what is now called the invisible church. Only in an all–African American gathering could one of their preachers speak about physical liberation. Sporadic efforts were made to suppress the invisible church and punish its leaders. Some slaves attended services conducted by their masters; others attended white churches. An estimated 468,000 Blacks were part of the regular churches in the South in 1860. Many who attended the white churches or their masters' services also attended secret meetings of Black Christian communities.

Biracial Worship

Biracial worship probably involved more Blacks than the invisible church. African Americans usually sat in separate sections of the church, often in the balcony. Episcopalians and Presbyterians usually had special services for the slaves after regular services; Methodist and Baptist preachers addressed special remarks to the Blacks after the main homily. Charles Colcock Jones, a Presbyterian minister in eighteenth-century South Carolina, methodically divided his area into stations. On appointed Sundays, Blacks could gather at the stations for singing and sermons suitable to their "circumstances and conditions." This kind of arrangement often ended the work of Black preachers, who were eventually outlawed in South Carolina. In eighteenth-century Virginia, African Americans were members of every Baptist congregation.

In evangelical churches, African Americans sometimes felt a brief sense of near equality, and even saw African Americans address white audiences. Like whites, they went to the communion table and agreed to church documents of incorporation. They shared love feasts, foot washing, and the hand of fellowship. Some were deacons, and often committees of African Americans were responsible for the conduct of African American members and made recommendations to the church's governing bodies. Within the Baptist and Methodist congregations, slaves could raise objections to the conduct of their masters. If the master was found at fault, he had to change his conduct or leave the congregation. If he left, he could not enter another congregation of that denomination. The practice in these denominations of communal judgment of conduct was strengthened by the presence of the African Americans, who had experience with this from their African heritage.

African American Catholics

There were some Black Catholics in North America during the colonial period. In 1785, John Carroll informed a Vatican official that there were three thousand African American Catholics in Maryland. There were also Black Catholics in areas held by Spain and France, particularly Florida and Louisiana, that would become parts of the United States. A priest was implicated in a planned insurrection in Maryland in 1739, and slaves who had been Catholics in Africa were apparently incited to revolt by priests in South Carolina in 1739 and 1740. Although there were a few cases of segregation in distributing communion in Catholic churches, the usual practice was not to form separate lines for communion or confession. African American sisterhoods and orders existed, and Blacks were members of the Society of Jesus. A few institutions or orders owned slaves, but this practice was eventually ended for practical and ethical reasons. Catholic theology had rejected slavery for centuries, as well-trained priests must have been aware, yet few of them spoke out against human bondage. John Carroll, the first American Catholic bishop, was critical of slavery. Later some of the most prominent Catholic families, such as the Carrolls and the Taneys, worked for voluntary emancipation. Some slaves attended mass because their masters required it but shared the rabid anti-Catholicism of southern evangelicals and would have preferred to worship with their peers at night in the woods or at least attend the more spirited Baptist or Methodist services. On the other hand, some were attracted by Catholic relics, incense, and feast days, perhaps viewing Catholicism as more akin to African piety than were Protestant groups. One of the most remarkable African American Catholics was a barber and hairdresser named Pierre Toussaint of New York City. He lived a life of heroic virtue and was eventually granted his freedom. He supported the wife of his former master, lent money to white and Black people in distress, and contributed to many charitable causes, including a Catholic school for African American children and an orphanage. Toussaint attended daily mass and risked his own health by nursing people of both races during the epidemics that visited the city.

African American Preachers and Congregations

By the end of the eighteenth century, Afro-American Christianity was not restricted to gatherings in remote places but appeared in some separate Black churches. From 1760 to 1790, a number of African American independent congregations emerged. In part, the racism of white evangelicals made necessary religious separatism. A number of Black preachers were licensed by their denominations. In Virginia's Westmoreland County, a Black named Lewis spoke to large crowds. Another, Harry Hoosier, or "Black Harry," traveled with Francis Asbury and other Methodist leaders. In 1773–1775 an African American Baptist church was gathered at Silver Bluff, South Carolina, and was shepherded by George Liele, a slave. The cornerstone of this church indicates it was founded in 1750. Freed by his master, Liele went to Jamaica as a missionary. Andrew Bryan, who had been converted by Liele, preached in Georgia despite great obstacles and founded a Baptist church in Savannah in 1788. Bryan and his brother twice suffered the lash and endured imprisonment for violating a law against slaves gathering to worship separately. In Savannah, a second African Baptist congregation was established in 1803, followed in a few years by yet a third. All three had Black pastors.

Black churches were usually found in southern cities and were controlled by free African Americans, even though slaves accounted for most of their members. On occasion a Black ministered to a mixed congregation. Many whites were very uncomfortable with the idea that African Americans were preaching the Gospel. Perhaps the greatest orator among these African American Baptist clergymen was John Jasper of Richmond, whose most noted sermon was "The Sun Do Move." After 1800 the greatest growth of Protestantism among slaves occurred in white churches, but the separate African American congregations were permitted their own preachers. Moreover, there continued to be Black preachers and exhorters who worked with African Americans in white-dominated congregations.

Black evangelicals enjoyed considerable autonomy until the alleged conspiracy of Denmark Vesey and other Charleston, South Carolina, Blacks was uncovered in 1822. Whites feared that seditious sentiments were spawned in all-Black churches. In Gabriel Prosser's revolt in Virginia in 1800, it was claimed that Prosser and his brother Martin, a preacher, used scriptural arguments to recruit followers. In 1816, a Camden, South Carolina, newspaper reported on a slave conspiracy in which "those who were most active occupied a respectable stand in one of the churches, several were professors [that is, Christians] and one a class leader."

In 1829, Charles Cotesworth Pinckney noted that whites opposed African American preachers because those preachers had more influence with slaves than did masters. A Charlestonian, Pinckney was probably referring to the common belief that an African Methodist congregation was believed to be at the center of what whites called the Denmark Vesey conspiracy in 1822. Vesey was a member of an African American Methodist congregation that was created by those who had withdrawn from white-dominated congregations. Vesey and his associate Peter Poyas were Methodist class leaders, and were alleged to be linked with a root doctor named Gullah Jack. A witness testified that Gullah Jack told him that if he kept a crab claw in his mouth, he could not be wounded. The healing techniques brought from Africa were probably no less effective than the blistering, purging, and bleeding employed by white physicians. It was not concern about the efficacy of tribal medicine that led whites to restrict the activities of "negro doctors." Whites were concerned about the influence root doctors had in the African American community and were determined to combat it.

In 1831, a Virginia slave and sometime Baptist preacher named Nat Turner led a rebellion in response to what he thought was God's call. He felt justified in shedding the blood of whites in an effort to free slaves. Turner was a millennialist who thought violence was necessary to hasten the coming of the millennium. Through visions and dreams, Turner claimed, God had made him a prophet empowered to free his people. He interpreted a solar eclipse, what he thought was a bit of the savior's blood he found on corn, and strange characters found on leaves as signs that the Day of Jubilee was near (Figure 2).

Whites were also concerned about the large numbers of African Americans who attended funerals; these large gatherings were seen as potential threats to public order. Funerals attracted many Blacks because they believed that the deceased was passing on to a better existence and because Africans traditionally placed great emphasis on funeral rites. In Virginia, there was an unsuccessful effort to require that African American funerals be led by white clergy.

In conversations with northerners, southern defenders of slavery and the subordination of free Blacks sometimes pointed to independent African American congregations with pride as well as suspicion. Many whites feared that abolitionist literature was being circulated in Black churches. African Americans successfully managed their own churches, giving them a sense of independence and self-worth. As a Charlestonian put it, the Black churches were "nurseries of self-government"; for that reason whites frequently discouraged their establishment. Though crowded conditions in biracial churches often prompted whites to build separate churches for African Americans, the majority of Christian slaves probably found it necessary to worship with whites most of the time.

African American Worship in the North

As African Americans in the North were freed after the American Revolution, Blacks there had an opportunity to decide for themselves where to worship. Blacks were frequently the objects of discrimination in mixed-race congregations, and many found it desirable to establish their own churches. In 1787 Richard Allen and Absalom Jones unsuccessfully challenged a rule of St. George Methodist Episcopal Church in Philadelphia that African Americans must worship in the church gallery. They built an "African Church," and a majority of members decided to follow Jones into the Protestant Episcopal Church of Saint Thomas. Allen founded a congregation for Black Methodists in 1794. He was noted for his Christian lifestyle and his

Discovery of Nat Turner.

Figure 2. Discovery of Nat Turner. Convinced that the second coming of Christ was at hand, "when the first should be last and the last should be first," Turner (1800–1831), a slave preacher, took up the "fight against the Serpent" by leading a slave revolt in Virginia. It occurred in 1831, lasted forty-eight hours, and spread fear among slaveholders. (Courtesy the Library of Congress.)

willingness to remain in Philadelphia during summer yellow fever epidemics to care for afflicted people of both races. Due to jurisdictional problems and discrimination, Allen founded the African Methodist Episcopal (AME) Church and was elected its first bishop at its initial conference in 1816. The denomination's first choice for bishop was Daniel Coker, who declined the honor and later went to Liberia as a missionary.

In 1830, Bishop Allen organized a "Negro Convention" for church leaders to coordinate efforts in fighting slavery, the first such convention. Bishop Daniel Payne played a major role in establishing Wilberforce University in Ohio in 1856, the first American college or university for African Americans. By 1850, there were one hundred AME congregations. Some of the AME ministers were not educated men, but they encouraged their members to acquire an education.

In New York City, another denomination, the African Methodist Episcopal Church Zion began to take shape in 1821. It began as a separate conference of the Methodist Episcopal Church and held its first conference as a denomination in 1828. James Varick was its first bishop. It has been known as the "Freedom Church," and included as members abolitionists Harriet Tubman, Sojourner Truth, and Frederick Douglass.

Affiliates of these churches were gradually organized in many northern cities, where clerical and lay leaders played important roles in struggles against racism and slavery. Nevertheless, they have been criticized by some historians because a desire for respectability may have sometimes restrained them in their struggle against racism and slavery. For example, the 1856 conference of the AME Church voted not to strengthen its stand against members holding slaves. The knew that some free Blacks were fictitious slave owners, technically holding slaves to prevent their sale into white hands. In this case pastoral and practical considerations seemed most important to these clergymen.

Not all Black Methodists were affiliated with these two African American Methodist denominations. By 1840, the white-dominated Methodist Episcopal Church had sixty-seven thousand African American members. Francis Burns became the first African American bishop of the northern Methodist Episcopal Church in 1852, and John W. Roberts became his successor in 1866. These men were missionary bishops and not permitted to supervise white clergymen.

The Baptist emphasis on the independence of each congregation made it easy for northern African Americans to establish congregations. These churches were established in protest against unfair treatment and were not a reflection of doctrinal differences with white Baptists. In 1805, Thomas Paul organized the African Baptist Church in Boston, later to be known as the Joy Street Church. Three years later, Paul also founded the Abyssinian Baptist Church, and Henry Cunningham established the First Baptist Church in Philadelphia in 1809. An all–African American Baptist denomination was not to emerge until the late nineteenth century. Until 1880, many Black congregations worked with white organizations and were linked to them via the African Baptist Missionary Society, whose emphasis was on bringing Christianity to Africa. Lot Carey became the first African American Baptist missionary in Africa in 1821. He was a founder of the African Baptist Missionary Society and was sent to Liberia by the American Colonization Society. After the North-South division among Baptists in 1845, the African Baptist Missionary Society was linked to the Southern Baptist Convention. By the 1830s there were all-Black Baptist associations. The American Baptist Missionary Convention emerged in 1840 and was active in New England and the Middle Atlantic states. More than two decades later, a northwestern and southern Baptist convention appeared, attended by African American Baptists from eight states.

Presbyterians and Quakers often welcomed African American worshipers, but did not attract them in large numbers. The Quakers made a greater effort than other denominations to educate African Americans. As a church, they came to oppose slavery in the mid–eighteenth century and organized the first manumission society in the United States.

Samuel R. Ward was probably the most prominent African American Presbyterian clergyman. Educated at the expense of abolitionist Gerrit Smith, Ward was a powerful and persuasive speaker who preached throughout central and western New York state, denouncing the Fugitive Slave Act of 1850. He ministered to a white congregation in South Butler, New York, for several years. On the eve of the Civil War, there may have been as many as twenty thousand African American Presbyterians. There were few Black Episcopalians; the first African American Episcopalian priest was William Peters in New York City. That church did not take a position on slavery and moved to prevent a Black priest, Peter Williams, from advocating abolitionist principles.

In Providence, Rhode Island, the first African American church was the interdenominational African Union Meeting House, founded in 1819. Sympathetic whites provided much of the money to build the church, and white ministers conducted its early services. To an extent, white backing for this venture reflected a desire to have Blacks leave other churches. Establishment of a separate church was considered a means of bringing Christianity to the many African Americans who would not worship in segregated churches. The African American community was partly motivated by a desire to use the building for the education of their children, as there were no public facilities for the education of African Americans in Providence until 1828. The establishment of the church was also an African American effort to find strength through unity at a time when many whites were growing hostile and violent toward Blacks. White immigrants built churches for similar reasons, to express cultural pride and to find strength through unity. This would be a common pattern in American religious and cultural history.

African American Churches and Self-Help

African American Protestants in the nineteenth-century North embraced the doctrine of human perfectibility that was proclaimed during the Second Great Awakening. They believed that God decreed that humankind would eventually enjoy complete happiness, and their churches urged members to lead moral lives and cultivate Christian virtues as a means of improving the race. Through moral improvement, African Americans would improve their own conditions of life, while demonstrating their equality to whites. Moral improvement societies were often formed, which not only attempted to uplift the race but fought slavery in the South and a caste system found throughout the United States. Until slavery was ended, they maintained, the American nation would not experience significant moral improvement.

Mutual aid and benevolence societies, formed in the 1830s and 1840s, attempted to demonstrate that the fate of each African American was intertwined with that of her or his Black community and with the entire race. These organizations assisted widows and orphans, looked after the disabled, aged, and sick, made loans, and sponsored schools, among other community services. Great emphasis was placed on offering educational opportunities and in sponsoring libraries. The constitution of the Pittsburgh African Education Association stated "that ignorance is the sole cause of the present degradation and bondage of the people of color in these United States; that the intellectual capacity of the Black man is equal to that of the white, and that he is equally susceptible of improvement." There were also literary, educational, and self-help associations for African American women. A journal describing the activities of a Baltimore African American Catholic society indicates it was active from 1843 to 1845 and had about 270 members. It operated a library, had charitable, devotional, and religious activities, and placed great emphasis upon music. Sometimes members broke into spontaneous song based upon scriptural verses.

Leaders of these African American associations were, often clergy or active church members. Churchmen also dominated the Black convention movement that began in 1830, when Bishop Richard Allen convened the first such meeting in Philadelphia. At these meetings, African American leaders considered common problems and attempted to coordinate their antislavery activities. There were annual meetings until 1835; thereafter there was a seven-year lull. The convention movement was revived by Samuel E. Cornish, a strong-willed New York Presbyterian preacher and editor. He worked to prevent followers of the radical white abolitionist William Lloyd Garrison from dominating the movement, but his position was more radical than that of a circle of Philadelphia-based Black leaders whose views were similar to those of moderate white abolitionists. Among the Philadelphia leaders were James Forten and Robert Purvis. Henry Highland Garnet, a Presbyterian pastor from Troy, New York, frequently offered scriptural reasons for a Black insurrection against slavery and attracted a substantial number of followers. Nevertheless, moderates, whose leadership included the great orator, writer, and abolitionist Frederick Douglass, were successful in persuading conventions to continue to rely upon moral suasion to end slavery.

African American denominations demonstrated their vitality in sending missionaries to the West Indies, where African Methodism was planted in many places. The missionaries were mainly concerned with converting heathens, but some believed that the islands offered Blacks a better life than African Americans could find anywhere in the United States. The success of these efforts was limited by the ability of the African American denominations to finance them.

Lemuel Haynes: African American Theologian

The first major African American theologian was New Englander Lemuel Haynes. Many trace the origins of African American Christian theology to the independent Black churches that emerged after the Civil War, but a strong case can be made that Haynes was the father of African American theology. This Black Congregationalist served white congregations from 1788 until his death in 1833. He emphasized individual liberty and equality and condemned slavery as a sinful institution. Haynes believed that the regenerated individual's actions would be characterized by universal benevolence. Influenced by the cohesion and harmony of Federalism, he thought that harmony and affection could mark the relationship between the races. Modern African American theology rejects his belief in "common sense" thought and insists on a Black hermeneutics, a distinctively African American style of interpretation, which stems from the fact that the Black experience has been different from that of whites.

African American clergy sometimes seemed to avoid pursuing positions to their logical ultimate consequence because they depended upon alliances with well-meaning but somewhat shortsighted whites. African American clergy carried great burdens as community leaders in the decades before the Civil War. They were the key figures in educational and self-help efforts, were involved in abolitionism, and often risked arrest by working in the Underground Railroad.

Ministry of Women

These churchmen were not without imperfections. Their record in the nineteenth century for permitting women to have significant roles in ministry was not much better than that of white, mainstream clergymen. Females had played important roles in African religion, and there were many prophetesses in the early African American Christian churches. The male clergy were generally successful in limiting the ministerial role of women to offering catechetical instruction to other women. However, there were female preachers, most of whom were Methodists. Many of them were traveling preachers who spoke and led prayer in groves and barns. Jarena Lee was permitted by Bishop Richard Allen to be an itinerant preacher, and in 1827 alone she traveled 2,325 miles. Lee, Zilphia Elaw, Amanda Berry Smith, and Julia Foote were four courageous African American women who experienced considerable resistance in finding ministering roles. Smith had an international reputation as a powerful preacher. It could be said that all four pursued entire sanctification as found in the Wesleyan perfectionist tradition. The spiritualism and religious enthusiasm they represented permeated early Methodism and was rooted in their African heritage. Elaw believed that one night she distinctly saw Christ walking toward her with open arms. Lee believed that God gave her "uncommon impressions" such as dreams and visions. These women believed that they had experienced a rebirth and were empowered by the indwelling of the Holy Spirit to live in holiness, free from sin. Believing that they lived in harmony with God's wishes, they held that God had commissioned them to preach. Lee was sanctioned as an AME traveling exhorter, but her efforts to persuade the church to commission women as ministers were voted down at the 1852 conference of the church. Elaw had no official standing but felt she was called to preach, and took her message to the South, where she could have been kidnapped and made a slave. Foote was read out of the AME church for preaching but eventually became its first female deacon in 1894. She played a part in the midwestern holiness revival in the 1870s. Foote, Elaw, and Lee left spiritual autobiographies as testaments to the spiritual liberation of African American women. Although they functioned as ministers, they were not ordained but traveled extensively as teachers and evangelists in the African Methodist Episcopal Church. The African Methodist Episcopal Church Zion ordained women by 1884.

The most famous African American female itinerant preacher was Sojourner Truth, who fearlessly attacked slavery and the inequality of women. To those who said women could not preach because Christ was male, she responded, "Where did your Christ come from? From God and a woman! Man had nothing to do with him." There were also deaconesses, sometimes called "church mothers." However, as the nineteenth century progressed, males were more and more successful in excluding women from the positions of deacon and preacher. Nevertheless, women played important roles in African American congregations, operating missionary societies and offering social services to the poor. Women found in their churches opportunities to develop leadership skills, and with time African American Christianity became more and more a female affair at the membership level, with women holding many leadership positions below the ministerial level.

Many slaves and free African Americans, whether worshiping in biracial congregations, in their own churches, or secretly and out of the sight of whites, usually found ways to adapt Christianity to meet their spiritual needs. It can be argued that Blacks only used Christianity as a vehicle for the preservation of African spirituality and religious usages. It is more likely that the slaves adopted the substance of Christianity, and within that framework were able to preserve the most important elements of their heritage. The two were not in diametrical opposition. The result was a remarkable example of how syncretism or blending of elements from two cultures can work without diminishing either element. Religion became a form of cultural resistance to racism and slavery. As noted, cultural resistance sometimes led to physical resistance. Some never resolved the question of why a good God could permit such an enormous evil as slavery to continue to exist. But many treasured the Christian doctrine that they were equal to whites in the sight of God. They developed the deep conviction that the God of Christian and Hebrew Scripture was primarily the God of the oppressed. In suffering, the faith and spirituality of many slaves and free African Americans was deepened.

Bibliography

Andrews, William L., ed. *Sisters of the Spirit: Three Black Women's Autobiographies of the Nineteenth Century*. Bloomington: Indiana University Press, 1986.

Baer, Hans A., and Merrill Singer. *African American Religion in the Twentieth Century: Varieties of Protest and Accommodation*. Knoxville: University of Tennessee Press, 1992.

Butler, Alfred. *The Africanization of American Christianity*. New York: Carlton Press, 1980.

Butler, Jon. *Awash in a Sea of Faith: Christianizing the American People.* Cambridge: Cambridge University Press, 1990.

————. "The Dark Ages of American Occultism, 1760–1848." In *Popular Religion in America: Symbolic Change and the Modernization Process,* ed. Peter W. Williams, pp. 58–78. Urbana: University of Illinois Press, 1989.

Clarke, Erskine. *Wrestlin' Jacob: A Portrait of Religion in the Old South.* Atlanta: John Knox Press, 1979.

Cottrol, Robert J. *The Afro-Yankees: Providence's Black Community in the Antebellum Era.* Westport, CT: Greenwood Press, 1982.

Davis, Cyprian. *The History of Black Catholics in the United States.* New York: Crossroad, 1990.

DuBois, W.E. Burghardt. "On the Faith of the Fathers." In *The Black Church in America,* ed. Hart M. Nelsen, Raytha L. Yokley, and Anne K. Nelsen, pp. 29–39. New York: Basic Books, 1971.

Eighmy, John Lee. *Churches in Cultural Captivity: A History of the Social Attitudes of Southern Baptists.* Knoxville: University of Tennessee Press, 1972.

Fordham, Monroe. *Major Themes in Northern Black Thought, 1800–1860.* Hicksville, New York: Exposition Press, 1975.

Frazier, E. Franklin. *The Negro Church in America.* New York: Schocken Books, 1963.

Frey, Sylvia. " 'God's Order': Gender and Religious Change in African American History." Unpublished manuscript, Institute of Early American History and Culture, 1994.

————. " 'The Year of Jubilee is Come': Black Christianity in the Plantation South in Post-Revolutionary America." In *Religion in a Revolutionary Age,* ed. Ronald Hoffman and Peter J. Albert, pp. 87–124. Charlottesville: University of Virginia Press, 1994.

Genovese, Eugene. *Roll, Jordan, Roll: The World the Slaves Made.* New York: Vintage Books, 1974.

Herskovits, Melville J. "Africanisms in Religious Life." In *The Black Church in America,* ed. Hart M. Nelsen, Raytha L. Yokley, and Anne K. Nelsen, pp. 44–48. New York: Basic Books, 1971.

Hine, Darlene Clark. "Lifting the Veil, Shattering the Silence: Black Women's History in Slavery and Freedom." In *The State of Afro-American History: Past, Present, and Future,* ed. Darlene Hine, pp. 223–252. Baton Rouge: Louisiana State University Press, 1986.

Johnson, Curtis D. *Redeeming America: Evangelicals and the Road to Civil War.* Chicago: Ivan R. Dee, 1993.

Kosmin, Barry A., and Seymour P. Lachman. *One Nation Under God: Religion in Contemporary American Society.* New York: Harmony Books, 1993.

Kulikoff, Allan. *Tobacco and Slaves: The Development of Southern Cultures in the Chesapeake, 1680–1800.* Chapel Hill: University of North Carolina Press, 1986.

Levine, Lawrence W. *Black Culture and Black Consciousness: African American Folk Thought from Slavery to Freedom.* New York: Oxford University Press, 1977.

Lincoln, C. Eric. *The Black Church Since.* New York: Schocken Books, 1974.

Lincoln, C. Eric, and Lawrence H. Mamiya. *The Black Church in the African American Experience.* Durham: Duke University Press, 1990.

Mays, Benjamin Elijah, and Joseph William Nicholson. *The Negro's Church.* New York: Russell and Russell, 1933.

Nash, Gary B. "New Light on Richard Allen: The Early Years of Freedom." *William and Mary Quarterly* Third Ser., 46 (April 1989): 332–340.

Oates, Stephen B. *The Fires of Jubilee: Nat Turner's Fierce Rebellion.* New York: Harper and Row, 1975.

Payne, Daniel A. *History of the African Methodist Episcopal Church.* 1861. Reprint, New York: Johnson Reprint Corporation, 1968.

Piersen, William D. "White Cannibals, Black Martyrs: Fear, Depression, and Religious Faith as Causes of Suicide Among New Slaves." *Journal of Negro History* 62 (April 1977): 147–159.

Raboteau, Albert J. *Slave Religion: The 'Invisible Institution' in the Antebellum South.* New York: Oxford University Press, 1978.

Saillant, John. "Lemuel Haynes and the Revolutionary Origins of Black Theology, 1776–1801." *Religion and American Life* 2 (summer 1992): 79–102.

Samford, Patricia. "The Archaeology of African American Slavery and Material Culture." *William and Mary Quarterly* 3rd. Ser., 53 (January 1996): 87–114.

Scherer, Lester B. *Slavery and the Negro Churches in Early America, 1619–1819.* Grand Rapids: William B. Eerdmans, 1975.

Shick, Tom W. "Healing and Race in the South Carolina Low Country." In *Africans in Bondage: Studies in Slavery and the Slave Trade,* ed. Paul Lovejoy, pp. 106–126. Madison: University of Wisconsin Press, 1986.

Sobel, Mechal. *The World They Made Together: Black and White Values in Eighteenth-Century Virginia.* Princeton: Princeton University Press, 1987.

Sterling, Dorothy. *The Making of an Afro-American: Martin Robison Delany, 1812–1885.* Garden City: Doubleday, 1971.

Stout, Harry S. "Heavenly Comet." *Christian History* 12 (spring 1993): 9–15.

Thomas, George M. *Revivalism and Cultural Change: Christianity, Nation Building, and the Market in the Nineteenth-Century United States.* Chicago: University of Chicago Press, 1989.

Thorton, John K. "African Dimensions of the Stono Rebellion." *American Historical Review* 96 (October 1991): 1101–1113.

Wade, Richard C. "Beyond the Master's Eye." In *The Black Church in America,* ed. Hart M. Nelsen, Raytha L. Yokley, and Anne K. Nelsen, pp. 63–76. New York: Basic Books, 1971.

Washington, Joseph R., Jr. *Black Religion: The Negro and Christianity in the United States.* Boston: Beacon Press, 1964.

———. *Black Sects and Cults.* Lanham, Maryland: University Press of America, 1984.

Wills, David W. "Beyond Commonality and Plurality: Persistent Racial Plurality in American Religion and Politics." In *Religion and American Politics,* ed. Mark A. Noll, pp. 199–224. New York: Oxford University Press, 1990.

Wilmore, Gayraud S. *Black Religion and Black Radicalism.* Garden City: Doubleday, 1972.

Woodson, Carter Godwin. *The History of the Negro Church.* Washington: Associated Publishers, 1945.

Three

Native American Religion

In the eighteenth century, Native Americans spoke about three hundred languages. There was no single Native American religion, but their religious beliefs had many similarities. They saw no separation between the physical world and the spirit world. Their social systems and cultures were permeated by a spirituality that cannot be isolated from them. They saw a unity of all things, and spiritual beliefs and rituals were related to every aspect of life. Unable to isolate this spirituality, their spokesmen have sometimes refused to describe their religion as something separate from the rest of life.

While Europeans built great churches and cathedrals to address a God in a different place, where they eventually hoped to reside, the Native American was at ease worshiping in a forest. While most Christian religions stress radical individualism, Native American spiritual ceremonies emphasize the welfare of the community. The Native American's whole world was alive and inhabited by spirit power, which also linked individual to surroundings.

Spirit beings could help but could also bring calamities, sickness, and death. Spirit power was a kind of cosmic energy and the source of abilities and knowledge. It was considered invisible but able to take on changing material shapes and was found in all things. The shaman or priest could fill an object with this power, which existed in ritual paraphernalia, such as masks and costumes. Shamans most often contacted the spirits in healing rituals, as well as hunting and agricultural rituals. They sought the help of spirits in taking the dead to the land of the dead. The Zuni believed that the souls of their deceased ancestors returned as parts of rain clouds. Sometimes spirits spoke through shamans. It was believed that spirits could guide individuals through dreams and visions, and a person could develop a strong lifelong bond with one spirit.

Creation Stories

Through legends, myths, and creation stories, Native Americans understood the world and their relationship to nature and others. Hopi and

Zuni legends portrayed the earth as their mother. Native Americans saw themselves as closely related to the earth—their ecological concerns were those of people caring for relatives. The Navajo creation story told how their people had passed though life in four worlds and were now living in a fifth, guarded by deities. The story taught that people encountered many problems of their own making and that the evils inherent in people must be controlled for happiness, harmony, and peace. Understanding human frailties, a Hopi axiom asserts that humans are clowns.

The Iroquois believed that in the beginning nature consisted of sky and water. A pregnant woman named Sky Woman, who lived in the sky, fell to the water but landed on the back of a snapping turtle. The mud placed there by a muskrat became the earth, on which Sky Woman fell. This basic story is found in numerous creation myths; North America is Turtle Island. According to the Iroquois, when the turtle stretched, there were cracks in the earth. The burial of Sky Woman's daughter in the earth made it possible for food to grow. Plants, animals, and streams were created by Sky Woman's sometimes wayward grandsons. The evil brother, Flint, was viewed as the source of healing power. The struggle of Sapling, the good brother, with Flint underscored the impossibility of eliminating evil and the need for divine intervention in battling it. In several petroglyphs, female symbolism was linked with earth and was the mother or source of life. In native languages, females and earth were linked as mothers, with earth epitomizing motherhood. The Native Americans' great reverence for nature grew out of their belief that all life flows from Mother Earth. The Moon was often referred to as grandmother, and governed women's bodily rhythms. The Sun was often seen as a male creative spirit.

Creation myths explained the existence of evil, held out the hope for curing sickness, explained why there were so many people and languages, and emphasized the need for cooperation among people. These myths allowed people to understand their deities and how best to please them. Not all myths were about creation. Some explained the power of good and evil, and many told about very self-centered tricksters whose misadventures created problems for humankind. The tricksters often seemed to be humanlike animals or humans who were given animal names because of their conduct.

Some Significant Rituals

Native Americans believed that spirit power, especially in the form of knowledge, could be acquired through chants, dance, prayer, and songs. Some maintained that certain sacred words must be said in exactly the same manner that they had been passed from generation to generation. When employing dance rituals, the Native American donned the costume and mask representing the spirit he desired to contact, and the dancer became a vehicle through which the spirit passed power to other members of the community. On the Great Plains, the sun dance was performed with gashes pierced in the male dancer's chest and back, and the pins or skewers in his flesh tied to a pole. He danced against ropes until freed from the pins or skewers. The participant suffered on behalf of the community and asked the Creator to assist him and the community. In this way, visions and sacred powers were acquired. Native Americans frequently entered sweat lodges in their quest for physical and spiritual health. The heat and steam were produced in various ways, including pouring water on hot stones. Participants meditated, prayed, sang, and bonded with one another.

Sacred tobacco pipes were smoked in a ceremony that explained the universe and man's relationship to it. In the end participants learned they were all related to one another. One explanation for the use of the pipe was that a supernatural buffalo cow woman gave it to Native Americans and instructed them in its use. Some believed the pipe was given them at creation; among its uses were healing and protection. Hopi priests smoked pipes in ritual chambers underground as a means of praying for rain. Tobacco was often offered to the spirits and carried messages to them. Sometimes dogs, who represented loyalty, were sacrificed to the spirits to demonstrate the fidelity of the community to their honored spirits. Today, some Christian clergy are interested in inserting the pipe ritual into communion services for Native Americans.

Some thought evil witches, or sorcerers, caused illness, and it was a common belief that illness resulted from an evil thought or action. Religious healers used different approaches to illness. Iroquois healers studied people's dreams, which reflected their desires. It was thought that illness could come from unfulfilled dreams. Some thought that illness occurred when the soul left the body at night but failed to return before the person awoke. In this case, healers sought to recover the lost soul.

Algonquian of the northeast woodlands had "False Face" curing societies, the faces cut from living wood. The masks were prepared by older women who were members of the Society of Faces, who also prepared medicines. Healing dances were held during the midwinter festival. There was a dance for men only, and the Fish Dance was performed by youth of both sexes and men.

Most Native Americans believed in a sacred mystery or sacred power, which is somewhat simplistically called the Great Spirit. It was seen as essentially unknowable; the Navajo spoke of the "Unknown Power," and the Hopi referred to the "Mighty Something." Native Americans believed that peace comes when one dwells in union with the Creator and lives in harmony and oneness with creation. Native Americans were not pantheists. Animals and natural phenomena were thought to have been created by the Great Spirit before people, reflecting and revealing some divine qualities. Partly for these reasons, their spirits were venerated, and Native Americans often addressed the creator through them. The Crow of the Yellowstone Valley believed they were guided by guardian spirits and venerated talismans that represented these spirits, such as the hair of the great warrior Red Plume.

Native Americans realized that they depended upon other species for life. Through their religions they paid their respects to all other living things as well as their spirits. An example of this phenomenon was provided by the Algonquian ritual that accompanied the killing of a bear; it included a respectful and ritualistic disposal of the bear's bones and skull. If performed correctly, the spirits of bears would permit them to later kill other bears for their sustenance. There were also sacred ways of fishing and hunting.

The myths of some Native American peoples taught that spirits gave their people certain plants and animals for their judicious use. Cherished stories often were used to explain the origins of certain crops. Some eastern Native Americans believed corn grew from the body of a dead woman, linking the fertility of the earth with the feminine, and teaching that death can serve to sustain and continue life. The Penobscot of New England saw this woman as a deity called First Mother, who planned her own death to make the soil fertile. Corn played a central role in the myths and rituals of many Native American peoples. To celebrate and give thanks for a corn harvest, Native Americans participated in the green corn ritual, whose roots were in the Mississippian culture that broke down with the coming of the European invaders. This ritual was later revived as part of religious, political, and military efforts to give new life to their cultures and resist white incursions.

Of equal importance were ceremonies relating to weather and the cycle of seasons. Renewal ceremonies held in the summer or December, as in the case of the Iroquois, reflected their thankfulness for the seasons and growth cycle and their hopes for blessings in the next cycle. In addition to addressing supernatural beings, thanks were also directed to all living earthly beings and things. For some, like the Arapaho, Lakota Sioux, Cheyenne, Shoshones, and Blackfeet, the sun dance was the renewal ritual and included petitions for the restoration of the health of a community.

Religious ceremonies marked birth and often reflected the newborn's connection with ancestors. Rituals also accompanied the naming of children. Various rites were designed to give children moral guidance and to prepare them for full participation in the ceremonial life of the community.

Kachina societies were used by the Hopi and some other southwestern peoples for this purpose. Puberty rituals were employed to prepare young women for motherhood and full participation in the life of the community. Females obtained the guidance of spirits, birds, and animals in becoming spiritually mature women.

When boys reached physical maturity, they went on vision quests or "lamentings," seeking supernatural beings who would lead them through life. On these spiritual retreats, they fasted and prayed for a number of days that the Great Spirit would send them wisdom through one of his creatures. A significant part of the community assisted in preparing for the quest, and the individual expected to gain knowledge and insights that would be of benefit to all. The most active force during the lamentation was silence, often considered the actual voice of the Creator. The young man might learn through a vision to use a special ritual or song, or to identify some object endowed with spiritual power for his personal use. Sometimes it was expected that he share his experience with others. It was generally expected that all men would participate in the quest, resulting in something like "democratic shamanism."

In the Great Lakes region, the young Ojibwa man may have been instructed in a vision to seek admission to the Medicine Lodge Society. Initiation ceremonies usually occurred twice a year in one lodge, considered a representation of the universe, and might last as long as eight days. The climax of the ceremonies was a ritual death followed by a spiritual rebirth marked by increased wisdom and spirituality. These ceremonies were not unlike rituals among white men's fraternal lodges. Funeral rites differed from people to people, but all honored the spirit of the dead and expressed the community's solidarity with the grieving family. Those who believed the spirit of the dead lingered on earth for a short time attempted to prepare the dead for the departure from the realm of the living.

Christian Elements in Native Religion

When they came in contact with white Europeans, Native Americans came to adapt some of their beliefs to make them comprehensible to Christians. The Christian devil was sometimes identified with their mythological figures. In the same way, the concept of the Christian God became the Great Spirit. The New York Iroquois False Face was adapted to facilitate Christian comprehension. Similarly, in the Southwest, the Arapaho developed a term for the Christian God. The Seminoles of Florida had a cultural hero they identified with Jesus Christ.

The Lakota of the northern plains used the term Wakan-Tanka, or "Great

Mysterious," as an adjective to mean the totality of sacred mysteries. These came to be translated as "Great Spirit," a name reflecting the Christian approach to God. At their Easter ceremony, the Yakis employed Christian symbolism and themes. They believed that at the time Christianity was founded, a wise woman taught her daughter to listen to a vibrating tree. The daughter learned from the tree about the Christian God and some Christian mysteries and that padres would bring this message to them. Those who rejected her teaching held a great departure ceremony and went to a kingdom beneath the earth and became ants. The contemporary Yakis were descendants of those who chose to wait for the Christian message. Hopi prophecies foresaw the eventual dominance of whites.

Over time, Christian Native Americans have contributed to the evolution of a syncretic blend of native religion and Christianity, which incorporates the strongest elements of each. A number of Native American prophets would attempt to revive traditional religion and customs by incorporating elements borrowed from Christianity.

Efforts to Christianize Indians

From the beginning of their contact with Native Americans, white Christians tried to convert them to Christianity. Unfortunately, whites usually equated accepting Christianity with abandoning native culture and living as white people. Some Christian beliefs conflicted sharply with the beliefs of Native Americans. The Navajo rejected the mass because they dreaded contamination through contact with the dead and saw Holy Communion as a cannibalistic rite. Their sexual spontaneity alarmed whites like Pilgrim leader William Bradford, who became convinced that Native Americans must be civilized for fear that they would have contact with white women. There were towns of "praying" or Christian Indians in Puritan New England where Christianized natives lived as second-class citizens. They served as an auxiliary military force and were practically discarded when no longer considered useful. Some early Virginians unsuccessfully tried to purchase Indian youths in order to Christianize them.

When some Native Americans within a tribe accepted Christianity, there were serious tribal divisions that weakened the community, clan government, and traditional practices. Sometimes, the appearance of Christianity simply accentuated existing divisions. When Christian missionaries had some success among Native Americans, it was often because Native Americans were moved by sincere missionary testimonies just as by descriptions of vision quests. Some accepted Christianity totally and rejected their old beliefs, but others embraced parts of it in the same manner that they incorporated new Native American practices. Some partially accepted Christianity so they could realize greater profits from relationships with whites. In the Southwest, the Spanish used the sword to force conversions. Many padres brought the Christian gospel to natives without the protection of Spanish arms, and not a few of them were killed. The priests were hated because they were the most serious threat to native culture. In 1680, the Pueblo Indians, led by shaman Popé, drove the Spanish out of their lands. They kept the Spanish at bay for twelve years and unbaptized the converts among them. In time native religion and Catholicism came to coexist among the Pueblo, as they do today, with some people participating in both. The Navajo aside, the Roman Catholic missionaries had significant success among Native Americans. Among the most successful was a Spaniard, Father Junipero Serra, who beginning in 1769 led a group of Franciscans in founding a chain of missions in California. A little more than a century later, Presbyterian lay missionary Sue McBeth came to work among the Nez Percé. Her community of Presbyterian Nez Percé stood aloof when federal forces crushed Chief Joseph's resistance in 1877.

Native American children who received Christian schooling found it necessary to turn their backs on most of their culture, and became adults who fit in neither the white man's world nor that of their ancestors. Christianity was seen by whites as a civilizing and detribalizing force. Protestant missionary Benjamin Whipple believed the Sioux could best be civilized and Christianized if they had less land, which would force detribalization. His work helped the U.S. government dispossess the Sioux of the gold-rich Black Hills, a sacred place beneath which the Sioux believed they had once dwelt. The white settlers who came to that area, Whipple thought, would be role models for the Native Americans.

Self-appointed white guardians of the Native Americans, such as Herbert Welsh, believed it was their mission to guide Native Americans "from the night of barbarism into the fair dawn of Christian civilization." Philadelphian Welsh was founder of the Indian Rights Association. Henry Dawes, author of the single most important piece of detribalizing legislation, wrote that the Indian "must be taught how to work, how to take care of himself, and then he must have the elevating influence of the Christian religion to inspire, and make him feel that to do this makes a man of him." The French Jesuit missionaries represented a partial exception to this white Christian ethnocentrism. They may not have embraced Indian culture, as Francis Parkman suggested, but they were less disparaging of Native American ways than English-speaking whites. Both the French missionaries and many Anglo-Saxon bearers of Christianity thought themselves sincere friends of the Indians. Some, like Isaac Jogues, were killed by the people they tried to convert.

Perhaps the most notable early Native American Catholic was the Mohawk Kateri Tekakwitha. A smallpox epidemic in 1660 took most of her family, and she was weakened and scarred by the disease. She was harassed due to her attachment to the new religion and disappointed her family when she refused to marry, preferring to be a bride of Christ. She fled to a Christian Mohawk community near Montreal, where she attended daily mass and subjected herself to painful penances such as burning herself with hot coals and sleeping on a bed of thorns. The Jesuits recorded that when she died at age twenty-four, her skin was restored to a healthy and youthful condition with the pockmarks disappearing. In 1980, the Catholic Church declared she was blessed, having led a life of heroic virtue. Catholic Native Americans have become devoted to her memory and see her spirituality and persistence as qualities to be emulated. Just as Catholicism became central to the lives of many Native Americans like Kateri Tekakwitha, Protestantism proved to be a source of meaning and solace for many other Native Americans. Facing removal to the Indian Territory, Cherokee Baptists under Reverend Jesse Bushyhead dismantled their church and laboriously transported it with them to Oklahoma.

The story of efforts to Christianize the Crow is not all that different from similar enterprises with other peoples. Roman Catholic missionaries often displayed great discipline and tenacity in their efforts to win Native American converts, and were sometimes more successful than their competitors. Father Pierre-Jean De Smet, a famous Jesuit missionary, first preached to the Crow of the Yellowstone Valley in 1842. Lutherans, Methodists, and Unitarians also preached to the Crow in the Big Horn Valley, but it was the Jesuits who succeeded in establishing a mission there in 1887. The Native Americans were impressed with the black robes' efforts to learn their language. The priests sought to win the conversion of tribal leaders in hopes others would follow the leaders' example. Some tribal leaders doubtless feigned piety in order to win concessions from white authorities and saw the church as offering them some protection from unreasonable authorities. There were Christian boarding schools for the children. A Baptist missionary opened day schools for Crow children in the early twentieth century, and won many converts because he made it possible for the children to live at home and still receive an education. The priests soon established day schools, but had lost their dominance among Christian Crow. By 1929, no Christian group had a substantial following among Big Horn Crow. There were about one hundred Baptists and fifty Catholics, with most of the remaining two hundred practicing native religion that centered on the use of peyote as a sacrament.

Federal authorities discouraged the practice of tribal religion on reservations, where Native Americans were encouraged to become Christians as part of the civilizing process. The Civilization Act of 1819 provided subsidies for Christian missionaries to educate Indian children as part of the government's efforts to detribalize Native Americans. The Grant administration placed entire nations under the jurisdiction of specific churches by appointing as federal Indian agents people nominated by those churches. Reflecting widespread anti-Catholicism, however, the Grant administration seized some Catholic missions and transferred them to Protestant groups. In *The Code of Religious Offenses* of 1883, the Bureau of Indian Affairs outlawed a number of Native American religious ceremonies. This policy of discouraging Native American religious practices continued well into the twentieth century. Circular 1665, issued by the Bureau of Indian Affairs in 1921, advised all superintendents and missionaries to discourage Indian dances. These restrictions ended in 1934 with the Indian Reorganization Act. In the 1970s, under legislation to protect endangered species, Native Americans were arrested for possessing eagle feathers for religious purposes. They were also arrested for using peyote in religious ceremonies.

Rebellion and Revitalization

In facing the many hardships that grew out of their encounters with Europeans, Native Americans sought strength and solace in their religions. In the mid–eighteenth century, a pan-Indian movement developed, with strong religious underpinnings, and would continue through the War of 1812. This intertribal movement focused on resisting the advance of the whites while strengthening commitment to Native American religion and culture. Above all, it was an effort to recover sacred power. The Great Spirit, it was thought, was angry because his people were too dependent on the goods of white traders and neglected traditional religious ceremonies. These rites seemed less important to Native Americans who wondered why shamans and healers were unable to cope with the deadly diseases that had felled tens of thousands of their people since the white Europeans arrived. These epidemics threw some Native American religions into disarray, and some questioned their traditional religious beliefs. The sense of coherence once provided by religion and tribal institutions was gone.

Nativist movements appeared that were intended to restore confidence in traditional religion and institutions and were directed against Native Americans who appeased the whites. A number of prophets emerged, and their visions and new rituals provided direction to this great revitalization movement. These prophets preached pure living, freedom from alcohol, Indian separateness, and brotherhood. Two important Delaware prophets were Papoonan and Neolin. As a young man living along the Cuyahoga River,

Neolin claimed to have visited heaven and seen hell. The Creator, he warned, would continue to punish his people unless they eliminated white influence among them, purified themselves by induced vomiting, and drove the whites out. His teachings reflected the influence of contact with Christianity in his condemnation of polygamy and references to hell and the evil spirit. Pontiac, the great Ottawa warrior, claimed to have been inspired by Neolin, but disagreed with him on the use of European weapons. This war leader laid siege to Detroit in 1763. The uprising known as Pontiac's Rebellion in 1763–1764 involved the Wyandot, Ottawas, Shawnee, and Delaware. The rebellion was at best a series of attacks that were not entirely orchestrated by Pontiac. After the rebellion he tried unsuccessfully to construct a confederation of tribes. There were pan-Indian conferences at Shawnee settlements on the Scioto (in Ohio) in 1769 and 1770, but they did not produce a substantial military force when Lord Dunmore's War erupted in 1774. It involved Shawnee, Mingos, Delaware, Wyandot, Ottawas, and Cherokee.

During the American Revolution, there were some uncharacteristic alliances between nativists and those assimilationists who favored close cooperation with the British. The Indians who opposed the United States sought spiritual support through traditional ceremonies. Northern radicals objected to the presence of Christian missionaries and urged the few Christians among them to return to Native American religion. The pacifist Moravian Delaware Indians suffered at the hands of the British and Wyandot, and were forced to abandon their homes in the Muskingum Valley; when these unarmed Moravians returned to this area they were massacred by Americans in 1782.

During the American Revolution, the Cherokee Nation negotiated agreements with the southern states, which militants rejected. They became the short-lived Chickamaugas. Radical Native Americans from the North sometimes fought by their side in the South, and some southern Native Americans later assisted the Shawnee, Wyandot, and Miami in battles that ended in the defeat at Fallen Timbers in 1794. In the latter campaigns, some of the Shawnee received spiritual guidance from a Mohawk woman, Coocoochee, and performed incantations that were usually followed by victory. The drinking and vomiting of a black liquid as a purification rite had developed among the Delaware at midcentury and was common in both North and South. The black drink was thought to strengthen warriors for war and sharpen the minds of tribal leaders for important deliberations.

The pan-Indian movement reappeared in 1805, but lacked the force of earlier efforts. It continued to be built upon a religious base provided by prophets. Its major religious spokesman was the Shawnee prophet Tenskwatawa, or the Open Door. Whites simply referred to him as "the

Prophet." Before his religious experience and conversion, he had been addicted to alcohol and led a dissolute life. During his spiritual awakening, he allegedly died and was taught how Native Americans could redeem or revitalize themselves. Whites, he said, were children of the evil Great Serpent and were to be avoided. There were other spiritual leaders, perhaps most important of whom was "the Trout," an Ottawa who acknowledged the one-eyed Tenskwatawa as his leader. The Trout forbade his followers to wear hats; his teachings reflect less Christian influence than those of the Prophet. Tenskwatawa spoke of a fiery hell, and his public ceremonies somewhat resembled camp meetings, with people weeping, trembling, and openly confessing their sins. The meetings of his Iroquois contemporary Handsome Lake and those of the Assinsink Munsees in the 1760s shared these characteristics. (Being completely surrounded by whites, Handsome Lake's followers did not play an active role in the early nineteenth century's pan-Indian movement.)

The Trout and Tenskwatawa said game would be plentiful again and warned against overhunting. All the pan-Indian revivals featured opposition to witchcraft, which they blamed for illness, and the witch-hunt was central to the Prophet's revival and even led to some deaths among the Delaware. The killing of accused witches led many Delaware to back away from Tenskwatawa's movement. The Prophet condemned chiefs who negotiated with the U.S. government, and opposed all efforts to induce Native Americans to live as white men. A third prophetic leader in the pan-Indian movement was the Potawatomi Main Poc, who continued to use alcohol after his conversion. He advocated temperance rather than total abstinence.

Tecumseh, half brother of the Prophet, emerged as the movement's military leader. In 1811, accompanied by some of the lesser Shawnee prophets, he traveled to the South, where he sought allies in a united Native American assault on the United States. Tecumseh was unable to revive the pan-Indian alliances of the past and did not win many firm supporters. He attracted the support of the Red Sticks, a militant Creek faction, bitter opponents of the whites' so-called civilizing mission and deeply committed to traditional Creek religion. A sharp division among Creeks existed before Tecumseh's appearance and would lead to a civil war in 1813. That war was touched off by the assassination of Little Warrior, a Red Stick leader who had journeyed north with Tecumseh. The Red Sticks adopted rituals they learned from Tecumseh, and their prophets devised additional new ceremonies. The accommodationists of the Creek National Council had their own prophets, one of whom claimed to have learned much from the Great Horned Serpents by spending much time on the floors of rivers.

When the War of 1812 erupted between the United States and Great Britain, Indian nativists took up arms against the United States. In the

North, Tecumseh and his followers allied with the British. Tecumseh died at the Battle of the Thames in 1813, wearing the uniform of a British brigadier general. That battle marked the end of effective Native American resistance in what would be called the Old Northwest. By and large, Tecumseh's followers were militants in revolt against the accommodationist and peaceful policies of their elders. Some Red Sticks were at his side, and some Shawnee joined the Red Sticks in the South. In 1814, General Andrew Jackson defeated the Red Sticks at the Battle of Horseshoe Bend. The American forces included five hundred Creek and Cherokee warriors. Tenskwatawa survived the war, lived for a time in Canada, and eventually became an accommodationist. He cooperated with federal plans for removal of Indians to the West.

A religious prophet emerged among the Cherokee two decades later. When the Cherokee were being removed from their homeland during the Trail of Tears in the 1830s, some Cherokee managed to find a home for themselves in the Smoky Mountains of North Carolina. Their leader was the prophet Yonaguska, who awoke from apparent death at his own funeral and announced that he had acquired wisdom in the land of the spirits. His followers are the ancestors of many of today's Eastern Cherokee.

Later Religious Movements

Aside from militant pan-Indian nativist religion, three significant new Native American religious movements were to develop: the Handsome Lake religion among the Iroquois of New York, the Ghost Dance religion among the Plains Indians, and the Peyote religion among many Western Indians.

Handsome Lake (1735–1815), or "the Life Giver," was an alcoholic Seneca. After a long illness and at the point of death, he had a sudden recovery and announced that four beings sent by the Creator had visited him. They told him the Creator was willing to give his people another chance to live properly and enjoy good lives. Handsome Lake was to take the Creator's instructions to all the Iroquois; these instructions were for all humankind. Like Neolin, he spoke of a place like the Christian hell where wrongdoers would suffer severe punishment. His belief that his deceased dog and dead relatives went to a marvelous and beautiful land reflected the influence of Christian thought. The Good Word, or Code of Handsome Lake, was to be recited by believers annually at a thanksgiving ceremony. It encouraged people to live in harmony, be helpful to others, and avoid alcohol and gossip. People were to be generous and compassionate; spouses were to be faithful and respect one another. Followers were expected to engage in traditional Iroquois religious rites. His followers became an influential force among the Iroquois and promoted renewed interest in traditional culture. This revitalization movement was accommodationist in nature and contained elements borrowed from Christians, especially the Quakers.

In the Northwest, there was accommodationist movement among the Tsimshian. Early in the century, prophets urged their people to find an accommodation between traditional ways and European culture. The work of the *bini,* or prophets, was completely negated in the 1830s when Anglican lay missionary William Duncan converted the high chief and many others. Duncan created a Christian community that still exists, and he functioned as their high chief.

During a total eclipse of the sun on January 1, 1889, a Nevada Paiute named Wovoka or Jack Wilson (1858–1932) was allegedly conveyed by spirits to heaven where he met God. He said that "God told me to come back and tell my people they must be good and love one another, and not fight, or steal, or lie." He was told that Native Americans must do the historic round dance. Wovoka taught that a new world would come about where there was no illness or old age and people would be rejoined by their deceased ancestors; those who did not heed his teachings would suffer and not enter this new world. Wovoka claimed to have received from God the power to control the weather and was designated copresident of the United States. He convinced some that he was invulnerable to gunpowder and could produce ice on a hot summer day.

The core of Wovoka's teachings was that everyone should lead a "clean, honest life," and he willingly shared his teachings with whites who came to him for guidance. His message spread among the Plains Indians. He told his followers to hasten the coming of the new world by performing the traditional round dance and performing other ceremonies. The dance was called by some the "Ghost Dance," because it involved resurrection of the dead. In this dance, which often produced trances and emotional catharsis, men and women danced together. The Ghost Dance or spirit dance was to be performed over five nights, with possible spirit encounters (Figure 3).

Wovoka also said that when this world ended it would shake mightily but his followers would not be hurt. The Lakota interpreted Wovoka's message to mean that they would be joined by their deceased loved ones. Some thought the plains would again be populated by game and buffalo. These were the ideas of an earlier Paiute teacher, Wodziwob, or Fish Lake Jo, who also prophesied that all whites would be destroyed. No version of the Ghost Dance religion suggested that whites would be killed off by Native Americans, but white authorities were concerned that this might be attempted. Wovoka's message was probably influenced by the earlier teachings of a prophet named Smohalla in eastern Washington and by

Figure 3. The Ghost Dance by the Ogallala Sioux at Pine Ridge Agency, Dakota. (By Frederic Remington.) Followers of the Paiute prophet Wovoka (1858–1932) performed a circular dance for several days in quest of visions. They believed in peaceful, virtuous living and hoped for the restoration of their lands and the return of deceased ancestors. (Courtesy the Library of Congress.)

Wodziwob, a prophet in western Nevada. Wovoka's approach was peaceful, but there emerged belief in an impenetrable "ghost shirt" that may have led some followers to consider a violent solution to their problems.

The Ghost Dance religion was warmly received in many places. Having experienced great mistreatment and humiliation at the hands of whites, many Lakota embraced the new rite on their reservations in the Dakotas. These people were facing disease, starvation, and death, and the government had cut their rations. Federal authorities forbade performance of the Ghost Dance, but it was performed anyway. Sitting Bull, an important military leader, urged his people to continue the rite as a way of protesting abuse and asserting their dignity as a people.

In late 1890, tensions heightened when one thousand federal troops were sent to the reservations to suppress an imagined uprising that white officials thought would be triggered by the Ghost Dance ritual. Sitting Bull was killed in a battle with native police, and Big Foot and over three hundred others who had surrendered to the military were slaughtered at Wounded Knee Creek. Nervous soldiers began to shoot four rapid-fire cannons into the camp when some Indians refused to surrender their rifles. Those who sought to flee were mowed down by these deadly weapons employing explosive shells. Some soldiers received military decorations for their valor. Small groups continued to perform the Ghost Dance ritual but did not emphasize the end of the world, and the dance is occasionally performed today. Wovoka continued to have some influence and supported himself by selling feathers and red ocher. Followers believed these items had healing qualities. Three months after his death in 1932, there was a small earthquake, which followers said he foretold.

Two less significant religious movements appeared in the late nineteenth century among Indians of the Northwest. Both were reactions against reservation life and white attempts to wipe out tribal life. The Dreamers and the Indian Shakers were founded by prophets who insisted that their people return to traditional ways of living, stressing the ascetic, contemplative life. The Dreamers were Sanspoils, Spanish-speaking Indians who lived on the north shore of the Columbia River. Their most important prophet was Skolaskin, who allegedly visited heaven after having died and lain motionless for at least a day. He successfully predicted the 1872 earthquake and its aftershocks. He developed his own criminal justice system, complete with a police force and jail pit. He was arrested and held at Alcatraz from 1889 to 1892 for disturbing reservation order. The Dreamers were soon called the Feather or Longhouse religion. Skolaskin eventually became a Roman Catholic and symbolically broke with his nativist past by cutting his long hair.

Another religion grew around the use of peyote, a small cactus used by Indians in Mexico and Texas even before the coming of whites—its use by some native peoples can be traced to pre-Columbian times. When ingested, the mescaline in the peyote produces hallucinations and euphoria, not unlike the effects of today's LSD or "acid." In the 1870s, some Native Americans on the plains and in Oklahoma were using peyote in religious rites. In addition to providing users with insights and visions, the plants themselves were thought capable of hearing and answering prayers. Sometimes the use of peyote caused muscle spasms and vomiting, but Peyotists insist its spiritual benefits far outweigh these side effects. Its use is not thought recreational; rather it is considered similar to the Christians' use of communion wine. Believers state that this ritual can restore health, particularly when the user also obeys the command to abstain from alcohol. There is medical evidence to suggest that peyote might be an excellent antidote for alcoholism. This religion often draws elements from Christianity and traditional Native American religion: Bibles and crosses were to be found on the plates containing peyote buttons. Some practitioners incorporated no Christian elements and relied upon traditional Native American usages. "Road men," or ministers, presided at the ceremonies and were assisted by drummers, fire men, and others. The ceremony began at sundown and lasted the night, and was followed by a common breakfast. The church conducted business in English, and sometimes Christ was said to have appeared in visions. The rite also incorporates purely Native American elements through the use of dances, drums, and traditional singing in native languages. Peyotists were to follow the "Peyote Road," which emphasized self-reliance, marital fidelity, brotherly love, concern for family, and avoidance of alcohol.

In the pre–World War II period, the religion experienced significant growth. When some states outlawed the use of peyote, Peyotists responded by forming the Native American Church in 1918. The church was to promote Christian morality through the use of the peyote sacrament. Peyotists hoped to enjoy the protection accorded religious observances by the First Amendment. In *Oregon Employment Division v. Smith* (1990), the U.S. Supreme Court upheld an Oregon law that outlawed peyote use. In response, Native Americans and civil libertarians succeeded in persuading Congress to pass legislation in 1993 making it more difficult for states to restrict the free exercise of religion. The following year, President William Clinton signed the American Indian Religious Freedom Act, which protects traditional religious practices, including the use of peyote. The U.S. Supreme Court declared this law unconstitutional in 1997.

The best examples of Native American religion combined a spiritual worldview with a heroism marked by both stoicism and combativeness. The virtues they emphasized were bravery, generosity, kindness, and serenity;

together they conveyed nobility upon believers. The social systems and religions of many native peoples accorded high status to those who gave much of their wealth to others; their religious values have been in stark contrast to many of the values of the dominant culture. Native American prophets often incorporated Christian images and ideas into their teachings, but their messages remained countercultural and subversive to the extent that they showed that the Christians could not live up to their own values. Today, bicultural spokespersons for Native Americans urge the emulation of some Indian values in an effort to help revitalize Western culture.

As modern Native Americans have attempted to find ways to coexist with or become part of the dominant society, they have reexamined their religious beliefs. This process has often led to the despiritualization or detraditionalization of their outlooks and undermined their customary way of life. Their communitarian outlook often conflicted with the extreme competitiveness demanded by capitalism. There have been intense federal efforts to detribalize Native Americans, one marked by the Dawes Act in 1887, and a more recent effort in the 1950s. Christians of European origins have also experienced damage to their religious values as a result of modernization, but the effect has rarely been as devastating. Native Americans are today actively working to preserve their languages because they are the vehicles of oral tradition and religious teachings.

Recent decades have also seen substantial increases in the number of people who identify themselves as Native Americans. In 1990, about 1.8 million people described themselves as Native Americans; this is in contrast to the estimated 350,000 Native Americans in the United States in 1900. Today many more young Native Americans are showing great interest in their heritage, and many traditional rites are being performed. A Hopi prophecy suggests that today's confrontation with whites is meant to purify the Hopi hearts by choosing the good that whites offer while resisting evil. They believe that in time a true white brother will join them if they have been purified by this experience. Otherwise, they would cease to be Hopi. There is reason to hope that Native Americans can find ways of preserving the essence of their rich religious heritage despite the corrosive power of modernity.

Bibliography

Ballantine, Betty, and Ian Ballantine, eds. *The Native Americans: An Illustrated History.* Atlanta: Turner, 1992.

Bonvillain, Nancy. *Native American Religion.* New York: Chelsea House, 1995.

Brown, Joseph Epes. *The Spiritual Legacy of the American Indian.* New York: Crossroad, 1982.

Calloway, Colin G. *The American Revolution in Indian Country: Crisis and Diversity in Native American Communities.* Cambridge: Cambridge University Press, 1995.

Deloria, Vine Jr. *God Is Red: A Native View of Religion.* Golden, CO: Fulcrum, 1994.

———. *Red Earth: Native Americans and the Myth of Scientific Fact.* New York: Scribner, 1995.

Dowd, Gregory Evans. *A Spirited Resistance: The North American Indian Struggle for Unity, 1745–1815.* Baltimore: Johns Hopkins University Press, 1992.

Gill, Sam D., and Irene F. Sullivan. *Dictionary of Native American Mythology.* New York: Oxford University Press, 1992.

———. *Native American Religious Action: A Performance Approach to Religion.* Columbia: University of South Carolina Press, 1987.

Hoxie, Frederick E., ed. *Encyclopedia of North American Indians: Native American History, Culture, and Life From Paleo-Indians to the Present.* Boston: Houghton Mifflin, 1996.

———. *Parading Through History: The Making of the Crow Nation in America, 1805–1935.* New York: Cambridge University Press, 1995.

Jennings, Francis. *The Ambiguous Iroquois Empire: The Covenant Chain Confederation of Indian Tribes with English Colonies.* New York: Norton, 1984.

Kehoe, Alice Beck. *The Ghost Dance: Ethnohistory and Revitalization.* Fort Worth: Holt, Rinehart, and Winston, 1989.

La Barre, Weston. *The Peyote Cult.* Norman: University of Oklahoma Press, 1989.

Loftin, John D. *Religion and Hopi Life in the Twentieth Century.* Bloomington: Indiana University Press, 1991.

Nash, Gary B. *Red, White, and Black: The Peoples of Early America.* New York: Prentice-Hall, 1982.

Nichols, Roger L. *The American Indian: Past and Present.* New York: McGraw-Hill, 1992.

Shorris, Earl. *The Death of the Great Spirit: An Elegy for the American Indian.* New York: Simon and Schuster, 1971.

Steele, Ian K. *Warpaths: Invasions of North America.* New York: Oxford University Press, 1994.

Underhill, Ruth Murray. *Red Man's America: A History of Indians in the United States.* Chicago: University of Chicago Press, 1953.

Vecsey, Christopher. *Religion in Native North America.* Moscow: University of Idaho Press, 1990.

Walker, Edward E., Jr. *Witchcraft and Sorcery of the Native American Peoples.* Moscow: University of Idaho Press, 1989.

Welsh, Herbert. "The Needs of the Time." In *Americanizing the American Indians: Writings by the 'Friends of the Indian,' 1880–1900,* ed. Francis Paul Prucha, pp. 96–99. Cambridge: Harvard University Press, 1973.

Williams, Peter W. *Popular Religion in America: Symbolic Change and the Modernization Process in Historical Perspective.* Urbana: University of Illinois Press, 1989.

Four

Societal Change and
the Second Awakening

In the first half of the nineteenth century, a market revolution and an equalitarian spirit swept across the United States. The years from 1820 to the mid-1840s have been called the Age of Jackson, but a more accurate designation is the Age of the Common Man. It was a time when the great majority of states democratized some of their institutions and would give the vote to almost all male, white adults. The political wisdom of the common man was proclaimed; many saw political parties as instruments of democracy. In the political realm, democracy was complemented by the Second Great Awakening, a massive religious revival that brought democracy to religion. It was a reaction against religious authority and emphasized the religious experience of the individual and the ability of ordinary people to find religious truth.

American churchmen and academicians frequently employed Scottish Common Sense philosophy to demonstrate that each person had the innate ability to grasp and apply self-evident principles, one of which was the existence of God. People could trust their perceptions and basic intuitions. It was a democratic epistemology, or approach to knowing, that, as Jefferson had suggested, enabled the plowman to think as clearly as the philosopher. Preachers of the Second Awakening proclaimed that America was a redeemed nation entrusted by God with bringing salvation, democracy, and progress to the world. The revivalists underscored the ability of saved individuals to attain perfection. This perfectionism was linked to the idea that the growth of the American people in perfection would lead to a thousand-year reign of peace and justice and the second coming of Christ. As a result of these developments, the American patriot of the revolution became the American Christian democrat in the Age of the Common Man.

Even churches not directly involved in the Second Awakening were influenced by republican currents of the age. Clergymen of many persuasions insisted that the American republic could not survive unless its citizens developed a stronger commitment to Christianity. The Universalists stood on a democratic theological platform, while they and Unitarians joined evangelical Protestants in the quest for social reforms. The Low Church Episcopalians reflected the republicanism of the age. Among Roman Catholics, laymen frequently asserted their right to control church property and sometimes even claimed the power to employ and dismiss priests. Within Lutheran and German Evangelical ranks there were debates about the value of revivalism and the extent to which these churches should embrace American ways.

Contact between democracy and faith often resulted in the liberalization of religion. It also had the effect of draining the democratic impulse of much of its potential for social and class conflict. The interaction between religion and the entrepreneurial spirit all too frequently resulted in religion being used to justify capitalism and prepare people to function in a market economy. The dislocations and anxieties produced by the market revolution predisposed some to religious conversion, and some clergymen complained of the selfishness and suffering that sometimes accompanied economic development. The market revolution seemed to quicken the pace of work and reduce human labor to a mere commodity. In the last analysis, evangelicalism would be embraced by the middle class because it seemed to justify the pursuit of self-interest, offered a higher standard of living, and called for self-improvement, hard work, frugality, and self-reliance. These qualities were praised by the revivalists, and temporal self-determination paralleled the spiritual autonomy proclaimed by evangelical spokesmen.

Impact of Economic Development

The years following the War of 1812 saw rapid economic development, characterized by the growth of industry, urban growth, and the spread of the market economy to most regions of the United States. These developments have been referred to as "the market revolution." It brought dramatic and often traumatic change to peoples' lives, affecting their politics and often their religious beliefs, livelihoods, and relationships with their families and communities. Many fiercely resisted those changes that came in the wake of economic development.

America's development as a capitalist nation was not accomplished without much pain and controversy. The market revolution positioned producers in competition with one another. Calculating egotism replaced the spirit of cooperation and interdependence. Farmers and mechanics lost a sense of independence as their welfare now was determined by impersonal economic forces. Journeymen, once proud of their skills and able to look to the day when as masters they might have their own shops, became wage laborers earning less than in the past. To survive, the master craftsmen who employed them found it necessary to pay them less, work them harder, and adopt the principle of division of labor, which meant the journeyman did the same few tiresome tasks all day long. He had been "deskilled." His workday was no longer somewhat relaxed and often pleasant. As the pace of work increased, there were few opportunities to socialize with patrons, other workers, or the master's family, which apprentices and journeymen had previously been made to feel almost a part of. Now they were simply sources of a commodity, labor. Prolabor ministers and some labor leaders used scriptural language to condemn "Mammonism" and emphasized interdependence of labor and employers and called for rebuilding Christian community. This approach made it impossible to discuss what was becoming the continual conflict of classes.

The structure of society changed rapidly with a greater concentration of wealth at the top. The number of people living in want and without labor-based claims to dignity increased alarmingly. The morality of economic decisions was now measured in terms of impersonal economic forces. Decisions dictated by considerations of supply and demand were not to be questioned. No longer in repute among those seeking economic development were the traditional views associated with what scholars now call "moral economy." It promised some independence and a decent living for working people. Clergymen in bygone days sometimes saw this as an extension of God-given natural law.

In the late eighteenth century and early years of the nineteenth century, many who had difficulty dealing with the stress and traumas that followed economic development embraced evangelical religion. Those who led the New-Light Stir sought to strengthen traditional communal values. They opposed the egoism and devotion to self-interest that marked the growth of the market economy. The Second Great Awakening was fueled in part by resentments brought about by the market revolution. The evangelical revival that emerged would, in time, serve the purposes of the market by urging people to build character traits that made them efficient producers.

Through diligence on the job, frugality, sobriety, and self-discipline, the sincere Christian demonstrated the presence of saving grace in his life and developed the character necessary to operate effectively in the market economy. Evangelicals saw individuals as being in command of their own fate, each one a free moral agent. In both the temporal and spiritual realms, the individual had the ability to rise in status through an act of the will. Clergymen were not critical of the self-interest that motivated wholesome economic activity, but they did complain about greed, financial chicanery, and economic exploitation. To an extent, some Christians had a quarrel with the secular sphere, but it turned out to be mostly a lovers' quarrel. The Mennonites and the Amish, neither of whom participated in the Second Awakening, did reject the market and modernity. The Stillwellites, a small Methodist splinter group, rejected industrial capitalism and projected a producerist philosophy in the pages of their newspaper. They were unhappy with the increasing respectability of Methodists.

Evangelical clergy offered a combination of Arminianism, millennialism, and insistence upon selfless benevolent activities on the part of committed Christians. Arminianism postulated that the individual could gain salvation by her or his own efforts. Many of those who came to the revivals were troubled by the new roles they were expected to play in the market-oriented economy of northeastern urban areas. Their evangelical preachers assured them it was not sinful to use all their energies to create wealth, so long as they did not cheat others and offered goods and services worthy of the prices they commanded. In this way, evangelical preachers were able to facilitate the transition of coastal towns and cities as well as commercial agricultural areas to the market economy. Many artisans, journeymen, and masters found this message convincing, and became Presbyterians and Congregationalists. Timothy Dwight went so far as to suggest that a thrifty, hardworking man could "live almost as he pleased," suggesting that a dedication to vocation would distract people from sin and toward useful activity. The evangelists urged laymen to demonstrate selfless benevolence by joining various benevolent societies devoted to stamping out vice and improving the lot of mankind.

In New England, another central focus of revivalist activities was the enlistment of people in a crusade to arrest the decline of the influence of organized religion and to create a Christian America. While many New England Calvinist clergy hoped revivalism would restore what they saw as eroding status and authority, clergymen wanted the full measure of power and standing enjoyed by their predecessors. Laymen who had been exhorted to take leading roles in voluntary benevolence were not as likely to dutifully await clerical guidance or view clergymen as intermediaries between God and men. Lyman Beecher, a Dwight student, was to become a leader of revivalistic activities in New England and the West. He was an unusually capable organizer, skillful at spreading the evangelical message through the printed word. In time, Beecher and others would successfully redirect evangelical efforts toward upholding the new economic order and removing "antimammon" elements from New Divinity theology.

In the South, both blacks and whites attended revivals in large numbers; frequently whites were outnumbered by blacks at these gatherings. Here and there mostly white congregations acquired spellbinding African American preachers. Egalitarianism and populism would characterize the early decades of the Second Great Awakening in the South and West.

The Second Awakening

Christianity's role in American life expanded greatly in the nineteenth century as evangelism came to dominate American Protestantism. For many, it was a means of revitalizing their belief systems, which seemed threatened by deism, western infidelity, economic development, and democratic challenge to established institutions. The Second Great Awakening, spanning the first half of the century, brought mass evangelism to almost every part of the nation. (Some have placed the Awakening in the years 1780–1830).

This great outburst of evangelical revivalism marked the democratization of American Protestantism. People rejected formal doctrines and selected their own religious spokesmen, who frequently lacked theological education, or even formal education beyond elementary school. Although Mormons and Methodists had hierarchies, the thrust of the revivalistic activities was democratic because the revivalists condemned social distinctions. All believers were encouraged to give testimony regarding their religious experiences. Spiritual ecstasy or the "enthusiasm" that the Puritans had so detested now became respectable. Traditional hymns often gave way to spirited songs that resembled African American spirituals. Not only the songs but the manner in which they were sung, and the emotions they unleashed, reflected the profound influence of African American spirituality on the Second Great Awakening. The impact of African American spirituality was particularly strong among early Methodists; the level of religious enthusiasm would later decline as Methodists acquired greater social status. Camp meetings could be seen as "festivals of democracy." Clergy were no longer viewed as mediators between God and man, and the impression was given that the revivalists had restored the Bible as the basis for belief. The primacy of the individual conscience was emphasized, and revivalists preached that holiness was reserved for the poor and humble in spirit rather than the proud and rich.

In the First Awakening, Baptist Isaac Backus had been able to accept class distinctions; in the Second Awakening Baptist leader John Leland heaped scorn on such distinctions. The Second Awakening has been discussed in terms of a battle between faith and reason, and this approach has considerable merit. It was seen foremost as a battle between classes. In a pamphlet defending camp meetings, Methodist Lorenzo Dow argued that those who criticized the meetings were "men of self-importance" who refused to mix with common folk in praising the Lord. Those involved in the Awakening saw their opponents as aristocrats, clerical elitists, and sinful plutocrats. Dow certainly would not have been mistaken for an aristocratic establishment cleric. He rode a swaybacked horse, carried an umbrella, and was filthy and unkempt. He had red hair to his shoulders and a harsh voice with a hypnotic quality; this strange countenance enhanced his image as a holy man. (In addition to preaching, he sold Dow's Family Medicine to support himself.) In 1804 alone, this barnstorming itinerant spoke at between five hundred and six hundred meetings, claiming that God had given him the power to read men's hearts. He was so effective that he toured England three times and covered ten thousand miles preaching in the United States. Preachers like Dow rejected many of the claims of lawyers and physicians, preferring home remedies and seeking ways to avoid the services of attorneys.

The Awakening not only reflected the democratic spirit of that age but intensified it. For a time, it threatened established social order, and deference broke down. The Awakening was also a period of antinomianism, when established sources of spiritual authority either crumbled or were revealed to have long since lost their power. Individuals found meaning, guidance, and sometimes prophetic power through this awakening. Casting aside established teachings and teachers, preachers of the Second Awakening found truth within themselves and tested it in their own unique spiritual experiences. The Second Awakening saw the enthronement of gnosticism, as many asserted that they derived special knowledge from their personal relationship with God; they chose to be guided by this knowledge rather than by external norms. The salvation was liberating; it gave them a new freedom from tradition, others, and even the community. Each believer was ultimately free to create a new theology and a new church. Initially, it did not involve self-worship but required great attention to one's inner life in order to experience God.

This awakening also came at a time when some clergymen felt that there was a noticeable decline in religious observance. As settlers moved west, they physically distanced themselves from contact with organized religion. There was great concern that the West could become godless territory unless religion were brought to it quickly. Methodist and Baptist preachers were promptly sent westward. Much of the complaining about the godless West came from other clergymen who believed the poorly educated Methodists and Baptists did more harm than good.

Advocates of deism and natural religion had few adherents in America, but represented to churchmen a cancerous state of mind that could grow unchecked if Christianity were not revitalized and brought to the unchurched. Equally alarming was the emergence of antitrinitarian or unitarian sentiment within Christian ranks, particularly in New England. This development seemed to call for a revival among the more traditional Christians. Lyman Beecher, a leading trinitarian, feared that without revivals the Unitarians would triumph. Beecher, however, could only accept rather tame revivals.

The "Great Revival" in New England and Nathaniel Taylor's Theology

In New England, the first stirrings of the Second Great Awakening occurred in Connecticut and New Hampshire in the late 1790s, during the so-called Great Revival. In 1801, Reverend Timothy Dwight of Yale delivered a series of intense sermons that resulted in the conversion of one-third of the student body. Many of those converted would become ministers. In the same year, Presbyterians and Congregationalists gathered in Dwight's parlor to work out the Plan of Union, whereby they agreed to cooperate in winning and tending to souls in western missionary areas. Dwight's activities and those of his followers made the New Divinity theology of Samuel Hopkins dominant in New England and other parts of the Northeast. This revival was characterized by restraint and, in its early years, an emphasis on man's depravity. Though some contemporaries separated the Great Revival and the Second Great Awakening, it is clear that they were of the same cloth, and the Great Revival was the opening stage of the Second Great Awakening in the Northeast.

Eventually, most New England revivalists moved toward building their evangelical appeals upon essentially Arminian foundations. Principal spokesman for this approach was Nathaniel Taylor, a New Haven pastor who became a theology professor at the Yale Divinity School when it was founded in 1822. Like Lyman Beecher, Taylor was a product of Dwight's Yale revival. According to his New Haven theology, found in *Concio ad Clerum* (1828), a human being was capable of avoiding sin, but became depraved by failing to exercise his power to do so. As he stated, "Sin is in the sinning." In advocating this elevated view of man's nature, Taylor departed from predestinarian thought and embraced the prospect of human perfection. He portrayed God as less remote, and people were seen as free and responsible. Just as a loving God sacrificed himself for humankind, people were expected to sacrifice for others. Human action could be efficacious in helping to bring about the Kingdom of God. Taylor's theology, like that of the Methodists, seemed well suited to the optimistic and egalitarian spirit of the Age of the Common Man.

The Awakening among Congregationalists and many Presbyterians in the Northeast focused on conversions and the pursuit of holiness and perfectionism. Its techniques were far more moderate than those found in the West or among the Presbyterian followers of Charles G. Finney, the most influential revivalist of the period. Many "awakeners" linked Taylor's perfectionism with postmillennialism. They argued that man must work to improve the world so as to hasten the coming of the millennium, a thousand-year period of peace and grace followed by the second coming of Christ. This desire to make men Christlike—to begin bringing the kingdom into being—paralleled the Methodists' yearning for Christian perfection. Methodists were converting vast numbers, relying upon a combination of perfectionism and revivalism. These two features most clearly marked the Second Awakening.

Methodist Revivalism

The needs that many fulfilled through various forms of folk religion were also met by the revivalists. They offered ordinary people the opportunity for contact with holy men, who were sometimes healers. Methodist evangelist Billy Hibbard included in his autobiography an account of a woman raised from the dead. Although other early Methodist preachers did not claim the power to heal, many claimed divine intervention in their dreams. These dreams provided advice or enabled them to predict the future. In making room for visions, signs, and wonders, these preachers gave legitimacy to contemporary folk religious beliefs. Revivalistic services provided people with ecstatic religious experiences, and shouting, sobbing, fainting, and falling were common. Enthusiastic religion seems to have been rife at a time when people were unsettled in their values, and republican American culture was still very much in a developmental stage.

Francis Asbury expected his preachers to lead celibate lives, enhancing their images as holy men. (Asbury intended celibacy only as a means to prevent them from putting down roots.) It has been estimated that half of his first six hundred preachers did not live to age thirty and that two hundred of them died during their first five years as preachers, so it was probably just as well that they did not wed. Methodist preacher Benjamin Abbott, who claimed to be gifted with prophetic dreams, in 1794 added an element of what has been called sacred theater: people were slain in the Spirit; "some lay in the agonies of death, some were rejoicing in God, others were crying for mercy."

Later in the nineteenth century, when Methodists came to enjoy greater prosperity and status, they no longer welcomed enthusiastic religious expression. As Methodist leaders and faithful rose in social status, there was less need for camp meetings and the alternative worldview plain folk created through them. By the late 1840s, there were permanent camp meeting sites that functioned in part as resorts. These permanent camp meeting sites were monuments to the fact that the Methodists had made peace with bourgeois America. Often their structures were elegant, and participation involved expenses beyond the reach of the poor.

While the Second Awakening had an important theological foundation, it was rooted in the great need many felt for contact with the sacred, for transcendence. Such a yearning for spiritual contact with God cannot be satisfied to any substantial degree by "rational" religion. Those who sought this intense connection with the divine found much of what they sought in revivals or folk religion.

Camp Meetings

The Second Great Awakening also had roots in southern revivals of the 1780s and 1790s, which were part of the New-Light Stir. The revivals were characterized by highly emotional manifestations of grace and conversion. These had marked the First Awakening in the South and would also characterize the second in the South and much of the West. To some extent, these "exercises" also appeared in the East. Many of these meetings were held outdoors. Their origin can be traced to the Scottish Presbyterian practice of "holy fairs" and "festal communions," common during the Great Awakening. Presbyterians continued to hold these meetings with decreasing frequency in the decades after the Great Awakening.

In 1800, after a decade's lull, a great revival movement was ignited in Logan County, Kentucky, that would burn long and bright in the South and West. At Gasper River Church, James McGready led four other Presbyterians and a Methodist in preaching a four-day revival. The camp meeting began here. These meetings were large and marked by a high degree of emotionalism. They were called camp meetings because many of those attending had traveled considerable distances and found it necessary to find shelter near the meeting site. Preachers strove mightily to convict listeners of sin and lead them to salvation in a few days. It was thought necessary to accelerate the usually protracted conversion process because there might not be another opportunity to bring these listeners to the Lord. Even during the first day of the meeting, McGready reduced many to shouting out, "What shall we do to be saved?" Preaching, praying, shouting, and singing continued throughout the four days from dusk to dawn. When the last day came, the "slain," those convicted of sin and groping for salvation, were lying about in agony throughout the camp, and there were many conversions. Before these individuals could be converted, they had to be convicted of sin—made to feel absolutely isolated and helpless to do anything about their sinfulness. When a person decided to leave her case completely in the hands of Christ, she had shown the faith necessary for conversion. This marked one's recognition, through the enlightenment of the Holy Spirit, that sins were forgiven and that God would love one forever. Some were not certain of the Holy Spirit's message, and would have to be told that they were indeed saved.

Among common manifestations or "exercises" at the meetings were falling, jerks, barks, ventriloquism, "tongue spieling" or glossolalia (speaking in strange tongues), seemingly uncontrollable laughing, and running. The barking exercise was usually "nothing but the jerks" in that the person affected often emitted grunts or barks. Some who were jerking or barking tried to run away from the Holy Spirit, but the preachers were certain that the runners could not escape the Spirit. Sometimes, however, the afflicted barked and dashed on all fours at a tree in order to tree the devil as dogs do when treeing an opossum. Some claimed to experience trances and visions. Those who experienced salvation stopped jerking and began singing, engaging in a heavenly dance, or emitted the "holy laugh." Preachers set the tone of these meetings carefully, as one person who could not control his own emotions might unleash mass hysterics. Many employed such emotionalism as seemed to serve their purposes, later calming the crowds with quiet prayer, apt stories, occasional dancing, or perhaps solemn prancing in the manner practiced by the Shakers. The emotionalism of the camp meeting provided a needed release for people frustrated with the problems of pioneer farming, and their emotional demonstrations were seen as proof of their conversion, which was necessary for entering an evangelical congregation.

Sellers of liquor, scoffers, and even prostitutes were often present at camp meeting sites, and some of these people were also overtaken by conversion. In addition to the preachers, there were lay exhorters who attempted to prepare people for conversion experiences. Along the periphery of the crowd, African American exhorters often appealed to blacks to renounce their sinfulness and seek salvation. Mourners, who acknowledged their sinfulness, often went to a central area, sometimes called the pen, where they were joined by song leaders and individuals who would pray over them.

A love feast occurred at the end of the camp meeting, at which the newly saved would give testimony and those present would be bathed in the warmth of mutual love and acceptance. People who had not experienced salvation could be present, and this experience might prepare them for salvation at a subsequent meeting. At a later point in time, camp meetings may have been influenced by practices at Methodist quarterly conferences as well as Baptist usages. Whatever ingredients helped shape camp meetings, they were an authentically American phenomenon.

Camp meeting revivals spread rapidly. Barton Stone, pastor of the Cane Ridge Presbyterian Church, had attended the Logan County revival and arranged for a Presbyterian meeting in August, 1801; it lasted six days and attracted between ten thousand and twenty-five thousand. (At that time, nearby Lexington had a population of 1,795.) The Cane Ridge meeting became the most successful and famous of all camp meetings. Though not specifically invited, Methodist clergymen appeared, and it became common at such meetings for ministers of several denominations to preach—often at once. Amid the ecstasy of believers, there began to develop an experimental, pragmatic approach to Christianity that was quite different from those found in Europe. A new understanding of Jesus also emerged. It was one that could not be found in churches; it depended completely upon a person's "one on one" personal encounter with Jesus. The western and southern camp meetings were thoroughly democratic affairs. They met the needs of plain folk, providing them with recreation, sociability, and above all a new approach to life. Camp meetings were especially attractive to plain folk who wanted respectability and orderly communities and rejected the excessive individualism and attendant culture of violence often found in frontier areas. All believers were considered equal, and the meeting represented their rejection of the layered social order frequently found in the West and on the southern frontier.

Awakening preachers no longer measured success in terms of acquiring things or positions in secular society. Believers had a new social status—a new distinctiveness—based upon the certainty of salvation, and available to them were opportunities to play leadership roles within their faith communities. Camp meetings provided them with the opportunity to reject selfish individualism and lives of excess and accept community and neighborly cooperation. The converted acknowledged that their old lives were without merit, and that they were embracing a more orderly and community-oriented existence. Conversion was also a rite of passage, a transition from the disordered moral laxness of the frontier to the order of community life. Western congregations, like many in the East, monitored and guided the behavior of their members. The church was the symbol of social order and stability. Mothers would bend every effort to complete the process of rearing children by seeing them proclaim their conversions and becoming church members. Raising children was like "raising a crop of corn," and the revivals served to harvest crops of souls. Within their new congregations, women had new status as saints and could express themselves in testimony or as song leaders.

The Second Awakening in the South

The Second Great Awakening made great headway in the South against formidable difficulties. Men's preoccupation with virility and honor worked against efforts to promote Christian humility, discipline, and benevolence. For southern men, reputation was most important; honor and status were important and emotions were freely displayed, not held in check. To lose honor was akin to being treated like slaves, who had been stripped of all honor. Preoccupation with honor spawned a culture of vengeance and violence. This tension between home-centered evangelical religion and masculine aggressiveness would continue throughout the century. Physical violence was frequently directed against evangelical gatherings. There were many unchurched areas in the South, and some of the unchurched whose way of life was threatened by evangelical preachers would ridicule their efforts and those who attended church meetings.

Attempts to establish Sunday schools were sometimes frustrated by a widely held belief that young people developed best when they suffered few restraints. Sunday schools seemed to threaten boys with effeminacy. There were never enough ministers or lay leaders, and the general lack of public schools made it difficult to recruit clergy and lay leaders. Moreover, most ministers, even some Methodist bishops, worked at farming or some other occupation during much of the week and were able to devote only part of their time to the ministry. Nevertheless, rapid growth of congregations continued even through the 1840s and 1850s; a number of denominational colleges also emerged, culminating in the founding of a major Methodist institution, Vanderbilt University, in 1873.

Southern evangelicals challenged the dominant culture of their region by denouncing dueling, Sabbath breaking, and the use of alcohol. Many evangelicals also claimed that dancing was sinful and that covetousness was at the root of the sinful lifestyle. Politicians were held in low esteem and preachers were critical of the judgment of voters because so many of them were unchurched. The will of the multitude could not be trusted, so democracy was of dubious value. Southern evangelicals pursued benevolence, but many of them were not convinced of the value of benevolent organizations. They thought it better that the individual go his or her own way in battling evil. Their experience with slavery led them to the conviction that some evils could not be overcome at a societal level. Moreover, many southerners feared that benevolent societies naturally prepared the way for organized abolitionism in the South. Still, there were societies dedicated to home and foreign missions, distributing Bibles, and assisting seamen and the deaf, blind, and insane.

Southern Baptists, using revivalism, experienced phenomenal growth and came to dominate their region. They took very seriously the great commission of the New Testament and sought to bring Christianity to all with whom they came into contact. They were convinced that they could plant a vibrant Christian civilization in the United States.

Revivalism was part and parcel of the Methodist tradition, and most Methodists felt no embarrassment with it. The southern Methodists experienced great growth in the years from 1780 to 1858, with two great surges of revivalism in years after the period most scholars assign to the Second Awakening, 1838–1844 and 1857–1858. Methodist evangelical efforts benefited from the church's organizational structure, which facilitated sending preachers into new areas. By 1860, the Methodist Episcopal Church was the largest denomination in the South, and the Baptists were the second largest group.

Southern Presbyterians also profited from the use of revivalism, but many of their clergymen found it objectionable. Clergy in communion with official Presbyterianism employed a significantly restrained form of revivalism if they chose to employ that approach at all. Those who fell out of favor formed separate Presbyterian organizations or joined other new churches.

Urban Revivals and Other Currents

There were some camp-meeting-like revivals in the East, appearing less than a decade after the Cane Ridge revival. Many urban revivals were conducted by the great Calvinist revivalist Charles G. Finney and his followers. Twenty years before Finney's conversion, the Methodists were already holding urban revivals and using techniques that would later be called Finney's "new measures." They held a notable revival outside Baltimore and one within sight of Yale in New Haven. In the cities, Methodists took the message to the poor and held services in prisons and almshouses. Methodists established Bible study groups, prayer groups for young people, Sunday schools, missionary aid societies, and lay testimonial services. In Baltimore, the respectable and prosperous were elected leaders among Methodists as well as other congregations, and there appears to have been no class antagonism. There and elsewhere, the Methodists attended to the spiritual needs of the poor, both white and African American. They preached that the rich must be good stewards of their wealth, and they did not charge pew rents, regarding it as an undemocratic practice.

In time, emphasis on stewardship gave way to the belief that God rewarded those who worked hard. When Methodist preachers came to see wealth as God's reward for diligence and hard work, they reduced the anxiety of entrepreneurs who had departed from community norms in order to prosper. Other revivalist religions would also come to embrace capitalism. Early Methodist preachers condemned extravagant living, theatergoing, slavery, lotteries, and preoccupation with accumulating money. Many of these were the sins of the wealthy. In New York City, Methodist ministers such as Nathaniel Bangs took religion to workers and the poor in the outer wards, where the gospel had seldom been preached. Bangs tried to restrain people's enthusiasm in worship, seeking decorum and respectability for what he saw as the religion of the common people. Bangs told the poor that Christ died for all and offered all pardon and peace. Elected agent of the Methodist Book Concern in 1820, he exercised great influence within the church through control of its publications. He declined the opportunity to become a Methodist bishop.

There were also unaffiliated lay preachers in New York, such as "mechanick preacher" Johnny Edwards, who founded a Church of Christ around 1808. Edwards preached from his wagon. On Wall Street, he used a three-foot tin trumpet to demand that the moneylenders repent their evil ways and turn to God. Though his predicted second coming of Christ did not occur in 1810, Edwards continued to be an active preacher for more than another decade. David Whitehead, another lay preacher, denounced the rich for establishing "robbery by law and a law for the protection of robbers."

Along the Erie Canal, evangelical Protestants launched efforts to bring the boatmen to God. These men and boys were sometimes disorderly, especially when lubricated with alcohol. Evangelicals saw them as a potentially serious threat to social order, and were genuinely concerned with the boatmen's spiritual welfare. In 1837, the Methodists and Presbyterians of western New York formed the American Bethel Society, with the objective of sending literature and missionaries to the boatmen. They also opened chapels where the boatmen were urged to worship. Merchants and other civic leaders often showed little interest in these missionary activities, refusing to consider the boatmen a threat to social order. When the evangelicals demanded that the boatmen not be required to work on Sundays, the Christian reformers encountered hostile responses. Although the canal continued to operate on Sundays, the reformers managed to somewhat reduce vice among the boatmen and rescued many boys from lives dominated by alcohol and other sinful ways.

Charles G. Finney

The "burned-over district"—so called because so many revivals swept across it—of western New York was the scene of frequent revivals. This area west of the Catskill and Adirondack Mountains had been swept by periodic waves of restrained, New England–style revivals in the first decades of the century. The completion of the Erie Canal brought great changes to the area as people flocked to find opportunity and new lives in upstate New York. By 1835, more than thirteen hundred revivals had marked the Second Great Awakening in the state of New York. The tempo of religious excitement was greatly accelerated as numerous sects appeared, such as the Disciples of Christ and the Millerites. Frequent revivalist campaigns set men to agonizing over their spiritual conditions and seeking moral purity and perfection.

The central figure in this spasm of revivals was Charles Grandison Finney, a lawyer and late convert to Christianity who was born again in 1821. He immediately abandoned his Adams, New York, practice to prepare to plead the Lord's case. Finney, who was to become "the father of modern revivalism," began studying theology under the local Presbyterian pastor and was preaching three years later. His revivals were very successful and Finney and the "new measures" he employed received national attention. He preached in plain language, as would a lawyer, often referring to sinners as "you" and sometimes mentioning a few by name. Finney's expositions of doctrine were clear and understandable, and he used examples familiar to his listeners. The business and professional classes were attracted by his almost businesslike approach. There was little of the emotional behavior characteristic of a western revival, yet Finney gave strong doses of "hellfire," and his style commanded full attention. He believed that "we must have exciting, powerful preaching, or the devil will have the people, except what the Methodists can save." Finney's protracted meetings lasted from four days to several weeks with nightly services, arranged to lead people to salvation in a relatively short period of time. In some ways, this was a camp meeting adapted to the needs of a more settled area. His most controversial practice was the use of the "anxious bench," where those seeking salvation gathered in front of the congregation.

Friends and neighbors often gathered around the anxious bench, praying that they would become sufficiently penitent to start a new life in Christ. Little was left to spontaneity. There were carefully defined rules of behavior, and plans were made to contain the enthusiasm of participants. As time passed, the same could be said of western and southern camp meetings. Techniques for planning and orchestrating revival meetings were soon borrowed by politicians and applied to political gatherings; conversely, the evangelists often borrowed techniques used by politicians in organizing political gatherings. It is no coincidence that this era of revivals and camp meetings also saw the birth of mass politics.

In formulating a theology, Finney came to advocate positions that seemed most helpful in winning souls. He did not consciously set out to make the Presbyterian view more acceptable to ordinary people in the Age of the Common Man, but he managed to do so. He removed the last determinism from what was already a softened Calvinism and arrived at a position similar to that of Nathaniel Taylor's New Haven theology. He taught justification by sanctification rather than by faith. Sanctification rested on human willpower assisted by God. The individual must decide to obey God, accept Christ as savior, and depend completely upon Christ. God would then grant a conversion experience, which included the beginning of sanctification.

There is no evidence that Finney attempted to emulate the Methodists in their theology and their revivalistic style, yet the similarities are striking. Like the followers of Wesley, Finney blended revivalism, Arminianism (the belief that individuals can win salvation by cooperating with God's grace), and perfectionism. His "new methods" were not new to the Methodists. They had long used protracted meetings in the East, and had pioneered in bringing revivals to the cities. They lacked the "anxious seat" or "mourners" bench, but their "call to the altar" was similar; the afflicted were asked to kneel in an open area before the altar where others prayed with them and instructed them. Finney was much criticized for permitting women to witness and pray in "promiscuous" assemblies. He differed with the Methodists in many respects, including matters of church polity (or organizational form) and sacraments. To varying degrees, Finney's approach was widely emulated in the East, particularly among Presbyterians and Congregationalists. After accepting an appointment in 1835 as professor of theology at the new Oberlin College in Ohio, Finney was in a position to directly shape the thinking and careers of a generation of vigorous evangelists who would blend individual salvation and social uplift in their sermons. Evangelical Oberlin was the first college to educate women and African Americans. Finney and his colleagues developed a doctrine of sanctification, contending that Christians must "aim at being perfect" and that men could rise higher and higher in search of perfection and in obedience to God's will. It was conceded that man would become perfect only in heaven. This approach to perfectionism was even more influential than that of Taylor in shaping the course of Protestant evangelism in the nineteenth century.

Perfectionism sprang from the shift from predestinarian theology to Arminianism. The individual was freed from anxiety over whether she or he had been predestined to salvation. It was taught that an individual best served God by developing moral character. It was not a matter of earning or investing in salvation; it was simply a question of serving and honoring one's maker. Attention shifted from metaphysics to common sense and from doctrine to behavior. Christ was seen as a role model, and many used the Bible as a source of inspirational stories.

Revivalism and Character

Once the evangelists accepted perfectionist theology, it followed naturally that they should dwell on social sins and man's efforts to remedy them through temperance and various benevolent activities. Northern evangelists often became involved in antislavery agitation. Sincere Christians prepared themselves for benevolence by developing character through rigid self-discipline. They were assisted in these efforts by their congregations, where it was not uncommon for Christian brothers and sisters to inquire into the spiritual condition of one another. Methodist class meetings were ideal for this purpose. Methodists were to avoid alcohol, dancing, extravagant dress, sharp business practices, and swearing. To one degree or another, all the evangelical denominations shared this discipline. Many were attracted to revivalism because they experienced considerable anomie or disorientation as the norms of the market economy appeared to displace traditional values. On balance, however, the nineteenth-century revivals facilitated the transition to that economy. Revivalists proclaimed that the character of a true man comprised traits useful to modern capitalism: thrift, diligence, reliability, sobriety, and industriousness. The most important characteristic of a Christian man was altruism or disinterested benevolence. By playing important roles in benevolent societies, entrepreneurs legitimized their conduct and newly won status.

There was much concern about the growing number of urban poor as well as concern about disorder and riots. Preachers of the Second Awakening emphasized to the poor and working class the importance of self-discipline and respect for those who rose in society through this virtue. Rich evangelical laymen were frequently reminded of their duty to employ the services of earnest evangelical craftsmen and shopkeepers. The preachers exhorted businessmen to offer employees sound advice, and lend them capital when warranted. If poor or unemployed artisans required assistance, it was expected that work rather than only money and commodities would be provided. These ideas became the framework for American middle-class ideology, the perfect handmaiden to modern capitalism.

An illustration of clergymen's role in nurturing modern capitalism can be found in their employment by what is now Dun and Bradstreet, the first agency to specialize in investigating creditworthiness. Its owners were the brothers Arthur and Lewis Tappan, evangelical laymen famous for their charitable activities. The Tappans employed clergymen as investigators.

Who could better detect flaws in character? The investigators particularly looked for signs of intemperance and unchecked sexual impulses. The Tappan brothers also founded a newspaper, the *Journal of Commerce,* to promote evangelical Christian virtues among businessmen.

Ralph Waldo Emerson, the great transcendentalist and former Unitarian minister, employed his many lecture circuit appearances to instruct Americans in the radical individualism of the emerging middle-class ideology. Though he had given to charities, he often wondered if his alms went for "the education at college of fools" or "alms for sots." In referring to the unfortunates of society, he asked, "Are they *my* poor?" and said that his only obligation was to be a chaste husband, support his family, and honor and look after his parents. Emerson's thought justified the predatory practices of the new entrepreneurs of the age, whom he even referred to as "monomaniacs" of the marketplace. Even if their activities smacked of banditry he thought that the net effect of their pursuits was positive in strengthening the national character. Somehow their behavior was in rhythm with the harmony of the universe; moralists who denounced them were out of touch with the universe's laws. He admired those who held wealth and power and admired people who could be called "pirates" and "bruisers."

Some clergymen worried that society was embracing aspects of a caste system and believed that the middle class was coming to see manual labor as demeaning, undignified and beneath them. A manual labor movement emerged to bridge the gap between the learned and those who worked with their hands. By combining book learning with manual labor, they argued that schools could help students become committed to republican egalitarianism and avoid caste prejudice and class hubris. The American founder of manual laborism was Reverend George Washington Gale, the Presbyterian minister who had converted Charles G. Finney. The Oneida Institute was founded in 1827 to implement his theories, which were also tested in other schools. These experiments failed for a number of reasons, including that they did not make money for the schools involved. Manual laborism and abolitionism shared basic beliefs in the equality of man and the dignity of physical labor, and its labor advocates usually became committed abolitionists. Some advocates of manual laborism saw it as a means to combat the perception that ministers, through their educations and involvement in feminized churches, were themselves effeminate.

Christian Benevolence

The chief organs of Congregationalist and Presbyterian evangelical cooperation were the American Board of Commissioners for Foreign Missions and the American Home Missionary Society. The ABCFM also sent missionaries to the so-called Five Civilized Nations and urged its missionaries to denounce the Native American practice of holding African American slaves. In 1859, it abandoned its missionaries among those Native Americans because the missionaries thought denouncing slavery interfered with saving Native American souls. Support of those missions was then assumed by the Old School Presbyterian Board of Foreign Missions, which had consistently instructed its missionaries to take a neutral position. The conservative Presbyterians were suspicious of innovations and wanted strict adherence to traditional doctrine and polity. Their stronghold was Princeton Theological Seminary.

The American Home Mission Society, assuming the responsibilities of two other bodies, supported western missionaries and fledgling churches. To raise money, its spokesmen often suggested that Christianity did not exist in places where they wanted to send missionaries, although Methodists and Baptists were already operating in many of those places. In 1831, the society supported 463 missionaries, who helped other societies by establishing local units of the temperance, foreign mission, Bible, education, and tract societies. Other cooperative enterprises were the American Sunday School Union and the American Bible Society, whose goal was to place a Bible in every American home. By 1833, the Bible society had been so successful in the West and Northeast that it was ready to focus on portions of the rural South. For a time, the northern Baptists provided substantial support to these cooperative ventures. Despite Presbyterian leadership of the cooperative enterprises, efforts to distribute Bibles and establish Sunday schools received considerable support from other denominations. However, the Methodists consistently preferred to deal with these concerns within the framework of their own denomination. The Methodists had their own Sunday school society, but they dissolved their Bible society in 1836 in order to support the American Bible Society. The cooperative ventures lost much support as the Baptists, Episcopalians, and Old Side Presbyterians substituted denominational efforts for them. Among the Baptists, some in the South and West opposed organized benevolence and missionary ventures altogether.

The cooperative spirit that led to the creation of evangelical organizations also led to the founding of a number of voluntary humanitarian ventures. Frequently, the same concerned Christians simultaneously sat on the boards of several evangelical and humanitarian societies. Humanitarian efforts included the American Education Society, the American Colonization Society, the American Peace Society, and the American Antislavery Society. Perfectionists, as well as other Protestants involved in these ventures, believed that the Christian must abandon selfish interests and develop "a preference for disinterested benevolence." Men of wealth took seriously New York clergyman Albert Barnes's statement that to be good Christians, the wealthy must devote their riches and talents to doing the Lord's work.

These Protestant humanitarians were intensely moralistic individuals who earnestly desired to uplift their fellow men. In the process, their moralism often got in the way of benevolence when it came to denouncing Catholicism and those who ignored their admonitions. Intense anti-Catholicism was a central and unifying characteristic of the evangelicals. Some of the humanitarians may have seen these efforts as essentially a means of preserving a threatened social order and their privileged places in it.

Formalists—those who placed much reliance on organizations to accomplish God's will—were convinced that they had a divine mission to Christianize the United States and the world and formed denominational and interdenominational benevolent organizations to move in this direction. Antiformalists distrusted these organizations. Among them were Anti-Missionary Baptists, and others who distrusted ecclesiastical organizations. To some degree, one could include the Disciples of Christ, whose main spokesman was Alexander Campbell, and the Churches of Christ, who followed Barton Stone. Deemphasizing creedalism, clericalism, and denominational organizations, they sought to return to the simplicity of the early church. Theirs was an American theology that took the doctrine of the priesthood of all believers very seriously; every man was essentially his own theologian.

The antiformalists thought the formalists overlooked the fundamental truth that the world cannot be improved until individuals were converted on a one-by-one basis. For a time, the Methodists supported the work of the American Sunday School Union, but they soon found it necessary to establish their own denominational organization. Some northern Baptists, particularly those in urban areas, were somewhat inclined toward formalism and could back the union. The American Bible Society had much support in both camps, with only the Old School Baptists remaining aloof. Antiformalists thought that the American Tract Society materials were too Calvinistic in tone. Antiformalists shared the concern of formalists that the Sabbath be kept holy, but they opposed efforts to force people to observe the Lord's day as steps on the road to a national church. Similarly, antiformalists who opposed the use of alcohol preferred the voluntarist Washingtonian movement to the American Temperance Society and American Temperance Union, both dominated by formalists.

Egalitarianism and Civil Religion

The evangelical theologies of Charles G. Finney and Nathaniel W. Taylor represented an accommodation with the American temper in the Age of the

Common Man. In their optimism, egalitarianism, and perfectionist ethos they reflected the spirit of the young republic. Through voluntary benevolent societies, evangelical Christians doubtless made a lasting contribution to shaping the American reform tradition. Their great accomplishment was generating interest in humanitarian causes designed to eradicate evils and to uplift God's children in the young republic.

It can be argued that this accommodation with prevailing American values was the beginning of a process whereby American Protestantism became the captive of secular American culture. Some argue that the effort to create a Christian America ended in producing a church largely stripped of an independent identity and mission. Alexis de Tocqueville, who wrote the most famous analysis of American society, described what would be called civil religion by noting that it enshrined the separation of church and state and the primacy of individual conscience. It stood as a bulwark against established religion. In focusing attention upon responsibilities toward community, it tended to diminish the antisocial consequences of an almost hyperindividualism. In these two ways, civil religion and religion itself functioned as the nation's chief defense against the erosion of republicanism. This French observer also thought that belief in human perfectibility had become an integral part of civil religion, although many American Christians did not embrace perfectionism.

The evangelical Christianity of the Second Great Awakening would become a key ingredient in the civil or public religion that would emerge full-blown in the second half of the nineteenth century. This amalgam of evangelical Protestant Christianity and American republicanism stressed the uniqueness and special role that God had marked out for the United States. It was God's providence, according to American civil religion, that Europeans migrate to this continent to establish a model for others in the ways of self-government and virtuous living. The nation's providential mission guaranteed its permanence and added a messianic dimension to American nationalism.

This sense of mission meshed fully with the evangelicals' attachment to perfectionism and their goal of bringing the Kingdom of God into existence on earth. This kingdom would first emerge in the United States and then extend its sway to other lands. It seemed to many that the United States was a redeemed nation that would be exempt from serious travail so long as it continued on the path of righteousness. The Bible was seen as a democratic handbook. It was necessary that citizens and legislators see that laws squared with divine law. Evangelicals believed they had a duty to reflect republican and Christian principles in their lifestyles. In a land where it seemed that every white male adult was a politician, it was necessary that evangelical Christians be serious participants in the political process.

The perfectionist theology of this Awakening led to an expanded version of American civil religion—one in which the nation became God's agent in pursuing justice and equality. This liberal version of the nation's legitimizing myth was not accepted by most Americans who were untouched by the Second Awakening.

The United States became God's "chosen nation," and many believed it had a mission or Manifest Destiny to extend its boundaries to encompass the entire North American continent. This prospect did not appeal to most northern evangelicals, who saw physical expansion as a means of enlarging the area under slavery. However, American civil religion was not the exclusive property of evangelical Christians; it became the cherished possession of almost all Americans. Even to those who had not given very careful thought to such matters, it seemed that God was somehow involved in the establishment of the United States. Some, like Daniel Webster, carried public religion to the point of arguing that prosperity was "a Divine imposition on our behalf." Abolitionist Wendell Phillips claimed that God supported American representative government and, thus, "The people never err. The voice of the people is the voice of God."

In this period, there was a convergence of religion and politics. Each party had its "creed," and elections could be likened to holy days in that work stopped and a public festival was observed. Rallies resembled services incorporating the peculiar rhetoric of each party—what literary critic Kenneth Burke called "secular prayer." Clergymen often gave election sermons in which the faithful heard how best to do the Lord's will through the ballot box. Parties provided followers with various combinations of these kinds of assurance—fraternal affirmation, purification, renewal, and hope. This practice was common among Methodists and New School Presbyterians. Accepting the theology of Nathaniel Taylor, the New-School Calvinists denounced slavery and favored interdenominational benevolent societies. Even Catholic and Episcopalian priests sometimes addressed public issues. The chief difficulty with civil religion, as pacifist and abolitionist William Lloyd Garrison noted, was that it left the impression that God approved of slavery, warfare, and other evils. He saw it as a covenant with the devil rather than God, and "a blasphemous conspiracy to maintain . . . slavery." African Americans rejected the claims of American civil religion, believing that there was no way the terms "America" and "justice" could be linked with one another.

Adventism, Millennialism, and New Churches

Millennialism and perfectionism were central elements in Protestant thought during the Second Great Awakening. Many believed that they must prepare for the thousand-year reign of Christian principles followed by the second coming of Christ by converting others, growing in perfection, and transforming society. The success of the revivals and the accomplishments of the benevolent societies led many to believe in the imminence of the second coming of Christ. There was a great deal more interest in the millennium than in any previous period in American history. It is possible to see in this movement frustrated, anxious people who used millennialism to solve problems related to their perceptions of the world. While some looked to a millenium growing out of revivals and reforms, others feared that the world was beyond repair. They expected the second coming to purge the world of evil and usher in the millennium. A great interest in millennialism occurred when many people thought that traditional ways of thinking and acting no longer seemed appropriate in dealing with change. Millennialism represented for them a framework for dealing with change and revitalizing their culture. In the South, millennialism was also employed to defend slavery. Southern Presbyterians noted that unfree labor had existed throughout history and suggested that the institution of slavery would continually improve as American society evolved toward the millennium. They touted slavery as a Christianizing agent and argued that Christian perfectionism would lead slaves to accept and internalize their duties. The popularity of this argument was not limited to southern Presbyterians.

Adventism was the belief in the imminent reappearance of Jesus Christ on earth. It promised its early supporters almost immediate contact with the divine as well as significant places in the Kingdom of God, which was to prevail on earth for a thousand years. William Miller, a Vermont farmer turned Baptist minister, calculated that the second advent of Christ would occur in 1843. When that year passed uneventfully, his followers pressed him to announce that the last day would be October 21, 1844. The Millerites were strongest in a geographical band that included New England, upstate New York, the Western Reserve of Ohio, and part of Michigan.

Miller believed that the humanitarian and evangelical reformers had prepared the way for his movement, but most of his followers thought that politics and reform efforts had failed. The coming apocalypse demonstrated that voluntary reform was unnecessary. Some sought to live in complete holiness, believing that the saved could avoid willful sin. Historical myths abound concerning the behavior of Millerites anticipating the last day and dealing with the Great Disappointment. It is alleged that some entered insane asylums while others committed suicide. Other tales tell of Miller's followers gathering atop hills or haystacks in white ascension robes. The truth of these stories is doubtful, but some Millerites stopped working, discarded social distinctions, and either practiced gluttony or stopped eating. A few crawled around like infants so that they could become like little children when the Kingdom of God was established. Miller died in 1849, and on his tombstone were the words, "At the time appointed the end shall be." After the Great Disappointment, most of Miller's adherents abandoned the movement. A few were "spiritualizers" and said the second coming had occurred on that date in a spiritual way. Some hard-core followers continued to be Advent Christians, as they called themselves.

A third group of Adventists came under the influence of Seventh-Day Baptists and denounced Sunday worship as a popish invention. They thought Christ had entered a "heavenly sanctuary," referred to in Hebrews 8:1, in preparation for a glorious return to earth. This third group would become the Seventh-Day Adventists by 1860.

Those who sought this intense connection with the divine often found much of what they sought in folk religion. These religious movements offered direct contact with the dead, and seemed to offer the greatest opportunities for achieving Christian perfection. There was a burning desire for connection with transcendence, manifested in a great interest in divine apparition in dreams, in healing, in the work of the adepts or practitioners of mysterious occult rites as well as the occult in general. The great optimism of the age, coupled for some with millenarian religious thought, may have given rise to religious expectations that could not be satisfied by conventional, rationalistic religion.

There were many indications of the persistence and popularity of folk religious beliefs in the early republic. As late as the 1850s and 1860s, federal censuses for Philadelphia revealed a number of people who claimed as occupations phrenologist, astrologer, healer, and herbal doctor. At the beginning of the century, Ezra Stiles, a leading New England clergyman, found it necessary to deny charges that he was either an adept or interested in the occult. Despite these denials, it is known that he collected books on the occult and admitted to a friend that he had "deeply studied" these writings.

Sometimes there were odd mixtures of Christian doctrines and folk healing beliefs that involved carrying out some rite while invoking the names of the members of the Trinity. People often sought hidden treasure after being guided by advice received in dreams or by knowledge acquired by reading or looking at something through "peep stones." Peep stones had holes in them through which one looked for treasure. Divining rods, still used today to locate underground water, were used to seek treasure. Some even sought the aid of the netherworld through cat sacrifices.

The middle class and upper middle class often showed great interest in spiritualism as a means of communicating with the dead. Spiritualism was marked by efforts to strip it of pagan aspects and to make it compatible with nineteenth-century science. Those who moved into spiritualism thought they were fulfilling, rather than abandoning, their Christianity. American Protestants had a great interest in divine intervention and in supernatural occurrences; great numbers attended spiritualist discussions throughout the United States. Most who attended these meetings or séances also attended their own churches on a regular basis. Spiritualists frequently argued that their movement strengthened Christianity by reinforcing belief in life after death.

By 1855, perhaps one million people out of a population of twenty-eight million would admit to more than a passing interest in spiritualism. Some who sought spiritual and physical perfection were attracted to the beliefs of the Austrian physician Franz Anton Mesmer (1734–1815), who based his healing philosophy on the belief in a fluid or substance variously known as animal magnetism, vital force, vital fluid, or divine electricity. It was essential that believers access that level of consciousness that exists just below the surface of ordinary consciousness in order to find the causes of illness. Some subjects were more readily "mesmerized" than others, and these people could be used to discover the reasons why others were ill.

There was often an informal alliance between followers of Mesmer and those of Swedish scientist and seer Emanuel Swedenborg (1688–1772). He claimed that God told him in a vision to "explain to men the spiritual sense of the scripture." Swedenborg found a new way of reading scripture that made the universe religiously intelligible. In some thirty works, this Swedish engineer insisted that God had "dictated to" him the true meaning and inner sense of scriptures. This seer claimed to have communicated with many famous people of the past, and his followers thought they could do the same. He also claimed to have visited heaven as well as other planets.

Swedenborgian gnosticism was based on the idea that the universe comprises several dimensions, among them the physical, mental, spiritual, and angelic. All dimensions are interconnected, with the welfare of one dimension depending on its being in harmony with the others. Swedenborg taught that the deity was an indwelling force and that an individual's health, prosperity, and spiritual welfare depends upon his mind and body being in harmony with one another and with the cosmos. He held that "love is the life of man" and that the human spirit is developed and refined through selflessness. Swedenborg claimed that he enjoyed full knowledge of "the inner sense of the Word of God." Swedenborgians believed that a person's physical well-being and prosperity depended on rapport with the universe. Divinity could be found in all things and within the person; once it was accessed through the mind, a person was on the road to almost limitless development. Swedenborgian millennialism was based on his teaching that the second coming of Christ had begun in the middle of the eighteenth century. There were probably never even ten thousand members of the New Church, or Church of the New Jerusalem, but many of these followers were highly educated individuals. By 1800, every American city of importance had at least one Swedenborgian church.

The Latter-day Saints

The Church of Jesus Christ of Latter-day Saints was organized in 1830 and took this name in 1838. Its early history reflects a high degree of syncretism or cultural blending between Christianity and occult elements of folk religion. It presents an example of a religion that, like Judaism, became "a people" and as such managed to survive. The Mormons, or Latter-day Saints, emerged with the publication in Palmyra, New York, of *The Book of Mormon* in 1830 (Figure 4).

Joseph Smith, the founder, from youth had been interested in treasure hunting and clairvoyance. At one time he was hired to seek treasure the Spanish had allegedly buried in Pennsylvania. Smith said that a supernatural being named Moroni told him where to find a book written on gold plates in an odd language. He was able to translate the book with the use of "peep stones" (they were named Urim and Thummim and were mounted in silver spectacle frames); the tablets were inscribed in what he called "reformed Egyptian" hieroglyphics. With respect to Urim and Thummim, it should be noted that there was then no clear line separating common belief in seer stones, spells, visions, and water witching from religion. Smith claimed to have learned that the prophet Mormon, one of the last of the Nephites, a lost tribe of Israel and God's chosen people, and his son Moroni, had written on the plates. This was the fifth, or American, gospel. It related their history and predicted the emergence of a new prophet, Smith. The salamanders or toads that guarded the engraved plates are associated in occult literature with divine messages.

For a time Smith performed healings. He once predicted that there would be a war between the states that would begin in South Carolina. In 1833, Mormon elders visited the Grant household in Erie, Pennsylvania, and healed a bedridden Mrs. Grant of severe rheumatism. Her son Jedediah subsequently became a preacher, the legendary "Mormon Thunder." Smith's inner circle later persuaded him to abandon healings. Church leadership would later distance itself from all aspects of folk religion. Joseph Smith attracted followers who, like himself, had not realized the American dream. Through their religion, Mormons sought community and power. Smith claimed that God gave him the blueprint to reform and reorganize the

C. C. A. Christensen.   Lith. F. F. Bording, Copenhagen.

Entered According to Act of Congress in the Year 1886, by C. C. A. Christensen, Ephraim, Utah.

The angel MORONI delivering the plates of the BOOK OF MORMON to JOSEPH SMITH jun.

Figure 4. The Angel Moroni Delivering the Plates of *The Book of Mormon* to Joseph Smith. Mormonism was founded on the night of September 21, 1823, when the angel Moroni thrice visited Joseph Smith, assured him his sins were forgiven, and told him about gold leaves or plates containing *The Book of Mormon*. Four years later, Moroni gave him the plates. (Courtesy the Library of Congress.)

world. With the assistance of a secret committee known as the Council of Fifty, he sought to organize a worldly substate.

Early Mormons sometimes spoke in tongues and prophesied. Speaking in tongues, or glossolalia, was the source of disputes, and was sometimes seen as a source of revelations that challenged the teachings of church leaders. In 1841, Joseph Smith discouraged the practice and sought to limit it to xenoglossia, the use of recognizable foreign languages. Brigham Young also discouraged glossolalia; by 1900 its practice among Mormons was very infrequent.

Members other than Mormon prophets sometimes asserted that they had received revelations from God. They shared the perfectionism of the age and claimed that each person was potentially a god in the making. God was originally a man on some other planet who passed through suffering, toil, and death before receiving exaltation. The saints, their term for Mormon believers, were to follow Christ in seeking truth, doing good, and enduring suffering. Truth, they believed, could be found through the Bible, *The Book of Mormon,* Smith's *Doctrines and Covenants,* the teachings of the church, and through what Brigham Young called natural revelation, which meant through reason and natural law. Eventually believers would be exalted. Young, espousing a doctrine that was not accepted by the church, said, "Adam fell that a man might be; and men are that they might have joy." This is sometimes called the happy, or fortunate, fall. Young may have identified Adam with God the Father, saying, "He [Adam] is our Father and the only god with whom we have to do." Use of the term "Father" may have only meant Adam was father of the human race. In their pursuit of perfection, Mormons were expected to refrain from using alcohol, tea, coffee, and tobacco. The practice of tithing developed at an early point in their history.

Mormons were millennialists. They believed it was their task to build a new Zion where the thousand-year reign of Christ would begin. They took David's interpretation of Nebuchadnezzar's dream to mean that they would constitute a sovereign state that would replace all others. This scriptural promise was contingent upon Mormons doing God's will; if they failed to obey they would be ruled by others. Red Israelites (Native Americans) would be converted to Mormonism in time to rejoice in the second coming of Christ. As a chosen people, Mormons would operate the Kingdom of God.

It was and remains a strongly patriarchal religion, emphasizing the governance of men over their families. Women could not join the church until they were married to Mormons. Male status and sanctity depended in large measure upon how many children they sired. In the early years of the church, the saints used communal familism to deal with the uncertainties and decline of communal values brought about by the capitalist transformation of American society. According to the "rule of consecration and stewardship," Mormons were to surrender their surpluses to the community for the welfare of the propertyless and needy Mormons. This rule was initially interpreted to mean that economic equality would prevail and that members would hold property in common. In time the practice of sharing one's surplus was abandoned, in part because it attracted some insincere converts. Resentful of husbands who turned over great amounts to the church, a number of wives resisted conversion.

Mormons tended to do business with one another and to be involved in some communal economic ventures. Following the law of consecration and stewardship, Mormons in Ohio and Missouri deeded property to their bishops, who then made those individuals stewards of this property. The prophet Smith led his followers into ill-fated land speculation and banking ventures. These practices caused resentment among their neighbors, first in the Kirtland, Ohio, area, where Mormons had their first settlement, later in Missouri, and then in Nauvoo, Illinois. Persecution of the Mormons was answered by the creation of the secret Danite Society, which was to enforce orthodoxy among Mormons and defend them from enemies. The society was unable to deal with unfriendly mobs, and a few of its members became thieves and thugs. In a town near Nauvoo, an angry crowd in 1844 murdered Joseph and Hyrum Smith while they were being held prisoner in a jail, awaiting trial on charges of having incited a riot.

Brigham Young assumed leadership of the movement at a meeting where some believers thought he literally spoke with Joseph Smith's voice. Some thought they saw Smith rather than Young speaking. Young led thousands of followers in a migration to the Great Salt Lake area, where a provisional state of Deseret (meaning honeybee, representing the ideal of industriousness) was organized. In 1853, there were about 30,000 Mormons in Deseret, or Utah; a year later, there were 38,627 members in all foreign countries—29,441 of whom were in Great Britain. It is estimated that between 1840 and 1846, about 17,000 Mormons migrated from Great Britain to the United States, and the majority of them probably moved to Utah.

There was a strong belief in a theocratic or church-dominated state, and Mormons in the nineteenth century tended to vote as a unit, following the leadership of their priesthood. The church was to dominate the public life of the Territory of Utah. In recognition of this fact, presidents sometimes appointed Brigham Young governor. The refusal of the Mormons to accept the authority of gentile officials resulted in President James Buchanan dispatching federal troops in 1857 and 1858 to demonstrate that federal power in the territory must be taken seriously. From the time that Utah became part of the United States in 1848, the Mormon leadership sought statehood

for Deseret of Utah. Barriers to statehood included the practice of polygamy, the role of church leadership in politics, and prejudice against Mormons. Soon after the church repudiated plural marriage, Utah become a state,
in 1896. The church continued to dominate the state for many years by insisting that Mormon candidates for public office first obtain permission to run for
the priesthood.

A dispute over the succession led to the emergence of another Mormon
body, the Reorganized Church of Jesus Christ of Latter-Day Saints. In 1860,
Joseph Smith III, son of the prophet, assumed leadership of this church,
headquartered in Independence, Missouri. It would come to reject some
controversial teachings and developments associated with the Nauvoo stage:
the plurality of gods, an earthly kingdom, and plural marriage (which had
originated with Smith but was not acknowledged until 1852). Baptism of
the dead was not explicitly condemned, but it fell into disuse. These moderate Mormons saw priestcraft in Brighamism, and they opposed concerted
political activity on the part of Mormons. About 5 percent of Mormon men
practiced polygamy until the church, under pressure from the federal government, abandoned the practice in the 1890s.

The prophet-president of the Church of Latter-day Saints was assisted by
twelve apostles. One apostle, Orson Pratt, functioned as a philosopher and
theologian and frequently challenged the views of Brigham Young. Pratt
admitted the superior authority of prophet Young, and was never excommunicated for his views. There were many bishops, each responsible for one
ward or congregation. Assisted by two "counselors," the bishop was to look
after the spiritual and material welfare of the congregation. Each household
would be visited by the bishop or his delegate. All worthy white males were
ordained as priests. From its beginning, the Mormon church had a very
ambitious missionary program. By 1870, about a quarter of the population
of Utah had been born in the United Kingdom.

Mormonism shared completely the populist character of the Second
Awakening. It should not be viewed as a religion with no connection to the
American mainstream; the major characteristics of the Second Awakening
were present in early Mormonism. In that sense, it is a quintessentially
American religion. Its preachers railed against the rich and proud and social
distinctions rooted in education, class, and money. Both Smith and Young
had a clear class bias against the oppressors of the poor and those who
possessed the advantages of profession, education, and wealth. They spoke
of the spiritual wisdom of the unlearned at the same time that they insisted
upon the teaching authority of their own hierarchy.

As saints, Mormons were expected to achieve perfection, but the route to
that blessed condition was not exactly like that of other Second Awakening

denominations. The prophet passed on "words of wisdom" regarding hot drinks, alcohol, and tobacco. Members were not regularly disciplined for sexual breaches, in part because Joseph Smith frequently broke what are now Mormon rules in that area. Mormons began as a group deeply committed to Jeffersonian republican values, but between 1830 and 1850 the hostility of others had the effect of bringing about an evolution toward an angry, alienated subculture.

In the beginning, the Mormons permitted African Americans to be priests, but Smith eventually began to weave racist views of them into his "Book of Moses" and "Book of Abraham." Mormons did not initially support slavery, but permitted it in Utah in 1852. Under Brigham Young, African Americans were barred from the priesthood, although there were always some white Mormons who criticized this position. In 1978, the church again admitted African Americans to the priesthood.

Women have been relegated to a secondary role in the affairs of the church. In the early church, Eliza R. Snow, known as "Aunt Eliza" and "Zion's poetess," spoke for women and intellectuals and led women in benevolent activities. She was a plural wife of Joseph Smith and a nonconnubial wife of Brigham Young. It can be argued that Smith intended to improve the status of women when he created for them the Relief Society. Through it, women raised funds for a variety of ventures and contributed substantially to building the Mormon kingdom in the desert. With time, the society fell more under the sway of the patriarchal leadership of the institutional church. At the local level, however, women in the society have retained some autonomy. Some of them hope that through continuous revelation, the church will eventually find it possible to admit them to priesthood.

Democracy, Antielitism, and Optimism

The Second Awakening differed from the Great Awakening in a number of respects. Its adherents did not insist upon an inflexible approach to the Calvinist doctrine of predestination; to varying degrees, they preached Christian perfectionism. Whereas the preachers of the Great Awakening reckoned success in terms of how many individuals claimed they had been saved and were anxious to own the covenant, clergymen associated with the Second Awakening thought in terms of building a mass movement and emphasized the number of congregations founded. Although the Presbyterians and Congregationalists often stressed traditional doctrines and the role of the clergy, other preachers of the Second Awakening underscored the importance of lay preachers. They were less concerned about adhering to what was then considered orthodoxy. This was also true of the Mormons and Millerites. Even though the Methodists had a hierarchy and the leader of the Disciples had difficulty accepting differences of opinion, both Methodists and Disciples capitalized on the democratic spirit of the age. They insisted on the importance of lay preachers and individual judgment. The American Revolution weakened appeals to tradition, authority, and educated elites. It greatly expanded the number of people who valued independent thought. It also emphasized the values of individualism, direct democracy, the primacy of the individual conscience, and localism.

John Leland, the period's leading Baptist, noted that those who possessed extensive educations differed among themselves on many theological matters. Therefore, it was clear to him that the untutored could reach valid theological decisions without the assistance of an educated elite. Unlike Isaac Backus, Leland saw no reason why individuals could not develop their own theologies within the broad framework of Baptist thought. Thus, it is not surprising that preachers of a democratized Christianity were very successful in reaching out to marginalized people. They identified the desires of ordinary people with the will of God. As a result of their evangelical efforts, their followers became convinced that they were indeed "somebodies" of importance and value.

Evangelical preachers were successful in binding their followers together into tightly knit, supportive communities. They persuaded their flocks to become involved in self-education and self-help activities, and to support various humanitarian causes. A contagious faith in the future of the American republic was conveyed, teaching that the common man, rather than traditional elites, was best equipped to deal with society's major problems.

Bibliography

Adams, Elizabeth T. "Divided Nation, Divided Church: The Presbyterian Schism, 1837–1838." *Historian* 54 (summer 1992): 683–696.

Anders, Sarah Frances, and Marilyn Metcalf-Whittaker. "Women as Lay Leaders and Clergy: A Critical Issue." In *Southern Baptists Observed: Multiple Perspectives on a Changing Denomination,* ed. Nancy Tatom Ammerman, pp. 201–221. Knoxville: University of Tennessee Press, 1993.

Anderson, Nels. *Desert Saints: The Mormon Frontier in Utah.* Chicago: University of Chicago Press, 1966.

Arrington, Leonard J. *Brigham Young: American Moses.* New York: Knopf, 1985.

Arrington, Leonard J., and Davis Bitton. *The Mormon Experience: A History of the Latter-day Saints.* Urbana: University of Chicago Press, 1992.

Baker, Jean. *Affairs of Party: The Political Culture of Northern Democrats in the Mid-Nineteenth Century.* Ithaca: Cornell University Press, 1983.

Barkun, Michael. *Crucible of the Millennium: The Burned-Over District of New*

York in the 1840s. Syracuse: Syracuse University Press, 1986.

Bilhartz, Terry D. *Urban Religion and the Second Great Awakening: Church and Society in Early National Baltimore.* Rutherford: Fairleigh Dickinson University Press, 1986.

Bitton, David. "The Mormon Past: The Search for Understanding." *Religious Studies Review* 11 (April 1985): 114–120.

Bradbury, M.L. "Structures of Nationalism." In *Religion in a Revolutionary Age,* ed. Ronald Hoffman and Peter J. Albert, pp. 236–289. Charlottesville: University of Virginia, 1994.

Brereton, Virginia Lieson. *From Sin to Salvation: Stories of Women's Conversions, 1800 to the Present.* Bloomington: Indiana University Press, 1991.

Bringhurst, Newell G. *Saints, Slaves, and Blacks: The Changing Place of Black People Within Mormonism.* Westport, CT: Greenwood Press, 1981.

Bruce, Dickson D., Jr. *And They All Sang Hallelujah: Plain Folk Camp-Meeting Religion, 1800–1845.* Knoxville: University of Tennessee Press, 1974.

Butler, Jon. "The Dark Ages of American Occultism, 1760–1848." 58–78. In *The Occult in America, New Perspectives,* ed. Howard Kerr and Charles Crow, pp. 58–78. Urbana: University of Illinois Press, 1986.

Carwardine, Richard J. *Evangelicals and Politics in Antebellum America.* New Haven: Yale University Press, 1993.

Cohen, David Steven. "The 'Angel Dancers': The Folklore of Religious Communitarianism." *New Jersey History* 115 (spring 1977): 5–20.

Coleman, Michael C. "Not Race, but Grace: Presbyterian Missionaries and American Indians, 1837–1893." *Journal of American History* 67 (June 1980): 41–60.

Conforti, Joseph A. "Mary Lyon: The Founding of Mount Holyoke College, and the Cultural Revival of Jonathan Edwards." *Religion and American Culture* 3 (winter 1993): 69–90.

Cross, Whitney R. *The Burned-Over District: The Social and Intellectual History of Enthusiastic Religion in Western New York, 1800–1850.* Ithaca: Cornell University Press, 1950.

Doan, Ruth Alden. *The Miller Heresy, Millennialism, and American Culture.* Philadelphia: Temple University Press, 1987.

Dorgan, Howard. *Giving Glory to God in Appalachia: Worship Practices of Six Baptist Subdenominations.* Knoxville: University of Tennessee Press, 1987.

Fuller, Robert C. *Alternative Medicine and American Religious Life.* New York: Oxford University Press, 1989.

Garrison, Winfred Ernest, and Alfred T. DeGroot. *The Disciples of Christ, A History.* St. Louis: Bethany Press, 1958.

Gilpin, W. Clark. "Recent Studies of American Protestant Primitivism." *Religious Studies Review* 19 (July 1993): 231–235.

Goodman, Paul. "The Manual Labor Movement and the Origins of Abolitionism." *Journal of the Early Republic* 13 (fall 1993): 355–388.

Hammond, Philip E., Amanda Porterfield, James G. Moseley, and Jonathan D. Sarna. "Forum: American Civil Religion Revisited." *Religion and American Culture* 4 (winter 1994): 1–23.

Handy, Robert T. *A Christian America: Protestant Hopes and Historical Realities.* New York: Oxford University Press, 1983.

Hannah, Walton. *Darkness Visible: A Revelation and Interpretation of Freemasonry.* London: Britons, 1966.

Harding, Vincent. *A Certain Magnificence: Lyman Beecher and the Transformation of American Protestantism, 1775–1863.* Brooklyn: Carlson, 1991.

Hatch, Nathan O. "The Christian Movement and the Demand for a Theology of the People." *Journal of American History* 67 (December 1980): 545–567.

———. *The Democratization of American Christianity.* New Haven: Yale University Press, 1989.

———. "The Democratization of Christianity and the Character of American Politics." In *Religion and American Politics,* ed. Mark A. Noll, pp. 92–120. New York: Oxford University Press, 1990.

Hewitt, Glenn A. *Regeneration and Morality: A Study of Charles G. Finney, Charles Hodge, John N. Nevin, and Horace Bushnell.* Brooklyn: Carlson, 1991.

Howe, Daniel Walker. "The Market Revolution and the Shaping of Identity in Whig-Jacksonian America." In *The Market Revolution in America: Social, Political, and Religious Expressions, 1800–1880,* ed. Melvin Stokes and Stephen Conway, pp. 259–281. Charlottesville: University of Virginia, 1996.

Hughes, Richard T. "The Apocalyptic Origins of the Churches of Christ and the Triumph of Modernism." *Religion and American Culture* 2 (summer 1992): 181–214.

Isaacs, Ernest. "The Fox Sisters and American Spiritualism." In *The Occult in America: New Historical Perspectives,* ed. Howard Kerr and Charles Crow, pp. 79–110. Urbana: University of Illinois Press, 1986.

Jackson, Rebecca. *Gifts of Power: The Writings of Rebecca Jackson, Black Visionary, Shaker Eldress.* Edited by Jean McMahon. Amherst: University of Massachusetts Press, 1981.

Juster, Susan. " 'In a Different Voice': Male and Female Narratives of Religious Conversion in Post-Revolutionary America." *American Quarterly* 41 (March 1989): 34–62.

Koritansky, John C. "Civil Religion in Tocqueville's *Democracy in America.*" *Interpretation* 17 (spring 1990): 389–400.

Kutolowski, Kathleen Smith. "Freemasonry and Community in the Early Republic: The Case for Anti-Masonic Anxieties." *American Quarterly* 34 (winter 1982): 543–561.

Long, Kathryn T. "The Power of Interpretation: The Revival of 1857–58 and the Historiography of Revivalism in America." *Religion and American Culture* 4 (December 1993): 107–132.

Loveland, Anne C. *Southern Evangelicals and the Social Order, 1800–1860.* Baton Rouge: Louisiana State University Press, 1980.

Maddex, Jack P. "Proslavery Millennialism: Social Eschatology in Antebellum Southern Calvinism." *American Quarterly* 31 (spring 1979): 46–62.

Mathews, Donald G. *Slavery and Methodism: A Chapter in American Morality, 1780–1845.* Princeton: Princeton University Press, 1965.

Matthews, Jean V. *Toward a New Society: American Thought and Culture.* Boston: Twayne, 1992.

McDannell, Colleen. *The Christian Home in Victorian America, 1840–1900.* Bloomington: Indiana University Press, 1986.

McKiernam, F. Mark, Alma R. Blair, and Paul M. Edwards, eds. *The Restoration Movement: Essays in Mormon History.* Lawrence, KS: Colorado Press, 1973.

McLoughlin, William. "Indian Slaveholders and Presbyterian Missionaries, 1837–1861." *Church History* 42 (December 1973): 535–551.

Miyakawa, T. Scott. *Protestants and Pioneers: Individualism and Conformity on the American Frontier.* Chicago: University of Chicago Press, 1964.

Moore, R. Laurence. "The Occult Connection? Mormonism, Christian Science, and Spiritualism." In *The Occult in America: New Historical Perspectives,* ed. Howard Kerr and Charles Crow, pp. 162–176. Urbana: University of Illinois, 1986.

———."Religion, Secularization, and the Shaping of Culture in Antebellum America." *American Quarterly* 41 (June 1989): 216–242.

Moorhead, James H. "Between Progress and Apocalypse: A Reassessment of Millennialism in American Religious Thought, 1800–1880." *Journal of American History* 71 (December 1984): 524–543.

Morse, Jedediah. "The Danger of Conspiracy." In *Anti-Masonry: The Crusade and the Party,* ed. Lorman Ratner, pp. 1–23. Englewood Cliffs: Prentice-Hall, 1969.

Numbers, Ronald L., and Jonathan M. Butler, eds. *The Disappointed: Millerism and Millenarianism in the Nineteenth Century.* Bloomington: Indiana University Press, 1987.

Pessen, Edward. *Jacksonian America: Society, Personality, and Politics.* Homewood, IL: Dorsey Press, 1969.

Ratner, Lorman. *Antimasonry: The Crusade and the Party.* New York: Prentice-Hall, 1969.

Richey, Russell E. *Early American Methodism.* Bloomington: Indiana University Press, 1991.

Robins, Roger. "Vernacular American Landscape: Methodists, Camp Meetings, and Social Respectability." In *Women in American Religion,* ed. Janet James Wilson, pp. 165–191. Philadelphia: University of Pennsylvania Press, 1980.

Schwartz, Gary. *Sect Ideologies and Social Status.* Chicago: University of Chicago Press, 1970.

Sellers, Charles. *The Market Revolution: Jacksonian America, 1815–1846.* New York: Oxford University Press, 1991.

Shiels, Richard D. "The Feminization of American Congregationalism, 1730–1835." *American Quarterly* 33 (spring 1981): 46–62.

Smith, Timothy L. *Revivalism and Social Reform: American Protestantism on the Eve of the Civil War.* New York: Harper and Row, 1965.

———."Righteousness and Hope: Christian Holiness and the Millennial Vision in America, 1800–1900." *American Quarterly* 31 (spring 1979): 21–45.

Snyder, Stephen H. *Lyman Beecher and His Children: The Transformation of a Religious Tradition.* Brooklyn: Carlson, 1991.

Stein, Stephen J. "Community, Commitment, and Practice: Union and Order at Pleasant Hill in 1834." *Journal of the Early Republic* 8 (spring 1988): 45–68.

Sutton, William R. "Benevolent Calvinism and the Moral Government of God: The Influence of Nathaniel W. Taylor on Revivalism in the Second Great Awakening." *Religion and American Culture* 2 (winter 1992): 23–47.

Vogel, Dan, and Scott C. Dunn. " 'The Tongue of Angels': Mormonism's Founders." *Journal of Mormon History* 19 (fall 1993): 1–34.

Way, Peter. "Evil Humors and Ardent Spirits: The Rough Culture of Canal Construction Laborers." *Journal of American History* 79 (March 1993): 1397–1428.

Whalen, William J. *Christianity and American Freemasonry.* Milwaukee: Bruce, 1958.

Wiebe, Robert H. *The Opening of American Society*. New York: Knopf, 1984.
Wigger, John H. "Taking Heaven by Storm: Enthusiasm and Early American Methodism, 1770–1820." *Journal of the Early Republic* 14 (summer 1994): 187–194.
Williams, Peter J. *Popular Religion in America: Symbolic Change and the Modernization Process in Historical Perspective*. Urbana: University of Illinois Press, 1989.
Wyatt-Brown, Bertram. "Religion and the 'Civilizing Process' in the Early South, 1600–1860." In *Religion and American Politics: From the Colonial Period to the 1980s,* ed. Mark A. Noll, pp. 172–198. New York: Oxford University Press, 1990.
Zwelling, Shomer F. "Robert Carter's Journey: From Colonial Patriarch to New Nation Mystic." *American Quarterly* 38 (summer 1986): 613–639.

Five

Women, the Churches, and Empowerment

Women and Christian Perfection

The Second Great Awakening enhanced the position of women within the churches and made possible a certain measure of female empowerment through the operation of benevolent societies. The public sphere has been defined as "the realm that was created when ordinary people emerged from their homes to engage in conversation." In a bourgeois public sphere, such as that found in America, there was strong opposition to authoritarianism, and conversation was rooted in what Jurgen Habermas termed "general and abstract laws" that had been learned in church or in the family. Women were active in these public conversations and helped shape its terms through the value-formation process that they dominated in the home. If politics is seen as the process of discussing public questions rather than the mere act of casting a ballot, the Second Awakening created an atmosphere in which women played a greater role in politics. Through the churches they became deeply involved in benevolent reform and they discussed these issues in the home. They attended public meetings at which questions such as slavery or closing businesses on Sunday were discussed. Considered the guardians of Christian and republican ideals, many accepted the idea that women should have strong opinions on some public questions, even if giving women the vote was thought to be out of the question.

The majority of people converted by Finney and other awakeners appear to have been the daughters and wives of businessmen. As many as two-thirds of those converted during the Second Awakening were women. Among New England Congregationalists, 59 percent of church members were women; during the Second Awakening that figure rose to 69 percent. Noted traveler Mrs. Frances Trollope remarked that she knew of no other country "where religion has so strong a hold upon the women, or a lighter hold upon men." In time, the content of sermons reflected the perspectives and concerns of women. A gentle Jesus was portrayed, rather than Christ as king and magistrate. Theologian Horace Bushnell dealt with concern for a child who died before baptism by suggesting that God could choose to regenerate that child as a fetus in the mother's womb. To a considerable extent, women made religion possible by providing most of the people who attended services. The church disenfranchised women, but it depended upon them for its existence. Though aware of this tragic paradox, women adhered to the church because it shared their perceived role of transmitting values to the next generation and because it offered them moral support amid the great difficulties associated with motherhood. As morality was associated with women's sphere, its place in the political and business spheres would be diminished. In the late twentieth century, the discussion of empowering women in politics and business has often not included consideration of restoring moral considerations in political and economic life.

Catherine Beecher, daughter of Lyman Beecher, advanced one of the most compelling arguments for Christian perfectionism. She rejected her father's doctrines of election and human depravity and insisted that God had created a perfect human nature; "the mind of man is perfect in its constituted powers," but people behave imperfectly because they lack knowledge and proper instruction. In *Religious Training of Children in the School, the Family, and the Church* (1864), she argued that people will move closer to perfection when they receive the benefits of sound Christian education. Her emphasis upon human perfectibility led her to enter the Episcopal Church in the 1860s. She was instrumental in opening the teaching profession to women, but the idea that female teachers should receive less compensation than men can also be traced to her. Another influential woman was Mary Lyon, who believed in equal education for women and founded Mount Holyoke Seminary in 1837. She also preached revivals on religious subjects. Mary Lyon had been raised as a Baptist, and converted to Congregationalism under the influence of her teacher, Reverend Joseph Emerson. Though not a minister, she was a member of the fellowship of New England's New Divinity clergy. She played a major role in the revival of the thought of Jonathan Edwards, whose works became read more frequently than in his own day. Lyon was attracted by Edwards's ideas of self-restraint, self-denial, and disinterested benevolence. Mount Holyoke trained hundreds of missionaries and many pious teachers who were later employed in public schools or other seminaries.

By joining a church before their husbands or parents, women exercised spiritual independence. In conversion, women surrendered themselves entirely to Christ, but this process often released a great deal of energy and a decline of self-consciousness. It was often an empowering experience that permitted them to sometimes engage in activities otherwise not thought suitable for women. Some became exhorters or published conversion stories. Conversion narratives sometimes were indirect attacks on the place of women in American society. They were often stories of women who lived a comfortable life, yet found something lacking. Through salvation, they made Christ, rather than husband and children, the center of their lives. When other members of the family followed them into the fold, they felt a significant sense of accomplishment.

The large number of female conversions may be attributed to the fact that women were feeling greater anxiety than normal because the status of women was deteriorating. Households were being physically separated from shops, and this had the effect of removing women not only from the source of the family's income but somewhat reducing their contact with the world outside the family and neighborhood. A study of the Second Awakening in Utica, New York, demonstrated that a woman was twice as likely as a man to be the first family member to join a church. Moreover, the middle-class church women of Utica had phenomenal success in evangelizing their sons and daughters. Their success appears to have been almost independent of the efforts of clergymen.

It is doubtful that there were great differences between the conversion experiences of men and women. Women were inclined to see God in personal terms as a revered and loving parent, and their conversion accounts were more emotional than those of men. Men often saw God as judge, king, and lawgiver. Both sexes had trouble admitting complete dependence on a all-sufficient God. These differences aside, there was essentially one, androgynous model for conversion; as Saint Paul said, "in Christ there is neither . . . male or female." Conversion represented spiritual empowerment for all, but especially for women, whom society had deprived of power. Women's conversion narratives often revealed conflict with fathers or husbands who had forbade them to attend revival meetings, and were often stories of female empowerment. In them, women defied tyrannical male family members, found the courage to write or speak to other women about their trials and religious experiences, became exhorters, and sometimes left home. These conversion accounts gave them an opportunity to vent anger and to unconsciously critique societal arrangements that demeaned them.

Women were told that it was their special role to set the household standard for piety and "domestick purity" and that they should bring about "the increase of our public charities." Women learned that evangelical values made it possible for them to exert greater control over their households and personal lives. They were viewed as best equipped to serve as guardians of morality, purity, culture, and patriotism. This doctrine of the separate spheres has been referred to as the cult of domesticity or that of "true womanhood" or motherhood.

The power women exercised in the home has been called "domestic feminism," to distinguish it from organized feminism. The cult of true womanhood was useful to patriarchy because it prevented women from challenging male prerogatives. Nevertheless, it can be seen as giving more status than women enjoyed in preindustrial society. Domestic feminism gave women a measure of autonomy in the home. Of course, middle-class women were most affected by these developments. Working-class women often worked in factories, took work into the home under an extension of the domestic system, or found it necessary to supplement family income by taking in boarders. The doctrine of the two spheres encouraged people to identify the work of men and wages with productivity, but women's work was not classified as productive. The bourgeois emphasis on politeness, evangelical benevolent reforms, and the prudery of the age—assisted by evangelical reform and spread of middle-class market values—may have somewhat reduced violent male behavior and prompted some to cease seeing women as sex objects.

Through revivals and sermons, women learned of their special role as guardians of gentility and spiritual values. They were expected to be "great sufferers." One prominent clergyman said the happiest home was one where a Christian woman radiated cheer though great suffering. Women took advantage of this trade-off to gain more control of household activities, such as child rearing, and to assert themselves in sexual matters. They used their status as the guardians of purity to reduce the number of pregnancies they endured. This was accomplished by abstinence, withdrawal, and, to an extent, probably by an increased abortion rate. In 1800, 55 babies were born per 1,000 people, a rate that declined to 43.3 by 1850. By the 1830s, literature on contraception and abortion was readily available, and practitioners were soon advertising in newspapers their willingness to perform abortions. Though women had a strong interest in limiting the number of their children, there were also economic reasons why most farmers and members of the middle class no longer needed large families. Middle-class men also had sound economic reasons for reducing the number of dependents they supported. To an extent the lower birthrate might have been the result of increased infanticide.

Legislation against abortion first appeared after the American Medical Association began a crusade against the practice in 1860. Abortions before quickening were not declared illegal because there was no accurate method of determining pregnancy before that time. Whether it was considered moral before quickening is open to question, but it is known that, by mid-century, one in five pregnancies were aborted.

Clergymen and women believed that what they considered an excessive interest in sex on the part of men was an index of the extent to which males needed to be civilized. Men were told by their clergy about the nobility of asexual love and made to feel guilty about their eroticism. To complement this view, many women accepted the idea that women lacked sexual feelings but were desirous of strong relationships built on asexual love. "True men" wished to grow in industriousness, sobriety, honesty, and frugality, but harnessing their sexual drive was most important and a barometer of progress they were making in other areas. Not only should men curb the sexual demands they made on their wives, they were to avoid the "vicious act" of masturbation, as it destroyed soul, mind, and body. "Lascivious day-dreams and amorous reveries" were dirty thoughts and to be avoided. Some thought that certain foods, for example meat, stimulated masculine sexual urges and should be forsworn. While curbing his erotic impulses, the true man must avoid effeminacy at all costs. Whiskers and beards were common then, and may have been fashionable in part due to the need to avoid appearing effeminate.

Women attempted to use churches, Bible and tract societies, Sunday schools, missionary alliances, and revivals to civilize males and society. Many clergymen and women thought that, due to his nature and contact with the market, man had too much of the "brute" in him and was insufficiently generous, cooperative, or community minded. Some blamed this largely on the competitiveness and calculating egotism of the market. As time passed most evangelical clergymen saw the market economy as an instrument of progress. Even if it had made some too selfish, it did demand of people a number of important and valuable traits: sobriety, reliability, industriousness, diligence, and frugality. One who possessed these traits could be said to possess *character*.

The Second Great Awakening gave women and evangelical clergy the means to promote qualities deemed more Christian and civilized. Through their dominance in household matters, women could attempt to raise children as they saw fit and lead their husbands to Christian purity, virtue, and altruism. It was necessary, however, for women to disclaim a high level of literary or critical abilities on their part. To be an ideal wife, according to Dr. Oliver Wendell Holmes, father of the famous jurist, a woman must be careful to give her husband cheerful surroundings and the opportunity to always be at his best. This meant she was never to embarrass her mate by appearing more intelligent or proficient than he. The senior Holmes had experienced childhood trauma when it became obvious that a female classmate was considerably brighter than he. Although women often found it necessary to offer their views in ways that did not offend sensitive men such as Holmes, they did contribute toward political discourse. They did not vote, but they were the conduits for reformist views that they heard in churches and meetings of various societies.

Revivalism made it easier for many middle-class women to accept the cult of true womanhood. They had been put on a pedestal as guardians of patriotism, gentility, and spirituality in return for noninvolvement in the economy and acceptance of unequal rights before the law. By receiving the home as their domain, middle-class women were actually given an opportunity to develop their powers in this sphere. In the absence of the household patriarch, women gained more control over their everyday lives.

An informal but important alliance was being formed by the evangelical clergy and women, who now dominated their congregations. Both were dedicated to the pursuit of morality and perfectionism. But both occupied only the fringes of a world increasingly devoted to the pursuit of wealth and unbridled—frequently unethical—competition for place and standing, and the world's goods. The clergy endorsed the moral superiority of women and in turn received their support in various benevolent activities. Although the clergy found it useful to ally with women, they held revivals as a means of increasing the male membership of their congregations, where men were frequently outnumbered. The somewhat drastic tactics the clergy employed were considered necessary to convert unchurched men. By bringing men into the churches, the clergy were improving their communities and incidentally making it easier for their congregations to pay bills.

A domestic religion emerged that centered on the mother and conferred a sacramental quality upon the home. The mother-child relationship rather than the patriarchal family was seen as the foundation of society. Domestic religion was defined and promoted in novels, women's magazines, and advice literature. Although it was the prerogative of the Protestant father to lead the family in prayer, it was the mother who instructed children individually in religion. She also helped them with their studies, using this opportunity to guide their spiritual development. Music and religious handicrafts were other instructional tools. Women usually did not speak of a stern, vindictive God, but told children about a loving and forgiving God. They urged their children to lead lives of private devotion, love, and self-sacrifice. Ministers and formal religion were secondary to this domestic religion. Through their experiences in parenting, they believed that just as youngsters could be led to civilized behavior, so too all society could be brought to a higher level of civilization through the application of Christian principles.

A form of domestic religion existed among Jewish women. They were not bound to study religion or carry out many public observances, but they were expected to transmit knowledge and piety to their children. In cases where husbands became Talmudic scholars and attended synagogue regularly, Jewish women not only had charge of the children's spiritual enlightenment but represented the family in the marketplace. They were better acquainted with the public sphere than their husbands.

A similar form of domestic religion did not appear among Roman Catholics until the 1880s, when some Catholics had sufficient income to live as Victorian middle-class families. There were differences between Catholic and Protestant domestic religion. Catholic women looked to Mary, the mother of Christ, as model and justification of their role. Because Roman Catholicism centered upon the sacraments, administered by priests, domestic religion was not considered as important as formal worship. Catholic women did not have their own journals, but there were Catholic women's novels, and women wrote for Catholic publications on themes that reinforced domestic religion. Protestants defined their domestic piety by mocking the Irish Catholic family, which they depicted as led by a drunken father with a mother who worked long hours in a factory. Similarly, Catholic domestic piety portrayed the Protestant family with a stern, unloving father, spoiled children, and mother who was completely absorbed in her social life.

Women's Benevolence Societies

Some women's societies were formed as early as the New-Light Stir. These benevolent associations were so successful that women were often forced to permit their organizations to be absorbed by male-dominated societies. However, not all of the women's societies were scrapped. The Female Charitable Society of Oneida County, New York, provided a salary that gave Charles Finney his start as an evangelist. (It was a woman, his fiancée, who first pressed for his conversion.) This charitable society eventually had seventy branches and in 1824 was renamed the Female Missionary Society of Western New York.

Through their activities in Sunday schools, missionary alliances, and other aspects of organized benevolence, women often exercised powers they could not otherwise possess. The charters of some of these groups permitted members to handle money and property and use the courts in a number of ways. Activities in these groups permitted members to develop a women's culture and sense of sisterhood. They affirmed one another in their femininity and worked to improve the lot of women and people in general. In working with the poor and outcast, they saw that other women shared their sense of oppression. Women frequently operated societies to help prostitutes, whose sad situations were often traced to men who led them astray or to unreliable or alcoholic husbands. As adherents to perfectionism, Christian women worked for the end of prostitution by uplifting and bringing prostitutes to salvation. They emphasized the curbing of immoral impulses and taught others the principles of Christian morality. Their crusade to bring about the triumph of "love over lust" epitomized their effort to uplift a corrupt society. Whether or not a community tolerated the existence of prostitution was an indication of its spiritual health.

The New York Moral Reform Society, under the leadership of Mrs. Charles G. Finney, worked to end prostitution through the efforts of agents, exhorters, and clergymen. Its goals were to bring the nation to moral purity and to help women who had been forced into prostitution. By 1840, there were 555 branches. In New York City, it attempted to close brothels and expose the men who visited them. They employed Reverend John McDowell, who had incurred the wrath of those who wanted to regulate rather than end prostitution. He had been indicted as a public nuisance, and his New York Magdalene Society had collapsed. McDowell's opponents were uneasy with the enthusiasm of the perfectionists and thought that the discussion of prostitution would lead to more women entering whoredom. Encountering opposition in their drive to end prostitution, these female Christian perfectionists became all the more convinced that revivals presented the best opportunities to civilize males and society. Through these activities, women were in fact preparing for organized feminism.

The New York Moral Reform Society published a periodical known as the *Advocate of Moral Reform*. Belonging broadened the role of its members in society, and through it women acquired and demonstrated leadership skills. They were competent in handling money, they hired and fired agents and other employees, they operated and even set type for the *Advocate*. Members traveled without male chaperons. The society spoke out on a number of social issues, and from time to time the *Advocate* revealed resentment of male domination. Although favoring women's rights, they did not formally affiliate with that movement. A number of other women's moral reform organizations emerged in the 1830s. Like the New York society, the Boston Female Moral Reform Society had a number of affiliates. These organizations hired mostly women, who carried out many functions usually reserved for men. There were some male employees, affording the women the opportunity to give orders to men.

Many Christian women's benevolent activities existed. Women could not openly protest their subjugation to men, but involvement in evangelical reform movements was a subtle but effective means of asserting their autonomy. Their most important reform activity was involvement in the temperance movement. Through it they could address problems created by the male drunkard, whom the New York women's temperance newsletter *Pearl* labeled "a deliberate, voluntary savage, and he treated his wife accordingly." Methodist women established the Women's Christian Temperance

Union in 1873, and it soon became the most important feminist organiza-tion in the United States. Many churches labeled drinking a sin; members of the WCTU saw drink as the root of most evils. The WCTU's most notable leader was its second president, the dynamic Frances Willard, who enjoyed many successes but was unable to persuade the membership to share her socialism or to shed some of the negative values then infecting American culture. With the slogan "Do-Everything," this organization spoke for women in many stations in life. Its leaders thought in terms of universal sisterhood and supported a variety of reforms. It stood for women's suf-frage and the right of women to address mixed assemblies, as well as opposition to the use of alcohol and drugs. Willard and the WCTU worked for stronger legislation against rape, improved conditions for women in prison, and supported the Knights of Labor. Unfortunately, it was never able to overcome the anti-Catholicism, fear of immigrants, or racism toward blacks that characterized the thinking of most middle-class Americans in the late nineteenth century. The WCTU was the most significant training ground for female leaders, and it provided them with a powerful platform from which to state their convictions on public questions. Through such philanthropic activities, women sought spiritual perfection (Figure 5).

Missionaries

Women's benevolence societies often raised funds for missionaries, and women often went to distant lands as wives of missionaries, serving not only as homemakers but as nurses or teachers. These wives often suffered the pain of separation from their children, left behind with relatives or sent home for schooling when they reached age ten. The mission press paid little attention to the wives other than to report that they died beautiful deaths in mission lands, noting that it was God's will that they die in a foreign land. There was a general impression that these missionary wives died young because they mistakenly took on tasks that exceeded their roles as home-makers. There is no evidence to suggest that they died much younger than their sisters in the United States.

Some wives functioned very effectively as missionaries after their husbands' deaths. In time, it became obvious that female missionaries were needed to deal with potential female converts. In 1861, the nondenominational Woman's Union Missionary Society of America for Heathen Lands was formed with the goal of recruiting single women for missionary work. By 1893, it had sixty-five female missionaries in Japan, China, and India. At least fifteen other—usually denominational—women's mission boards were organ-ized. Through these boards, women acquired leadership skills they later em-

Figure 5. Frances Willard. Frances Willard (1838–1898), president of the Women's Christian Temperance Union, called for women's suffrage so women could bring about "Home Protection" by banning the trade in strong drink. She encouraged women to embrace many reforms and inspired them to develop a sense of moral and political mission. (Courtesy the Library of Congress.)

ployed in other church forums. Women in American churches took pride in supporting this "work of women for women," and thought it important that the work was "performed in a women's way." Sixty percent of all American missionaries were women by 1893, a figure that included women married to clerical missionaries. In 1880, the Methodist Episcopal Church General Conference refused to create the office of deaconess. Of course, women were doing all the work of deaconess in mission lands. The conference reversed its decision in 1888.

Political Concerns

Though disenfranchised, women carried their benevolent and reformist concerns into the political arena by way of petitions and literary efforts. By petitioning local, state, and federal governments they expressed their opinions on a variety of subjects including temperance, the extension of slavery into the territories, the regulation of asylums and prisons, women's property rights, and Indian removal. By the thousands, evangelical women participated in elections by attending rallies, barbecues, and other functions. They made and carried banners and sought ways of influencing the political opinions of those who could vote.

Public opinion on political matters was formed in the streets, at rallies, in the newspapers, and at the meetings of benevolent societies. In all these places, women played major roles in political life. The conscious inclusion of women in political rituals began in 1840, when Whigs urged them to participate in political events. Some women assisted the Whigs through their writings. Notable among them was Lucy Kenney of Virginia, who supported Democrat Andrew Jackson in the 1830s before giving the Whigs her allegiance. It was thought that women would not be swept away by partisanship but, as custodians of American virtues, would be able to identify the most suitable candidates, who naturally would be Whigs. A doctrine of female civic duty was emerging. Daniel Webster noted that "there is one morality for politics and another morality for other things"; the great orator thought it was women's special role to bring the two standards together into one universal code of ethics. Whigs thought that a patriotic women would teach her children love of the republic and their party.

The Democrats were hesitant to bring women into the political arena, but by the late 1840s they were recruiting female supporters. During the Civil War, women frequently attended Republican gatherings, and there were even some women at Democratic functions. As women entered the realm of politics, the role of "true motherhood" was being expanded into the doctrine of benevolent femininity. By supporting benevolent enterprises and virtuous politicians, women had a civilizing influence upon society and politics.

Feminization of Culture

Women came to exert great influence on American popular culture in part due to the loss of status and authority experienced by liberal Protestant clergy. Disestablishment and the growth of democracy diminished the authority of the clergy, especially New England Congregationalists. Stripped of much authority and economic power and facing the prospect of relatively short tenures, these clergymen came to emphasize feminine values, those of the majorities in their congregations. The sternness, toughness, and intellectual rigor that once characterized Calvinism—considered "masculine" characteristics—eventually gave way. Now faith was defined in terms of civic responsibility, solid family morality and togetherness, and regular participation in church activities; liberal Protestantism was redefined in terms of sentimental and "feminine" qualities. This development was influenced by the emergence of the market revolution and mass culture. Once an authoritative institution with considerable independence, the church—both liberal and evangelical—would be reduced to taking its cues from the evolving mass culture. For many northern clergy, this meant not challenging slavery; in the South it required embracing the vile institution. The adoption of market values led to measuring piety by the number of people attending church functions.

As mistress of the household, the woman was expected to become a competent and enthusiastic consumer. Women also produced and consumed the literature being produced then, for the first time, to be sold to a mass market. The female author was no longer an aberration; hers was a respected place in society, and she had great influence. As the principle consumers of mass culture, women were able to shape it to satisfy feminine sensibilities. In the process American culture was to be feminized. Old values, threatened by capitalist development, were sentimentalized. This process represented a half-hearted resistance to the inevitable victory of the market revolution. Literary women such as Sarah Josepha Hale of *Godey's Lady's Book* sought to influence society in many positive ways, but they were unable to effectively address the fundamental changes that grew out of the market revolution, one of which was the degradation of the labor of many women. These writers sought to strengthen qualities such as supportiveness and the nurturing of others in developing maturity and Christian virtue.

Female writers and their ecclesiastical supporters lacked real power and sought to make themselves emotionally indispensable because they were a major civilizing force. Editor Hale insisted that fundamental Christian purity existed in the feminine sphere and should be used to reform society at large through such movements as temperance, improving women's education, and women's suffrage. As caretakers of the American version of Christian culture, women came to dominate local libraries and to produce the bulk of novels and short stories that appeared in this first age of mass marketing. In these roles, women assumed some of the moral authority once held by the liberal clergy—who now depended upon women for status and their livelihoods. The women now almost spoke for their churches, and in this way wielded new power. They did not affirm patriarchy, gently suggesting that men assume more feminine qualities, and that Christian perfection could enable women to rival the angels in virtue. The downside of women's newfound power was that they tended to substitute a theology of feeling for rationalist theology, and thus contributed to an anti-intellectualism that was to be a powerful tool in the hands of many whose only interest in Judeo-Christian values was to bend them to serve their selfish purposes. This unfortunate development in liberal Protestantism corresponded to a similar phenomenon flowing from the evangelism of the Second Awakening.

Seeking Women's Rights

The principal goal of the women's rights movement was to acquire the vote, and within the churches it was important that women address mixed audiences and be ordained. Many women were awakened by perfectionist theology to a fuller understanding of their capacity to do good. They were certain women could at least match the efforts of men in doing good. For these women, it was important to escape the bondage of the cult of true womanhood. When they became involved in reform activities, they expected the right to address mixed assemblies, but were rebuffed. Some who fought to do so, such as Quakers Sarah and Angelina Grimké, were inspired by biblical rather than Finneyite thought. Angelina had been a Presbyterian before joining the Society of Friends. When she broke with her Presbyterian congregation over slavery, her former minister, who was privately critical of slavery, thought she had been deluded by Satan. The church session expelled her for nonattendance and failure to attend the ceremony of the Lord's Supper. Angelina's *Appeal to the Christian Women of the South* was forcefully written and was based on the hope that moral suasion could end slavery.

Margaret Fuller was a central figure among the transcendentalists and a powerful advocate of women's rights. Transcendentalism was not part of the Second Awakening; rather it was an outgrowth of Unitarianism, which transcendentalists saw as cold, excessively formal, and too cerebral. Ralph Waldo Emerson, the chief founder, argued that divinity can be found in nature and in one's intuition. They believed that an oversoul dwells within all people, and that the individual is most in touch with the spirit within when living spontaneously and in harmony with nature. Transcendentalism was a philosophy and faith, but it was not a formal religion. Informal gatherings for discussion came to be called the Transcendentalist Club, and from 1840 to 1844 it published a literary review, *The Dial.* Margaret Fuller was its first editor, and Emerson was responsible for it in its last two years. Fuller had carefully studied the Bible and found truth in Christ's ethics, but she saw no reason to affiliate with any particular church. However, she believed that the Swedenborgians and Quakers had the most satisfactory views on women. Remarkably well educated by her father, she led "conversations" or discussion groups on a variety of topics for five years. She left Boston in 1845 to become the first woman to write for Horace Greeley's *New York Tribune.* In the previous year she published *Woman in the Nineteenth Century.* In it she insisted women must fulfill themselves on their own terms and not in subordination to men. This can be done if a woman lives "*first* for God's sake. Then she will not make an imperfect man her god."

Lucretia Mott of Philadelphia, a Public Friend (the Quaker equivalent to a minister), was a leading abolitionist and spokesperson for women's rights. Mrs. Mott insisted upon righteous living, denounced sectarianism, and thought authority flowed from true principles rather than public offices. Since the time of their founder, George Fox, Quakers had believed in the spiritual equality of women, even though they did not accord women equality in church governance. Within the Society of Friends there was a parallel organizational structure for women, through which females carried out benevolent activities, developed leadership skills, and acquired experience handling money. Lucretia Mott used the doctrine of women's spiritual equality to insist upon their secular equality. She thought that the churches and clergymen bore much of the responsibility for the subjugation of women. While the franchise, equal pay for women, and other measures were important to her, Mott thought the greatest task of the women's movement was to liberate women from a paralyzing and enervating view of themselves.

Discord over the role of women and their right to speak in abolitionist circles led to the formation of the nineteenth-century women's rights movement. Lucy Stone was one of the first women to discuss women's rights before a mixed assembly, speaking in her brother's church in Gardner, Massachusetts. Her father, whose mood changed from shame to pride and affirmation, was present to hear her speak. Massachusetts Congregational clergy were unsuccessful in preventing Sarah and Angelina Grimké from addressing mixed audiences. Methodist women took their inspiration from Susanna Wesley, mother of John Wesley, who found it necessary to educate her son on the subject of the equality of women. Within the African Methodist Episcopal Church, some women were gifted preachers, but after 1840 its hierarchy opposed ordaining women. Nevertheless, Sojourner Truth continued to demonstrate extraordinary ability to interpret the Bible, and Harriet Tubman found in Scripture the strength she needed to lead slaves out of the South to freedom.

The churches were feminized to the extent that more women than men attended, and that much of their mission was providing succor for the weak, poor, and oppressed. However, the churches remained under patriarchal control, and women would experience many difficulties expanding their roles in making church policy or becoming ordained ministers. Antoinette Brown, ordained the first American woman minister in 1853, had studied at Oberlin College, where Finney was a professor and later president. Finney once said that the employment of women as preachers was an aberration. Brown was a Congregationalist; by 1900 that denomination had forty female ministers. Presbyterians, the other large historic American Calvinist denomination, did not ordain women until 1956. Due to their tradition of separatism, Southern Baptists ordained more women as deaconesses and eldresses than did their northern brethren. After northern and southern Baptists divided over slavery, this practice declined among Southern Baptists. The northern Baptists would be called American Baptists. Today some Baptists ordain women, but the Southern Baptist Convention has not endorsed the practice. Holy Ghost churches—holiness and pentecostals—have long ordained women, but today this practice seems to be in decline among them.

A number of women were ordained in the Unitarian and Universalist churches; their inspiration would have been more Christian than specifically Finneyite. Olympia Brown was the first woman in the Universalist clergy and was active in the National American Woman Suffrage Association. Wesleyan Methodists, who seemed to be most in harmony with Wesley's views on complete sanctification, perfection, and opposition to slavery, were ordaining women beginning in the 1860s. (It was in a Wesleyan Methodist chapel in Seneca Falls, New York, in 1848 that the women's rights movement was formally organized with the writing of a Declaration of Principles.)

The first female member of the Methodist Episcopal Church to become a minister was Anna Howard Shaw, ordained in 1880. She was also a physician and later served as president of both the Women's Christian Temperance Union and the National American Woman Suffrage Association. That same year, the local preacher's license of Margaret ("Maggie") Newton Van Cott was revoked because women were showing increased interest in becoming Methodist ministers. Her license had been granted in 1869. Anna Oliver functioned as pastor before Shaw, but appears to have been unlicensed. Amanda Smith, an African American evangelist, assisted Oliver in her Passaic, New Jersey, church. Oliver was the first female to hold a theology degree, graduating from Boston University in 1876. That institution claims Betsy Dow as its first theology professor. Dow taught at Newbury Seminary in Vermont, which later became part of Boston University. In 1924, the northern Methodists decided women could be local preachers, but could not advance beyond that point.

There has been a relationship between women entering the ministry and entering other professions. During World War II and the late 1940s, the number of women ordained and those entering other professions increased. A decline followed in the fifties and sixties, with the number of female ministers in 1970 being smaller than their number in 1950. By then the Methodists and Presbyterians were ordaining women, and the Episcopalians, Lutheran Church in America, and American Lutheran Church admitted women to clerical ranks in the 1970s. Female ministers found employment, but it took them longer to become senior or sole pastors with their own churches.

Women had greater success exercising religious power when they functioned within marginal religions, small groups distanced in beliefs and history from most larger denominations. Often women attained leadership roles through their personal qualities and the promise to place followers in immediate touch with the divinity. This was the case in spiritualism, where women are still dominant, and in Shakerism and Christian Science. Mother Ann Lee, founder of the Shakers, taught that the second appearing of Christ would be in female form and that there was a dual Mother-Father God. After her death, she came to be seen as a semidivine figure who reflects the characteristics of Holy Mother Wisdom, who is associated with the Heavenly Father. In time Mother Wisdom was employed to teach conventional female virtues. Women continued to have influence in the religion, primarily as deaconesses, but theirs became a secondary role.

In spiritualism, the role of medium possessed a gender identification that could be traced to ancient origins. Spiritualism was intensely anticlerical and antiauthoritarian. These qualities made it attractive to opponents of patriarchy, and they made it impossible for men to exercise power in the movement. Their antiauthoritarianism underpinned the opposition of many spiritualists to slavery. Ellen Gould Harmon White also claimed special spiritual gifts and in 1860 founded what would become a much larger denomination, the Seventh-Day Adventist Church. In the late nineteenth century, Mary Baker Eddy established Christian Science upon a spiritualist foundation and was able to institutionalize the role of women by providing for an equal number of male and female readers.

Emma Curtis Hopkins was editor of the *Christian Science Journal,* but she broke with Eddy in the mid-1880s. She founded a college in Chicago to train Christian Science leaders, and the Hopkins Memorial Association, later to become the Christian Science Association. Hopkins recruited women for church leadership positions and fashioned a theology that gave women the central role in the salvation drama. Like Eddy, she referred to God as Father-Mother, but she went on to teach that the Mother-Spirit would overcome the concept of sin. Scripture, she argued, taught the "seed of the woman" would destroy the serpent. It can be argued that she was the first American female theologian. New Thought writers call her "teacher of teachers," as most New Thought groups can be linked to her or her students. Among these organizations were Divine Science, the Unity School of Christianity, and Religious Science. Women were to dominate the early New Thought movement.

Phoebe Palmer, a woman working to uplift New York City's poor, would play a significant role in the blossoming of the holiness movement, also known as Holy Ghost religion. In 1854, Methodist women working through their denomination's Ladies Home Missionary Society established the Five Points House of Industry for the poor in a New York City neighborhood notorious for crime, street gangs, and poverty. Schooling, day care, bathing facilities, and low-rent apartments were made available. People learned baking, sewing, and cobbling there, and women gained experience preaching. Antoinette Brown worked at Five Points for a time after leaving Oberlin, along with Phoebe Palmer, who did more than any other person to found the holiness movement. These Christian women had been active in that area since 1843.

Palmer began her ministry by presiding over small prayer meetings and soon joined her husband in preaching at revivals. She was joined by Amanda Smith and other female revivalists, and in 1859 she published a book defending the female ministry, *The Promise of the Father*. The holiness movement that Phoebe Palmer cultivated offered opportunities for female leadership and empowerment because it emphasized individual holiness over institutional authority. This approach to religion had theological roots in Wesleyan thought and some of Finney's lectures, and has been known as "true holiness" and "entire sanctification." It was developed through faith and represented a "higher life, a second gift or blessing from the Spirit. It liberated people from sinful earthly desires, and its recipients sometimes felt the pure love of God. They had been given pure hearts and enjoyed in considerable measure "entire sanctification" or "sinless perfection." In this way, holiness perfectionism loosened the control of the congregation over the lives of those who had received the second blessing. Charles G. Finney believed that he had passed through a "second conversion" and preached about the benefits of the second gift of the Holy Spirit.

Palmer taught that the second gift came as a fire sent by God to cleanse and transform the soul. She answered those who argued that she should not teach or preach by proclaiming that she was filled with the Holy Spirit, and thus commissioned to teach and preach. Holiness perfectionism had a strong appeal to women who resented male authority and the restrictions placed upon them by congregations. Some Methodists, following the logic of Wesley's teachings, were to accept the right of women to preach in the Spirit. The holiness movement would attract large numbers of followers in the late nineteenth and twentieth centuries. In the early twentieth century, Pentecostalism would grow out of the holiness movement and would provide opportunities for female leadership.

There was an anticlerical strain in the women's rights movement. Some shared William Lloyd Garrison's contempt for the churches because of their equivocal positions on slavery. Others were angry that churchmen sought to consign women to a second-class status. Lucretia Mott, a Public Friend, complained at a women's conference that the Bible had been distorted and the "pulpit has been prostituted."

Elizabeth Cady Stanton was very anticlerical and noted that as a girl she barely averted being converted. She studied biblical treatment of women and published *The Woman's Bible,* which appeared in two parts in 1895 and 1898. Written by a number of women, it scoffed at the virgin birth and labeled parts of Scripture fantastic and incredible. A great storm of criticism did erupt when it appeared.

The Second Great Awakening enhanced the position of women within the churches and made possible a certain measure of female empowerment through the operation of benevolent societies. Women played a greater role in politics; they did not vote but participated in political discourse in other ways. Through the churches they became deeply involved in benevolent reform, and they discussed these issues in the home. Women often attended public meetings at which such questions as slavery or closing businesses on Sunday were discussed. Entrusted with protecting and teaching Christian and republican ideals, it was possible for women to voice strong moral concerns regarding a number of public questions even though they were denied the franchise.

Bibliography

Anders, Sarah Frances, and Marilyn Metcalf-Whittaker. "Women as Lay Leaders and Clergy: A Critical Issue." In *Southern Baptists Observed: Multiple Perspectives on a Changing Denomination,* ed. Nancy Tatom Ammerman, pp. 201–221. Knoxville: University of Tennessee Press, 1993.

Berg, Barbara J. *The Remembered Gate: Origins of American Feminism, the Woman and the City, 1800–1860.* Oxford: Oxford University Press, 1978.

Blauvelt, Martha. "Women and Revivalism." In *Women and Religion in America.* Volume 1, *The Nineteenth Century,* ed. Rosemary Radford Reuther and Rosemary Skinner Keller, pp. 46–100. San Francisco: Harper and Row, 1981.

Branson, Susan. "Women and the Family Economy in the Early Republic: The Case of Elizabeth Meredity." *Journal of the Early Republic* 16 (spring 1996): 47–71.

Brereton, Virginia Lieson. *From Sin to Salvation: Stories of Women's Conversions, 1800 to the Present.* Bloomington: Indiana University Press, 1991.

Briggs, Sheila. "Women and Religion." In *Analyzing Gender: A Handbook of Social Science Research,* ed. Beth B. Hess and Myra Marx Feree, pp. 408–441. Newbury Park, CA: Sage, 1987.

Conforti, Joseph A. "Mary Lyon: The Founding of Mount Holyoke College, and the Cultural Revival of Jonathan Edwards." *Religion and American Culture* 3 (winter 1993): 69–90.

Cott, Nancy F. *The Bonds of Womanhood: 'Woman's Sphere' in New England, 1780–1935.* New Haven: Yale University Press, 1977.

Culver, Elsie Thomas. *Women in the World of Religion: From Pagan Priestesses to Ecumenical Delegates.* Garden City: Doubleday, 1967.

DeJong, Mary. "Introduction: Protestantism and Its Discontents in the Eighteenth and Nineteenth Centuries." *Women's Studies* 19 (winter 1991): 99–118.

Evans, Sara M. *Born for Liberty: A History of Women in America.* New York: Free Press, 1989.

Flexner, Eleanor. *Century of Struggle: The Woman's Rights Movement in the United States.* Cambridge: Harvard University Press, 1959.

Fuller, Margaret. *Woman in the Nineteenth Century.* New York: Norton, 1971.

Gimelli, Louis B. " 'Borne Upon the Wings of Faith': The Chinese Odyssey of Henrietta Hall Shuck, 1835–1844." *Journal of the Early Republic* 14 (summer 1994): 221–245.

Green, Nancy L. "The Making of the Modern Jewish Woman." In *A History of Women: Emerging Feminism from Revolution to World War,* ed. Genevieve Fraisse and Michael Perrot, pp. 213–227. Cambridge: Harvard University Press, 1993.

Hardesty, Nancy. *Women Called to Witness: Evangelical Feminism in the Nineteenth Century.* Nashville: Abingdon Press, 1984.

Isaacs, Ernest. "The Fox Sisters and American Spiritualism." In *The Occult in America: New Historical Perspectives,* ed. Howard Kerr and Charles Crow, pp. 79–110. Urbana: University of Illinois, 1986.

Jackson, Rebecca. *Gifts of Power: The Writings of Rebecca Jackson, Black Visionary, Shaker Eldress.* Edited by Jean McMahon. Amherst: University of Massachusetts Press, 1981.

Juster, Susan. " 'In a Different Voice:' Male and Female Narratives of Religious Conversion in Post-Revolutionary America." *American Quarterly* 41 (March 1989): 34–62.

Kerber, Linda K., Alice Kessler-Harris, and Kathryn Kish Sklar. *U.S. History as Women's History: New Feminist Essays.* Chapel Hill: University of North Carolina Press, 1995.

Lebsock, Suzanne. *The Free Women of Petersburg: Status and Culture in a Southern Town, 1784–1860.* New York: Norton, 1985.

Lerner, Gerda. *The Grimke Sisters of South Carolina: Rebels Against Slavery.* Boston: Houghton Mifflin, 1967.

Lewis, Jan. " 'Of Every Age, Sex, and Condition': The Representation of Women in the Constitution." *Journal of the Early Republic* 15 (fall 1995): 359–387.

Mohr, James C. "The Historical Character of Abortions in the United States Through World War II." In *Perspectives on Abortion,* ed. Paul Sachdev, pp. 3–15. Metuchen, NJ: Scarecrow Press, 1985.

Riegel, Robert E. *American Women: A Story of Social Change.* Rutherford, NJ: Fairleigh Dickinson University Press, 1971.

Ryan, Mary. *Cradle of the Middle Class: The Family in Oneida County, New York, 1790–1865.* Cambridge: Cambridge University Press, 1981.

———. "A Woman's Awakening: Evangelical Religion and the Families of Utica, New York, 1800–1840." In *Women in American Religion,* ed. Janet James, pp. 89–110. Philadelphia: University of Pennsylvania Press, 1980.

———. *Women in Public: Between Banners and Ballots, 1825–1880.* Baltimore: Johns Hopkins University Press, 1990.

Schneider, A. Gregory. "Social Religion, the Christian Home, and Republican Spirituality in Antebellum Methodism." *Journal of the Early Republic* 10 (summer 1990): 163–190.

Shiels, Richard D. "The Feminization of American Congregationalism, 1730–1835." *American Quarterly* 33 (spring 1981): 46–62.

Smith, Page. *Daughters of the Promised Land: Women in American History.* Boston: Little, Brown, 1970.

Smith-Rosenberg, Carroll. "Beauty, the Beast, and the Militant Woman: A Case Study in Sex Roles and Social Stress in Jacksonian America." In *An Interdisciplinary Approach to American History,* Volume 1, ed. Ari Hoogenboom and Olive Hoogenboom, pp. 219–237. Englewood Cliffs, NJ: Prentice-Hall, 1973.

Welter, Barbara. "The Feminization of American Religion, 1800–1860." In *Clio's Consciousness Raised,* ed. Mary Hartman and Lois Banner, pp. 135–137. New York: Harper and Row, 1973.

———. "She Hath Done What She Could: Protestant Women's Missionary Careers in Nineteenth-Century America." In *Women in American Religion,* ed. Janet Wilson James, pp. 111–117. Philadelphia: University of Pennsylvania Press, 1985.

Woloch, Nancy. *Women and the American Experience.* New York: Knopf, 1984.

Zikmund, Barbara Brown. "The Struggle for the Right to Preach." In *Women and Religion in America.* Vol. 1, *The Nineteenth Century,* ed. Rosemary Radford Reuther and Rosemary Skinner Keller, pp. 193–241. San Francisco: Harper and Row, 1981.

Six

Reform, Political Divisions, and Disunion

Religious ferment contributed mightily to an outburst of reformist energy in the first half of the nineteenth century. A link between religion and reform was forged that would persist through the twentieth century. Ugly eruptions of nativism were rooted in religious animosities. Religious connections were strongly linked to political affiliations. The division of churches over slavery snipped important ties that bonded North and South and contributed to the coming of the war between the states. Religious bodies on both sides supported their respective war efforts, assured people God was on their side, and marshaled people and resources to deal with human problems that grew out of the war. Abraham Lincoln, a profoundly religious man without denominational membership, dramatically reshaped American civil religion.

The Protestant Reformers

A great reforming impulse swept the land early in the nineteenth century. In its duration and impact, this period of reform remains unparalleled in American history. Reformers examined every aspect of life, offering prescriptions for improvements that they believed would bring about a veritable heaven on earth. This ferment of reform grew out of a faith in progress nurtured by the eighteenth-century Enlightenment, the democratic ideals of the revolution, and, especially, the Christian idealism of the Second Awakening. The latter was the essential ingredient. Even though Christians of all stripes were involved in these movements, evangelical Protestantism proved to be the driving force behind this remarkable outburst of reforming zeal. The roots of the social Christianity that appeared later in the nineteenth century are to be found here, along with the wellspring of subsequent American reform thought and movements. The Progressive movement of the early twentieth century, with its emphasis upon uplift and efficiency, owes much to this period.

The unique role of Unitarians, though not as great or indispensable as that of evangelical Protestants, deserves special mention. This form of Protestant Christianity grew out of Congregationalism, denied the Trinity, and appealed especially to the prosperous and educated. Far from a cold, uninspiring faith, Unitarianism kindled in many a passion for moral reform. William E. Channing, a founder, and his followers were involved in a plethora of uplifting efforts, including the common school movement, humane care of the insane, the peace movement, and antislavery. They were sincere opponents of slavery, but most of them would not be radical abolitionists. These were refined, upper-class people who found the rhetoric of William Garrison too harsh and distasteful.

It has been argued that Protestant involvement in reform movements grew out of the desire of some clergy to reassert their leadership. They sought to provide a conservative counterbalance to what they thought was Jeffersonian radicalism rooted in the pagan philosophy of the French Revolution. They believed that their political influence and social status had declined. The ascendancy of Jeffersonian republicans was blamed for ushering in disorderly settlement of the frontier, intemperance, excessive acquisitiveness, pandering to the clamoring of the common man, harmful political factionalism, and the diminished influence of religion. Convinced that some link between the church and the state was necessary to insure morality and stability, they embarked upon moral crusades in order to restore their influence, uplift others, and save the republic from godless radicalism. This was doubtless the view shared by many Congregationalists and by some Presbyterian and Dutch Reformed clergymen. In 1827, Ezra Stiles Ely of Philadelphia's Old Pine Street Church spoke for these troubled clerics when he openly called for a "Christian party in politics." By the time he made this appeal, however, Protestant benevolence was clearly motivated by perfectionist and evangelical zeal rather than by fear of declining influence and dreams of restoring some form of theocratic control over society.

Moreover, the interdenominational ventures were dominated by Presbyterians, most of whom did not share the Congregationalists' yearning for semiofficial status. They did, of course, expect harmony and cooperation between church and state. Baptists who cooperated in many interdenominational ventures feared close connections between church and state, as did Methodists who pursued their perfectionist visions through denominational efforts and occasionally through participation in joint ventures.

The evangelical perfectionists believed man could become Christlike. They felt they had an obligation to eradicate social evils and uplift their fellow men. Reverend Albert Barnes of New York City was typical of those who emphasized the connection between individual salvation, the welfare of the community, and the possibility of a socioeconomic millennium.

Through laboring for humanitarian causes, these evangelical clergymen expressed the freedom from sin they had found through conversion and showed that they had overcome calculating expediency and selfishness. Just as they had overcome individual sinfulness, they believed that social ills were easily curable. They believed that Protestantism was responsible for all worthwhile movements of the age. Religious periodicals were filled with news of the activities of humanitarian societies because their readers were involved in these organizations and thought reform a natural adjunct to evangelical Christianity. Moreover, they saw the societies as workshops in Christian republicanism where the well-disposed, bound together by shared commitment and Christian love, worked to reduce misery and improve common conditions without encountering the social tensions and divisiveness that characterized American society and politics. These organizations were microcosmic models of the Christian republic they hoped would emerge. This hope for a Christian America was closely related to the millennialist beliefs of these evangelicals. By working toward a perfect society they hastened the second coming.

Christianity and the Social Order

The Christian reformers were concerned with increasing social disorder and friction between classes. Reforms were often aimed at bringing about greater social cohesiveness and bridging the gap between rich and poor—necessary prerequisites for creating a Christian America. Pacifying and uplifting the lower classes was essential to Christian reform; mass conversion to Christianity would save society from the evils of mobocracy. Entrepreneurs saw evangelical religion as a way to influence the lives of their employees and the working class. In preindustrial society, employers were in daily contact with all their employees. Some employees, particularly apprentices, lived with the employer. In the industrial age, this close tie no longer existed. By supporting evangelical religion, employers not only uplifted their employees but were able to combat alcoholism, inefficiency on the job, and social disorders. At a personal level, the entrepreneur embraced revivalism when he learned that the clergy did not see his efforts as being motivated by greed. Evangelical religion showed employers how to reconcile economic aggressiveness with the requirements of the Christian conscience. Entrepreneurs were also attracted by the evangelical's praise of meritocracy. The evangelical clergy and the politicians in league with them wanted an organic, hierarchical society but did not expressly call for deference or social hierarchy. Rather, they praised those who had accumulated wealth and accepted social distinctions based on merit.

Missionary Activities

Conversion was, of course, the central reform. Officials of the American Home Missionary Society proclaimed that "the Gospel is the most economical police on earth." The American Tract Society argued that conversion would bring fellowship and a sense of interdependence to rich and poor alike. In 1829, it printed about 6 million pieces of religious literature, and the American Bible Society produced 344,500 Bibles. Similarly, the American Board of Commissioners for Foreign Missions aimed to not only evangelize heathens abroad but to transform America. They hoped to combat secularism and divisiveness at home by providing examples of missionary-induced change abroad. These benevolent organizations reflected a transatlantic interest in benevolence on the part of evangelical Protestants. There was a genuine Atlantic community of reformers. Americans pursued English initiatives in the cases of the missionary, tract, and Bible societies, and the English found a useful pattern in American temperance activity. In these areas, as well as in pursuit of universal peace and opposition to slavery, American and English reformers, the Protestant evangelicals influenced by the ideas of William Wilberforce, worked together. It seems that Americans excelled as agitators, while the English were better organizers. Works on American evangelical theology often were to find their way into English rectories, much to the chagrin of Anglican traditionalists.

Sabbatarianism

One of the most important, though generally unsuccessful, Christian reform movements was Sabbatarianism, which gained momentum in the 1820s. Sabbatarians were largely Presbyterians and Congregationalists. Many observers inaccurately saw this crusade as one more attempt of prosperous snobs to interfere with the lives of others. Efforts to promote Sabbath observance by preventing distracting activities contributed to a growing anticlericalism by the early 1830s. The failure of this effort and rising anticlericalism convinced its supporters that the United States was becoming a godless nation and that politics was meaningless and corrupt. Most Sabbatarians were anti-Jacksonians, and their most important political spokesman was Senator Theodore Frelinghuysen, Henry Clay's running mate in 1844. Jacksonian Richard Johnson of Kentucky, vice president under Martin Van Buren, was the most outspoken political opponent of the Sabbatarian crusade. In some ways Sabbatarianism was "America's first great antimodern crusade." It had a certain anticommercial animus. This drive was responsible for many of the Sunday blue laws that have lasted into the twentieth century.

Humanitarian Reforms

Filled with desire to bring salvation to others and improve the world around them, Christian reformers became involved in numerous humanitarian efforts. Evangelical Christians, particularly Presbyterian clergymen, opposed Andrew Jackson's Indian removal policy. Others participated in the movement to improve prison conditions and promote the reform and rehabilitation of prisoners. Reformers insisted that every person had the capability to live a good life if so desired; prisons were to be places where individuals could change their values and experience spiritual redemption. Reformers opposed physical punishment (even the corporal punishment of children), preferring the mental coercion of solitary confinement to such punishments as flogging.

Dorothea Dix, a spinster Unitarian schoolteacher, launched a lifelong crusade—a "holy cause," in her words—for compassionate treatment of the insane. Her work led to the founding and improvement of mental hospitals in many states. Friends (Quakers), committed pacifists, were joined in the early nineteenth century by other Protestants in opposing warfare. William Ladd, a wealthy layman, took the lead in forming the American Peace Society in 1828. Educational reform attracted great support because it promised to remedy many social evils. It was considered the "universal antidote" to end corruption in government, crime, poverty, and immorality. Unitarian layman Horace Mann played the central role in the drive for better education and common or free schools. Generations of students would learn traditional Protestant virtues through moral lessons contained in the famous readers of Reverend William Holmes McGuffey. The Reverend Samuel Reed Hall pioneered in the training of teachers and wrote a number of textbooks for use in the schools. Teachers were frequently ministers or young men preparing for the ministry. A nondenominational form of Protestantism was taught in the schools, and only a few Protestants thought this practice improper.

Christian reformers also believed that temperance had the characteristics of a universal antidote. Drunkenness was considered a prime cause of civil disorders, crime, poverty, and godlessness. Temperance advocates initially denounced rum and hard liquor, but in time many insisted upon total abstinence from all alcohol. Emphasis shifted from attempts to secure voluntary temperance to efforts to secure legislation against the liquor traffic. Opposition to alcohol was the most important of the evangelical reforms; revivalists invariably included this topic in their preaching. The teetotaler's pledge was a sign of salvation, and the decision to make it followed an emotional upheaval in the same way that conversion followed emotional turmoil and resolution. In both conversion and the acceptance of teetotalism, the sinner decided to start a new life.

The Washington Temperance Society was founded in 1840 by six reformed drunkards. Its mass meetings were similar to revivals, but it did not have a religious base. Its leaders usually became deeply spiritual people, but they were frequently churchless. Washingtonians relied upon persuasion rather than legislative action to accomplish their goals.

The United Front

The evangelical united front was a network of interrelated, interdenominational Christian reform organizations. Officers held annual meetings in New York during the second week of May, when the American Bible Society held its annual meeting. Sometimes at these Anniversary Week meetings, a speech would be met with the highest possible evangelical sign of approval—silence combined with sobbing! Only men attended these meetings. Wealthy individuals such as the Tappan brothers supported the efforts of the evangelical united front, but member organizations also attempted to raise donations from those they helped. By the late 1830s, the influence of the united front would diminish. Sectarianism caused some to withdraw from agencies or establish rival societies. Many Americans feared the united front was an effort of the evangelicals to impose uniform views on all and acquire too much power. It appeared that the American Sunday School Union sought to dominate education because it looked forward to the day when it would be the main supplier of books for the common schools.

Reform in the South

Not enough is known about the Christian reform efforts in the South. We know that northern evangelicals felt a need to instruct and uplift southerners even before they decided southerners must be persuaded to abandon slavery. Southern evangelicals were active in efforts to end dueling, horse racing, and gambling. They confronted a subculture that placed a premium on honor, manhood, and local autonomy. For southern men, manliness and reputation were all-important. In a sense, life was a continuing play in which one displayed generosity, physical force, courage, conspicuous consumption, some learning, a bit of hedonism, and paternalism in order to win the approval of peers. The evangelical clergy were usually part-time preachers who found it necessary to devote most of their time to earning their livings. The lack of common schools meant that reform literature would reach relatively fewer readers in the South. Baptist and Methodist congregations often were divided over whether intemperate church members should be expelled. In many poor, backcountry areas, the distilling of whiskey was the best method of earning money from a cash crop because it was almost impossible to take crops to distant markets, and temperance smacked too much of Yankee intervention.

Southern Baptists did not commit themselves to total abstinence until 1886. Anti-Missionary Baptists viewed temperance as the intrusion of educated snobs into local and family affairs. Emphasis on local autonomy prevented legislation regulating the sale and consumption of liquor. Pacifism also won few converts in a region where militia service was an avenue of social advancement. In an area known for brutal fights, self-restraint resembled cowardice. Some southern men resented and discouraged their wives' involvement in religion and the reform movements associated with it. They saw clergymen as possible threats to their authority and feared that women's involvement in benevolent reform could lead them to question male dominance and possibly come to oppose slavery.

Dorothea Dix had southern allies, and temperance had some strong champions south of the Mason-Dixon Line. In terms of timing, the southern urban areas were only a little behind their northern counterparts in establishing voluntary benevolent societies. In the towns, ambitious merchants, craftsmen, and mechanics often opposed card playing and billiard saloons and formed benevolent societies rather than agree to militia service. The most popular reform in the South was temperance, but only 10 percent of the nation's pledges were found there in 1831, a time when that section had a quarter of the nation's free population. Many southerners doubtlessly identified this panoply of reforms with the Yankee's inclination to preach to others. They pointed to evidence of the Yankees' tendency to rely upon compulsion as northern reformers looked to the state to restrict the liquor trade, force school attendance, and limit Sunday activities. Southerners came to associate these reforms with abolitionism because abolitionists almost invariably backed other humanitarian reforms.

Abolitionism

Abolitionism, the strident demand for the immediate end of slavery, was particularly appealing to Quakers, transcendentalists, Unitarians, and evangelical Protestants who embraced the revivalistic and perfectionist views of Finney and Taylor. William Lloyd Garrison, who denounced the churches for their reluctance to condemn slavery, claimed the allegiance of many abolitionists. Although he heaped scorn upon the institutional churches, Garrison's opposition to slavery was rooted in deeply held Christian principles.

A larger number of abolitionists looked to men such as Reverend Theodore Dwight Weld, a Finney disciple, and the Tappan brothers, prominent evangelical lay spokesmen and reformers, for leadership in combating what they believed to be the foulest sin of all—human slavery. Weld evangelized in the Midwest and was particularly effective in places where New Englanders had migrated. Married to feminist and abolitionist Angelina Grimké, and sporting porcupinelike hair that seemed to go in every direction, Weld developed compelling antislavery arguments that converted a considerable number of lawyers to abolitionism. It was his practice to debate lawyers in the communities he visited, and he invariably converted opponents to abolitionism. There were no constitutional steps against slavery that abolitionists could realistically demand other than the exclusion of slavery from the territories and the end of slavery and the slave trade in the District of Columbia. These steps would not touch slavery where it flourished in the South. Consequently, Christian abolitionists strove mightily to convict slaveholders of sin in hope that they would repent and end the hated "peculiar institution."

It is possible that the invective of the abolitionists had the opposite effect—ending debate of the matter in the South and driving southerners to defend slavery as a positive good rather than a necessary evil. The perfectionism of the Christian abolitionists led them to bend every effort to combat this great obstacle to human perfection. African American abolitionists Henry Highland Garnet and David Walker also employed evangelical rhetoric in their assaults on slavery. Evangelical reformers believed that all Christians bore responsibility for the continued existence of this great social evil and were charged by the Almighty with the sacred obligation of eradicating it. The Christian reformers based their pleas for abolition on natural law and the Bible.

The spread of antislavery sentiment within the churches brought about sectional divisions in the three main evangelical churches, the Methodists, the Baptists, and the Presbyterians. Antislavery agitation among northern Presbyterians was a major factor in leading the Old School Presbyterians, who controlled the denomination's general assembly, to excise four New School synods in 1837. Southerners generally supported Old School Presbyterianism. The New School Presbyterians organized their own general assembly; it split over slavery in 1857. In 1861, the Old School Presbyterians formed sectional organizations after their general assembly, dominated by northerners, adopted a resolution supporting the Union.

The Baptist national associations divided along sectional lines in 1845, and the Southern Baptist Convention (SBC) was organized in that year. The Southern Baptists held that slavery was a civil matter that churches should not address, but William B. Johnson, the first president of the SBC, proclaimed that Southern Baptists were at last free "to promote slavery." The northern and southern Baptists divided in 1844. Since the break, Southern Baptist growth has exceeded that of northern Baptists sevenfold. Southern Baptists emphasized evangelization and eschewed taking positions on social questions that might have divided their communities or put off potential converts. Emphasis upon democratic church organization has meant that Southern Baptist churches mirrored the political and social views of their communities.

It was frequently argued that religious divisions along sectional lines would contribute to the division of the Union. In the early 1830s, Amasa Converse used his *Southern Religious Telegraph* to warn that "to condemn slavery as a sin under all circumstances would divide the church and to that extent the nation." Just prior to his death, Henry Clay told the editor of the *Presbyterian Herald* that loss of Presbyterian unity damaged the Union. The divisions among the three large evangelical churches exposed serious moral divisions between North and South and contributed to the coming of political disunion.

Evangelical Protestantism was a significant unifying force, as many Americans in both sections believed that God had given the United States a special mission in the world. Religion had freed them from sectional tribalism. Schisms growing out of the debate over slavery caused bad feelings between the sections and foreshadowed the moral rift that existed by the Civil War. Increasingly, southern evangelical clergymen came to the defense of slavery. The stridency of the abolitionists as well as what seemed to be a need for social cohesion in the face of potential slave revolts partially account for this development. Southern clergymen pointed out that the Bible described no slavery-free societies, and that natural law as well as Scripture suggested that inequality was a natural condition. Northern talk of a higher law than statute law seemed to southerners the height of arrogance, and they saw proponents of higher law as using this theory to override specific scriptural justifications for slavery. Northerners, on the other hand, came to see southern clergymen as the tools of politicians who wanted religious schisms to prepare the way for secession.

Nativism

The rise of Roman Catholicism was viewed by the Protestant reformers as a deadly cancer threatening the republic; some thought it even more dangerous than slavery. Anti-Catholicism was a Protestant and Anglo-Saxon tradition. Many Protestants believed that there was a papal plot to send Catholic immigrants to America so that the church could take over the republic by way of the ballot box. It was said that northern political machines and southern politicians were parties to the plot. Anti-Catholicism's prominence in the years after 1830 can be attributed in part to the phenomenal growth of Catholicism. At the time of independence Catholics were a tiny minority. By 1830 immigration had swelled their number to 318,000; by 1860, there would be 3.1 million. Protestant reformers saw Catholicism as a threat to republican freedom and a sinister challenge to their vision of a Protestant America united in the quest for human perfection and progress. Moreover, they saw in Catholicism a major threat to their ideas regarding families and true womanhood. The celibacy of priests and sisters was seen as unnatural. Sisters were particularly detested for not taking their "proper places" in families. Sometimes the sisters were viewed as victims, but Mothers Superior were detested as they wielded considerable power and usually were not particularly submissive women. Because they saw Catholicism as a tyrannical, ungodly, "soul-corrupting, soul-destroying influence," many Protestants had no doubt that their efforts to limit the influence of Catholics was a major reform effort. It was incomprehensible to these sincere reformers that some thought their efforts an affront to basic American values. They urged fellow Protestants not to vote for or employ Roman Catholics. Public schools were expected to teach an interdenominational form of Protestantism and emphasize the evils of the "whore of Babylon," the Roman Church. It was expected that access of Catholic chaplains to public institutions would be barred or severely limited.

By combating the growth of Catholic influence, these reformers intended to purify America. Somehow, stirring up hatred of Catholicism and Catholics would work God's will in America and destroy this "abomination of abominations." Anti-Catholic leaders were affronted by the presence of Roman Catholics because they threatened American homogeneity. The problem was, as Catholics quickly pointed out, that a homogeneous American culture had never existed. Catholics, whose religious culture was pluralistic in many ways, thought pluralism a normal condition.

Although it is impossible to justify efforts to limit the rights of others, these Protestant reformers sincerely saw Catholicism as a threat to American institutions and their vision of a Protestant America. Evangelical women, themselves disenfranchised, were more violent than men in their denunciation of Catholicism. Nativists noted that the Roman Church was allied with some of the most repressive regimes in the world and that the papacy was a declared enemy of republicanism. The structure of the church itself was highly authoritarian, with all power flowing from its earthly head, the pope, through bishops who expected obedience of the lower clergy. Nativists fretted over the fact that so many bishops and priests were foreigners; indeed, foreign mission societies contributed extensively to the American church. It was also observed that the immigrant Irish often lived in poverty and were involved in crime and violence—as though these unwelcome newcomers somehow preferred misery, disorder, and lawlessness. That the Catholic immigrants tended to vote for the Democratic Party, which was most open to cultural pluralism, was also alarming to reformers who dreamed of a homogeneous Protestant America.

Newspapers and periodicals were founded with the express purpose of combating Catholicism. Many pamphlets and books were written in this effort, and Samuel F.B. Morse proved to be one of the most prolific writers in the cause. Another prominent anti-Catholic propagandist, Lyman Beecher, extolled in his *Plea for the West* (1835) the value of public schools where Catholic children could be weaned away from the faith of their parents and thoroughly Americanized. Propagandists sometimes made crude charges of immorality and sexual perversion between priests and nuns. Although these fabrications were thoroughly refuted by respected Protestant leaders, this salacious literature had a great appeal.

Sometimes, hatred of Catholicism led to violence. In 1834, Lyman Beecher preached three anti-Catholic sermons in Boston that led to the burning by a mob of the Ursuline Convent in nearby Charlestown. Anti-Catholic violence occurred frequently enough that Catholics encountered great difficulty in purchasing insurance for their church buildings. In Philadelphia, two churches, a convent, a school, and the homes of hundreds of Irish were burned in 1844; sixteen died in those riots. Anti-Catholic violence had a long history in New York City, where there were ten such riots between 1806 and 1858. The riots of 1853 were occasioned by the arrival of papal nuncio Gaetano Bedini, who had come to visit the American church. His appearance was taken as proof that there was a papal plot to subvert the American republic. In Cincinnati, police found it necessary to fire into an angry mob in order to protect him. It is an interesting commentary on the period that the American Catholic bishops, who regarded abuse as part of their priestly vocation, did not sympathize with Bedini, who seemed too concerned for his own safety.

Anti-Catholic violence marked the 1850s. In 1855, twenty died in a Louisville anti-Catholic riot, and riots in Baltimore and New Orleans in the next year also ended in deaths. In addition to verbal and physical harassment, Roman Catholics suffered abuse from aroused state and local authorities. In Massachusetts, the legislature moved to fire foreign-born public employees and established a commission to investigate convents for evidence of immorality. The commission turned up no scandals in the convents, but its tactics proved a great embarrassment to nativists. Moreover, it developed that some of these guardians of propriety used commission funds for immoral purposes. In Pittsburgh, nativist mayor

Joe Baker ordered the arrest of Bishop Michael O'Connor for permitting sewage from a Catholic hospital to enter a public sewer. Sitting as judge, Baker fined the bishop twenty dollars.

Disputes over educational policies added fuel to the flames of anti-Catholicism. It was the general practice that nondenominational Protestantism be taught in schools supported with public funds. In this respect, a functional Protestant establishment existed in the schools. So long as the beliefs of a particular denomination were not advanced, most Americans believed that this practice did not violate the provisions of state constitutions commanding separation of church and state. Textbooks referred to Catholics as "Papists" or "Romanists," and their religion was called "Popery." Catholics were portrayed frequently as deceitful, unreasonable fanatics. When Catholic bishops demanded that unbiased materials be used and that Catholic children be permitted to bring their own Bibles to school, the Protestant reformers saw these demands as efforts to control public education. When Roman bishops demanded a share of educational funds for Catholic parochial schools, reformers called it a plot to destroy public education, which they viewed as the swiftest agent for Americanizing the children of immigrants.

The efforts of Christian reformers had several unintended consequences. By attacking chattel slavery, they indirectly provoked moral sanction for "wage slavery" in northern factories and mines. Apologists for slavery, such as George Fitzhugh, contrasted the plight of slaves and northern "wage slaves" and insisted that black slaves enjoyed better living conditions than most immigrant laborers in the North. In attacking this position, abolitionists often found it necessary to posit that the condition of northern factory and mine laborers was morally acceptable. In its emphasis upon self-discipline, individualism, and voluntary choices, the evangelical movement was congenial to the rapid development of the market economy in nineteenth-century America. Evangelicals realized the importance of meritocracy and endorsed Daniel Webster's argument that money was the "life-blood" of civil society. Webster suggested that the absence of prosperity threatened the stability and welfare of society. The marketplace, evangelical clergy believed, offered many opportunities for self-improvement. They saw a Christian's pursuit of wealth as anything but greed. By the 1840s, however, a significant number of Protestant clergymen criticized the unquestioned acceptance of social and economic change as signs of societal and religious progress. The materialism, self-confidence, and unfettered freedom of this democratic age seemed to nurture spiritual complacency.

Religion and Political Life:
Evangelicals and Whigs

Religious values had a profound effect upon affiliations under the second party system, which prevailed from the late 1820s to the mid-1850s. (Some doubt the durability of the first party system and call the later arrangement the "first permanent party system.") Ethnocultural values were generally more important than economic and sectional factors in influencing party allegiances. Religion proved, in the last analysis, generally more influential in determining party allegiance than ethnic origins.

In the North, those whose religious experience was shaped by the Second Great Awakening tended to support the Whig Party. These evangelicals were usually joined in their backing of the Whigs by Quakers, Unitarians, and others who shared their perfectionism and ardent desire to reform the world around them. Evangelical Episcopalians were inclined to be Whigs and later Republicans. Whig leader Henry Clay became an Episcopalian in 1847. The Whig Party was a modernizing party. It was more inclined to legislative activism than the Democrats, and the evangelicals and their allies found it a ready instrument to make men virtuous. Though not an antislavery party, it was less racist than the Democrats and somewhat more compassionate toward Native Americans. To evangelical Whigs, the church and state should work together in uplifting men and society. They envisioned an organic, homogeneous society united by general acceptance of republican institutions and Anglo-Saxon Protestant religious values. At the state level, they worked against the liquor trade, to curb violations of the Sabbath, and discourage the operation of Roman Catholic schools. Some evangelicals, believing that the Whigs displayed insufficient zeal in attacking slavery, played important roles in forming the Free-Soil Party in 1848. Its founding convention in Buffalo resembled a great evangelical revival.

Like the evangelicals, the Whig Party had difficulty accepting a pluralistic America and did not welcome Catholic immigrants, particularly Irishmen. In the 1830s, about 4 percent of the population was foreign born. Most of these immigrants were Protestants and were employed as farmers, white-collar workers, or skilled workers. They were largely from northern Ireland, England, or Scotland. Whigs could welcome most of these immigrants; the Catholic Irish were another matter. In the 1840s, there was a great increase in immigration, and by the 1850s, 15 percent of the population was foreign born; worse, most were poor, Catholic, and Irish, having fled famine and destitution. There were also large numbers of Germans. In some cities there were more immigrants and their children than there were old-line Americans.

Immigrants seemed difficult to assimilate. Old-line American workers believed the unwanted immigrants drove down wages and preferred criminal ways. It was true that the dramatic increase in crime appeared to be associated with immigrants, who were arrested in large numbers. It did not occur to old Americans to look for a link between crime and poverty. Many immigrants were also benefiting from what poor relief then existed. Evangelicals believed that the "filth of Europe" were mainly responsible for crime, intemperance, Sabbath breaking, and a general increase in immorality. Considered in this light, the debate over temperance involved more than the evils of drink. A man's position on this question indicated whether he welcomed these foreigners and whether he thought the state should legislate morality.

Their minds fixed on a vision of a harmonious, homogeneous society, Whigs saw political parties as divisive influences and viewed their own political activity as a distasteful necessity. They saw the presidential campaign of 1840 as a great contest of good and evil. The depressed economy was a sign of God's displeasure with a sinful nation. The Whigs were proud of William Henry Harrison's piety and their own righteousness and support of temperance. They associated the Democrats with irreligion, Sabbath breaking, Roman Catholicism, and the mistreatment of Native Americans.

Congregationalists and New School Presbyterians were strongly inclined to support the Whigs. Scotch-Irish and Scottish Presbyterians, who frequently led anti-Catholic movements and mobs, were usually Whigs except in a few areas where their resentment of English dominance was particularly strong. Scandinavian Lutherans were also inclined to back the Whigs. Moravians and River Brethren, German pietistic sects, supported the evangelical Whigs. Many northern Baptists, particularly those who were relatively prosperous or lived in urban areas, cooperated in interdenominational humanitarian and reform ventures and gave their votes to the Whigs. Unlike Baptists who lived on the margins of society or in the South, these Baptist Whigs were quickly moving away from an antiformalist religious position.

New England Baptists did not believe Jackson was a genuinely pious man, but they praised John Quincy Adams because he referred to God's "divine superintendence" over the nation. The general's anticlericalism and participation in duels also troubled the Baptists; their clergy urged them not to vote for swearers, adulterers, gamblers, or intemperate men. These Baptists had entered the mainstream of American society. They were now socially respectable and joined other evangelical Protestants in voting for Whigs. They called for the teaching of Protestant principles in the schools, an end to Sunday mails, and legislation assisting foreign missionaries and opposing intemperance and blasphemy. The Baptists had contributed greatly toward the emergence of radical individualism but also saw religion as a social principle that would unite society and promote benevolence. By defending religious individualism, their leaders were defending the religious rights of other Protestant dissenters. Whigs often portrayed Democratic leaders as atheists and religious perverts in order to win the evangelical vote. In 1840, Whig publicists made much of the fact that General William Henry Harrison, their candidate for president, had attended Methodist revival meetings in Cincinnati that year and regularly attended services in his parish Episcopal church.

Quakers and Unitarians tended to vote for Whigs. The northern Methodists shared many of the views of evangelicals and gave more support to the Whigs than to the Democrats, but their southern brethren tended to be Democrats. In places in the South where Methodist competition with Baptists was acute, the Methodists tended to be strongly Democratic. This remained true in some places by the late 1850s. In the North, Methodists who remained uncomfortable with the market revolution were frequently strong Jacksonians. Methodists who were becoming economically and socially respectable had far fewer misgivings about the market revolution and backed the Whigs, whom they saw as the party of economic and moral progress. Methodist tradesmen who accepted market values and hoped to climb the social ladder were frequently Whigs. Wesleyan Methodists were firm supporters of the Whig Party.

There was a tendency for Disciples of Christ to back the Whigs, but a substantial number of them supported the Democrats because they thought the Whigs too inclined to interfere in matters best handled by the family or individual. A study of Northampton County, Pennsylvania, demonstrated that Moravians and Presbyterians—as might be expected—backed the Whigs. However, the German Reformed did not conform to this pattern. They joined the Lutherans and Catholics in supporting the Democrats. There, both parties backed protective tariffs and internal improvements. The Whigs supported voter registration legislation that would be to the disadvantage of Germans and Irish, and they also called for temperance legislation.

Antievangelicals and Democrats

The Democrats drew greatest support from antievangelical elements and antiformalist evangelicals. Among them were Old School Presbyterians, Old School Dutch Reformed, Roman Catholics, and most German Lutherans, including Missouri Synod Lutherans. For Dutch immigrants, the Old School Dutch Reformed Church made possible cultural maintenance and separatism. Catholicism and Lutheranism also provided immigrants with an opportunity for a certain degree of cultural separatism. Something like a Catholic melting pot existed, in which immigrants experienced partial assimilation by participating in American Catholic culture.

These religious communities were more liturgical than the evangelicals and were inclined to revere long-standing doctrines of their respective faiths. Scholars have also referred to nonevangelical Protestants as "ritualists." These nonevangelicals were joined by Baptists of southern origins and some northern Baptists who feared evangelical efforts to promote a union of church and state. They saw in evangelical and Whig proposals efforts to restrict individual liberties. Anti-Missionary Baptists were also inclined to support the Democrats. Although the German Reformed were anti-Democrat in a later period, they tended to support the Democrats at this time, partly out of fear of Whig nativism. A certain undercurrent of nativism existed among Democrats, and most of them defended slavery and embraced racism. There were some antislavery Democrats, who also were not evangelicals.

The Democrats gained considerable support from those northern Methodists and Baptists who lived on the fringes of society and had not yet won social respectability. They worried about the power of ecclesiastical organizations and saw federal spending for internal improvements, the tariffs, and the federally chartered Bank of the United States as steps taken to help the northern financial elite at the expense of common folks. These general patterns of religious commitment and party allegiance were not found in every locality. A study of voters' allegiances in Prince Edward County, Virginia, in 1840 revealed that Baptists were only a little more Democratic than were voters in general in this Democratic county, and Presbyterians were more Whiggish than others. The Methodists were strongly Democratic there. These results indicate that local connections and issues as well as kinship were important in shaping voter allegiance. Nevertheless, religion remained an important variable in explaining party allegiance in that locality.

Jews tended to give the Democrats strong support. By the 1840s, Jewish support in New York City was so important that Democratic leaders often attended Jewish community social activities. Its political leader was Major Mordecai Manuel Noah, publisher of a Democratic newspaper. He was active in politics from youth, when he was rewarded with the militia rank of major in 1803, until his death in 1851. Whigs made his ancestry an issue; Jewish politicians elsewhere would encounter similar problems. In Georgia, Dr. Philip Minis killed a legislator in a duel for calling him "a damned Jew [who] ought to be pissed on." After 1860, Jews divided their allegiance between Democrats and Republicans, with local concerns determining their party affiliations.

Many groups supporting the Democrats recognized that the United States had long been a pluralistic society and saw no reason why it should cease to be one. Of course, some of the Democrats who welcomed the newcomers did not do so on the basis of deep commitment to principle. More than a few

Democratic politicians harbored private prejudices against the immigrants and only appeared to be friendly to them because it was politically expedient. In a number of states, Democrats not only welcomed the immigrants; they fought to enfranchise those who declared their intention to become citizens. Democrats feared the tendency of Congregationalists and some Presbyterian clergy to meddle in politics: they warned their Catholic allies not to permit the priests to emulate the political activities of Calvinist ecclesiastics. Democrats wished to thoroughly separate church and state and believed that the state should interfere with the individual as little as possible.

Moreover, they were suspicious of legislative activism and revered Jefferson's call for minimal government. Like Jackson, they saw themselves as the heirs of old-style republicanism and feared that too much economic change threatened the ordinary individual. They were alarmed by the overly rapid development of the market economy and opposed government efforts to promote economic development. Such governmental activity frequently fostered corruption and undermined the independence and equality that made republicanism possible. Generally distrustful of evangelical efforts to tamper with the personal affairs of others, most Democrats were unfriendly to temperance proposals and other humanitarian reforms backed by Protestant reformers.

By legislative inaction, Democrats wished to enlarge the sphere of human liberties for white males. Through a more active approach to legislation, Whigs hoped to promote virtue and eradicate evils. Whigs claimed that legislation to protect certain industries through tariffs or to assist banks or railroads would promote a healthier economy. Democrats were more inclined to let each interest fend for itself. They thought economic legislation was designed only to aid special interests.

An Ethnocultural Interpretation

Ethnocultural historians postulate that evangelicals or pietists tended to support the Whigs, while ritualists or antievangelicals were inclined toward the Democrats. Evangelicals or pietists and liturgicals or antievangelicals are designations for opposite groups held together by common values and worldviews which both repelled and attracted individuals. Hence, a Roman Catholic would identify with the liturgicals and would support Democrats, but his association with the Democrats would also be influenced by the fact that evangelicals, usually Whigs, constituted a negative reference group. Not all New School Presbyterians associated with the Whigs, nor were all Missouri Lutherans Democrats. Nor should the terms "evangelical" and "liturgical" be considered mutually exclusive: many religions had both liturgical and evangelical emphases. These terms are used only to reflect what appeared to be the principal orientation of a group. Occasionally some highly evangelical groups backed the Democrats, such as the Anti-Missionary Baptists. Such groups are sometimes called "salvationist pietists," because they emphasized belief and personal salvation rather than using government for social engineering.

In the South, religious values often did not significantly influence political affiliation. The establishment there was Jeffersonian and slaveholding, with the Scotch-Irish closely linked to it. Irish Catholics were allied to the Democratic leadership of the South. Otherwise, it seems that out-groups gravitated to the Whig Party. For example, Louisiana's French Catholics were Whigs, as were many German immigrants there. The Whig coalition of groups that for one reason or other were uncomfortable with the southern establishment was a potent political force capable of defeating the dominant elements at the polls.

Political Realignment in the 1850s

The second party system collapsed in the mid-1850s, no longer able to contain mounting sectional tensions, burdened by widespread antiparty sentiment, and strained by a great surge of nativist hysteria. Many believed the parties differed little from one another. Party leaders were viewed as unresponsive to their constituencies, and self-serving if not corrupt. Politicians embraced expedient, unprincipled approaches to fundamental problems. Many people looked for new political leadership untainted by association with the old political establishments. The collapse of the second party system coincided with the passage of Stephen Douglas's Kansas-Nebraska Act in 1854. In order to win acceptance of the measure, Douglas included the provision that the territories would be initially open to slavery and that the Missouri Compromise, which had barred slavery in that area, was void. The territorial legislatures, according to his doctrine of popular sovereignty, should be free to decide whether or not to permit slavery. Many northern Democrats left their party, charging that Senator Douglas and President Franklin Pierce had sold out to southern interests.

The national Whig Party expired during this debate as northern Whigs denounced the measure, and southern Whigs hastened to defend slavery, soon joining the Democrats. The demise of the Whig Party owed a great deal to the fact that antiparty sentiment was particularly strong among the Whigs' constituency. Moreover, many who had supported Whigs had become disenchanted with the party due to its weak anti-Catholic stance. Without this strong nativist dissatisfaction with the party, it is likely that the

Whigs could have survived the crisis of the mid-1850s. Hostility toward Roman Catholics and foreigners reached flood-tide proportions. In the 1830s, half a million immigrants came to the United States; the next decade saw a million come. Before the 1850s were concluded, a million and a half additional immigrants had arrived, a large proportion of them Catholics. In some places, Catholics were becoming active in politics. Many native Protestants were alarmed by the size of the immigrant tide and especially fearful of what they viewed as a Catholic drive to destroy free institutions. Catholic bishops demanded a share of public educational funds for parochial schools and complained when priests were not permitted to minister to Catholics in prisons and public charitable institutions. Catholic inmates were usually required to attend Protestant worship services. These demands were perceived to be naked attempts to breach the wall that separated church and state.

Many Whigs abandoned their party because it was insufficiently opposed to Catholicism. Fearful of becoming a minority party, professional Whig politicians attempted to avoid the temperance question. They often shied away from measures designed to damage parochial schools or prevent Catholic bishops from controlling the property of local churches. Some took to "twisting the British lion's tail," buying Irish votes, and distributing pork and bread in immigrant neighborhoods. The Whigs occasionally made anti-Catholic utterances to retain evangelical support but usually refrained from legislative action. Many evangelical Whigs were not fooled by these tactics. They were particularly distressed that the party professionals wooed Catholic votes in the 1852 election and that the presidential nominee that year, Winfield Scott, was willing to educate his children in a convent. Moreover, General Scott had not harassed the Roman Church in Mexico during the war there. A number of Protestant Democrats became caught up in the nativist excitement and were outraged when President Franklin Pierce appointed James Campbell, a Catholic, postmaster general.

The Know-Nothings

Many who were alarmed by the Catholic threat drifted into secret lodges opposed to foreign-born Catholics. The Know-Nothings derived their name from an oath they took to answer questions about the society by saying they knew nothing about it. These lodges soon became involved in politics, running candidates under the American Party label or endorsing nativists on other tickets. Between 1853 and 1856, the Know-Nothings were the fastest growing political movement in America, surpassing even the growth of the Republican Party, which ultimately absorbed it. In 1854 it carried Delaware and Massachusetts with large majorities, and also polled a majority in

Maine. Forty percent of Pennsylvania's voters backed these nativists. One hundred Congressmen won their seats with Know-Nothing votes, and the party elected eight governors in 1854 and 1855.

During the political crisis that followed the Kansas-Nebraska Act, the Know-Nothings were often allied with the Republicans, a party composed of former Whigs, Democrats, and Free-Soilers and opposed to the extension of slavery into the territories. By 1856, it was clear that most northerners were more concerned about southern aggression and the extension of slavery into the territories than with the Catholic threat. Within the new party, there had been serious debate over whether to emphasize nativism or slavery extension. Though some antislavery radicals like William H. Seward were not unfriendly to the Catholic Church, many strong antislavery men opposed nativism only because it distracted attention from the more serious problem of keeping slavery out of the territories and resisting efforts of slaveholders to dominate the union. The determination of these men and events in Kansas shifted Republican attention to the antislavery question. Open warfare between proslavery and antislavery settlers there as well as federal assistance to the proslavery element left the Republicans little choice. By the 1856 presidential nominating convention, the party was firmly committed to making opposition to slavery in the territories its central concern and was able to absorb most Know-Nothings. Catholicism seemed a remote threat: many thought that the slaveholders were governing the country and in a position to deprive citizens of their liberties. Nativism remained an important though secondary concern for the Republicans.

Those Know-Nothings not absorbed by the Republican Party nominated former president Millard Fillmore in 1856; he would attract 22 percent of the popular vote. To confuse matters, Louisiana Know-Nothings permitted Creole Catholics to join their party, a move bitterly criticized by many northern Know-Nothings at the convention. John C. Frémont was the Republican nominee. Fillmore backers insisted Frémont was Catholic. Colonel Frémont was Protestant, but he had been married before a priest and his father was Catholic. Some Republican spokesmen found it necessary to assure voters that Frémont was more hostile to immigrants and Catholics than the former president was. Buffalo's Catholic bishop thought the Republicans were more anti-Catholic than the American Party. Analysis of Pennsylvania voting in the election of 1856 suggests that German Lutherans and German Evangelicals voted for the North American Party candidate for president. For the most part, northern Know-Nothings joined the Republicans, and the South became the focus of Know-Nothing activity. The North American Party attracted more than 40 percent of the southern vote in 1856. Later, many former American Party members claimed they had supported the nativist organization out of fear that radical antislavery men would dominate the Republican Party and endanger the Union. Once the nativist hysteria had subsided, few were willing to admit that they had once been affiliated with a party devoted to depriving others of political rights and economic opportunity.

The Republicans were a northern party, and their constituency was essentially that of the northern Whigs, with some additions. It was the party of evangelical Protestants and their reformist allies. Whereas Whigs attracted only a respectable majority of Methodists, Republicans had overwhelming Methodist support. In 1856, some Methodists held prayer meetings to petition God for the electoral success of Frémont, the Republican presidential candidate. Baptists of New England origins were now becoming firmly Republican; the Whigs had tended to win only the support of those Baptists who were involved in interdenominational humanitarian ventures or were prosperous urban dwellers. Terrified by the Catholic threat, many northern Baptists and Methodists joined the Republicans. The majority of northern Baptists and Methodists were Republican in part because they had prospered and no longer saw themselves as cultural outsiders. "Old School" Presbyterians can be seen as liturgicals, while "New School" Presbyterians were pietists and warm supporters of the Second Awakening and revivalism. Free Will Baptists were strong pietists, and Primitive Baptists can be seen as more liturgical than the former. Pietists or evangelicals were often nativists, prohibitionists, and sometimes abolitionists; they were inclined to be Whigs and Republicans. In the North, the Democrats looked to liturgical and antievangelical elements for support. Their losses in the North were balanced by their nearly complete dominance of the South, where former Whigs marched behind the Democratic standard to defend slavery and southern rights.

Religion in the Civil War

The causes of the Civil War are complex, and involve much more than the debate over the morality of human bondage. Yet the war is inconceivable without the controversy over slavery. As the years passed, more and more northerners found slavery morally unacceptable. Northerners were at least equally concerned by what they saw as southern efforts to control national affairs and establish slavery in the federal territories. Few of those who questioned slavery—even many abolitionists—believed that African Americans were equal to whites. Many abolitionists, though contending that blacks were an inferior human strain, argued that free blacks must enjoy equal rights under the law.

Churchmen in both North and South contributed greatly to the debate over slavery. Southern ecclesiastics played leading roles in defending slavery and referred to biblical passages as a means of justifying it. By midcentury, they ceased defending it as a necessary evil; they joined politicians in calling it "a positive good." Reverend James Henley Thornwell, a noted South Carolina Presbyterian, reflected the thinking of southern churchmen when he declared in 1850 that slavery was not only sanctioned by Christ and his apostles, it was a valuable school in which people are prepared for their life and eternity. Saint Paul, he explained, explicitly did not refuse fellowship with slaveholders.

A literal or narrow interpretation of the Bible yielded information useful to slavery's defenders and provided little of value to sustain abolitionists. This might explain in part the attachment of Southern Baptists to inerrancy. Southern preachers were strong advocates of southern rights. Many of them called for secession after the election of Abraham Lincoln in 1860. Like southern clergy, northern ministers exerted great influence as society's arbiters of morality. A considerable number of them refrained from condemning slavery. Some, like John Henry Hopkins, presiding bishop of the Protestant Episcopal Church, defended slavery on biblical grounds. Others were convinced abolitionists who bent every effort to persuade others of their moral duty to combat slavery and consider slaveholders great sinners.

Northern critics of slavery were untroubled by the ability of southern clergy to cite scriptural passages in support of slavery. They maintained that slavery violated the spirit of Christianity and that Christian principles must be applied anew to each age and its institutions. These theological liberals contended that revelation was continuous and progressive, demanding that man attain higher goals in successive ages in response to God's call. It was in this spirit that James Russell Lowell wrote about the antislavery movement in 1844:

> By the light of burning martyrs
> Jesus' bleeding feet I track,
> Toiling up new Calvaries ever
> With the cross that looks not back;
> New occasions teach new duties
> Time makes ancient good uncouth;
> They must upward still and onward,
> Who would keep abreast of truth.

While southern clergymen employed scriptural literalism to defend slavery, many northern clergymen liberated themselves from literalism by proclaiming that the Bible's central doctrine was the law of love. The unfolding of this principle and the application of the law of love to human problems amounted to progressive revelation. With time, people were able to grasp more of God's eternal design; certainly preservation of the Union and the end of slavery were chief elements in God's plan for humankind. Even before the Civil War began, Henry Ward Beecher told a congregation on January 4, 1861, that the whole nation was guilty of perpetuating slavery, "and every one of us is more or less, directly or indirectly, willingly or unwillingly, implicated in it." The individual did not achieve conversion and rebirth alone: it was a corporate matter. Conversion, rebirth, freedom, and justice are only achieved through the action of a nation. Individual salvation, he claimed, was a function of the rebirth of the nation.

The most radical ecclesiastical position on slavery was taken by the Church Anti-Slavery Society, founded in 1859 by Reverends Henry Beecher of Connecticut and George Cheever of New York City. Its spokesmen argued that rebellion was sufficient justification for ending slavery in the South. It worked closely with radical abolitionist William Lloyd Garrison and demanded equal treatment of African American troops. It opposed Lincoln's reelection because his plan for reconstructing the South left too much to be desired. There were never more than a few hundred members of this organization, but, as the war progressed, more and more northern Protestants came to share many of the society's views. A sermon B.H. Nadal gave to his New Haven Methodist congregation did not depart from mainstream thought. If the Union lost the war, he asserted, "the civilized world would leave the broken remnants of human rights clutched in the hands of a few Negroes . . . and it would prove that all our notions and hopes in regard to a personal and righteous God have been a dream." Such sentiments may have been best expressed by the erudite Julia Ward Howe, a respected and well-educated lay preacher and women's rights advocate. She wrote these revered words after she had visited an army camp near Washington in 1862 (Figure 6).

> Mine eyes have seen the glory of the coming of the Lord;
> He is trampling out the vintage where the grapes of wrath are stored;
> He hath loosed the fateful lightning of his terrible swift sword;
> His truth is marching on.
>
> I have seen Him in the watch-fires of a hundred circling camps;
> They have builded Him an altar in the evening dews and damps;
> I can read His righteous sentence by the dim and flaring lamps;
> His day is marching on.

Figure 6. Julia Ward Howe. Julia Ward Howe (1819–1910), author of "The Battle Hymn of the Republic," was one of the best read people of her age. With her husband, Samuel Gridley Howe, she edited the Boston journal *Abolitionist*. Howe used her talents and knowledge as a reformer, women's suffragist, advocate of African American rights, and poet. (Courtesy the Library of Congress.)

Southern churchmen were no less willing to see God's hand in the Confederate war effort or accept much of the credit for bringing it about. They had clothed the social system of the South in the garb of scriptural justifications and questioned the virtue of its northern critics. Southern churchmen saw southerners as God's chosen people: they were virtuous and God-fearing, while northerners were tyrannical, barbarous, moneygrubbing, and hostile. Federal troops were accused of being brutal and wicked. As southern nationalism evolved, southern Christianity took on the dimensions of a folk religion, and God was viewed almost as a tribal god—Jehovah of the Old Testament, stern, direct, the god of battles. Sophisticated approaches to theology were looked upon with more and more suspicion. As early as 1850, a prominent Presbyterian explained the struggle between North and South in terms that prefigured the rhetoric of southern preachers during their war for southern independence. He thought the North represented the forces of atheism and the South stood for Christianity. Southerners were seen as the defenders of liberty and order against northern Jacobins, atheists, and socialists.

In 1862, southern Old School Presbyterians denounced the federal government as despotic and proclaimed that the war was a struggle "not alone for civil rights, and property, and home, but the religion, for the Church, for the gospel." In 1864, the southern Presbyterians asserted that "it is the peculiar mission of the southern Church to conserve the institution of slavery." Baptist clergy and churches reflected the social and political views of respective areas in the Confederacy. Southern Baptists consistently defended slavery and the confederacy, and the Southern Baptist Convention called upon its adherents to observe fast days. It even prayed against the enemies of the South, "trusting that their pitiless purposes may be frustrated," and that happiness and prosperity could again be enjoyed under two governments. Some southern churchmen saw a Confederate victory as ushering in the millennium, which would have an exalted place for slavery.

Although he affiliated with no denomination, Abraham Lincoln was a profoundly Christian man who studied Scripture and looked for signs of God's will. He agonized over the suffering caused by the war, but never questioned God's justice or that the Almighty had reason to permit the nation's "fiery trial." Lincoln believed it divine will that the nation must save the united republic, "this last best hope of earth," but he found it difficult to fathom God's overall design. He often told associates that he was more interested in being on God's side than in enlisting God on his side. Regarding those who were certain God willed that the war be fought to end slavery, Lincoln observed that "if it is probable that God would reveal his will to others on a point so connected with my duty, it might be supposed he would reveal it directly to me." Early in the war, he made "a solemn vow to God" that he would move against slavery as soon as a major Union victory provided an occasion for such a step. Certainly, he came to believe, it was God's plan that slavery be ended.

In the Gettysburg Address, Lincoln changed the meaning of American history, American civil religion, and the revolution in asserting that the nation was "conceived in Liberty, and dedicated to the proposition that all men are created equal." With these words, historian Garry Wills asserts, Lincoln gave the Constitution a new meaning. Lincoln's second inaugural address reflects this belief as well as the depth of his thoughts regarding God's sovereignty and justice. In it he noted that the prayers "of neither [people] has been answered fully." Among God's purposes in the war, Lincoln thought, was to punish the American people for slavery and that "He now wills to remove [slavery]." Northern Protestant clergy saw Lincoln's death on Good Friday, 1865, as the last sacrifice necessary to purify the nation and qualify it to take up its sacred mission of bringing liberty to the people of the world.

The Martyred President and
Civil Religion

The martyred Lincoln would ultimately ascend to preeminence in the American civil religion: He would occupy the place of an almost-divine agent who was sacrificially slain—slain but still present in American life. Benedict Arnold was displaced by John Wilkes Booth as the Judas figure. In Lincoln, the nation had a noble symbol of unity, equality, and sacrifice. He embodied the American dream in that he rose from humble origins to become president. Memorial Day was invested with a sacred character, as people in both sections honored warriors who gave up their lives for what they considered America's highest ideals. The votaries of the American civil religion—the politicians, teachers, clergy, and other public figures— found in the Civil War many rich symbols to invest American culture and the American nation with a sacred character.

Impact on Southern Religion

Having passed through defeat in war and the humiliation of Reconstruction, southerners clung to the somewhat primitive religion of the past, a symbol of the South's separate identity. Adherence to their religion was a means by which individuals attested their loyalty to the South. For their part, the Southern Baptist churches consoled their people and helped Confederate veterans abandon the ways of soldiers and resume civilian lives. As the North seemed to drift toward liberal religion and greater theological sophistication, southerners adhered to the faith of their fathers. They alone, they believed, kept the true faith in a nation dominated by materialistic, possibly satanic, Yankees. Like the people of Israel, these chosen people suffered because God expected much more of southerners than of other people, church members were told, and God chastised the South for not living up to the high standards established for it. The South had been brought low because there had been too much gambling, drinking, swearing, and indulging in the sins of the flesh. If the South obeyed its puritanical tribal God, the day of deliverance when it would shake off Yankee domination would be hastened. Hence, the post–Civil War years saw a renewed emphasis upon personal morality and growing public opposition to such personal sins as sexual indiscretion, gambling, and drinking. These beliefs came to constitute a civil religion for the South and were found in undiluted form in the faith of Southern Baptists.

The dominant religion in the South, the Southern Baptist denomination was the church of common white folk, and it upheld white supremacy and white dominance. Southern Baptists believed that God had led the South through the sufferings of the war in order to strengthen and purify them. Southern Baptist leaders believed that their people possessed a "certain depth of soul" that equipped them for their special mission of building a flourishing Christian civilization in the United States. They were to maintain the purity of their society by practicing a holy separatism from the rest of the United States. The end of the Confederacy had been a creative death through which the South was reborn, while the North emerged from the war with its soul mortgaged to materialism and mammon. The southerners' convictions were a source of great satisfaction because they knew that they had been entrusted with a special mission and that they, more than other Christians, most closely resembled the primitive church. This worldview, promoted particularly by Baptists and Methodists, transformed the South into the nation's most religious region.

Bibliography

Baker, Jean H. *Affairs of Party: The Political Culture of Northern Democrats in the Mid–Nineteenth Century.* Ithaca: Cornell University Press, 1983.

Balmer, Randall. *Mine Eyes Have Seen the Glory: A Journey into the Evangelical Subculture in America.* New York: Oxford University Press, 1989.

Barnes, Gilbert H. *The Anti-Slavery Impulse, 1830–1844.* New York: Harper and Row, 1933.

Baum, Dale. *The Civil War Party System: The Case of Massachusetts, 1848–1876.* Chapel Hill: University of North Carolina Press, 1984.

Billington, Ray A. *The Protestant Crusade, 1800–1860.* Chicago: Quadrangle, 1964.

Budd, Richard M. "Ohio Army Chaplains and the Professionalization of Military Chaplaincy in the Civil War." *Ohio History* 102 (spring 1993): 5–19.

Carwardine, Richard. " 'Antinomians' and 'Nominalists': Methodists and the Market Revolution." In *The Market Revolution in America,* ed. Melvyn Stokes and Stephen Conway, pp. 259–281. Charlottesville: University of Virginia Press, 1996.

———. *Evangelicals and Politics in Antebellum America.* New Haven: Yale University Press, 1993.

Cheney, Mary Randall. *Life and Letters of Horace Bushnell.* New York: Arno Press, 1969.

Chesbrough, David B., ed. *'God Ordained This War': Sermons on the Sectional Crisis, 1830–1865.* Columbia: University of South Carolina Press, 1991.

Cole, Charles C. *The Social Ideas of the Northwestern Evangelists, 1826–1860.* New York: Columbia University Press, 1954.

Davidson, James West. *The Logic of Millennial Thought: Eighteenth Century New England.* New Haven: Yale University Press, 1977.

Davis, Cyprian. *The History of Black Catholics in the United States.* New York: Crossroad, 1990.

Dillon, Merton. *The Abolitionists: The Growth of a Dissenting Minority.* De Kalb: Northern Illinois University Press, 1974.

Diner, Hasia R. *A Time for Gathering: The Second Migration, 1820–1880.* Vol. 2. *Jewish People in America.* Baltimore: Johns Hopkins University Press, 1992.

Eighmy, John Lee. *Churches in Cultural Captivity*

Foner, Eric. *Free Soil, Free Labor, Free Men: The Ideology of the Republican Party Before the Civil War.* New York: Holt, Rinehard, Winston, 1970.

Formisano, Ronald P. *The Birth of Mass Political Parties: Michigan, 1827–1861.* Princeton: Princeton University Press, 1971.

———. "The New Political History and the Election of 1840." *Journal of Interdisciplinary History* 33 (spring 1993): 661–682.

———. *The Transformation of Political Culture: Massachusetts Parties, 1790s–1840s.* New York: Oxford University Press, 1983.

Foster, Charles I. *An Errand of Mercy: The Evangelical United Front, 1790–1837.* Chapel Hill: University of North Carolina Press, 1960.

Fredrickson, George M. *The Inner Civil War: Northern Intellectuals and the Crisis of the Union.* New York: Harper Torchbooks, 1968.

Freehling, William W. *The Road to Disunion: Secession at Bay, 1774–1854.* New York: Oxford University Press, 1980.

Gabriel, Ralph Henry. *The Course of American Democratic Thought.* New York: Ronald Press, 1956.

Galli, Mark. "The Gallery: Firebrands and Visionaries, Leading People in Religion and Politics During the Civil War Era." *Christian History* 11 (1992): 16–19.

Gilbert, Arthur. *A Jew in Christian America.* New York: Sheed and Ward, 1966.

Goen, C.C. *Broken Churches, Broken Nation: Denominational Schisms and the Coming of the Civil War.* Macon: Mercer University Press, 1985.

Goodman, Paul. "The Manual Labor Movement and the Origins of Abolitionism." *Journal of the Early Republic* 13 (fall 1993): 355–388.

Griffin, Clifford S. "Religious Benevolence as Social Control, 1815–1860." In *Ante-Bellum Reform,* ed. David Brion Davis, pp. 81–96. New York: Harper and Row, 1967.

Gusfield, Joseph R. "Temperance, Status, Control, and Mobility, 1826–1860." In *Ante-Bellum Reform,* ed. David Brion Davis, pp. 120–139. New York: Harper and Row, 1967.

Handy, Mark Y. *A Christian America: Protestant Hopes and Historical Realities.* New York: Oxford University Press, 1984.

————. "The New Infidelity: Northern Protestant Clergymen and the Critique of Progress, 1840–1855." *Religion and American Culture* 1 (winter 1991): 203–226.

Hill, Samuel S. "The Story Before the Story: Southern Baptists Since World War II." In *Southern Baptists Observed,* ed. Nancy Tatom Ammerman, pp. 30–46. Knoxville: University of Tennessee Press, 1993.

Holt, Michael F. *Forging a Majority: The Formation of the Republican Party in Pittsburgh, 1848–1860.* New York: Wiley, 1978.

————. *The Political Crisis of the 1850s.* New York: Wiley. 1978.

Howe, Daniel Walker. "The Market Revolution and the Shaping of Identity in Whig-Jacksonian America." In *The Market Revolution in America,* ed. Melvyn Stokes and Stephen Conway, pp. 259–281. Charlottesville: University of Virginia Press.

————. "Religion and Politics in the Antebellum North." *Religion and American Politics,* ed. Mark A. Noll, pp. 121–145. New York: Oxford University Press, 1990.

Huston, James L. "Economic Change and Political Realignment in Antebellum Pennsylvania." *Pennsylvania Magazine of History and Biography,* 113 (July 1989): 347–395.

Jensen, Richard J. "The Religious and Occupational Roots of Party Identification: Illinois and Indiana in the 1870s." In *Beyond the Civil War Synthesis: Political Essays of the Civil War Era,* ed. Robert P. Swierenga, pp. 255–273. Westport, CT: Greenwood Press, 1975.

John, Richard R. "Taking Sabbatarianism Seriously: The Postal System, the Sabbath, and the Transformation of American Political Culture." *Journal of the Early Republic* (winter 1990): 517–568.

Johnson, Curtis D. *Redeeming America: Evangelicals and the Road to the Civil War.* Chicago: Ivan R. Dee, 1993.

Kelley, Robert. *The Cultural Pattern in American Politics, The First Century.*

Lannie, Vincent P. "Catholics, Protestants, and Public Education." In *Catholicism in America,* ed. Philip Gleason, pp. 45–57. New York: Harper and Row, 1970. New York: Knopf, 1979.

Lazerow, Jama. "Spokesmen for the Working Class: Protestant Clergy and the Labor Movement in Antebellum New England." *Journal of the Early Republic* 13 (fall 1993): 323–355.

Mayfield, John. " 'The Soul of a Man!' William Filmore Simms and the Myths of Southern Manhood." *Journal of the Early Republic* 15 (fall 1995): 477–500.

McInerney, Daniel J. " 'A Faith for Freedom': The Gospel of Abolition." *Journal of the Early Republic* 11 (fall 1991): 371–393.

McPherson, James M. *Battle Cry of Freedom: The Civil War Era.* New York: Oxford University Press, 1988.

————. *The Struggle for Equality: Abolitionists and the Negro in the Civil War and Reconstruction.* Princeton: Princeton University Press, 1988.

Moorhead, James H. *American Apocalypse: Yankee Protestants and the Civil War and Reconstruction.* New Haven: Yale University Press, 1978.

————. "Preaching the Holy War." *Christian History* 33 (1991): 38–41.

Murrin, John M. "Religion and Politics in America from the First Settlements to the Civil War." In *Religion and American Politics,* ed. Mark A. Noll, pp. 19–43. New York: Oxford University Press, 1990.

Noll, Mark A. "The Puzzling Faith of Abraham Lincoln." *Christian History* 33 (1991): 10–20.

Padgett, Chris. "Hearing the Antislavery Rank-and-File: The Wesleyan Methodist Schism of 1843." *Journal of the Early Republic* 11 (spring 1992): 63–84.

Perry, Lewis. *Radical Abolitionism: Anarchy and the Government of God in Antislavery Thought.* Ithaca: Cornell University Press, 1973.

Queen, Edward L. *In the South the Baptists Are the Center of Gravity: Southern Baptists and Social Change, 1930–1980.* Brooklyn: Carlson, 1991.

Quist, John W. " 'The Greatest Majority of Our Subscribers Are Farmers': The Michigan Abolitionist Constituency of the 1840s." *Journal of the Early Republic* 14 (fall 1994): 325–358.

Rosenberg, Ellen M. *The Southern Baptists: A Subculture in Transition.* Knoxville: University of Tennessee Press, 1989.

Rothman, David J. *The Discovery of the Asylum: Social Order and Disorder in the New Republic.* Boston: Little, Brown, 1971.

Sachar, *A History of the Jews in America.* New York: Knopf, 1992.

Scott, Jeffrey Warren, and Mary Ann Jeffreys. "The Gallery: Fighters of Faith." *Civil War History* 11 (1992): 34–37.

Scudder, Horace Elisha. *James Russell Lowell: A Biography.* Grosse Pointe, Michigan: Scholarly Press, 1968.

Shade, William G. "Pennsylvania Politics in the Jacksonian Period: A Case Study, Northampton County, 1829–1844." *Pennsylvania History* 39 (July 1972): 313–333.

————. "Society and Politics in Antebellum Virginia's Southside." *Journal of Southern History* 53 (May 1987): 163–193.

Shattuck, Gardiner H., Jr. "Revivals in the Camp." *Christian History* 10 (1991): 28–38.

Smith, Timothy L. *Revivalism and Social Reform: American Protestantism on the Eve of the Civil War.* Nashville: Abingdon Press, 1957.

Swierenga, Robert P. "Ethnoreligious Political Behavior in the Mid–Nineteenth Century: Voting, Values, Cultures." In *Religion and American Politics,* ed. Mark A. Noll, pp. 146–171. New York: Oxford University Press, 1990.

————. "Religion and Immigration Behavior: The Dutch Experience." In *Belief and Behavior: Essays in the New Religious History,* ed. Philip B. Vandermeer and Robert P. Swierenga, pp. 164–188. New Brunswick: Rutgers University Press, 1991.

Swift, David E. *Black Prophets of Justice: Activist Clergy Before the Civil War.* Baton Rouge: Louisiana State University Press, 1989.

Tharp, Louise Hall. *Three Saints and a Sinner: Julia Ward Howe, Louisa, Annie, and Sam Ward.* Boston: Little, Brown, 1956.

Thistlethwaite, Frank. "The Anglo-American World of Humanitarian Endeavor." In *Ante-Bellum Reform,* ed. David Brion Davis, pp. 63–81. New York: Harper and Row, 1967.

Turner, Helen Lee. "Fundamentalism in the Southern Baptist Convention: The Crystallization of a Millennialist Vision." Ph.D. dissertation, University of Virginia, 1990.

Tyler, Alice Felt. *Freedom's Ferment: Phases of American Social History from the Colonial Period to the Outbreak of the Civil War.* New York: Harper Torchbooks, 1944.

Wilentz, Sean. "Slavery, Antislavery, and Jacksonian Democracy," In *The Market Revolution in America,* ed. Melvyn Stokes and Stephen Conway, pp. 202–223. Charlottesville: University of Virginia Press, 1996.

Wills, Garry. *Lincoln at Gettysburg: The Words That Remade America.* New York: Simon and Schuster, 1992.

Winston, Diane. "The Southern Baptist Story." In *Southern Baptists Observed,* ed. Nancy Tatom Ammerman, pp. 12–29. Knoxville: University of Tennessee Press, 1993.

Wyatt-Brown, Bertram. "Religion and the 'Civilizing Process' in the Early South, 1600–1860." In *Religion and American Politics,* ed. Mark A. Noll, pp. 172–195. New York: Oxford University Press, 1990.

Seven

Postbellum African American Religion

The end of slavery did not bring an end to racism or substantial improvement in the physical quality of life for African Americans in the South. Lacking money, property, and access to many occupations, southern Blacks passed from being slaves of individuals to figuratively becoming the slaves of society. Racism was intensified as whites reacted against Reconstruction regimes. The emergence of pseudoscientific racial theories intensified prejudice throughout the nation, and the migration of Blacks to the North in search of economic opportunity was met with hostility, particularly on the part of those who feared their economic competition.

The termination of hostilities and emancipation of slaves made possible the growth of the African Methodist Episcopal Church and the AME Zion Church in the South. There was a multiplication of African American Baptist churches as restrictions on Black churches ended and African Americans left white-dominated congregations. Not wishing to worship with Blacks, southern whites often assisted African Americans in forming their own congregations. Northern white churches carried out missionary and benevolent activity in the South, but their efforts were too frequently tinged with condescension.

Missionary Activities

Northern Protestant churches provided solid support for the radical Republicans' Reconstruction plans in the South. Protestant philanthropists believed that a federal military presence was necessary in the states of the Confederacy until southerners had repented their past deeds and were willing to permit African Americans to live in true freedom and dignity. White violence against Blacks and the Black Codes passed by legislatures seemed to offer solid proof that southerners had not abandoned their "lost cause," and that extended protection of the freedmen was necessary. The northern churches launched major programs to assist the freedmen, with the Congregationalists, Presbyterians, and Methodists particularly active in establishing schools. However, northern Baptists and Methodists did not show an interest in merging with African American counterparts on the basis of equality. Both the AME and the AME Zion churches showed interest in merging with the northern Methodists, in part because this would open theology schools to African American seminarians. They requested that African American bishops be treated as equals in a merged church. The American Home Missionary Society, dominated by Congregationalists, launched the largest educational effort. By 1867, it had 528 teachers in the South. Among the surviving schools it helped establish are Fisk and Atlanta universities, Talladega College, and Hampton Institute. Most of the teachers in the lower schools established by the northern church were women. These women endured harassment as well as the most primitive living and working conditions in order to teach African American youngsters. Hampton Institute in Virginia and other institutions established by northern white benevolence were built on the principle of African American inferiority. They were to teach "the habits of labor" to a people who had much experience with work and had shown considerable ingenuity in carrying out the tasks assigned to them. It was assumed the African Americans needed the guidance of paternalistic northern white Protestants in all matters of importance. Immediately after the war, Dr. Nathaniel Colver, a famous Chicago Baptist professor then in his seventies, founded the National Theological Institute for African Americans; it would be the core of what was later Virginia Union University. White paternalism resulted in a bitter dispute in the 1890s, as African Americans who wanted to control their own destinies proved that they could maintain their own school in Lynchburg. Among African Americans, the quarrel between accommodationists and self-help advocates produced two separate Baptist conferences and two barely viable schools.

Institutions for African Americans produced lawyers, politicians, ministers, and merchants, with Hampton Institute a pattern for many of them. In 1884, Tuskegee Institute was founded in Alabama under Booker T. Washington, Hampton's most famous alumnus. Like Hampton, Tuskegee would become the model for other institutes. It was a social settlement, church, and school. Tuskegee included Phelps Hall Bible School; it sponsored summer chautauqua-style mothers' meetings, a Temperance Legion, social societies, and YMCA work. Washington also superintended settlements at Cotton Valley, Society Hill, and East Tallassee, Alabama.

These southern African American social settlements were the models for African American missions and settlement houses established in northern cities, including the New York Colored Mission (1865), "Tennesseetown" in Topeka (1890), and Henry Street House in New York (1906). African American institutional churches reflected the experiences of the southern settlements and the missions. Worship and concern for members of a particular congregation differentiated the institutional church from the settlement house, which served a clientele and assigned a secondary position to religion. The first AME institutional church and social settlement was established in Chicago by Reverend Reverdy Ransom. He obtained a building with a twelve-hundred-seat auditorium that provided a gymnasium, kindergarten, employment service, clubs for boys and girls, and a print shop. In 1902 he tried to mediate between strikers and African American strikebreakers. His attacks on the rackets resulted in the dynamiting of his church. In 1904, he found it necessary to move to Massachusetts to work under a more sympathetic bishop. His successor was ordered to "make it a regular A.M.E. church [and] cut out the social foolishness." Ransom brought the concept of the African American institutional church to Boston and New York. He became a leading AME bishop and a prominent Christian Socialist.

The End of Reconstruction and Emergence of White Supremacy

The 1877 inauguration of President Rutherford B. Hayes, a devout Methodist, marked the end of Reconstruction. In order to obtain southern Democratic assistance in winning the disputed election of 1876, Hayes agreed, among other things, to remove the last occupation forces from three southern states. Had the election not been disputed, the former general still would have favored an end to Reconstruction. Many northerners and church members had become disillusioned with Reconstruction. They incorrectly blamed the corruption that characterized most Reconstruction regimes on the freedmen. It was also believed that the federal presence in the South provoked whites to resist and abuse African Americans. If troops were withdrawn and the federal government abandoned efforts to monitor race relations, many thought that responsible southern whites would come to power and accord Blacks the protection of the law. A large proportion of middle-class northern Protestants, disturbed by the presence of immigrants, took a more sympathetic view of southern whites. The complaints that these northerners had about immigrants were similar to the disparaging comments of southern whites about Blacks.

Southern white churches made some efforts to care for the African Americans, but public sentiment made it impossible to do much more than establish separate organizational units for them. The white churches, especially Southern Baptists, stood for racial separation and white supremacy.

African Americans were frequently pushed out into their own congregations, though a number of them remained in communion with the Southern Baptists. Today there are about seven hundred African American congregations in the Southern Baptist Convention; Southern Baptists continue to defend racial separation in worship because African Americans and whites have different liturgical styles.

Soon after the Civil War, it became clear that southern African Americans and whites would not worship together. For example, the white minister of the Bull Swamp Baptist Church in South Carolina built a new church around 1873, suggesting that the African Americans use the old church. When African Americans did worship with whites it was expected for Blacks to enter the building last and sit in the rear. A fixed order existed for baptismal ceremonies: white women first, then white males, then African American women, and finally African American men. Throughout the South, African Americans withdrew into their own independent churches. In 1876, the Raleigh *Biblical Recorder* said that for African Americans and whites to worship together was like "fire and gunpowder [occupying] the same canister in peace." In 1892, the *Christian Index,* published in Atlanta by Baptists, defended the lynching of African American men as an expression of the whites' respect for their women. Thomas Dixon, a former pastor, wrote novels that proclaimed the inferiority of African Americans and the danger that the South could someday be dominated by mulattoes. D.W. Griffith, maker of the Klan-glorifying film *Birth of a Nation,* was the son of a Baptist minister. There were some white ministers who stood before crazed mobs and denounced lynchings, and a number of them supportively accompanied African Americans to the gallows. The Methodist General Conference came out against lynchings in 1912.

Church bodies denounced books teaching that African Americans lacked souls and were not human. A white clergyman could be "moderate" on the race question and still insist on white supremacy and support complete racial separation in worship, schools, and social matters. By the early twentieth century, very few northern Christians were critical of the separate but equal policy.

Desiring complete separation of the races in worship, the southern Methodists organized the Colored Methodist Episcopal Church in 1870; by 1918 it had 350,000 members. (The northern Methodists had provided a separate conference for African Americans in 1866.)

Booker T. Washington and W.E.B. Du Bois

The Supreme Court in *Plessy v. Ferguson* (1896) ruled it lawful to provide separate but equal railroad accommodations for African Americans. This became the legal justification for Jim Crow legislation regulating interracial relations. Many African American church people found it necessary to follow Booker T. Washington in accepting racial segregation and staying out of politics. Washington believed it very foolish and unproductive to raise questions about social equality. He counseled his people to concentrate on improving their economic condition by learning trade or agricultural skills. He was the dominant African American spokesman between 1890 and 1915 and enjoyed the support of most black clergy. Washington and his followers took an accommodationist view in large measure as a means of obtaining support for African American education. Edgar Gardner Murphy, an African American Episcopal priest in Montgomery, claimed his people were willing to give up the vote so whites would no longer fear African American domination and would become sympathetic toward them. Other African Americans shared his view.

Washington's most severe African American critic was the historian W.E.B. Du Bois, the first African American to earn a doctoral degree from Harvard. Du Bois called for the most capable "Talented Tenth" among African Americans to lead their people in obtaining full citizenship and combating Jim Crowism, or segregation. Du Bois was the key figure in the founding of the National Association for the Advancement of Colored People in 1909. A year later the National Urban League was created. Both groups rejected the accommodationism of Booker T. Washington; nevertheless, accommodation was a popular approach to white racism and the socioeconomic problems of African Americans. To a considerable degree, this outlook characterizes the policy of the National Baptist Convention, USA, today.

African American Catholics

There were relatively few Black Catholics, except in Louisiana, and a number of former slaves defected from the Roman Church. Catholics had attempted to establish schools for the freedmen, with some separate churches built for Blacks. Resistance on the part of white communicants frustrated the program to assist and evangelize African American Catholics as called for by the Second Plenary Council of U.S. bishops in 1866. At that council, the bishops, at the request of Roman authorities, discussed means of meeting the spiritual needs of African Americans. Though some bishops had a low opinion of the abilities of Blacks, the bishops were concerned with their spiritual welfare. With some anger, they rejected the Vatican's suggestion that a prefect apostolic or national coordinator be appointed to look after the spiritual welfare of African Americans. Among those supporting the suggestion were Baltimore archbishop Martin J. Spalding, the author of this idea, and Augustin Verot of St. Augustine, one of two bishops whose previous warm support of slavery had displeased the Holy See.

In the year prior to the Third Plenary Council of 1884, the archbishops were instructed to meet and discuss the apostolate to African Americans; these instructions included a statement of Rome's displeasure that little progress had been made and that suggestions sent after the last plenary council were ignored.

During the nineteenth century, the most effective work of evangelization was done by the African American orders for women, founded before the Civil War, and by the Sisters of the Blessed Sacrament for Indians and Colored People, founded by a wealthy heiress, Mother Katharine Drexel, in 1891. The community of African American sisters was the Oblate Sisters of Providence, founded in 1829, whose first superior was Mother Elizabeth Lange, a Cuban born of Haitian parents. The Mill Hill Fathers, an English missionary order, as well as the St. Joseph's Society of the Sacred Heart (Josephites), the Holy Ghost Congregation, and the Society of Missionaries of Africa (White Fathers) also worked with African American Catholics.

Efforts to recruit an African American priesthood met with only limited success, due in considerable part to racism. In the early twentieth century Father John A. Bureke, organizer of the Catholic Board of Negro Missions, suggested that married Black men be ordained deacons, and he called for renewed efforts to recruit Black priests. Rome endorsed efforts to recruit Black priests but did not endorse a married deaconate. In 1919, it instructed American archbishops to denounce the anti-Black riots that followed World War I.

Among the first African American priests in the United States, the three Healy brothers were most notable. They entered the Catholic Church while attending Holy Cross College. James Augustine Healy became bishop of Portland, Maine, in 1875 and was known as an effective preacher and administrator. Father Alexander Sherwood Healy earned a doctorate in Rome, was briefly chancellor in Boston, was rector of the cathedral there, and served as the bishop's theologian. Patrick Francis Healy, a Jesuit, taught at Holy Cross College, St. Joseph College, and at Georgetown College, where he was vice president, vice rector, and president. Georgetown did not admit Black students until after World War II. Though light-skinned, the Healys were known to be Blacks. They were not involved in African American Catholic groups.

Father Augustus Tolton founded an African American parish in Chicago. A former slave from Missouri, he was refused admission to seminaries in the United States and studied in Rome, where he was ordained in 1888. It was fortunate that he had the protection of Roman authorities. As pastor of a Black parish in Chicago, he shared in his people's poverty and had much difficulty raising money, although Mother Drexel gave his parish $30,000. His mother served as his housekeeper, and he felt isolated—being one of about twenty-seven African American priests—and knew that he was always under the scrutiny of fellow priests.

There were a number of African American parishes, and membership in them probably contributed to a sense of autonomy for the parishioners. The foundation of separate parishes was consistent then with the Catholic practice of national parishes for white ethnic groups. In Cincinnati, the archdiocese established St. Ann's parish for Blacks even though some Irish Catholics threatened violence if the church was erected. Despite the existence of St. Ann's parish and school, a number of African American Catholics attended other Cincinnati parish churches.

Daniel Rudd was the most prominent African American Catholic layman in the late nineteenth century. He owned and published the *American Catholic Tribune,* which was successively published in Springfield, Ohio, Cincinnati, and Detroit. Probably funded by Cincinnati archbishop William Henry Elder, Rudd went to Lucerne, Switzerland, to participate in an international congress sponsored by the Vatican to fight slavery and the slave trade. Rudd became the U.S. spokesman for Charles Martial Allemand Cardinal Lavigerie, the main force behind the congress. He was also active in organizing the first congress for African American lay Catholics that met in Baltimore in 1889. In 1919, he received money from the bishop of Little Rock to attend a meeting of the NAACP; however, the bishop did not want Rudd to act as an official representative of the diocese at the meeting.

In the early twentieth century, African American laymen repeatedly demonstrated their commitment to the church, but they also demanded an end to discrimination within the church and more schools for African American children. They denounced the decision of the Catholic University of America to no longer admit African Americans and criticized the Josephite order for not educating more African American candidates for the priesthood. In the 1920s, the Vatican raised questions about the treatment of African Americans within the American church and praised those bishops who admitted Blacks to their seminaries. Unfortunately, the American church reflected all too well American attitudes on racial matters, and little progress was made in improving the condition of Black Catholics. There was African American interest in having their own bishop, an idea similar to the demands of some white ethnics for national churches with their own bishops. Rome rejected this suggestion, as it had similar requests by white ethnic groups. In the 1980s, this suggestion appeared in the form of a request for a separate African American rite, which would be distinct from the Latin rite to which most Catholics belong.

The Catholic Church had limited success attracting African Americans in the United States until the middle of the twentieth century, when it achieved a substantial increase. Some African Americans entered the Catholic Church then because it had pressed for desegregation in the South since the 1940s. Non-Catholic African American children were permitted to attend Catholic schools in both the North and the South. Some families entered the Roman Church by becoming acquainted with it through its schools. Within the worldwide Catholic communion, there were many African American saints and role models. By the 1990s there were a number of African American bishops, one of whom presided over the archdiocese of Atlanta. There were relatively few African American priests, making it necessary for African American parishes to rely upon white clergy. By 1990, 8.4 percent of churchgoing African Americans were Roman Catholics. No other white-controlled church could claim as many African American adherents.

African American Protestant Churches

African Americans preferred Black Baptist and Methodist affiliations, in part because these churches in some ways offered means of expression and fulfillment not accorded them in white-dominated churches and society. Both denominations also offered laymen many opportunities to become leaders and preachers. Most Black Southern Methodists affiliated with one of the two independent Black Methodist churches. Both the African Methodist Episcopal Church, founded in Philadelphia in 1816, and the AME Zion Church, formed in New York in 1820, rapidly acquired new members south of the Mason-Dixon Line.

A Colored Primitive Baptist Church was organized in 1865, and a number of independent African American Baptist associations emerged. By 1895, there was a National Baptist Convention, USA, with many Black Baptist congregations remaining independent. Within the denomination, there was a women's convention, through which women sought gender equality and empowerment. They fought the dominant society's image of immoral, lazy Black women and avoided the image of the silent helpmate, while standing as full partners of men in the battle against racism. A serious dispute over whether the denomination should cooperate with white Baptists and over control of the denomination's printing firm led in 1915 to the formation of the National Baptist Convention of America. The cooperationists retained control of the older body. In 1958, the National Baptist Convention, USA, had about 26,000 churches; two years earlier the National Baptist Convention of America reported 11,398 member churches. By one count, there were at least thirty-four completely Black denominations and sects in the United States in 1948.

There was an active holiness movement within AME ranks in the late nineteenth century, and one of its most effective unordained preachers was Amanda Berry Smith. One AME bishop claimed he had learned more of practical value in homiletics from her than from any other person. African American holiness and Pentecostal churches grew rapidly in the twentieth century. These churches and sects tended to be otherworldly in that they usually did not become involved in politics, but instead sought to improve the lot of their people by addressing personal problems such as gambling, drinking, dancing, smoking, and illicit sex. The most important of the Black Holy Ghost churches was the Church of God in Christ, formed in 1895. Its larger portion later became Pentecostal. In 1982, the Church of God in Christ had 9,982 member congregations. For a time, it claimed a substantial number of white members. Two other Black Holy Ghost churches were the Pentecostal Assemblies of the World and the Fire-Baptized Holiness Church. Many who joined these African American churches were saying, in effect, "Father, give us power."

Both of these approaches to religion—holiness and Pentecostalism—had great appeal for the dispossessed of both races. They offered religious ecstasy, the pursuit of spiritual perfection, and often the healing of sicknesses. Many left the historic African American churches when congregations became more ritualistic and formal in order to satisfy the need of the African American middle class for restrained and "dignified" religion. (Many members of the African American upper middle class would in time leave Black churches to become Anglicans, Presbyterians, and Congregationalists.) African American migrants from the South often found northern African churches too formal and sought spiritual nourishment in the storefront churches of the holiness and Pentecostal people. African Americans played central roles in the great charismatic revival of the early twentieth century. Indeed, they often guided whites in opening to the Spirit and acquiring its second blessing. Some white Pentecostal denominations have their roots in interracial Pentecostal experiences.

Today, there are about 6 million African American Pentecostals. Of late, a few of them have become involved in what has been called High-Church Pentecostalism. They use chalices, vestments, and borrow other features from the Episcopalians and Catholics. Their bishops sometimes wear garb very similar to that of Roman Catholic prelates. Their leaders indicate that their priestly garments have African origins, noting that the book of Exodus discusses the color of garments. They recite the Nicene Creed and sometimes use Catholic manuals in their services. Though using some high-church practices, they continue to permit women to preach. The three small denominations that embrace high-church practices are the United Pentecostal Churches of Christ, the Pilgrim Assemblies International, and the Full Gospel Baptist Church Fellowship.

While the churches were dominated by the African American middle class, the smaller faith communities or sects appealed more to poor African Americans. In these social and religious communities there was an intense sense of solidarity. Members saw themselves as a unique, frequently despised people. Special efforts were made to welcome the poor and "outcasts" because creating a haven for poor Blacks was at the core of their reason for being. Then as now, creed is more important than membership, and a member can be forgiven any sin. Older members have a special status and can refer to others, even the pastor, as "boy" or "girl." The possession of wealth threatens cohesiveness, as the upwardly mobile frequently distance themselves from these communities. The faith community demands total commitment on the part of its members to its values and organized activities. More than merely a church, it is a small community that gives each member a social niche and a variety of wholesome social relationships. Its members may be "deprived" in the sense of having few of this world's goods, but they enjoy the riches of a full life in a supportive community.

The uneducated holiness and Pentecostal exhorters set off the creation of many African American spirituals. These people were wise in the ways of the world, having much experience in ghetto or rural African American life. Some had been criminals. Often they had been or still were singers or jazz musicians. They could speak with authority to the prostitute, the gambler, the robber, the murderer, or the adulterer. Frequently they put their words to music. This music combined the blues, jazz, traditional African American music, and often urban themes. The urban slum with its desperation, depersonalization, vices, and statuslessness was fertile soil for holiness and Pentecostal religion and for a new form of gospel music. Socioeconomic forces all but imprisoned many African Americans in the ghettos, preventing them from moving away from holiness and Pentecostal religions. They have evolved out of what one could call a sect stage to become churches, but have not outgrown their theological radicalism. They still address the needs of the poor and oppressed, but the salvation of these people involves more than religion; it awaits a changed society.

Within the ranks of African American Pentecostals, women sometimes have the opportunity to function as ministers. However, it is likely that they would be called "teachers," while males doing the same things are called "ministers." In some churches there is a dual hierarchy, an arrangement whereby the female leaders are not subject to orders from the men. Nevertheless, few ministers in the Church of God in Christ favor women's ordination. On the other hand, 90 percent of the ministers in the African Methodist

Episcopal Church favor women's ordination. Perhaps the superior education of the latter and their greater exposure to professional women account for the difference.

The accomplishments of African American churches were remarkable. Before the Civil War, the percentage of churched Blacks was half that of whites in the South. By World War I, there were proportionately more Black than white church members there. Despite great poverty and other grievous hardships, African Americans managed to organize congregations, erect humble buildings as symbols of faith, and engage in self-help activity. These communities of faith provided solace and fellowship to those who struggled to exist in a hostile nation. African American churches also made possible the maintenance of an independent cultural and social life. They were the first institutions completely owned by African Americans. Through control of the churches African Americans gave expression to and perpetuated their culture. Individuals who, due to racism, might otherwise have been completely beaten in life had an opportunity to express themselves, show leadership, and be esteemed by others as deacons, financial board members, choir members, Sunday school teachers, or missionary society members.

Black churches were community centers as well as places of worship. They often took the place of theater, dance hall, and other places of commercial recreation where African Americans were not welcome. Churches often offered many debates, plays, recitals, lectures, and suppers. In the South, the African American churches were the centers of social and community life, and they have enjoyed high attendance rates.

African American clergy, though modestly educated, possessed great power in a Black community with few other professionals. The churches provided leadership in economic cooperation and opportunities for the continual development of African American culture. Their periodicals helped knit together the community and served as outlets for talented writers.

Black clergy have sometimes been criticized for a degree of anti-intellectualism, but it was necessary that they focus on the immediate and the practical. One wonders to what degree anti-intellectualism mirrored the condition of many southern white clergy. African American clergymen have been criticized for pursuing accommodationist policies and urging acceptance of present difficulties in order to win a greater reward in the next life. A few, such as AME bishops Henry Turner and Jabez P. Campbell, rejected this role and denounced white hypocrisy. Turner thought return to Africa was the best course for his people; their only other choice was to "get ready for extermination."

Yet the counsel of Christian resignation had scriptural roots. One wonders what a more assertive, activist course could have accomplished in an age when Jim Crow segregation was the rule and church burnings and lynchings not uncommon. Moreover, southern white churches provided no model of social activism for Black clergy to emulate. Despite heavy burdens laid upon their people, these men taught forgiveness, repentance, and ultimate deliverance. Though generally lacking the theological training of most white clergy, these Black preachers understood more about basic Christianity than did many white ministers and laymen. They often focused on human rights and the dignity of all men. The quarrels between modernists and fundamentalists of the twentieth century did not interest them, and some were touched by the emergence of neoevangelicalism that has occurred since the 1940s. The theological debates among whites had too much to do with words and abstractions; the African American's religious concerns were more in touch with reality and substantive concerns. Yearning for liberation, they saw that doctrinal correctness was much less important than correct practice.

The African American church played a central role in interpreting Western, Enlightenment thought and Christian thought and culture for African Americans. It was necessary for African American clergy, whose lives were fully rooted in the experience of their people, to interpret Enlightenment ideas for their people by employing models based on both suspicion and hope. They identified the racist elements of this thought while finding features that were liberating and genuinely progressive. Similarly, they criticized racists' misuses of the story of Ham, the Tower of Babel, and house codes in 1 Peter, while exulting in the true message of Christian scriptures.

Black philosopher Cornel West has borrowed the term "organic intellectuals" to describe the holistic approach to learning represented by the clergy and some African American intellectuals. Life in the neighborhood kept the preacher-scholars in touch with Black realities and concerns. Their hermeneutics, or interpretive principles, were based on suspicion and hope, and were populist in the best sense of the term. This approach is best exemplified by the sermons of Reverend Dr. Martin Luther King, Jr., who drew a parallel between the African American people and the Jewish people in their journeys to the promised land. He urged his people to follow the examples of Amos and Jesus in acting on their own behalf. The hermeneutics of hope and suspicion is also found in the Nation of Islam.

Marcus Garvey

After the passing of Bishop Turner in 1915, the mainline African American churches seemed less inclined to boldly demand respect for the rights of their people. The leadership and congregations were often concerned with pursuing middle-class respectability. There were always more than a few African American preachers willing to denounce injustice. In the early 1920s, the Universal Negro Improvement Association (UNIA) claimed half a million African American members. It was founded by a pan-Africanist and layman, Marcus Garvey, who taught that Jesus was a Black man. He urged talented African Americans to return to Africa to help improve societies there. He instilled in the organization's members pride in being Black, and he publicized African American achievement. His most determined opponents were upper-middle-class African Americans who feared that his activities would bring derision and slow assimilation to the race.

The UNIA emphasized education, religiosity, and self-help, and had several economic ventures. In a case involving one of those enterprises, Garvey was sent to federal prison in 1923. It has been argued that he was railroaded by federal authorities.

The African Orthodox Church was connected to the UNIA. Garvey lieutenant and Episcopal priest George Alexander McGuire was consecrated bishop by a Syrian Orthodox archbishop. Bishop McGuire told his people to forget about white gods and return to their African roots to come in contact with the true God, who was Black. Despite McGuire's wishes, Garvey made it clear that membership in the UNIA did not require membership in the African Orthodox Church. Clergy members of the UNIA performed a valuable service for the African American churches in reminding their clergy that their mission extended beyond leading flocks to eternal salvation; it was necessary to assist people in improving their economic situations. One minister said it was necessary to arouse the African American people "to holy unrest" with their spiritual leaders. At Liberty Hall in Harlem in 1923, Garveyite Baptist minister William Henry Moses told the crowd that it was a good sign that people were denouncing preachers who avoided controversy; he stated that those rendering the criticism had heard the truth.

Migration North

African Americans migrated to the North in vast numbers during the twentieth century. There was a great movement from rural areas to cities, both in the North and South. These migrants were attracted by industrial jobs and better living conditions. During the Great Depression, many moved because northern states offered greater assistance to the poor and unemployed. Many people lost contact with religious communities as a result of their migration. A million African American migrants moved north in the 1950s; by 1965, about half of the nation's African Americans lived in northern cities. There they faced de facto segregation of schools, segregated neighborhoods, frequent unemployment, and deplorable living conditions in urban slums. Filled with residents overwhelmed by anger, frustration, and unfulfilled expectations, many northern ghettos in the 1960s erupted in fiery riots, during which substantial parts of their own neighborhoods were destroyed. The worst of these riots occurred in the Watts district of Los Angeles in 1965, and in Detroit and Newark in 1967.

Martin Luther King, Jr.

Despite the occasional caution of its leaders, a large portion of African American Christianity strongly resisted racial prejudice and segregation. Usually led by clergy, they stood as prophetic witnesses insisting that a Christianity that condones or coexists with slavery or racism stands as an enormous distortion of true Christianity. As in the case of largely Caucasian churches, internal politics and rivalries sometimes prevented African American Christian churches from taking a united position in support of the civil rights movement led by Reverend Martin Luther King, Jr. Angered by King's criticisms of his accommodationism and leadership style, Reverend Joseph Jackson of Chicago, head of the seven-million-member National Baptist Convention, USA, denounced King and the movement.

Jackson called for a much more gradualist approach to improving the lot of African Americans and emphasized efforts to develop their own communities and resources. Jackson was an ally of Chicago mayor Richard Daley, one of the last major machine politicians. In 1961, forces supportive of the movement almost succeeded in unseating Jackson; they would form the Progressive National Baptist Convention.

The civil rights movement had widespread support in other African American denominations. Suffering came to be seen by many African American leaders as redemptive. Martin Luther King, Jr., the young Baptist preacher who came to lead the civil rights movement of the 1960s, taught this lesson through his life, in which he was incarcerated many times, faced many dangers, and was finally murdered. King based his approach to the civil rights movement on the gospel and belief in nonviolence, a philosophy he absorbed by studying the works of Thoreau, Tolstoy, and Gandhi. From the great Protestant theologian Reinhold Niebuhr, he learned that men of God had often made the mistake of trusting reason over faith and that evil was pervasive—a grim, stark reality. Trusting in the power of the gospel, he acknowledged that he had repeatedly made the mistake of expecting too much support from white clergy.

Some might mark the beginning of the movement in December 1955, when African Americans began to boycott buses in Montgomery, Alabama. Dr. King, a beginning pastor, felt called by God to play a leading role in the movement. He said it was as if God were saying to him: "Martin Luther, stand up for righteousness. Stand up for justice. Stand up for the truth. And lo I will be with you, even unto the end of the world." King was a prophet of peaceful resistance who looked forward to an integrated America where all people would enjoy the same rights. He opposed Black separatism and clung to the belief that the American dream could be realized by all. Speaking in Greenwood, Mississippi, King addressed the question of force and insisted that the power of human souls was far greater than that of guns, bombs, and armies. Young African American members of the Student Nonviolent Coordinating Committee stood in the rear of King's church audience and hooted derisively, "Oh, de *Lawd*, de *Lawd*, now!" They had come to doubt the initial philosophy of their own organization, and had found the arguments of Malcolm X, another African American leader, very persuasive.

As leader of the movement King's life would be repeatedly threatened, and he would spend many days in southern jails, places where African Americans had often been beaten and sometimes killed. King founded the Southern Christian Leadership Conference, which would be dedicated to nonviolence and integration. He insisted that human possibilities and values and socioeconomic uplift for all must be given priority over "getting and spending." King insisted that all people were their neighbors' keepers and that all are interdependent under the "Fatherhood of God and the Brotherhood of Man." King's courage and his appeal to essential Christianity led many white Christians to rally to his side. Civil rights marches became redemptive experiences as thousands of rabbis, white Christian laymen, ministers, priests, and nuns joined King in what could be called applied Christianity. On August 28, 1963, with the Lincoln Memorial as backdrop, King gave his famous "I have a dream" speech to the thousands who had come for the March on Washington. Other clergy who spoke to the crowd that day included an Episcopal bishop, the Catholic archbishop of Washington, and the Stated Clerk of the United Presbyterian Church.

The passage of the Civil Rights Act of 1964 and the Voting Rights Act of 1965 were among the achievements of the movement, though they cannot be attributed to one man, extraordinary leader that King was. Dr. King was slain in Memphis, Tennessee, on April 4, 1968. Though some have suggested that the time has come for secular leadership of the movement, leadership has remained in the hands of a number of highly effective clergymen, the most notable of whom was Reverend Jesse Jackson, a major contender for the 1988 Democratic presidential nomination. The liberating message of Dr. King has been fully developed by a number of African

American theologians, the most significant of whom was James H. Cone. Another spokesman for "Black theology" is Cornel West, who influenced Cone's thought when they were colleagues at Union Theological Seminary. The root of their thought is that African American clergy should forge a strong link to Christ by identifying completely with the poor rather than through denominational organizations. By the time of King's murder, many African Americans, especially the young, had turned away from his message of nonviolence. They believed African Americans were being asked to bear too much suffering in order to win white support.

National Black Evangelical Association

African American evangelicals formed the National Black Evangelical Association (NBEA) in 1963, with Reverend William H. Bentley of Chicago as its first president. At its 1975 convention, the NBEA emphasized pan-Africanism, social action projects, counseling at the street level, and assistance for African American youth. There has been a lively debate within the NBEA over whether it should develop a theology rooted in the African American experience. Critics of experiential theology worried that a clash between the Bible and Blackness could end in reducing the importance of Scripture. By 1980, the "theology-culture rift" led three conservative board members to offer their resignations. Some called for a statement endorsing inerrancy. Those calling for an experiential theology, rooted in the praxis of the African American people, were led by former president Bentley, as well as Cone, probably the most important scholar involved in this debate.

In *Black Theology and Black Power* (1969), Cone argued persuasively that integration involves accepting the white man's definition of African Americans; it involves admitting to inferiority. African Americans, he believed, must come to prize their Blackness. Cone asserted that integration cannot come about until whites can honestly affirm the beauty of Blackness, and that reconciliation is an impossibility until every African American has been liberated from racism and oppression. Black theology, he noted further, is a revolutionary body of thought devoted to the unity of Black people struggling to end racism.

Islam and Malcolm X

Another major expression of African American religiosity, African American Islam, would emerge in northern cities. Wallace D. Fard and Elijah Poole founded the Nation of Islam in 1931. Fard appeared in Detroit in 1930 as an Arab peddler. To be known to followers as "Honorable Master

Fard Muhammad," he gathered and instructed a number of followers, Fard disappearing four years later. Poole became the movement's sole leader using the name Elijah Muhammad, "Spiritual Leader of the Lost-Found Nation in the West." Elijah Muhammad later taught that Fard, his master, was Allah himself. After Elijah's death, his son Wallace D. Muhammad also insisted that Fard was Allah but added that he spoke to Fard on the telephone rather than through prayer.

The Nation of Islam taught that Allah created the earth 63 trillion years ago in a big bang. The first man he created was Black, who was good and beautiful. An evil "big head scientist" named Yakub bred inferior beings who were lighter and lighter, until whites emerged. They were a weaker and vicious hybrid. Blacks were superior to whites in all respects, but were conspired against by whites in league with the devil for six thousand years. The Bible was a "poison book" and "the graveyard of my people." Whites used Christianity to subdue and enslave Blacks. Allah ordered Elijah Muhammad to lead the "Lost-Found Nation of Islam" out of its difficulties.

Elijah Muhammad called upon his people to avoid whites in all ways, but the whites employed the prospect of integration in order to prevent African Americans from realizing their full potential. The time would come when Allah would entrust the governance of the world to African Americans. Muhammad wanted one to five states for African Americans; his chief follower, Malcolm X, called for nine or ten. Elijah Muhammad's teachings are contained in *The Supreme Wisdom: Solution to the So-Called Negroes' Problem.* The Muslims sponsored weekly radio programs and published magazines and tabloids. Guards in dark suits constituted the movement's militia, the Fruit of Islam.

Some Black intellectuals were attracted to Islam in the 1960s, but the vast majority saw it as a threat to long-term aspirations. Speaking at Princeton, Thurgood Marshall, a famous Black lawyer and later associate justice of the U.S. Supreme Court, stated that the Muslims were "run by a bunch of thugs organized from prisons and jails, and financed, I am sure, by Nasser or some Arab group." The Nation of Islam drew heavily from the poor and marginalized. It promised salvation only by separation from the "white devils" and acknowledged that nothing in the previous religious lives of converts was worthwhile.

Criminals and drug addicts often have embraced the Nation of Islam because it has helped them shed their bad habits and avoid lawbreaking. The Nation of Islam explained that white racism was responsible for their problems, and soon became a major force among the nation's prison population. It offered prisoners a way to change their lives through rigid standards for personal living and morality. Islam instilled great pride in being

Black. Its earliest members were recent migrants from the South, and it attracted more male members than female members. The movement's greatest attractions have been its emphasis on African American self-awareness and passion for solidarity. In becoming a Muslim, a person changes completely, embracing a new homeland, a new family, and new values. He or she is no longer a Negro, trying to live the life whites have assigned, but a Black person, and as such partly divine and a natural leader, a ruler of the world.

The movement grew slowly, centered mainly in Detroit and Chicago. Rapid growth occurred after the airing of a television program about the movement reported by Mike Wallace. Whites were alarmed by what they saw and accused the Black Muslims of being racists, wondering aloud whether communists were behind the movement. African Americans in the ghettos came to the movement in large numbers, eventually in the hundreds of thousands.

Elijah Muhammad's chief assistant was Malcolm X, who led Temple 10 in New York City. Malcolm, formerly Malcolm Little, grew up near Lansing, Michigan. His father, Earl Little, was involved in Marcus Garvey's Universal Negro Improvement Association, and he took young Malcolm to Garveyite meetings. Little died after being run over by a streetcar; Malcolm later insisted his father had been murdered by white racists. This conclusion was based in part on his belief that Klansmen had torched their home in Omaha. Malcolm became a pimp and street hustler, and spent time in prison where he read widely and was converted to the Nation of Islam. He changed his name to Malcolm X, as Black Muslims do not wish to retain the surname of the masters of their ancestors (Figure 7).

Malcolm was a powerful and cogent speaker and attracted many converts, among them the heavyweight boxer Cassius Clay, who took the Islamic name Muhammad Ali. While Elijah Muhammad taught passive rejection of white racism, Malcolm X thought some self-assertion should be involved in the rejection. He ridiculed King's doctrines of nonviolence and love for white neighbors, stating that only fools "could love someone who has treated them as the white man has treated you." He felt this type of militancy would help members grow in self-respect. Malcolm's enigmatic comment about chickens coming home to roost in reference to the assassination of John F. Kennedy led to a period of imposed silence. When it expired, he broke with the Nation of Islam, stating his disapproval of Elijah Muhammad's personal life. Malcolm took a new name, el-Hajj Malik el-Shabazz, a name he first used when touring Egypt in 1959. He was to back away from blanket indictments of all whites, although he continued to disagree with the views of Martin Luther King. While King called for nonresistance and integration, Malcolm would not abandon the right of

Figure 7. Malcolm X. Malcolm X (1925–1965) was the leading spokesman for the Nation of Islam but eventually broke with that organization to found the Organization of Afro-American Unity. A revolutionary, persuasive speaker, and a man of intelligence and character, he infused other blacks with pride and militancy. (Courtesy the Library of Congress.)

self-defense, and he espoused separatism. He also advocated a form of Black power that alarmed whites. His philosophy of Black nationalism called for African Americans to control the politicians and politics of their communities, and served notice that African American communities would no longer take orders from white outsiders.

Malcolm X traveled to Africa twice, interacted with some New York City Trotskyite intellectuals, and came to see the African Americans' fight for freedom as part of a worldwide movement in which the oppressed confront their oppressors. He was able to see the possibility that some kind of integration might exist in the distant future, and he was not opposed to allying with oppressed whites if they ceased to act like racists. Commenting on his altered view of whites, he admitted that he had been wrong in hurling sweeping indictments against all of them; he saw this as no different than whites making blanket indictments of all African Americans. He believed that the Nation of Islam would bring about his death. Malcolm X was assassinated on February 21, 1965, while speaking in a Harlem ballroom. Three young members of the Nation of Islam were convicted for the murder. Many of Malcolm's followers in his Organization for Afro-American Unity insisted that this explanation was too convenient, suggesting that the FBI had reason to be rid of Malcolm.

The Autobiography of Malcolm X appeared shortly after his death. It would be embraced by young African Americans who had grown impatient with Martin Luther King's reliance on nonviolence and passive resistance. While King would be viewed as one of the nation's greatest leaders, Malcolm X would be ranked with him as one of the civil rights movement's two great African American leaders.

Elijah Muhammad died in 1975, and most of his followers became orthodox Sunni Muslims. Wallace Muhammad, son of Elijah, encouraged followers to venerate the memory of Malcolm, and the Harlem mosque was renamed in his honor. About twenty thousand remain in the Nation of Islam under the leadership of Louis Farrakhan, organizer of the 1995 "Million Man March" in Washington, an effort to inspire African American males to be effective parents and role models.

The Black Messiah

In Detroit, Reverend Albert B. Cleage, Jr., created the Shrine of the Black Madonna. He realized that a cult demanding that African Americans separate from Christianity and embrace Islam would never be an effective instrument for improving the situation of African Americans. He saw more promise in a marriage between African American separatism and a Christianity that worshiped a Black Messiah. He preached that Jesus was a Black revolutionary—a Zealot—who sought to liberate the Black nation; his essential ideas appeared in *The Black Messiah* in 1968. He believed that African Americans had to shed the chains of self-hate before they could worship a Black Messiah. Worshiping a Black Messiah meant they now would be able to look back in time beyond enslavement to their African heritage with great pride and courage. He also taught that Israel was a Black nation in biblical times. Cleage, a former United Church of Christ minister, has not had great success in building the Black Christian Nationalist Movement.

Other Cults

There have been a number of other African American cults; among the most interesting are those of Father Divine, Sweet Daddy Grace, and several groups of Black Jews. Father Divine began life in Georgia as George Baker. He lived in great poverty and studied a number of cults and noted that they raised people's hopes and then disappointed them. For a time he was the messenger for a cultist named "Father Jehovah," who called himself Father Eternal. Baker was a mystic teacher, spiritualist, and a Pentecostalist. In his native state he was tried for insanity and forced to leave. In New York City, he saw many cults and puzzled over what he could do to improve the condition of downtrodden African Americans. In Brooklyn he changed his name to Major J. Divine and set up a religious community. Seeking a greater opportunity to experiment and think, he and his wife purchased a home in Sayville on Long Island and established his Peace Mission there in 1919. He gained a reputation as a man of great wisdom and as an effective employment agent. Many flocked there for free chicken dinners and to be in his presence. By the end of the twenties, there were also white followers.

It was claimed that Divine healed people of physical infirmities as well as sinful ways of life. He reformed criminals, drug addicts, and prostitutes. He demanded brotherhood, peace, and purity in thoughts and actions. Racism was forbidden and followers were not permitted to utter the words "white" or "Negro." Lust, dancing, copulation, and marriage were also forbidden because they would only increase suffering in the world. He worked to reduce racial tensions and helped elect reformer Fiorello La Guardia to the office of mayor. In 1931, he moved back to Harlem, where he was later brought to trial as a public nuisance. The death of a prejudiced judge was seen as a demonstration of Father Divine's power. The guilty verdict was overturned upon appeal. Divine urged African Americans to improve their condition through self-help and founded a number of economic cooperatives. He viewed his movement as efforts to feed, clothe, and provide jobs and shelter for his followers. He supported private property and urged his followers to emulate people like Henry Ford, yet he briefly flirted with communism. In 1936, he helped establish the All People's Party in Harlem; among its candidates for office were Vito Marcantonio, a white communist, and Angelo Herndon, a Black labor organizer and communist.

Divine never claimed to be a god, but his followers wanted a heaven on earth and were certain he was god, a belief he did not dispute. Divine lived surrounded by great wealth and elaborate ritual. Twenty-five secretaries noted his every comment and action. His followers believed that association with him produced physical health, prosperity, and peace. In 1941, he moved to Philadelphia but there continued to be a "heaven" in Harlem. He died in 1965, leaving branches of his movement in northern and western cities and on farms in New York state. Mother Divine, his widow, took up leadership of the movement. It is impossible to estimate the number of his followers. In this and other African American cults, great stress is placed on African American consciousness. The charismatic leader is given wealth and power, things his followers desperately desire. The leader acts as their surrogate, and through him the faithful have some experience of wealth and power.

In this case and in the religion of Daddy Grace, the prophet-messiah becomes a god who rules over his own world. As in the African American churches, the central focus is upon creating an ethos that enables Blacks to live in dignity, self-respect, and integrity. It provides them with the belief that they possess power and are able to take control of their own lives. Other religions do the same things for whites. The differences between African American churches, sects, and cults are class orientation and matters of degree.

Charles Emmanuel "Sweet Daddy" Grace probably came from the Azores or Portugal, was exposed to holiness and Pentecostal religion, and established the United House of Prayer for All People and made himself a bishop. Grace claimed he was white and insisted that salvation came from him. He claimed that he manifested the spirit of God, and some of his people saw him as god. Followers were expected to contribute their money and obey. They were also to purchase the products he sold that possessed healing power: stationery, facial creams, talcum powder, soap, cookies, coffee, tea, the *Grace Magazine,* and hair dressing. They were expected to genuflect and pray before his picture. Daddy Grace preached and visited congregations in twenty eastern cities and conducted very lively services, in which people danced ecstatically to spirited music. He was a master of pomp, orchestrated grand parades, and performed interesting ceremonies. Baptism could be done with a fire hose. He died in 1960 a rich man. There were 111 churches and missions at that time. The House of Prayer movement continued and a new headquarters and senior citizens' home were opened in Washington in 1969.

Additional churches were built and there is now a seminary in Virginia.

William S. Crowdy, a former cook, founded the Church of God and Saints of Christ, a group of Black Jews centered in Washington, D.C., and Belleville, Virginia. He claimed it had been revealed to him that African Americans are Jews, descendants of the lost tribe of Israel, and that the first Jews were Black. His followers use the Old and New Testaments and practice circumcision, baptism, foot washing, and the holy kiss. In Philadelphia, another group is called the Church of God; its prophet was F.S. Cherry. His followers believe that the first inhabitants of the planet were Black. They accept Christ but substitute the passover for communion, and do not observe Christmas or Easter. Members are forbidden to marry outside the cult. A third group was incorporated in Harlem in 1930. The Commandment Keepers of the Living God claim to be the descendants of King Solomon's union with the Queen of Sheba. They consider themselves Ethiopian Hebrews, not Negroes, and, following their leader Rabbi Wentworth A. Matthew, do not welcome the term "Black Jews." They keep kosher, and in most respects are similar to American Conservative Jews. Rabbi Matthew claims to possess an ancient Hebrew formula that enables him to raise the dead, heal illnesses, and transform enemies into friends.

The African American cults are evidence of a people that is seeking community and a solid basis for expression of its profound moral sense. They are also evidence of the anomie African Americans experience in a still hostile environment. Like holiness and Pentecostal sects, they point to a great desire to give fuller expression to historic African spirituality. A problem is that in their diversity they divide rather than unify the community.

The years since the Civil War have seen enormous growth in the number of African American denominations and places of worship. The explosion of Black Pentecostalism early in this century touched off a similar development among whites. Indeed, the history of white Pentecostal bodies can often be traced to Black churches. The African American church has served as the nucleus of African American culture and life in the United States. It has offered a safe haven in a society dominated by a different, and often hostile, culture. African religion provided support and reinforced self-esteem during the long reign of Jim Crow in the South, and it—particularly through Black Pentecostalism—provided Black migrants to northern cities with spiritual homes. Like their shackled ancestors, post–Civil War African American Christians saw themselves as a saved, chosen people, not because they had suffered or were black but because their lives and history seemed to reflect the salvation story found in the Bible.

In broad terms, the debate between Booker T. Washington and W.E.B. Du Bois continues in the churches. Most small Black Pentecostal denominations, as well as many Black Baptists, concentrate on self-help at the individual and community level and usually avoid direct involvement in politics.

Others actively pursue civil and human rights objectives through involvement in the political process. The separatism prescribed by Marcus Garvey and his African Orthodox Church is today most forcefully advocated by Black Islamic clergymen, particularly Louis Farrakhan. Clergymen remain spokesmen for African American communities, even though some Black intellectuals and academicians challenge their continued leadership. Though the place of religion in the lives of many whites has diminished, African American religion remains vigorous and plays a central role in the lives of most Blacks.

Bibliography

Banks, Adelle. "Pentecostals Dress Like Catholic Bishops: High-Church Group Says Garb Is Linked to Its African Heritage." *National Catholic Reporter* 31 (February 24, 1995): 3.

Banks, Samuel L. "Dr. Martin Luther King, Jr., Remembered: The Fractured Dream." *Journal of Negro History* 67 (fall 1982): 195–197.

Branch, Taylor. *Parting the Waters: America in the King Years, 1954–63.* New York: Simon and Schuster, 1988.

Butler, Alfoyd. *The Africanization of American Christianity.* New York: Carlton Press, 1980.

Davis, Cyprian. *The History of Black Catholics in the United States.* New York: Crossroad, 1990.

Farley, Ena L. "Methodists and Baptists on the Issue of Black Equality in New York, 1865–1868." *Journal of Negro History* 61 (October 1976): 374–392.

Garrow, David J. *Bearing the Cross: Martin Luther King, Jr., and the Southern Christian Leadership Conference.* New York: William Morrow, 1986.

Grundman, Adolph H. "Northern Baptists and the Founding of Virginia Union University: The Perils of Paternalism." *Journal of Negro History* 63 (January 1978): 26–41.

Hackett, David G. "Gender and Religion in American Culture, 1870–1930." *Religion and American Culture* 5 (summer 1995): 127–157.

Haley, Alex. *The Autobiography of Malcolm X As Told to Alex Haley.* New York: Ballantine Books, 1992.

Harris, Robert L., Jr. "Coming of Age: The Transformation of Afro-American Historiography." *Journal of Negro History* 67 (Summer 1982): 107–121.

Jaffe, James. *The American Jews.* New York: Random House, 1968.

Lackner, Joseph H. "The Foundation of St. Ann's Parish, 1866–1870: The African American Experience in Cincinnati." *U.S. Catholic Historian* 44 (spring 1996): 13–36.

Lincoln, Carl Eric. *The Black Muslims in America.* Boston: Beacon Press, 1961.

Luker, Ralph E. "Missions, Institutional Churches, and Settlement Houses: The Black Experience, 1885–1910." *Journal of Negro History* 69 (summer–fall 1984): 101–113.

Mays, Benjamin E., and Joseph William Nicholson. *The Negro's Church.* New York: Russell and Russell, 1969.

Nelsen, Hart M., Raytha L. Yokley, and Anne K. Nelsen. *The Black Church in America.* New York: Basic Books, 1971.

Paris, Arthur E. *Black Pentecostalism: Southern Religion in an Urban World.* Amherst: University of Massachusetts Press, 1992.

Raboteau, Albert J. *A Fire in the Bones: Reflections on African American Religious History.* Boston: Beacon Press, 1995.

Reid, Stephen Beck. "Endangered Reading: The African American Scholar Between Text and People." *Cross Currents* 44 (winter 1994–95): 476–487.

Rosenberg, Ellen M. *The Southern Baptist: A Subculture in Transition.* Knoxville: University of Tennessee Press, 1989.

Stump, Roger W. "Regional Contrasts Within Black Protestantism: A Research Note." *Social Forces* 66 (September 1987): 143–151.

Washington, Joseph R., Jr. *Black Sects and Cults.* Lanham, MD: University Press of America, 1984.

West, Cornel. *Prophesy Deliverance: An Afro-American Revolutionary Christianity.* Philadelphia: Westminster, 1982.

Williams, Melvin D. *Community in a Black Pentecostal Church: An Anthropological Study.* Prospect Heights, IL: Waveland Press, 1974.

Wyatt-Brown, Bertram. *Honor and Violence in the Old South.* New York: Oxford University Press, 1986.

Eight

Beyond the Mainstream: Immigrants, Nativism, and Cultural Conflict

During the nineteenth century, Americans prided themselves upon their willingness to welcome people possessing quite dissimilar cultures. Yet many who boasted of this willingness to accept people from other lands also expected the newcomers to quickly shed their cultural peculiarities and live like the majority of Protestant Americans. Those who persisted in retaining cultural patterns that differed significantly from the norm were often the victims of prejudice, discrimination, and sometimes nativist violence. In addition to this external pressure, there was the natural desire of many among the cultural minorities to accommodate as much as possible to the ways of their adopted land. Among German Lutherans, who suffered little from nativism, there was a continuing debate over the extent to which they should become like evangelical, Anglo-Saxon Protestants. Within the early American Catholic Church, there was conflict over assimilation between Anglo-Saxon Catholics and their French allies, on the one hand, and the Irish newcomers, on the other. In the late nineteenth century, the Catholic Church, the largest Christian denomination in the United States, would be disturbed by serious disagreements between conservatives and Americanizers. While debating its role in the United States, the Roman Church continued the enormous task of meeting spiritual and other needs of tens and sometimes hundreds of thousands of new Catholic immigrants who arrived from many different lands each year.

Immigration was a major force in nineteenth-century American history and fueled religious conflict. It was not until the late eighteenth century that the word "immigrant" existed in the English language. In the broadest sense it was meant to distinguish bearers of foreign culture from original inhabitants—meaning those who arrived in the United States before 1790. In a cultural if not a statistical sense, the word "immigrant" included all children of immigrants. According to national mythology, the United States is a melting pot, which assumes that assimilation happens quickly here. Assimilation can be considered to take place on two levels. On a cultural level, it involves learning the language, developing a loyalty to the nation and its basic institutions, and accepting certain values such as the American success ethic. More essential is structural assimilation. This takes place when other Americans cease to consider the person of foreign extraction a bearer of foreign culture, and the immigrant and his descendants no longer think of themselves as members of a distinctive group.

In the years between 1815 and 1914, 50 million people left Europe; 35 million came to the United States. The Irish and Germans dominated the first waves of immigration. British, Scots-Irish, Scots, and some Germans quickly achieved both levels of assimilation. Others, particularly the Irish, did not pass both tests by the late nineteenth century. After 1880, a new and much larger wave of immigrants came to the United States. These "new immigrants" were from southern and eastern Europe. They would face more serious problems than did earlier immigrants in their efforts to become a part of American life. Their cultural backgrounds differed sharply from those of original Americans. A large majority of the new immigrants were Roman Catholics, and many others were either Eastern Orthodox or Jewish. Between 1880 and 1910, 1.5 million Jews—mostly Orthodox—settled in the United States. Few observers of American society would maintain that structural assimilation had taken place for the new immigrants.

Daniel Patrick Moynihan and Nathan Glazer noted in *Beyond the Melting Pot* that the melting pot simply "did not happen." Not only did immigrants bring different languages and often strange cultures to America, they usually settled together in cities and lived in crowded, unsanitary, crime-ridden neighborhoods. To old-stock Americans, these newcomers brought crime and vice to America. They took the jobs native Americans did not want— the unskilled, monotonous, low-paying jobs in industry, both in the city and in rural areas. Their presence and the ethnocentrism of old-stock Americans, as well as lingering misgivings about urbanization and the development of impersonal, massive industries that mostly relied on unskilled labor, provoked "a crisis in the whole American social order."

Many Protestants were not nativists but were friendly to Catholics and Jews. Some native Catholics were very critical of immigrant Catholics. Likewise, when desperately poor Eastern European Jews arrived in the late nineteenth century, the established American Jewish community did not always welcome them. Sometimes the Roman Church behaved in a manner that invited hostility. Priests who got along with Protestants were called "Protestant priests" by New York archbishop John Hughes. All too often, some Catholic spokesmen suggested that American culture was inferior to European culture. German Catholics seem to have been the greatest offenders in this respect. Protestants were understandably put off by the suggestion that the Roman Catholic Church was the one true church, and were offended by the singing, dancing, and drinking that characterized the "continental Sunday" the immigrants brought from Europe. Within the ranks of both Jews and Roman Catholics there was sometimes a spirited debate over Americanization. Members of both religious groups suffered discrimination and prejudice, particularly when the nation was passing through difficult years.

Judaism

Immigration swelled the ranks of the American Jewish population; by the end of the century Judaism was by any measure one of America's major religious bodies. By 1880, there were 250,000 Jews in the country, the vast majority of whom were German Jews who were culturally assimilated with relative ease. Many of the rabbis and laymen brought from Germany the spirit of Reform Judaism. Influenced by the rationalism of the Enlightenment and the higher biblical criticism of the nineteenth century, they moved to strip their faith of anachronistic elements that they thought were no longer justified. Hoping to westernize Judaism and make it compatible with the modern world, they saw no reason for the preservation of its ethnic dimension and defined the faith in universalistic terms. In Germany, middle-class Jews hoped that these moves would solidify their status and bring about their acceptance as full-fledged Germans. As Ashkenazic Jews climbed the occupational ladder in the United States, they had similar motives for making Judaic worship somewhat similar to Protestant worship.

The leader of these reforming rabbis was Isaac Mayer Wise, who came from Bohemia in 1846. He permitted men and women to sit together during worship, eliminated some prayers he considered no longer relevant, and used a choir and organ. Wise denounced Jews who played cards or did business on Sundays, and attempted to lead the congregation in applying biblical principles to everyday life. His efforts to reform the lives of his people led to a temporary division of his Albany congregation and his disownment by the conservatives. The division was healed, and Wise moved on to a congregation in Cincinnati in 1854. The Queen City on the Ohio River became the center of Reform Judaism in the United States, and the Hebrew Union College was founded there in 1876.

Some Jews, though not thoroughly Orthodox, were very uncomfortable with Reform practices and beliefs and looked for another means of expressing their Judaism. They eventually found spiritual home in the Conservative movement, whose evolution could be traced to the graduation of the first rabbis at Hebrew Union College in 1883, when the caterer at the graduation banquet mistakenly served shrimp as part of the first course. Subsequently, Conservative and Orthodox forces established a Jewish Theological Seminary Association in New York in 1885, but the new seminary barely managed to survive. Conservatives' numbers eventually increased substantially, especially when many of the children of Eastern European Jewish immigrants joined their ranks in the twentieth century.

Anti-Semitism

American Jews had long suffered some discrimination, even prior to the coming of the Eastern European Orthodox Jews. Jews in the early republic had not enjoyed full political rights, but gradually those barriers were removed. In many places it was common practice to provide Christian religious instruction in public schools, a practice Jews thought illegal. Sunday blue laws in many states obviously worked to the disadvantage of those who observed the Sabbath on Saturday and kept their shops open on Sunday.

The late 1870s saw a rise in anti-Semitism that continued well into the twentieth century. The presence of Eastern European Jews does not alone account for its increase in the late seventies, but its persistence and growth can be partly attributed to gentile fears of these newcomers. Some Eastern European Jews were socialists or anarchists. Gentiles tended to exaggerate the extent of political radicalism among Jews as well as to have contempt for their different ways. Another major factor may have been that many were jealous of the accomplishments of German Jews, who had come earlier in the century. It was at this time that many adopted a stereotypical view of Jews as pushy parvenus who conspicuously consumed the world's goods in a lavish manner. They were depicted as wearing glasses, shabby trousers, and unattractive black coats. Sometimes the stereotype was altered to include dressing in a garish manner. The stereotypical Jew spoke broken German and English.

The Gilded Age in the late nineteenth century was a time when almost all ethnic groups had more than their share of rude parvenus; frequently others projected their insecurities onto the Jews. In 1877, the Grand Union Hotel in Saratoga refused to serve Jews. Hotel management claimed that its business was suffering because gentiles objected to the fact that it was patronized by Jews. It has been said that the hotel posted signs saying "No Jews or Dogs Admitted Here." Other resort hotels would soon follow this policy of discrimination. In the same year, the New York Bar Association refused to admit a Jew; a year later a City College fraternity did the same thing. Some hotels, resorts, private clubs and schools, college fraternities, and professional groups were closed to Jews.

Anti-Semitic views often surfaced in connection with agrarian radicalism and became especially pronounced in the Populist movement of the 1890s. Most of the Populist leaders who showed signs of anti-Semitism had never actually known Jews and simply reflected a low-grade anti-Semitism that was found throughout America. Neither the Populist Party nor any other party or significant social movement relied upon anti-Semitism as a major tactic. By the end of the century, there were relatively few instances of anti-Jewish violence. Occurrences of discrimination were much more frequent.

To educate and affirm Jewish collegians in their Jewishness and to help them grow as practicing Jews, Rabbi Benjamin M. Frankel founded the Hillel Foundation at the University of Illinois in 1923. He soon persuaded B'nai B'rith to support Hillel, and it was planted on other campuses.

In 1917, there were 3.5 million Jews and nineteen hundred synagogues in the United States; American Jews had become a considerable segment of the national population. Jews had developed organizational skills to contribute to the improvement of society and safeguard their own interests. Early in the twentieth century, the American Jewish Committee emerged to represent Jewish concerns in the United States and abroad. It was elitist and exclusive in nature, not popularly elected. A small executive committee guided it, setting procedures and policies. The murder conviction of Leo Frank in Georgia, essentially because he was a Jew, led in 1913 to the foundation of B'nai B'rith's Anti-Defamation League as a means of combating prejudice and discrimination.

Anti-Semitism was sometimes denounced by non-Jews before World War I; after the war, these defenses became more frequent. In 1920 the Federal Council of Churches adopted a strong position against anti-Semitism and denounced such views as "so preposterous as to be unworthy of credence." A year later, a committee of 119 prominent Christians, including former presidents William Howard Taft and Woodrow Wilson, took a firm stand against anti-Semitism.

The revival of the Ku Klux Klan in the 1920s in the North as well as the South brought with it a revival of anti-Semitism. Several right-wing movements in the 1930s incorporated anti-Semitism in their programs. The most prominent anti-Semitic spokesman in that period was Father Charles Coughlin, whose radio addresses eventually blended anti-Semitism with anticommunism and inflationary economic policy, although his early pronouncements did not emphasize anti-Semitism. For a time Coughlin had an enormous radio following for his denunciations of Franklin Roosevelt and the New Deal and advocacy of inflationary monetary policies. He also ranted against communism, low wages, the lack of a secure means of supporting a family, Wall Street, monopolies, and concentrations of wealth. In

1936, he was a major backer of the Union Party, which ran William Lemke for president. He appeared to support Benito Mussolini's fascism and came to advance anti-Semitism, prompting his bishop to end his broadcasts in 1942.

Although popular for a time, Coughlin never reflected Catholic social thought. Concerned that some people would think he did, Cardinal Patrick J. Hayes of New York instructed Father Joseph Moody to write a booklet in which he demolished the anti-Semitic comments found in *Social Justice,* Coughlin's publication.

In the last two decades there has been a troubling tendency for anti-Semitism to appear in the rhetoric of some radical African American spokesmen, most notably minister Louis Farrakhan of the Nation of Islam. Overlooking the long-term commitment of Jews to African American rights, Farrakhan and others associate Jews with American capitalism and the economic exploitation of blacks.

Jewish Efforts at Assimilation

Just as it appeared that Reform Judaism would dominate American Judaism, a tide of Eastern European Jewish immigrants would add new strength to the forces of Orthodoxy, or traditional Judaism. Late-nineteenth-century Europe experienced a great increase in anti-Semitism, which was particularly vicious in Eastern Europe, with violent outbursts and pogroms against Jews in Austria and Russia. After the bloody outbreaks of 1881, Russia limited Jews to a Pale of Settlement, imposing a variety of onerous restrictions on them. Some Eastern European Jews had made their way to the United States before 1880 and established a number of synagogues, first in New York City, in 1852. The next great influx of these Jews began around 1881. A half million came by 1900; another 1,250,000 came by 1914. They spoke Yiddish, a medieval German dialect with Hebrew characters and some Hebrew words, were desperately poor, and clustered in northeastern cities. Unlike the German Jews who spread across the country, the new immigrants had no choice but to settle in East Coast cities, lacking money and marketable skills. They represented an entirely different and, critics thought, more primitive strain of Judaism than had been commonly observed in the United States.

Established American Jews felt threatened by these Yiddish-speaking coreligionists with their fierce devotion to Orthodoxy and often deep learning in the Talmud. Their presence, it was feared, would fuel anti-Semitism and threaten the respectability of Jews already here. American Jews at first rejected the newcomers. The *Milwaukee Zeitgeist,* a Jewish paper, called them "uncouth Asiatics." Many feared that American Christians would have a lower opinion of Israelites as a result of contact with Eastern European Jews.

Despite their disdain, the Americanized Jews soon organized efforts to uplift and assist their Yiddish-speaking brethren. Fearing in part that the newcomers would become burdens upon society, the older Jewish community established schools, orphanages, recreational facilities, hospitals, and homes for delinquents and unwed mothers. In the 1880s, American, British, and French Jewish philanthropists financed efforts to place Eastern European Jews in agricultural communities. This concept also had the support of a number of the new immigrants, including some intellectuals. Of the sixteen communities founded in that decade, only the Alliance community in New Jersey survived.

The new Jewish immigrants accepted this help and also established their own self-help organizations. In addition, they moved to assure the preservation of their own culture by establishing schools and Yiddish publications. Rabbi Kasriel Sarasohn, who fled Russia, founded the first Yiddish daily, *Yiddishe Tageblat* (Jewish Daily News). Though many other immigrant rabbis wanted their people to be socially isolated, Sarasohn opposed ghettoization. The paper had great influence and its opinions were widely discussed. Sarasohn was also active in establishing contacts with Reformed Jewish leaders, and was a founder of what became known as the Hebrew Immigrant Aid Society (Figure 8).

Resenting the condescending attitudes of American Jews, Orthodox Eastern European Jews established parallel hospitals and social agencies and organizations in an effort to limit the influence of American Jews. A number of schools operated after public school hours and offered in summary form the elements of a traditional Jewish education. In 1896, the first yeshiva, an Eastern European Jewish high school, was founded; it would eventually become part of the nucleus of Yeshiva University. All these activities on the part of the new Jews helped them move beyond culture shock and served as instruments of Americanization.

The well-assimilated Jews spent great amounts of money attempting to assist and uplift their Eastern European cousins. However, their benevolence took place within an American framework for understanding philanthropy and charity rather than the traditional Jewish approach. It mandated that charity was a social obligation and should be used for the benefit of the poor. Under the best conditions, the donor and recipient should not know one another. The philanthropy of American Jews directed toward new Jewish immigrants was intended to manage and uplift them, and was essentially an effort at social control. It smacked of the Gospel of Wealth: the recipient should become worthy of assistance, which the donor used to manipulate him for his own good. This is not to suggest that within other contexts Jewish philanthropy was not more altruistic and in keeping with Hebrew

Figure 8. Jewish Males at Prayer. This photograph of seven Jewish men and a boy at prayer was made in 1901. It was estimated that the Jewish population in the previous year was about 1,085,135. Of the approximately 200,000 children, somewhat less than half received much formal or informal religious instruction. Though passing on specific tenets was not easy, the rich Jewish ethical heritage was to flourish. (Courtesy the Library of Congress.)

tradition. This philanthropy was consistent with the essence of Judaism; it meant doing good for others.

Zionism

Zionism, the quest for a national homeland, became attractive to some American Jews partly as a response to anti-Semitism. Many Yiddish-speaking Jews became Zionists, asserting that Palestine should become the homeland for the world's Jews. Theodor Herzl, a secular Hungarian Jew and noted Vienna newspaper correspondent, was convinced by the Dreyfus case in France that European Jews needed a Jewish state in Palestine. His book *The Jewish State,* published in 1896, became the credo of the movement. A year later, the first Zionist congress was held in Basel. Though Isaac Wise and other Reform leaders called upon their followers to vigorously fight Zionism, the movement gained many adherents among Eastern European Jews in the United States. In its early years, it did not attempt to keep Jewish culture alive in America or work for an acceptable form of assimilation. Its focus was on a national state for Jews. There seemed to be no easy way to reconcile that dream with the real opportunities life in American offered Jews. Jewish socialists opposed Zionism, as did a number of Orthodox leaders.

In 1914, there were about twelve thousand Federation of American Zionists members out of a Jewish population of 3.5 million. In that year Louis Brandeis, who would become the first Jew on the Supreme Court in 1916, assumed leadership of the provisional executive committee of the federation. He admired the Zionists in Palestine, seeing them as uncorrupted, hardworking, and courageous. He liked the idea that their work was experimental and consistent with his conviction that small societal units should be relied upon whenever possible. With the help of Harvard philosophy professor Horace Kallen, Brandeis Americanized Zionism, insisting that American Zionists need not leave the United States. He argued, "To be good Americans, we must be better Jews, we must become Zionists." Brandeis conferred respectability on Zionism. In 1917 he won President Wilson's support for Great Britain's enunciation of the Balfour Declaration, wherein Great Britain endorsed the concept of a homeland for Jews in Palestine.

While Brandeis favored both Zionism and assimilation, other Zionists resisted assimilation. In 1912, the Zionist Organization of America created Hadassah, whose goal was to instruct children in Zionist and Jewish ideas in the home. One of its publications spoke of "defeating assimilation" by returning to the basic features of Jewish life. By the late 1990s this women's organization had over 380,000 members.

Upward Social Mobility and Assimilation

Orthodox Jews from Eastern Europe also experienced upward social mobility. Though not as employable as German Jews, they did possess some nonagricultural skills, which the Irish and Italians generally lacked. In New York and Brooklyn, many Jews possessed experience in the needle trades. Large numbers of new Jewish immigrants started their economic and social ascent with difficult and low-paid jobs in the garment industry, often with Jewish employers. The owners of these "sweatshops" made the workers supply their own needles and thread and paid them as little as possible while demanding long hours and breakneck speed. The workers had little choice but to succeed in America; they could not return to Eastern Europe.

Children of the new immigrants were quick to seize educational opportunities, often becoming teachers, lawyers, and physicians. So many Jews were entering colleges that some institutions set quotas for them. The emphasis Jews traditionally place on education doubtless contributed to their success, but this factor can be overemphasized. Their determination to succeed might also be measured by the fact that far fewer Jews in late-nineteenth-century New York died of alcoholism or sexually transmitted diseases than members of other white ethnic groups. They worked hard and accepted the concept of deferred gratification.

Significant assimilation of Eastern European Jews began with the second generation, children of the new immigrants. This generation left the ghetto and settled in middle-class neighborhoods. They abandoned Yiddish and some elements of Jewish culture, often embarrassed by their parents' language and way of life. Among the first to leave were the "alrighters," Jewish nouveaux riches who were most embarrassed by the old culture and often practiced conspicuous consumption, a behavior pattern found in all American ethnic groups. They built impressive synagogues or temples, but their allegiance was often to Conservative Judaism. Some thought that Reform Jews seemed nonreligious and that Orthodoxy offered them more religion than they wanted. They were joined by less prosperous and somewhat less assimilated Jews. The lower birthrate of the second generation is another indication of assimilation.

Their neighborhoods, often called "gilded ghettos," were largely Jewish and were served by many voluntary Jewish organizations. Economic progress and assimilation did not alter important family relationships. The father remained the patriarch, and the mother dominated everyday home life. The first-generation father, perhaps a garment worker, may have spent much time studying the Torah and in the synagogue. The second- and third-generation fathers were often remote and awesome figures. They spent great amounts of time at the office, having limited contact with their children.

The third generation had more gentile friends and neighbors. A 1961 study of Jews living in small New York state communities found that half said their closest friend was a Christian. Intermarriage increased, and they worried that their children would wed non-Jews. They had stronger communal bonds than the second-generation Jews, but religious observance among them declined. Nevertheless, these Jews insisted that religion, rather than culture, bound them together. Like the old German Jews, they retained a religious identity but would not accept a separate social identity. Most were nonobservant but kept kosher for their parents. They observed traditional holidays, retained circumcision, held memorial services, and often sent their children to Sunday school to study Jewish history and culture.

The temple frequently remained the center of Jewish life, largely because the third generation wished to pass on to its children the symbols of ethic identification. Sometimes this was reflected in a revival of synagogue membership, but the reason for this may not have been as much a renewed interest in religion as a framework for making sense of life and dealing with transcendence. By the 1960s, living in America had produced more structural assimilation, and some Jews no longer could be thought of as part of the Jewish population. The professional lifestyles of many limited community involvement. Yet interest in religion and in Jewish literature and culture increased. The number of people affiliated with synagogues declined as younger Jews often declined to join. Nevertheless, among those who were members, interest in religion deepened. The young people who did not join often had a deep interest in spiritual matters but thought they knew enough about Judaism to work out their own belief systems, which remained fundamentally Jewish. There was also an intensified interest in Jewish culture reflected in Jewish studies programs and the teaching of Hebrew in some universities. The quality of Jewish schools increased but fewer students attended. Few Jewish organizations served nonkosher food at their functions, and many stores owned by Jews now closed on Saturday. Assimilation has increased, but there remains a deepening of interest in what could called intrinsic Jewish culture.

Jews and Social Concerns

In the political arena, American Jews have usually allied with those they saw as being committed to reform and human betterment. Though there are various interpretations of "chosenness," most Jews agree that at the least it means being called to high ethical standards and to work for the betterment of humankind. Jewish Americans have contributed more than their share to education, science, the arts, and entertainment. Their philanthropy has been unmatched by any other religious community. Jewish charities constitute over two thousand organizations, not including unions and fraternal and mutual benefit societies. Individual Jews could not meet the obligations of their religion or win the respect of other Jews without becoming involved in philanthropy.

Jews have identified more closely with liberalism than other groups. They have been particularly involved in the battle against racial segregation. Eighty percent of Jewish voters supported Hubert Humphrey for president in 1968, and two-thirds backed George McGovern in 1972, despite his bungling of the Israel question. It had been suggested that Jewish liberalism would diminish as their assimilation increased, but this has not been the case. Apparently, liberalism among Jews does not appear to increase with synagogue attendance. Still, those fully involved in the synagogue are twice as likely to be liberal as other Americans. The tendency toward liberalism may be related to Judaism's affinity for cosmopolitanism and humanism as well as the historic identification of persecuted Jews with reform causes. They have come by identification with the underdog honestly.

Today, there some important Jewish neoconservatives, but they do not have a significant following among Jews. There are also a few politically conservative Jews who believe that the African American civil rights movement has gone too far.

Since the late nineteenth century, Jews have made efforts to assist the urban poor and organized labor. Josephine Goldmark was a major figure in the National Consumers League and other Progressive era reform organizations. Lillian Wald is remembered for founding New York's Henry Street House. Wald, a student nurse, was asked in 1893 to teach a class of immigrants at a Jewish Sabbath school. She was so appalled by the poverty, sickness, and squalor she found in that East Side neighborhood that she and a Christian classmate from nursing school established this community center.

In recent years, Jewish Americans have been deeply involved in the civil rights struggle, the New Left, and feminism. Perhaps as many as two-thirds of the whites who fought segregated transportation in the South as "freedom riders" were Jewish. During 1964's Freedom Summer, Andrew Goodman and Michael Schwerner were killed in Mississippi. In the first half of the 1060s, up to half the leadership of Students for a Democratic Society was Jewish, and Jews dominated the free speech movement at Berkeley. Among leaders of the contemporary feminist movement were Betty Friedan, author of *The Feminine Mystique,* Shulamith Firestone, Susan Brownmiller, Karen Lipschutz De Crow, and Gloria Steinem.

Jewish Women

Jewish women played important roles in secular reform activities. They have often joined in the struggle against sexism and patriarchy by attempting to improve their situation within Judaism. Beginning in the 1870s, congregations organized sisterhoods. These organizations were involved in charity, decorating the altar, secular education, Bible classes, theater parties, book clubs, teas and luncheons, and dinner dances. They worked to increase fellowship within congregations and encourage temple attendance. While never formally petitioning for a greater role for women in worship and operation of the congregations, sisterhoods demonstrated in many ways that women were as capable as men. The role of women was denigrated in all three forms of Judaism, with Reform Judaism offering them the most opportunities and Orthodoxy providing the least.

Because political radicalism advocated sexual equality, many women joined political organizations and led nonreligious lives. Frequently they were reacting against Orthodoxy. Ester Luria was a well-educated socialist who escaped from Siberia to the United States in 1912. She wrote many articles about the accomplishments of women for a Yiddish monthly before disappearing in the 1920s. Emma Goldman was another secular woman who became a prominent anarchist. Often women became active in trade unions with hopes of filling leadership positions. Leah Morton, another nonobservant Jew and social worker, expressed her ambivalence toward Judaism in *I Am a Woman and a Jew,* published in 1926. Early in life she rejected the religion of her parents, but in her thirties she developed an interest in Jewish practices. Though not religious, she acknowledged that her Jewishness was deeply rooted in her memories and heart. Clara Lemlich Shavelson was a remarkable labor leader, whose career as an activist began in 1909 when she inspired twenty-five hundred workers to take an oath of solidarity in Yiddish. She also fought for women's rights and against racism and anti-Semitism. Shavelson later ran unsuccessfully for public office as a communist, and founded the Emma Lazarus Federation of Women's Clubs, which became a leading vehicle for the activism of Jewish women. Though her approach was secular, she worked to preserve Jewish culture because she believed it would inspire commitment to progressive goals.

In 1987, the weekly *Reform Advocate* conducted a poll of Jewish women that revealed that they believed women had greater spiritual insight than men. Since the late nineteenth century, Jewish women had been told that they were the defenders of the faith and were to protect and perpetuate Jewish values through their domestic roles. This was the Jewish equivalent of the cult of domesticity or true womanhood. Assigned this role, many women found it difficult to break with traditional practices. Perhaps the results of the 1987 poll reflect the fact that Jewish women had internalized this mission.

Early in the twentieth century, women came to dominate the educational, social, and charitable activities of their congregations. The National Council of Jewish Women grew out of a congress of Jewish women held in conjunction with the World Parliament of Religions at the World's Columbian Exhibition in Chicago in 1893. Hannah Solomon, who organized this congress, suggested the national council's formation and served as its founding president. Rosa Sonnenschein's *American Jewess* became the first publication in English for American Jewish women. An early Zionist, she insisted that Jewish women should not depart from Hebrew ways in order to adopt American culture.

In 1921, Martha Neumark's request for ordination was rejected by Hebrew Union College even though the Central Conference of American Rabbis had ruled that women could not be denied ordination. Another woman was denied ordination in 1939 by the otherwise progressive Stephen Wise. Women sought inclusion in *minyan,* the ten Jews necessary for worship, and formed their own Sabbath *minyans.* Sally J. Preisand became the first female Reform rabbi in 1972; women were admitted to the cantorate in the next year. Ten years later there were fifty female rabbis in Reform ranks. One of them, Rabbi Laura Geller, has explained that the beginning passages of Genesis need to be understood in a broad way. She pointed out that in the beginning, all people were created in the image of God; God could be seen as both father and mother. Some radical temples changed the language of worship in order to address complaints raised by women.

In 1985, Amy Eilberg became the first Conservative rabbi; the cantorate was opened to women in 1985. By the end of the eighties, there were eleven other rabbis. By this time, women held a significantly larger share of leadership positions in Jewish voluntary agencies. The improvement of their status within Orthodoxy may await strengthening of the movement's progressive wing, which lost some ground in the 1980s. However, Orthodox women now serve on governing boards, are permitted to have their own prayer groups, and may carry Torah scrolls around synagogues as part of rituals.

American Jews are not a monolithic community. They differ among themselves in numerous ways. Most identify their religiosity with ethical behavior rather than with formal worship, and do not see life in America as living in religious exile. The leaders of the major Jewish organizations have supported the hard-liners in Israel over the moderates, but many American Jews have strongly backed the peace process of Shimon Peres and the late

Yitzhak Rabin. American Jews have a low birth rate, and this suggests their proportion in American society is likely to diminish. Some think American Judaism is in crisis because fewer people attend services regularly and many Jews are marrying gentiles and have no ties to organized Jewry. They fear that intermarriage threatens the continuity of Jewish culture in America. Most American Jews, however, see assimilation as a blessing.

Roman Catholics

Roman Catholicism in the late nineteenth century continued to experience phenomenal growth, stimulated by continued increases in immigration. The annexation of Louisiana, Florida, Texas, California, and New Mexico also added considerably to the nation's Catholic population.

In the last two decades of the century, Catholic newcomers from southern and eastern Europe outnumbered those migrating from Ireland and Germany. Among the new Catholic arrivals were Italians, Poles, Lithuanians, Ukrainians, Slovaks, Slovenes, Ruthenians, Hungarians, and Czechs. In 1870, there were 4 million Roman Catholics in the United States, a number that swelled to 12 million by 1900. The number of priests increased from two thousand in 1860 to twelve thousand in 1900. Many clergymen came from Ireland, Germany, France, and Belgium, and most were members of religious orders. Similarly, thousands of religious sisters and brothers crossed the Atlantic to staff the schools, hospitals, orphanages, industrial schools (then called "protectories"), and other charitable facilities maintained by the American church.

Often the church had little choice but to operate these costly institutions despite the existence of public facilities. Roman Catholics were frequently denied assistance by Protestant charitable agencies. Protestants made frequent efforts to cripple the Catholic schools, the last major effort being an Oregon law that gave the state control of all schools within its boundaries. The U.S. Supreme Count invalidated the Oregon law in 1925. Public funds were frequently used to fund Protestant schools. For example, Presbyterian and Baptist schools were funded in Chicago beginning in 1834, a practice that did not end there until 1910. Nondenominational Protestantism was taught in many public schools, and disparaging views of Catholicism were offered. Roman Catholic priests were frequently denied the right to visit parishioners in public hospitals and asylums. In Boston, long an anti-Catholic citadel, priests were not permitted to enter municipal orphanages and hospitals until 1879.

Funds to operate the extensive Catholic network of institutions came from the church's own people, largely poor and underprivileged. Nevertheless, not all Catholics were poor. While destitute Irish immigrants had little choice but to cluster in urban areas, a number of Germans became farmers or lived in rural villages and towns. Germans often came with marketable skills and were able to acquire property more rapidly than the Irish. By 1900, there was an American Catholic middle class composed of the children of German and Irish immigrants. About a fifth of Catholics of Irish and German backgrounds held middle-class jobs, but most held low-paying jobs.

The Catholic Church provided a haven for despised foreigners. Unwelcome in the larger culture, foreign-born Catholics frequently clung to the church as a way of asserting their own cultural identities and defining themselves in relation to a hostile mainstream culture. Many who found refuge in the church had not been very religious at home. This was also true of old immigrants. Many Irish had little contact with the church before the revivals of the late nineteenth century; in America the church became their refuge. Italians, known for their anticlericalism at home, likewise often drew closer to the church in America.

The Demands of Nationalities

The late nineteenth century was a period in which anti-Catholicism was a strong force. Many Protestants saw the most important application of the biblical Great Commission being the conversion of Roman Catholics. The success of their labors was one reason for the ethnic conflict that appeared among American Catholics. There was much concern over the loss of immigrant Catholics to indifference or to other faiths. Estimates of how great the leakage was in the late nineteenth century ranged from hundreds of thousands to millions. The highest estimates are based on the faulty assumption that everyone coming from a supposedly Catholic country was Catholic. For example, some have mistakenly thought that everyone coming from Ireland was Catholic, even though large numbers of Scots-Irish came to America. More than a few immigrants abandoned the faith as a means of obtaining social and economic advancement in a land where hostility to Roman Catholicism sometimes seemed almost part of the national creed.

German ecclesiastics argued that defections among their people occurred because too little had been done to maintain German Catholic culture and because Teutonic clergy were not sufficiently represented in the American hierarchy. About seven hundred thousand German Catholics came between 1865 and 1900. They chafed under the rule of Irish bishops and resisted being part of Irish-dominated parishes. In 1884, over eighty German priests complained to the Vatican that German parishes often did not have the same privileges that the Irish parishes enjoyed. In Germany, the St. Raphael Society was formed to assist German Catholics in America, and in 1890 it met in Lucerne, Switzerland. There it was decided to ask Pope Leo XIII for separate schools and parishes for Germans and other nationalities in the United States. In the 1920s, Polish leaders, backed by the government of Poland, made a similar request. In neither case did the Vatican respond affirmatively. However, bishops frequently decided to establish separate parishes for different nationalities.

German bishops and priests argued that language was the best guardian of faith and insisted upon their own parishes and schools. German leaders argued that their parishes were essential as fortresses of faith erected against other Germans who would lure people to Protestantism, skepticism, and political radicalism. Because German Catholics wanted parishes that were miniature societies, their parishes had more subunits than those of the Irish or most other Catholic ethnics. In addition to the usual cluster of devotional confraternities and sodalities, their parishes had cultural and musical societies, military units, and life insurance groups. Some parishes had bands and drum and bugle corps. It is likely that rural German Catholic communities in the Midwest had a greater participation in the sacraments than urban German parishes. Nevertheless, devotion to the church was strong in both settings and was also reflected in the financial offerings of parishioners.

American Catholics had difficulty understanding the spirituality of Italian Catholics. Southern Italians brought with them an intense devotion to Our Lady of Mount Carmel, and many of them commemorated her feast day, July 16, with elaborate and colorful celebrations. A church by that name in east Harlem was the center of a great annual celebration that began with a solemn high mass and a procession. There was music, food, fireworks, many decorations, and gambling. People came from considerable distances to celebrate with family and friends. The observance lasted at least several days, and often much longer. Life in America was difficult for these sons and daughters of Italy, and it was essential to attend the *festa* and ask the Madonna to intercede on their behalf with her son, Christ. People who rarely came to mass stood barefoot on hot pavement outside the church, waiting to participate in the procession.

The wealthy and prominent who paid for much of the festivities led the procession, and penitents brought up the rear. People carried wax candles to present to the Madonna. Some lugged huge candles as they had major requests. Many went to confession before approaching the Madonna and her child. Christ and his saints were not remote to these people; many called the Madonna "mama." They knew that spirituality must be communal; it was not an individual matter and involved mutual forgiveness. These Italian Americans knew that even Christ and the Madonna had suffered, and they believed that suffering linked them to the divine. Many who attended the *festa* only came to church at important times, such as baptisms and marriages, yet thought of themselves as solid Catholics, and their basic values did reflect the vital elements of Catholicism. Celebration of the *festa* was also a way to express pride in their ethnic heritage.

The Irish, Poles, Lithuanians, and other Catholic ethnics attended parishes that served as centers of social and cultural life as well as religious centers. Those who did not speak English often were the most thoroughly organized, as they attempted to defend and preserve their own culture. Through their church they also found assistance in Americanizing without abandoning their faith or national origins.

Historians frequently refer to ethnic neighborhoods, yet seldom did one group constitute a numerical majority in an area larger than half a square mile. Residential ghettos were usually not the case; there were cultural ghettoes organized around parishes. People spoke of Irish, German, Polish, or Italian neighborhoods because residents associated almost entirely with people of the same national origins.

Before parishes even existed, various ethnic groups founded mutual benefit societies that sought opportunities for worship according to their national customs. These societies often acquired land for parishes and organized parishes dominated by lay trustees. Though the Italians had mutual benefit societies, their parishes were usually organized by the clergy, not organized lay trustees. A similar situation would later prevail among Mexicans. Poles revamped their natural practice of having noblemen rather than bishops dominate parishes; lay committees replaced noblemen.

In the twentieth century, there have been racial confrontations between white Catholics and African Americans. For Catholics, there was an earlier "race" problem, which marked the years before 1940, characterized by suspicion and distance between the various white Catholic ethnic groups. Just as Poles were expected to attend their nationality's parish, African American Catholics were expected to live, work, and worship with other Blacks.

The church lost many adherents through disputes over ownership of church property and governance. There were numerous secessions of ethnic parishes, which usually ended in their return to the Roman Catholic fold. In the 1890s, Polish parishes in Scranton, Buffalo, Chicago and other northeastern cities cut ties with Catholic bishops, and a Polish National Catholic Church emerged in 1904. Francis Hodur functioned as its first bishop until his death in 1953. Hodur had been consecrated bishop in 1907 by the Old Catholic bishop of Utrecht. Membership never exceeded 5 percent of Polish Americans. There was also a Lithuanian National Church founded at about the same time, and several independent Slovak and Lithuanian parishes. Although a Polish national church was established, the vast majority of

Poles submitted to governance by a largely Irish hierarchy and agreed to turn church deeds over to the bishops. Reverend Vincent Barzynski and the Resurrectionist Order ministered to Poles in the Chicago area and elsewhere. In Chicago, Poles reached an arrangement with the archdiocese wherein the archbishop held the deeds to churches and the Resurrectionists were assured the right to administer those parishes for ninety-nine years. The Polish National Alliance reflects the hostilities that grew out of the Poles' encounter with the American church, and the Polish Roman Catholic Union represents Poles who are not anticlerical.

Relations with Eastern European Catholics of the Eastern or Byzantine rites were complicated by the opposition of American bishops to married clergy and the desire that these immigrants enter the Latin rite. Uniate rites acknowledged the authority of the pope but retained usages common to the Orthodox tradition, among these the right of priests to marry. There was also a problem of overlapping jurisdictions. In the Middle East and Eastern Europe, Catholics in the same cities and provinces often had different bishops, depending on their ethnic backgrounds and rites. American bishops could not imagine functioning under these conditions. Beginning in 1891, about 225,000 Ukrainian Catholics found it necessary to join the Russian Orthodox Church. Local control of property was a key issue and was seen as a way to resist absorption by the Latin rite. Some Ukrainians established an independent church. Hundreds of thousands of Eastern rite Catholics as well as Poles, Slovaks, and Lithuanians, left the Roman Catholic Church. They refused to abandon a congregationally controlled parish in favor of complete submission to the principle of a hierarchical church. This can be seen as part of a revolt against "hibernarchy," an Irish-dominated American hierarchy.

Many Catholics, it was argued, were lost to the faith when they moved to rural areas where there were few Catholics and no priests. Catholic immigrants who were part of the westward movement would find fewer and fewer Catholics as they traveled west. There were reasonably well-established dioceses on the Pacific Coast; however, those dioceses would be desperately short of clergy until well into the twentieth century. Some efforts were made to create immigrant Catholic communities in the Midwest and West, which were expected to become the nuclei for further Catholic settlement. As late as 1953, no priests were located in 26 percent of the counties of the United States, most frequently in the South and West.

The church's most serious failure in retaining and meeting the spiritual needs of immigrants was in its work with Hispanics, many of whom lived in western areas with few priests. The problem was compounded by the fact that few Hispanic men entered the priesthood. Since the 1920s, the church had trained lay catechists to work among Hispanics, mostly of Mexican origins. In 1945, the National Catholic Welfare Conference organized the Bishops' Committee for the Spanish-Speaking, dominated for a quarter century by Archbishop Robert E. Lucey of San Antonio. Lucey used the committee to defend the rights of Hispanic farm workers and migrant workers and to fight the injustices they faced. Not until 1970 did Hispanics begin to enter the hierarchy, when Patrick Flores, of migrant worker stock, became archbishop of San Antonio. A scarcity of Hispanic vocations and very little knowledge of Catholicism on the part of Hispanics made it difficult for the church to reach them. They are now the most rapidly growing ethnic group of Catholic background, but the church has been unable to restrain their movement into conservative Protestant, often Pentecostal, sects. This development parallels a similar situation in Latin America, where it is possible that Protestant evangelicals will soon deprive Catholicism of its once dominant position. In 1980 there were 15 million Hispanic Americans, and it is expected that there will be 35 million in the year 2000.

Women Religious

The success of Catholic schools and other institutions—hospitals, orphanages, and charitable operations—was made possible by the hard work and devotion of thousands of sisters and nuns. These women were devoted to serving God through the church and they took seriously their vows of obedience. Nevertheless, their leaders sometimes found it necessary to resist what they considered abuses of ecclesiastical power. These conflicts were often a reflection of the sometimes tense relationship between the sexes that characterized all of American society. Women religious leaders were frequently extraordinarily gifted people whose intelligence and skills rivaled those of any male. Their disputes with ecclesiastical authorities often involved natural reactions against high-handed conduct on the part of patriarchal male clergy. Bishops found it necessary to remove a number of mothers superior and abbesses who had the temerity to resist bullying or to assert the basic rights of their sisters. On occasion sacraments were withheld from the sisters until they were brought into line. When Mother General Catherine Connor of the Kentucky Sisters of Loretto succeeded in obtaining an ecclesiastical investigation of the arbitrary actions of Louisville bishop George William McCloskey, she was removed from her office even though the investigator found merit in her complaints. Her successor, Mother Praxedes Carty, found it necessary in 1894 to visit the apostolic delegate in Washington to request that McCloskey's interdict (ban on administration of the sacraments) be lifted. The delegate ordered the interdict lifted, but McCloskey lived to bedevil the sisters for another five years. His death was noted thusly in the sisters' records: "Our dear Bishop and exerciser is dead, and Mother General Praxedes is one of the chief mourners at his funeral."

Mother Theresa Maxis Duchemin, an African American who founded three communities of white nuns, quarreled with her Michigan bishop and lived in Canadian exile for eighteen years before she could return to Michigan in 1885. Another spirited founder was Mother Margaret Anna Cusack of the Sisters of Saint Joseph of Peace; frustrated by the high-handed actions of a bishop, she found it necessary to leave her adopted church. The sisterhoods usually succeeded despite episcopal opposition and harassment.

The women religious (sisters and nuns) seem to have been oblivious to true womanhood or the cult of domesticity. Whatever their tasks, running asylums, hospitals, schools, or other institutions, they accomplished them with or without the help of men. Often bishops and pastors simply got in the way, or worse, actively impeded their efforts. However, the early church was understaffed and faced a plethora of pressing obligations; in this situation the women religious were blessed with a degree of autonomy that often permitted them to blossom as administrators or professionals.

The 1884 decree of the American bishops mandating the establishment of a Catholic school system meant that, in time, the overwhelming majority of women religious would be teachers. A study of women religious in Massachusetts showed that in 1870 they were spread out among a great variety of occupations; in 1940 the great majority was concentrated in teaching. (The same study demonstrated that religious brothers were paid about twice what the sisters received for teaching.)

The Americanism Controversy

Efforts of some Catholics to make accommodations with American culture led to conflict within the American church. Although the great majority of prelates were theologically conservative, they were sharply divided over the extent to which the church should cooperate with non-Catholics in civil and social matters and accommodate itself to American culture in ways that did not diminish their Catholicism. The liberals or Americanizers were led by the aggressive and articulate John Ireland, archbishop of St. Paul. His closest collaborators were Bishop John Keane Bishop of Richmond and First Rector of the Catholic University of America and Monsignor Denis O'Connor, rector of the American College in Rome and a protégé of James Cardinal Gibbons, the highest ranking American Catholic. The cardinal generally associated himself with their efforts, and John Lancaster Spalding, Bishop of Peoria, was usually in sympathy with them. They gloried in

American democratic institutions and practices. Like Isaac Hecker's Paulists, they saw no incompatibility between Catholicism and democracy and insisted that the church prospers most where separation of church and state is observed. Father Hecker was a onetime transcendentalist who converted to Catholicism and founded a religious order devoted to winning Americans to Catholicism. He had a positive view of human nature, was uncomfortable with some devotionalism, and emphasized the importance of following the promptings of the Holy Spirit through one's conscience.

The liberal bishops opposed continuation of foreign cultures under the aegis of Catholicism and demanded rapid assimilation of immigrants. Many American-born Catholic laymen shared this opinion. Some, like Ireland, supported the Republican Party, mainly in an effort to assure that no single party came to expect complete Catholic support. The Americanizers did not denounce public schools, avoided unnecessary quarrels with Protestants, and sought to cooperate whenever possible with non-Catholics in promoting useful causes. They thought it counterproductive to condemn relatively harmless fraternal orders that had secret oaths and quasi-religious rituals. Many were willing to seek an accommodation with modern science and were open to at least considering new developments in theology.

On the question of the vote for women, the hierarchy did not split on liberal-conservative lines. Gibbons spoke to the first antisuffrage convention, but conservative bishop Bernard McQuaid joined liberals Spalding and Ireland in supporting the National American Woman Suffrage Association. The church taught that women were called by God to be mothers and that they were often more moral and religious than men. It was the Catholic version of the cult of domesticity. In Catholic circles it has been referred to as "pedestal Mary," meaning women should emulate the mother of Christ and occupy pedestals, removed from much of everyday life.

The titular head of the Catholic conservatives was New York's archbishop Michael A. Corrigan, but their chief spokesman was his friend Bernard McQuaid, bishop of Rochester. The German bishops of the Midwest, who particularly detested John Ireland, were solidly conservative and vocal critics of the Americanizers. Though the Germans did not always find full support coming from Irish conservatives in efforts to win greater privileges for German parishes and ecclesiastics, they could count on the solid opposition of the Americanizers. The conservatives wanted rigid enforcement of church restrictions against secret societies and were openly critical of public schools. Though completely loyal to the United States, they did not sing the praises of the doctrine of separation of church and state; they thought that some American institutions and practices could be improved upon.

A number of episodes revealed the depth and nature of the philosophical divisions within the American hierarchy. The most serious blow to the Americanizers came as a consequence of a debate in France over the translated edition of Walter Elliott's biography of Father Hecker. This discussion over what the French called "Americanism" hinged upon the acceptability of Hecker's belief that, whenever possible, the church should accommodate itself to democracy and the modern age. Also in dispute were Hecker's praise of separation of church and state in the United States and his emphasis on how the individual is prompted by the indwelling Holy Spirit. In 1899, Leo XIII condemned "Americanism" in *Testem Benevolentiae*. He defined "Americanism" as serious departures from Catholic orthodoxy in order for the church to respond to the needs of the times. The pope added that the encyclical was not intended to be a criticism of "the characteristic qualities which reflect honor on the people of America . . . or the laws and customs that prevail" in the United States.

Liberals insisted that the heresies described in the encyclical did not exist in the United States. Yet the papal letter was doubtless intended as a rebuke to the liberals, and the conservatives in the hierarchy considered it a great victory. O'Connor and Keane lost their positions, and Father John A. Zahn, an Ireland friend, was ordered to withdraw from distribution and sale his book *Evolution and Dogma*. Later, the Holy See moved to rehabilitate Keane, appointing him archbishop of Dubuque. However, the bull of appointment was accompanied by a personal letter from Leo XIII instructing him to protect his people from the heresy of Americanism. In 1910, Rome required that all priests and seminarians take an oath against modernism.

Catholicism at the Parish Level

The Bureau of the Census reported in 1906 that there were more than 14 million Catholics in the United States, many of them immigrants with Catholic backgrounds but no real commitment to Roman Catholicism. The great accomplishment of the American church was in persuading vast numbers of them to actually become Catholics. Some immigrant groups seemed almost ignorant of Catholicism. In 1888, Archbishop Corrigan of New York estimated that "there are 80,000 Italians in this city, of whom only two percent have been in the habit of hearing mass." The same was said of French-Canadian immigrants. Mexicans carried on devotional practices in their homes, particularly honoring Our Lady of Guadalupe, but were not accustomed to attending mass and receiving the sacraments. The Catholic parish offered the immigrants, in the words of sociologists Roger Finke and Rodney Stark, "an encapsulated social structure—a kind of parallel Catholic America," where they found comfort and affirmation.

The church was carrying on its own revivalist campaign rivaling that of the Second Great Awakening. It extended from about the middle of the nineteenth century well into the twentieth century. Indeed, parish missions or revivals were very common as late as the 1950s. The American Catholic revivals were at least as successful as the devotional revivals that occurred in France and Ireland in the late nineteenth century. The parish missions were given by traveling revivalists who usually belonged to religious orders. Typically, a parish mission lasted about two weeks. It would begin with a week for women, who were expected to persuade their husbands to attend the second week. Parishioners were reminded of the wages of sin and led to return to the sacraments. Many adult immigrants made their first communions at the missions. Today revivals and missions continue in abbreviated form.

Though Roman Catholics frequently quarreled among themselves, they made every effort to present a united front when dealing with Protestant America. There is no way of estimating how much anti-Catholicism contributed to building solidarity among Catholics. It was an ever present element in American life and did not begin to lose force until after the middle of the twentieth century. High-water marks of anti-Catholicism were the activities of the American Protective Association in the 1890s, the Ku Klux Klan in the 1920s, and the great outburst that met the nomination of New York governor Al Smith for the presidency in 1928. It was not until 1960 that the first Roman Catholic, John F. Kennedy, was elected to that office. Anti-Catholicism was not confined to rubes who yearned to burn crosses or thought Al Smith would install the pope in the White House. It was consistently found among intellectuals and liberal Protestants who saw the hierarchical and authoritarian Catholic Church as a grave threat to American democracy.

The first half of the twentieth century could be called the brick-and-mortar phase of American Catholicism. It was an age when many new parishes were created, while schools and colleges, orphanages, hospitals, and other institutional edifices appeared. These buildings were signs of a parallel Catholic society that was to exist until the 1960s, when American Catholics became full-fledged members of the American mainstream.

The American Catholic Church only appeared to be a vast, unchanging, monolith. Despite hierarchical and authoritarian governance, the church, since the 1920s and 1930s, was experiencing change that would prepare it in some ways for the emphases on liturgical renewal and lay participation that would grow out of the documents of the Second Vatican Council (1962–1965). A strong liturgical reform movement explored ways to change and enhance worship, and a variety of social action programs laid a foundation for the social teachings of Vatican II.

Eastern Orthodox Christians

Immigration also greatly increased the number of Eastern Orthodox Christians in the United States. By 1900, they may have numbered one hundred thousand, with many more to follow. The first Orthodox in the United States were the Russian Orthodox, who had been active in Alaska since the 1790s. Their first diocese was located in Sitka, Alaska, in 1848, and subsequently moved to San Francisco in 1872 and to New York City in 1905.

The Orthodox trace their roots to the apostles and consider themselves the original Christians. The decisive breach in relations between the Roman Catholics and Orthodoxy occurred in 1054. Orthodox churches are part of the Orthodox Catholic Church of the East, and the patriarch of Constantinople is first among equals in this family of churches. Their churches usually have onion-shaped cupolas or domes; the Slavic Orthodox churches have three-crossbar crosses. The Orthodox are similar to Roman Catholics in a number of respects, but may be somewhat less legalistic and more mystical. The Orthodox Holy Liturgy resembles the Catholic mass, but their communion bread contains yeast, unlike the Catholic host. The Orthodox have fast regulations more demanding than those of Roman Catholics. They also have the same sacraments, as well as bishops, priests, nuns, and monks. They use icons but forbid the use of statues in churches. They use the ancient Julian calendar and administer some of the sacraments in ways that significantly vary from Roman Catholic usage. Priests may marry before taking orders, but their bishops cannot be married. Orthodox bishops have more power and independence than Roman Catholic bishops. Although all Orthodox communions acknowledge that the universal patriarch in Constantinople is to be accorded greater honor than other bishops, he cannot involve himself in ordinary affairs of the various communions.

Orthodoxy is a large family of different communions most often organized along ethnic lines. In addition to Russian and Greek Orthodox, there are Ukrainian, Romanian, Bulgarian, Georgian, Albanian, Cypriot, Czechoslovakian, and Polish Orthodox. Even this is not an exhaustive list. Some of these nationality groups have several versions of Orthodoxy.

By 1938, there was a Ukrainian church in the United States; most of its membership came from a mass exodus of Carpatho-Rusyns from a Catholic Eastern rite loyal to Rome. About 65 percent of the membership of today's Orthodox churches in the United States is composed of former Eastern-rite Catholics who found it impossible to deal with American Catholic, Latin-rite bishops.

The Russian Orthodox made repeated efforts to unify the Orthodox in the United States, all to no avail. As a result of the October Revolution in

1917, the Russian Orthodox in the United States would be distracted for decades by the question of their relationship to the patriarchate of Moscow. The autocephaly, or independent authority, of the American church was not recognized by Moscow until 1970. The American church then took the name the Orthodox Church in America.

Like other religions transplanted from Europe, the American Russian Orthodox found it necessary to accommodate to American ways. It reduced its activities to Sunday liturgy and a few holy days. A large number of its members did not attend services regularly. It was still dependent on émigrés to staff many of its churches and teach in its seminaries. Traditionally, the church was deeply rooted in monasticism, but the monastic tradition was not strong among the Russian Orthodox in America. Conservatives within the church thought it was surrendering to secularism. They also were alarmed that modernist religious thought was making inroads among the clergy.

In 1970, there was a severe shortage of priests, with only 174 of 411 parishes claiming resident priests. In comparison, the Greek Archdiocese had priests for all but 41 of its 420 parishes. Russian Orthodox claimed eight hundred thousand adherents in the United States, in comparison to 1.6 million members of the Greek Archdiocese.

Though not the first Orthodox here, the Greeks would grow to become the largest Orthodox community in the United States. Many of the Orthodox new arrivals found homes and bone-tiring employment in mining or iron and steel towns and cities. The experience of many of these groups was marked by much internal squabbling, not unlike the often fierce intra-Catholic and intra-Jewish disputes of those years.

In the early years of the Cold War, much of Eastern Europe was ruled by communist regimes. This created problems within some of the churches here as some members wanted to sever ties with the church in the mother country. With time, they created schools, seminaries, ecclesiastical organizations, and by the 1960s and 1970s some were using English in their divine liturgies. They adopted American usages such as church dinners, parish organizations, mixed choirs, and church pews.

Today, the Greek Orthodox Archdiocese of North and South America has about 1.3 million adherents in the United States and another 600,000 in Latin America and Canada. All together, there are roughly 4 million Orthodox Christians in the United States. Some of them are still ruled by hierarchies in their native countries. In December, 1994, there was a conference in Ligonier, Pennsylvania, to consider unity among the Orthodox in the United States. While the patriarchate of Constantinople has expressed concern that this was a move toward independence from its authority, some American Orthodox have suggested that the mother see of Orthodoxy has shown an inclination to interfere inappropriately in affairs in the American Orthodox churches.

It took time for the Orthodox to be assimilated, and there were two much larger Caucasian ethnocultural groups that were not integral parts of mainstream America—the Jews and the Roman Catholics. Each group suffered from prejudice and discrimination but nevertheless managed to build a thriving subculture, and their members experienced significant upward social mobility. There were serious debates within American Judaism, Catholicism, and Eastern Orthodoxy over the extent to which each group should seek to assimilate with the larger culture, as well as serious ethnic divisions within these subcultures. Within Catholic and Jewish subcultures, women sought to expand their roles and authority in ways similar to the efforts of their sisters in the American mainstream. Each would play significant roles in American political life.

Bibliography

Abell, Aaron. *American Catholicism and Social Action: A Search for Social Justice, 1865–1950.* Garden City: Hanover House, 1960.

Antler, Joyce. "Between Culture and Politics: The Emma Lazarus Federation of Jewish Women's Clubs." In *U.S. History as Women's History: New Feminist Essays,* ed. Linda K. Kerber, Alice Kessler-Harris, and Kathryn Kish Sklar, pp. 267–295. Chapel Hill: University of North Carolina Press, 1995.

Archdeacon, Thomas J. *Becoming American: An Ethnic History.* New York: Free Press, 1983.

Barry, Coleman J. "German Catholics and the Nationality Controversy." In *Catholicism in America.* ed. Phillip Gleason, 65–80. New York: Harper and Row, 1970.

Braude, Ann. "The Jewish Woman's Encounter with American Culture." In *Women and Religion in America.* Volume 1, *The Nineteenth Century,* eds. Rosemary Radford Reuther and Rosemary Skinner Keller, pp. 150–192. San Francisco: Harper and Row, 1981.

Craig, Robert H. *Religion and Radical Politics: An Alternative Christian Tradition in the United States.* Philadelphia: Temple University Press, 1992.

Day, Dorothy. *The Long Loneliness: An Autobiography.* San Francisco: Harper and Row, 1981.

Dershowitz, Alan M. *The Vanishing American Jewish Identity for the Next Century.* Boston: Little, Brown, 1997.

Eisen, Arnold M. *The Chosen People in America: A Study of Jewish Religious Ideology.* Bloomington: Indiana University Press, 1983.

Elazar, Daniel J. "The Development of the American Synagogue." In *American Synagogue History: A Bibliography and State-of-the-Field Survey,* ed. Alexandra Sheckert Korros, pp. 23–53. New York: Markus Wiener, 1988.

Ellis, John Tracy. "American Catholics and the Intellectual Life." In *Catholicism in America,* ed. Phillip Gleason, pp. 10–27. San Francisco: Harper and Row, 1970.

Ewens, Mary. "The Leadership of Nuns in Immigrant Catholicism." In *Women and Religion in America*. Volume 1, *The Nineteenth Century,* ed. Rosemary Radford Reuther and Rosemary Skinner Keller, pp. 101–149. San Francisco: Harper and Row, 1981.

Finke, Roger, and Rodney Stark, *The Churching of America*. New Brunswick: Rutgers University Press, 1992.

Fuchs, Lawrence H. *The Political Behavior of American Jews*. Glencoe, IL: Free Press, 1956.

Gilbert, Arthur. *A Jew in Christian America*. New York: Sheed and Ward, 1966.

Glanz, Rudolph. *The Jewish Woman in America: Two Female Immigrant Generations, 1820–1929*. New York: KTVA Publishing House, 1976.

Glazer, Nathan. *American Judaism*. Chicago: University of Chicago Press, 1957.

Gleason, Philip, ed. *Catholicism in America*. New York: Harper and Row, 1970.

Greene, Victor R. *American Immigrant Leaders, 1800–1910: Marginality and Identity*. Baltimore: Johns Hopkins University Press, 1987.

Gurock, Jeffrey S. "The Orthodox Synagogue." In *The American Synagogue: A Sanctuary Transformed,* ed. Jack Wertheimer, pp. 37–84. Cambridge: Cambridge University Press, 1987.

Hennesey, James. *American Catholics: A History of the Roman Catholic Community in the United States*. New York: Oxford University Press, 1982.

———. "Roman Catholics and American Politics, 1900–1960: Altered Circumstances, Continuing Patterns." In *Religion and American Politics,* ed. Mark A. Noll, pp. 302–321. New York: Oxford University Press, 1990.

Holy Transfiguration Monastery. *A History of the Russian Church Abroad and Events Leading to the American Metropolia's Autocephaly*. Boston: Holy Transfiguration Monastery, 1972.

Joselit, Jenna. "The Special Sphere of the Middle-Class American Jewish Woman: The Synagogue Sisterhood, 1890–1940." In *The American Synagogue,* ed. Jack Wertheimer, pp. 206–230. Cambridge: Cambridge University Press, 1987.

Karp, Abraham J. "Overview: The Synagogue in America—A Historical Typology." In *The American Synagogue,* ed. Jack Wertheimer, pp. 1–34. Cambridge: Cambridge University Press, 1987.

Kenneally, James. "Eve, Mary, and the Historians: American Catholicism and Women." In *Women in American Religion,* ed. Janet Wilson James, pp. 191–206. Philadelphia: University of Pennsylvania Press, 1980.

Kolmer, Elizabeth. "Catholic Women Religious and Women's History: A Survey of the Literature." In *Women in American Religion,* ed. Janet Wilson James, pp. 127–140. Philadelphia: University of Pennsylvania Press, 1990.

Kramer, Judith R., and Seymour Leventman. *Children of the Gilded Ghetto*. New Haven: Yale University Press, 1961.

Kraut, Benny. "Ethnic-Religious Ambiguities in an Immigrant Synagogue: The Case of New Hope Congregation." In *The American Synagogue,* ed. Jack Wertheimer, pp. 231–273. Cambridge: Cambridge University Press, 1987.

Leahy, William P. "American Jesuits and the Social Apostolate: The Origins and Early Years of the Institute of Social Order." *Mid-America* 73 (October 1991): 227–241.

Levinger, Lee J. *Anti-Semitism in the United States: Its History and Causes*. Westport, CT: Greenwood Press, 1972.

Liberles, Robert. "Conflict over Reforms: The Case of Congregation Beth Elohim,

Charleston, South Carolina." In *The American Synagogue,* ed. Jack Wertheimer, pp. 274–296. Cambridge: Cambridge University Press, 1987.

MacEeoin, Gary. "Lay Movements in the United States Before Vatican II." *America* 165 (August 3–10, 1991): 61–65.

McAvoy, Thomas T. *The Great Crisis in American Catholic History, 1895–1900.* New York: H. Regency, 1957.

McGreevy, John T. *Parish Boundaries: The Catholic Encounter with Race in the Twentieth Century Urban North.* Chicago: University of Chicago Press, 1995.

Murray, Henry. *Do Not Neglect Hospitality: The Catholic Worker Movement and the Homeless.* Philadelphia: Temple University Press, 1990.

Nugent, Walter T.K. *Modern America.* Boston: Houghton Mifflin, 1973.

Oates, Mary J. "Organized Voluntarism: The Catholic Sisters in Massachusetts, 1870–1940." In *Women in American Religion,* ed. Janet Wilson James, pp. 141–170. Philadelphia: University of Pennsylvania Press, 1980.

O'Brien, David J. "Catholicism and Americanism in the 1930s." In *Catholicism in America,* ed. Philip Gleason, pp. 101–114. New York: Harper and Row, 1990.

———. *Isaac Hecker: American Catholic.* New York: Paulist Press, 1992.

Pratt, Norma Fain. "Transitions in Judaism: The Jewish American Woman Through the 1930s." In *Women in American Religion,* ed. Janet Wilson James, pp. 207–228. Philadelphia: University of Pennsylvania Press, 1980.

Rosenberg, Stuart E. *America Is Different.* London: Thomas Nelson and Sons, 1964.

Rozenblit, Marsha L. "Choosing a Synagogue: The Social Composition of Two German Congregations in Nineteenth-Century Baltimore." In *The American Synagogue,* ed. Jack Wertheimer, pp. 327–362. Cambridge: Cambridge University Press, 1987.

Sachar, Howard M. *A History of the Jews in America.* New York: Knopf, 1992.

St. John, Robert. *Jews, Justice, and Judaism.* Garden City: Doubleday, 1969.

Sarna, Jonathan D. "Seating and the American Synagogue." In *Belief and Behavior,* ed. Philip B. Vandermeer and Robert P. Swierenga, pp. 189–206. New Brunswick: Rutgers University Press, 1990.

Slobin, Mark. *Chosen Voices: The Story of the American Cantorate.* Urbana: University of Illinois Press, 1989.

Spalding, Thomas W. "German Parishes East and West." *U.S. Catholic Historian* 44 (spring 1996): 37–52.

Thompson, Margaret Susan. "Women, Feminism, and the New Religious History: Catholic Sisters as a Case Study." In *Belief and Behavior,* ed. Philip B. Vandermeer and Robert P. Swierenga, pp. 136–163. New Brunswick: Rutgers University Press, 1990.

Waxman, Chaim I. *America's Jews in Transition.* Philadelphia: Temple University Press, 1983.

Weigel, Gustave. *Churches in North America, An Introduction.* Baltimore: Helicon Press, 1961.

Williams, Peter J. *Popular Religion in America: Symbolic Change and the Modernization Process in Historical Perspective.* Urbana: University of Illinois Press, 1989.

Nine

Socioeconomic Change and Politics

Religion played a major role in American political life in the late nineteenth and twentieth centuries. It strongly influenced party affiliations and voting patterns. It was the source of serious social divisions as well as prejudice and discrimination against adherents of some faiths. Scholars insist that it effected upward social mobility, but it is not altogether clear how this happened. Religion also inspired efforts to alleviate poverty, assist the poor, and battle for the rights of working people.

While some clergymen and churches sought to improve the status of workers and ease the sufferings of the poor, others supported the status quo, opposing unions, strikes, and social legislation. Many Christians accepted social Darwinism, a secular ideology that applied Darwinian evolutionary thought to the development of society. According to this view, the wealthy were the most fit, and the poor were unfit. Many attempts to assist the have-nots were viewed as mistaken benevolence that actually encouraged the poor to persist in unproductive behavior. Evangelist Samuel P. Jones announced that "God projected this world on the root-hog-or-die-poor principle. If the hog, or man either, don't root, let him die."

Problems of an Urban, Industrial Society

The late nineteenth and early twentieth centuries witnessed great changes in the American social order. The United States had become an urban, industrialized nation. It is estimated that 40 percent of working-class families lived in poverty in 1880; about that many more were not far from the clutches of poverty. Accompanying these developments were poor and unsafe working conditions and labor-management strife. American Protestantism was strong in rural areas and small- and medium-sized cities. Its ideology was congenial to rural people and the middle class, but it did not address the problems of immigrants, industrial labor, or the urban poor. Indeed evangelical Protestants were often hostile to labor unions, tending to believe that the poor were responsible for their own problems. There were efforts to reach out to the urban masses, but they were more successful among middle-class people than among the poor. Charles G. Finney had preached in the great cities, only to find he was more effective in other environments.

In the late nineteenth century, Protestants again attempted to assist, uplift, and evangelize city dwellers, but they were most successful in ministering spiritually to the needs of urban, managerial, middle-class congregations. These people had a vested interest in the status quo; they were self-satisfied and easily identified their activities with God's ways. Heirs to the Second Great Awakening, they had lost their spiritual cutting edge. They saw nothing wrong with American society that good people like themselves could not fix with a little goodwill. Their theology legitimized America as it was.

The most important preacher of the period was Reverend Henry Ward Beecher, of Plymouth Congregational Church in Brooklyn. He earned about $40,000 a year from his speaking engagements. He defended his parishioners from the charge that they were money-grubbers, arguing that creating wealth develops character. Riches were most useful in doing God's work, and the ability to produce wealth was a valued God-given talent. His sermons were essentially an extended self-help manual. Beecher dwelt upon how to prevent failure, emphasizing the need to honor parents and to subordinate oneself to employer, country, and the needs of the community. Attentiveness to the needs of the poor was a paramount obligation of those blessed with this world's goods.

Beecher's position was similar to that of Russell Conwell, a Philadelphia Baptist, who delivered six thousand times his famous sermon "Acres of Diamonds." Conwell called on people to earn money so they could use it for good, adding that it was sinful to accumulate wealth only for one's own use. Beecher turned away from hellfire-and-damnation sermons, arguing that a God of love would not be too hard on people he created in his own likeness. Endorsing the work ethic and drawing upon social Darwinism, Beecher thought that working-class demands for better living conditions and wages showed that those who raised these points were unfit for the race of life.

His views were representative of many middle- and upper-class Protestant clergy and laymen. Most Protestant clergy shared Beecher's dislike of unions and strikes. During the railroad strike of 1877, one Protestant publication suggested that the only response to this crisis was the use of guns, grapeshot, and bayonets. Another added, "There are times when mercy is a mistake." Most ministers took such positions because they did not understand the working class. Some, like Methodist William Carwardine, later changed their views when they grasped both sides of the question. He defended the workers during the Pullman strike of 1894.

Catholic clergy, who should have been better acquainted with the working class, frequently denounced unions and strikes. In part this reflected the conservatism of the Vatican as well as an effort to avoid further alienating the American Protestant middle class, many of whom already had a strong distaste for Catholicism. However, in 1888, James Cardinal Gibbons succeeded in convincing the Vatican to rule that workers could join the Knights of Labor. In 1891, Pope Leo XIII issued *Rerum Novarum,* an encyclical that recognized the rights of working people. It was welcomed by priests who were friends of labor, but the pope's suggestion that Catholic laborers' societies be created did not seem applicable to the United States, where Catholics were a distinct minority.

Roman Catholics, who did successfully attend to the spiritual needs of innumerable urban congregations, frequently offered a social message similar to that of Beecher, Phillips Brooks, and other prominent Protestant clerics. It was a Catholic view that God permits poverty as a means of fostering Christian virtues. The poor learned perseverance and the theological virtues of faith and hope, while the rich grew in the virtue of charity as they worked to relieve the sufferings of the less fortunate. In 1890, *Catholic World* noted that the three men Christ brought back to life were rich men. Bishop John Spalding, a prominent Catholic spokesman, told a Notre Dame graduating class that the American economic system worked well, while Archbishop John Ireland told Catholics that money should be associated with energy and will, that it was not evil. Cardinal Gibbons also praised Andrew Carnegie's Gospel of Wealth.

The Sisters of Charity, the Sisters of Mercy, and a number of other male and female religious orders are credited with enormous accomplishments in meeting the religious and material needs of the poor and the working class (Figure 9). Few of them denounced the economic system or offered solid support for unions. The same can be said of most Protestants who attended to the needs of the poor and working classes. There were isolated individuals and groups who were led by their Christian convictions to denounce the system that produced poverty and to support unions. The Catholic *Boston Pilot* published anonymous articles on labor that dealt with the conditions endured by workers, and Milwaukee's *Catholic Citizen* called upon the church to more closely identify with the poor and labor. Two Protestant laymen and a Catholic founded the Christian Labor Union in 1872 as a means of bringing Christian principles to bear on the social question.

Terence V. Powderly, head of the Knights of Labor, and Mother Mary Jones, a famous labor agitator, said their labor principles were based on the gospel and their religious convictions. Both remained only nominal Catholics because the church was too closely identified with defending the status

Figure 9. Roman Catholic Sister. Roman Catholic sisters, like the one shown here working with the urban poor, served in many capacities including assisting the poor, nursing, and teaching, and made possible their church's extensive social and educational activities. Their superiors were frequently remarkable women who possessed strength of character and substantial leadership and administrative skills. (Courtesy the Library of Congress.)

quo. Jones said that Christ built a revolutionary organization based on the efforts of the twelve workingmen he selected. She told workers to "pray for the dead and fight like hell for the living." She died at age one hundred in 1930, and American Federation of Labor president William Green led the mourners at her funeral mass. These people were forerunners of the Protestant Social Gospel, the union priests, and the efforts of John Ryan and others to apply Catholic social teachings to the problems of poverty and working people in the United States.

Many inner-city Protestant churches followed their congregations by withdrawing to the suburbs. Some maintained inner-city missions, which generally were short-lived and unsuccessful. Members of the mission congregations had no influence in the affairs of the mother church; they certainly did not sit on its board. In Muncie, Indiana, the downtown churches remained financially strong while workers settled at some distances from them. To reach these workers in industrial suburbs and as a means of social control, industrialists made it possible for the downtown churches to establish new churches in working-class neighborhoods. In the 1890s, church growth there exceeded population growth.

Some missions were as successful as institutional churches, which attempted to address the social, economic, and spiritual needs of the poor. Reverend Edward Judson, a Presbyterian, was the most prominent spokesman of the institutional church. Institutional churches offered drama clubs, athletic programs, choral societies, reading rooms, penny savings associations, nurseries, employment bureaus, medical clinics, concerts, industrial education, cooking classes, and lecture series. Judson spent much time in the necessary activity of raising money and expressed concern that he was evolving into a social worker rather than a minister of the gospel. Temple University in Philadelphia grew out of a Baptist institutional church. The most famous of these churches was under the care of Reverend Thomas K. Beecher in Elmira, New York; Mark Twain, Beecher's brother-in-law, described it in *Curious Dreams and Other Sketches.* Another well-known inner-city church that did not remove to the suburbs was St. George Episcopal in New York City. It became an institutional church, with expenses met by financier J.P. Morgan. The Vanderbilts supported another New York City institutional church, St. Bartholomew Episcopal. Some of these churches evolved into social service agencies.

The American Christian Commission, an outgrowth of the Civil War U.S. Christian Commission, was another effort to reach out to the urban masses. It published a periodical, the *Christian at Work,* and urged churches to follow the European practice of having deaconesses or members of sisterhoods visit the homes of the poor. There was much criticism of this idea, but by 1900 Methodists, Lutherans, and German Reformed were using deaconesses to minister to the urban poor and working classes, while Episcopalians, Congregationalists, and Baptists were moving in that direction. A number of missions, homes for working mothers, soup kitchens, employment services, and children's hospitals were formed.

The Salvation Army and the Young Men's Christian Association (YMCA) were two agencies imported from England that became active in American cities. The Salvation Army was founded in London in 1868 by a former Methodist preacher, "General" William Booth. Catherine Mumford Booth, his spouse, was an intelligent and persuasive preacher and advocate of women's rights; the success of the army was due as much to her efforts as to his leadership. In 1880, the army was brought to the United States and began to provide work, food, and shelter for the poor. The army sent visiting nurses to the poor and established a few farm colonies where urban poor could be rehabilitated. The Booths' chief American mentors were evangelists James Caughey, Charles G. Finney, and Phoebe Palmer, the prominent holiness movement leader. Catherine Booth defended Palmer in her pamphlet *Female Ministry*. Ballington Booth, the general's son, took charge of American operations in 1886 and greatly expanded the agency's operations. In 1896, he quarreled with his father and established a rival agency, Volunteers in Service to America, which stressed work with ex-convicts and unwed mothers.

The first YMCA in the United States was formed in Boston in 1851, and the first YWCA followed in 1855. The "Y" emphasized athletic recreation as a means of keeping people away from sinful ways. Many people were brought to Christianity through its Bible classes and nondenominational religious services.

Revivals, the establishment of institutional churches, and a variety of Christian outreach efforts enjoyed considerable success in the nation's cities. Census Bureau religious data for 1890 and 1906 demonstrates that the proportion of the population identified as adult church members was higher in cities than in rural areas. The percentages for the principal cities for 1890 and 1906 were 37.9 and 46.9, respectively; comparable figures for areas outside those cities were 31.2 and 39.1.

The Social Gospel

A number of clergymen attempted to apply the gospel to social and economic problems of that period. Their efforts came to be called the Social Gospel movement, though the term itself was not widely used until the early twentieth century. The movement was inspired in part by similar developments in Europe, especially England. In Boston, Congregationalist Reverend Jesse Jones called for an eight-hour workday and said that churches must show as much concern for the laborer as for the interests of the employer. Jones is considered the forerunner and father of the Social Gospel movement. In 1872, he was among the three founders of the Christian Labor Union. Its journal, *Equality,* offered a socialist outlook until the movement's collapse a few years later. Another Congregationalist, Theodore Munger, developed a "New Theology" as the basis for a nonsocialist approach to the Social Gospel. While acknowledging the rights of the individual, Munger insisted that each must accomplish his goals within a framework that takes into account the good of the family and the nation. His efforts to balance the principle of individualism with those of equality and community (or brotherhood) took shape in *The Freedom of Faith.*

The year 1884 saw the publication of a controversial little book entitled *Being Christian,* by Washington Gladden, a young minister in Columbus, Ohio. Gladden stated that it was the duty of a Christian to love his neighbor as himself; accepting a certain body of doctrines was less important. He believed that society must be reformed along Christian lines, and held that this was as important as saving individual souls. Gladden rejected socialism as well as laissez-faire economics and insisted that workers had the right to organize and strike. He was critical of clergymen who would not speak out about the rights of workers to a just wage or to organize and strike. The labor-management disputes of the 1890s convinced Gladden that the nation would descend into chaos unless Americans developed a sense of community through the Christian church. Gladden asked the American Board of Commissioners for Foreign Missions to reexamine its decision to accept what the minister considered tainted money from John D. Rockefeller.

Reverend Josiah Strong was another leader of the Social Gospel movement. He left his position as secretary of the Evangelical Alliance to lead other clergymen toward socially responsible positions. Strong argued that the church would occupy an insignificant place in society if it refused to support reform or take an interest in the advancement of civilization. Strong drew a sharp distinction between traditional Christianity and adherence to the gospel, an occurrence that was most rare. This clergyman is also remembered for his strong nativist views; he worried about the impact of the new immigrants from southern and eastern Europe and was not friendly to Catholicism. Gladden, on the other hand, openly denounced the American Protective Association, an anti-Catholic organization that briefly had half a million members. Strong was a vocal advocate of creating an American empire, and in this was not alone among Social Gospel advocates. Many of them welcomed the Spanish-American War in 1898.

Boston's William Dwight Bliss joined the Episcopal bishop of New York in creating the Church Association for the Advancement of the Interests of Labor in 1887, which grew to a substantial membership. Bliss said, "I was made a Christian by Karl Marx, and a Socialist by Jesus Christ." Bliss later founded the Society of Christian Socialists and edited its short-lived journal, *The Dial;* in it he advocated a gradualistic approach to socialism. Still later, he founded the American Fabian Society, patterned after the British Fabians, an organization of very pragmatic socialists. Another Christian socialist was Reverend Franklin Sprague, a Michigan Congregationalist. He insisted that man must choose between God and mammon. Charles M. Sheldon, a Congregationalist minister in Topeka, Kansas, published the novel *In His Steps* in 1896. By 1965, 8 million copies had been sold. (This record for the sale of novels was eventually surpassed by *Peyton Place.*) *In His Steps* addressed social concerns and moral betterment, and raised the question, "What would Jesus do?" Sheldon took a conservative approach to reform and did not call for child-labor or wages-and-hours legislation. Reverend George D. Herron, a Congregationalist who taught at Grinnell College in Iowa, wrote an influential series of small books to publicize the Social Gospel and was also a most effective public speaker.

Christian socialists among the Catholic clergy included Thomas McGrady of Bellevue, Kentucky, and Thomas Hagerty, ordained in Chicago and serving in Texas and New Mexico. Both were suspended from the active ministry for their socioeconomic beliefs. McGrady edited the *Voice of Labor* and drafted the constitution for the Industrial Workers of the World (IWW, known as the Wobblies). He later taught Spanish under an assumed name in Chicago and ended his days as an alcoholic on that city's skid row.

Social Gospel ministers also appeared in the seminaries, where they saw to it that concern for social responsibility was part of the clergy formation process. The seminaries responded by offering courses in sociology and ethics. Seminarians were encouraged to see their work as much more than converting and shepherding souls; they were to help bring the Kingdom of God to earth. Seminary professors became leaders of the movement; the most important of them was Walter Rauschenbusch, a German Baptist at Rochester Theological Seminary, whose writings had a profound effect upon the next generation of Protestant clergy. His works reflected his eleven year experience as a pastor in New York City's Hell's Kitchen. Rauschenbusch is considered the most influential writer and theologian of the Social Gospel movement. Unlike some, he did not subordinate individual salvation to social reform or the salvation of society—individual salvation came first. In 1893, he organized the Brotherhood of the Kingdom to focus attention on bringing the kingdom into existence on earth. Those seeking to bring about the Kingdom of God, he said, would find that religion touches every aspect of life. He came to believe that many of the principles of the Social Gospel appeared to have been accepted, and he announced in 1912 that American political life was partly Christianized.

Another influential figure was Episcopal layman Richard T. Ely, economics professor at Johns Hopkins University and a prolific writer. Ely was linked to social reformers in the Roman Catholic fold through Father John J. Ryan, the most important American exponent of Catholic social thought in the early twentieth century.

The Social Gospel movement had blind spots in respect to women's suffrage and race. Its leaders saw the typical Victorian nuclear family as a model for the organization of society. They were blind to the limitations this arrangement placed upon women. The movement's leaders did not become active in the drive for women's suffrage, and many, including Rauschenbusch, opposed it. At the grassroots level, however, many clergymen supported the right of women to vote. The most prominent woman in the Social Gospel movement was Vida Scudder, a Christian socialist, but she did not address women's issues in her book On Journey, which dealt with her early life.

These were extremely trying years for Native Americans, Orientals, and African Americans, but these marginalized groups were not aided by the Social Gospelers. Unfortunately these Christian leaders accepted the idea that African Americans had a limited potential for growth, and they supported the doctrine of separate but equal as enunciated in *Plessy v. Ferguson* in 1896. They applauded Booker T. Washington's willingness to support separation of the races and reliance upon white benevolence. Separation, they believed, was the natural way of dealing with racial differences. Washington Gladden and Lyman Abbott believed that another century would pass before the nation would make much progress in dealing with racial questions, and they were correct.

Studying Limestone County, Alabama, historian Richard C. Goode has suggested that the Social Gospel was at the root of the Southern Alliance and southern Populism. Joseph Wheeler, the district's congressman, claimed that the Alliance was the "voice of God, creating the highest possible attainment in the perfection of government." Its leaders insisted it was founded on Christian principles and sought privilege for no one, with social justice for all. They attacked the maldistribution of wealth and sought the reformation of society along basic Christian principles, thus ending social and economic inequality. The Alliance was not linked to denominational religions, as the Southern Baptists, Methodists, and Presbyterians supported the status quo.

Women were so active in social reform in twentieth century America that it has been suggested that they dominated reform movements. The National Consumers' League (NCL) was led by women and was an important reform force in the Progressive era. It was especially interested in improving factory working conditions and in ending child labor. The National Child Labor Committee had its headquarters in the same New York building as the NCL and two reform periodicals, *Survey* and *Outlook*. It grew out of meetings of women who were concerned about working conditions of women, and was encouraged by Episcopal priest James Otis Huntington, a founder of the Church Association for the Advancement of the Interests of Labor. In 1899, Florence Kelley, a Philadelphian nourished in Quaker and Unitarian reform traditions, was appointed general secretary of the NCL. Members used their power as consumers to reform factories and retail outlets. They patronized only stores that treated their employees fairly and purchased only merchandise produced in "fair houses," factories that observed state factory legislation and were fair to their employees. Trade unions helped the NCL prepare a list of these places. Eventually the league authorized fair houses to display a white NCL label on their products. The league had thirty thousand members by 1913 and was by no means limited to Protestant women. Josephine Goldmark, a Jew, was an officer of the organization, and James Cardinal Gibbons, by becoming a vice president of the Maryland league, encouraged Catholic women to become involved. J. Regis Canevin, Roman Catholic bishop of Pittsburgh, also urged Catholic women to join.

The work of Miriam Van Waters, a Ph.D. in anthropology, also reveals an ecumenical dimension. Her desire to do good sprang from the liberal Protestantism she learned from her father, an Episcopal priest. Like Kelley, this Portland, Oregon, native sought support for her work on behalf of juveniles by developing connections with women's organizations across the nation. She had considerable success in Los Angeles, but political disputes destroyed her experimental school for troubled girls. In 1932 Van Waters began twenty-five years as head of the Massachusetts Reformatory for Women in Framingham. Critics thought she coddled the prisoners, and she was dismissed in 1949. Her defenders included Jewish, Protestant, and Catholic clergy, an order of Catholic sisters, the YWCA, and the Massachusetts Council of Churchwomen. She mounted a forceful defense of her work and was restored to the superintendency of the reformatory. Her career, like those of Kelley, Jane Addams of Chicago's Hull House, and other female reform leaders, underscores the importance of an informal national network of women's church and social service organizations. In addition to receiving political and financial support from these organizations, women reformers drew emotional support and genuine sisterhood from these contacts.

Cooperative Protestantism

The Social Gospel movement, along with the missionary movement, led to increased cooperation among Protestant denominations. Washington Gladden called for cooperation, and Josiah Strong wanted federative arrangements so the Christian church could better serve humanity. In 1901 the National Federation of Churches and Workers was founded, but denominations did not send official representatives to it until its 1905 conference. That meeting developed plans for the Federal Council of Churches, which came into being in 1908. Thirty-three denominations joined initially, but it was only an advisory body. The council turned its attention immediately to social concerns, in 1909 adopting a report entitled "The Church and Modern Industry." This report was practically written into the Methodists' Social Creed and was endorsed by the YMCA and YWCA, a move that provoked businessmen to threaten not to donate to local units that supported the report. In 1910, a committee of the federal council investigated the Bethlehem Steel strike, denouncing the seven-day week and twelve-hour day as "a disgrace to civilization." There could be no mistaking the fact that the primary concern of cooperative Christianity was extending gospel principles to social and economic activities.

Most of those affiliated with the federal council also believed that a unified Christianity was necessary for the establishment of the Kingdom of God on earth. To a degree, they also were favorable to a rapprochement with the Roman Catholic Church. They wished Catholic modernists well, and theologian Newman Smyth even hoped for the day when a "modernized Pope" would convene a general council to consider the relationship of the Christian church and the modern world. The Social Gospel outlook and zeal to apply Christian principles to social issues came to dominate the twentieth-century mainline churches and the National Council of Churches, successor to the federal council.

Similar outlooks characterized the official social teachings of the international Roman Catholic Church since Leo XIII's *Rerum Novarum,* and would underpin social teachings of the American Catholic bishops after World War I. The extent to which these views made their way into local churches is difficult to assess. Similarly, there is no precise method for determining how the progressive views of mainline Protestant churches influenced the sermons of local pastors.

In the area of social thought, American Catholics made great headway. Before Leo XIII's social encyclical, American Catholics were not organizationally or intellectually in a position to apply progressive social doctrines to conditions in the United States. The key figure in building an intellectual framework for serious Catholic participation in the discussion of social questions was John J. Ryan of Milwaukee. He maintained cordial relations with Protestant social gospel professor Richard T. Ely, who wrote a preface for Ryan's dissertation, *The Living Wage,* when it appeared in print in 1906. He found that neo-Thomist thought, a revival of interest in the theology and philosophy of Thomas Aquinas, and recent papal declarations provided an excellent foundation for progressive Catholic social thought.

Ryan worked with the National Conference of Catholic Charities and the American Federation of Catholic Societies. He emphasized the need to improve the lot of labor, and worked to establish a genuinely Christian America where the dignity of all would be respected. In his writings, Ryan blended contemporary American reform thought with Catholic social teachings. Though not a Christian socialist, he believed workers should play a role in the management of industry. He also was active in supporting progressive legislation in Minnesota. In 1919, he wrote for the American bishops the "Bishops' Program of Social Reconstruction." The most advanced document yet produced by American Catholics, it placed the hierarchy on record as supporting progressive reforms in the 1920s. Among other things, it called for control of monopolies, legislation regulating utility prices, public housing, a minimum wage, and insurance against unemployment, sickness, and old age.

The National Catholic War Council, which published the report, soon became the National Catholic Welfare Conference, and Ryan became head of its social action department. In 1931, Ryan's efforts to marshal Catholic support for social justice programs was assisted by the appearance of Pope Pius XI's *Quadragesimo Anno,* which marked the fortieth anniversary of *Rerum Novarum.* Using the new encyclical, other declarations, and natural law, Ryan built strong arguments for the rights of labor and state intervention in the economy. His support of Franklin Roosevelt's New Deal was unwavering, and he was called "the New Deal's Ambassador to Catholics."

J. Bryan Hehir, a Boston priest working for the National Conference of Catholic Bishops, is today's best representative of the tradition of John J. Ryan. He had a significant influence on the bishops' far-reaching and progressive pastoral letter on war and peace. He was an associate secretary in charge of the U.S. Catholic Conference (USCC) Office of International Justice for eleven years, until 1984, when he became secretary for the more inclusive Department of Social Development and World Peace.

A number of other priests were also social activists; among these "labor priests" the most interesting probably was Charles Owen Rice of Pittsburgh. Rice joined picket lines, spoke at rallies, ran labor schools, and helped workers organize. In 1937, Catholic laymen founded the Association of

Catholic Trade Unionists, which helped workers organize and functioned as a pressure group within many of the major unions. Baroness Catherine de Hueck was a member and the founder of Friendship Houses, where whites came to dwell among African Americans as a means of fighting racism and expressing solidarity with them. In 1933, the Catholic Worker Movement was founded by Dorothy Day and Peter Maurin, a French hobo, thinker, poet, and peasant. Day, a Catholic convert, was a journalist and former Marxist who sometimes wrote for *Commonweal.* The movement produced a monthly newspaper, the *Catholic Worker,* which sold for a penny an issue. They considered it a "call to perfection," and it was soon selling 150,000 copies. The movement had a few farm communes and operated houses for the poor in many cities.

More than any other group or person, Day served as the conscience of American Catholicism. She taught its members the importance of living the Beatitudes and voluntary works of mercy. Every person, especially the poor, she believed, must be treated as Christ should be treated. "He was the I.W.W. who was tortured and lynched out in Centralia and Everett," she said. "There was never a Negro fleeing from a maniacal mob whose fear and agony and suffering Christ did not feel."

The Catholic Worker Movement's emphasis on pacifism produced several of the leaders of the antiwar movement in the 1960s, one of whom was the Jesuit Daniel Berrigan, who was sent to prison for his antiwar activities. The American branch of the international Pax Christi has become the most prominent Catholic advocate of Christian pacificism. Though not absolute pacifists, the bishops have criticized the arms race and development of nuclear weapons. That Roman Catholics can openly take these positions indicates that they have finally been admitted to the American mainstream, no longer having to prove they are 110 percent Americans by taking very hawkish positions.

Under the aegis of Catholic Action, laymen were beginning to play important roles in the church and preparing to assume still more responsibilities. Catholic Action refers to the sharing by the laity in the apostolic mission of the hierarchy.

Nowhere was it stronger than in Chicago, where auxiliary bishop Bernard J. Sheil worked with Catholic labor activists, especially in the steelworkers' and meatpackers' unions. He founded the Catholic Youth Organization in 1930 and the Sheil School of Social Studies, which emphasized ecumenism, support of organized labor, and interracial activities. The rector of St. Mary of the Lake Seminary in Chicago, Reynold Hillenbrand, developed labor schools for Catholic unionists and a Summer Social Action School for clergy that influenced clergy from other dioceses. John Egan, a

Hillenbrand protégé, worked to build and spread the Christian Family Movement, known for its then controversial efforts to fight poverty and racism. More than a century old, St. Vincent de Paul Societies in most parishes gathered clothing, food, money, and sometimes furniture for the use of the poor. Catholic Action programs have also been active in addressing the problems faced by Hispanics. César Chavez began his career as an organizer of farm workers through one of these efforts.

Religion and Voting Behavior

In the late nineteenth century, religion was the principal determinant of voting behavior. More than a set of doctrines and liturgical practices, it was a "perspective, a frame of reference for the organization of experiences." People used religion to achieve their goals and to preserve and extend their values. Political parties were social forces through which voters related to the larger society. Particularly in the Midwest and East, voter commitments to parties flowed from ethnocultural loyalties. As noted earlier, this has been true of party affiliations since the 1820s, but it was particularly true in the late nineteenth century. Party positions on specific economic issues influenced the choice of relatively few voters under normal circumstances. Most voters selected their parties on the basis of religious and ethnic commitments, subsequently adopting the economic policies of their respective parties. Religion was the main source of political conflict.

Pietistic Protestants tended to support the Republicans, while liturgical Protestants and Roman Catholics backed the Democrats. These groups are sometimes referred to as evangelicals and antievangelicals or ritualists. The broad perspectives encompassed in the liturgical and pietistic mind-sets tended to transcend organizational lines. Ritualists, the opposite of pietists, emphasized acceptance of doctrine and prescribed manners of worship. Adherence to tradition was very important to them. The ritualists or liturgicals often were members of hierarchical churches and stressed acceptance of authority. On the other hand, the pietists placed a premium on conversion experiences and rejected ritualism. Above all, they were concerned with "right action," while ritualists were concerned with "right beliefs." The pietists or evangelicals thought it their duty to battle sin in the world and lead others to salvation through moralistic crusades. Although liturgicals or ritualists did not approve of sin, they thought that only God possessed the power to purge the world of evil. Pietists thought the state and voluntary groups should be concerned with promoting morality, while the liturgicals thought that only the church should deal with these matters.

In describing this continuum of opinion from pietist to ritualist, historian

Paul Kleppner has contended, "The more ritualistic the religious orientation of the group, the more likely it was to support Democrats; conversely, the more pietistic the group's outlook, the more intensely Republican its partisan affiliation." Membership in an ethnic group could reinforce one's political orientation, but religion was the most important factor. Thus, German Evangelicals supported the Republicans while Lutherans were inclined to support the Democrats.

Pietists were convinced that God's law and their values were being attacked by those with different social customs and mores. Native pietists often found themselves involved in a crusade against immorality; this effort frequently became intertwined with opposition to certain foreign elements. Immigrant pietists were able to identify this crusade against ungodly ways with hostilities brought from the Old World, such as between Scots-Irish Presbyterians and Irish Catholics. Catholic or Lutheran schools were seen by many evangelicals as barriers to Americanization, institutions designed to foster and preserve unacceptable value systems. The pietists sought the aid of the state in stamping out what they considered immorality or unpatriotic views. Key among their demands were temperance legislation and Sunday blue laws. The pietists appeared not to have noticed that American Catholics had launched a massive crusade against strong drink, one that would rival in extent today's Catholic campaign against abortion. Although liturgicals did not defend drunkenness, many of them opposed the intervention of the state in matters of morality, charging that the fanatical pietists were interested in depriving others of personal liberty. Liturgicals also resented evangelical harassment of parochial schools and limitations on Catholic and Lutheran clergy in public penal institutions.

The following groups were pietistic or evangelical: Methodists, Congregationalists, Universalists, Unitarians (though neither Universalists nor Unitarians had conversion experiences), German Evangelicals, Free Will Baptists, and Quakers. Lutherans and Roman Catholics were the main liturgical groups. Episcopalians were also liturgical, but many of them, due to their wealth and standing, supported Republicans. Members of the Disciples of Christ had conversion experiences but often resented evangelical efforts to legislate morality, and supported Democrats. New School Presbyterians tended to support Republicans while Old School Presbyterians tended to back Democrats.

In a study of voting patterns in Connecticut, New Jersey, and New York in the years 1893–1896, historian Samuel T. McSeveney affirmed the importance of religion and ethnicity in influencing voting. He indicated that political "behavior was rooted in the group experience of religious, ethnic, and racial communities and that national issues . . . neither shaped the original political identifications of most voters, nor, except under unusual circumstances, altered identification." Though he did not build his analysis within the liturgical versus pietist framework, his results have warranted its use. Frederick C. Luebke reached similar conclusions in his study of German voting patterns in Nebraska between 1880 and 1900. He also did not use the liturgical versus pietist model, but he did point to the pietism and moralism of the groups that supported the Republicans and the relative rigidity in practice and belief of the Lutherans and Catholics. In Nebraska, the principal cultural issues that bound the liturgicals to the Democrats were opposition to women's suffrage, Sabbatarianism, temperance legislation, and Republican efforts to injure sectarian schools.

Ethnocultural issues tended to dominate at times when the differences between parties were not great and there were not serious economic difficulties. In times of economic crisis, the importance of ethnocultural factors temporarily diminishes.

Many German liturgicals were attracted by Republican presidential candidate William McKinley's linkage of prosperity to the protective tariff. It was charged that Democratic tinkering with tariff legislation helped bring on the panic of 1893. Many German liturgicals were repelled by Democratic free-silver doctrine in 1896, and some others decided McKinley might be correct in calling for a high tariff. Even during these depression years, ethnocultural factors were important in accounting for the realignment of these groups. Many liturgicals were repulsed by 1896 Democratic presidential nominee William Jennings Bryan's pietistic rhetoric and decided to support McKinley. Conversely, many pietists joined the Democratic Party due to Bryan's crusading style.

Most pietists remained Republicans until the Franklin Roosevelt realignment, but the GOP also enjoyed considerable liturgical support. The Democrats had both liturgical and pietistic support and would continue to claim the "solid South." As a three-time presidential nominee, Bryan attracted a number of pietists—particularly westerners—to the party. Although the realignment of politcal parties in 1893–1896 produced a less coherent political system in that the great majority of pietists were not found in one party and many liturgicals backed Republican urban machines, the Republicans were able to break the delicate equilibrium of the late nineteenth century and clearly emerged as the dominant party. (Although Grover Cleveland was the only Democratic president of the period, the parties were reasonably well balanced, with Republicans enjoying a slight edge.) Despite the loss of some pietistic supporters, Republicans were able to win almost undisputed majority status by exploiting economic questions and courting liturgical voters.

This accomplishment is particularly impressive in view of the fact that the Democrats in these years continually discussed Republican nativism and the alleged links of the GOP to the American Protective Association, an anti-Catholic group founded in 1887 and momentarily powerful in the 1890s. Its members took a secret oath to "strike the shackles and chains of blind obedience from the hampered and bound consciences of a priest-ridden and church-oppressed people." In 1893 the APA invented a Leo XIII encyclical stating that "it will be the duty of the faithful to exterminate all heretics found within the jurisdiction of the United States." One APA leader insisted the pope had seven hundred thousand trained troops awaiting his orders in U.S. cities. The mayor of Toledo accepted this far-fetched story and wanted the National Guard to protect his city. The APA also spread lurid stories of priestly lust and the kidnapping of thousands of white American women. It should be noted that a number of Protestant spokesmen denounced this secret organization. Many Catholic spokesmen suggested that such fanaticism could not command the support of large numbers of Americans for any considerable length of time. The APA was responsible for violence in a number of places in 1894 as well as some loss of life; after that it faded into obscurity.

In the Progressive era, newcomers often distrusted those who urged temperance legislation and supported social work programs, seemingly designed to strip immigrants of all vestiges of their European pasts. Some progressives urged Anglo-Saxon Protestants to breed more in order to at least keep up with the less desirable population increase of Italians and southern Europeans. Theodore Roosevelt also thought increased old-stock breeding was necessary to retain Anglo-Saxon dominance. Roosevelt had come from a long line of wealthy Dutch landowners. Republican progressives could not understand the immigrant's attachment to the urban political machine, which sometimes provided the newcomers with jobs, food, or intercession with the criminal justice system. In some places, Republicans did not need to appeal to anti-Catholicism and xenophobia. Republicans dominated Pittsburgh and Philadelphia and could count on Catholic and immigrant votes. Progressives were often at a loss to understand the strong attachment of many immigrants to the Roman Catholic Church or Eastern Orthodoxy. Edward A. Ross, a leading progressive writer, denounced the immigrant's "pigsty mode of life" in his *Old World in the New*.

Progressives frequently demanded an end to voting by unnaturalized immigrants, calling for voter registration laws to prevent election fraud. Some progressives saw the women's vote as a way to temporarily dilute the impact of immigrant voting. Of course, the pattern of anti-foreign, anti-Catholic, anti-Jewish prejudice was not clearly demarcated between Democrats and Republicans. The anti-Semitic persecutors of Leo Frank, a Jew unjustly accused of murder and lynched in Georgia, were Democrats. The revived Ku Klux Klan in the South disliked Jews and Catholics almost as much as blacks. Democratic president Woodrow Wilson, who appointed a Jew to the Supreme Court and relied on a Catholic executive secretary, harbored anti-Catholic prejudices that became apparent in his second term. Despite these Democratic lapses, the new immigrant of the North usually had little choice but to make the Democratic Party his home. Nativism remained strong within the Republican Party, and GOP leaders such as Senator Henry Cabot Lodge championed legislation to restrict immigration. Many German Protestants also continued to vote Democratic in the early twentieth century.

Restriction of immigration became a popular subject in the 1880s. Chinese immigration was ended in 1882, and an agreement with Japan in 1907 all but ended Japanese entrance into the United States. A number of restrictions were adopted during World War I. In 1921 Congress enacted a measure that established admission quotas for different nationalities. This temporary measure was replaced by the National Origins Act of 1924. Substantial quotas were established for northern and western Europe, with much smaller quotas for southern and eastern Europe. The measure was a device to reduce the number of new immigrants coming into the United States. Asians were totally excluded. Advocates of immigration restriction hoped that these measures would preserve Protestant, old-stock dominance of American society.

The use of the terms "pietist," "evangelical," "liturgical," and "ritualist" does not imply mutually exclusive categories. The term "pietist" is not used to deny that Catholics and Lutherans had numerous devotional practices; use of the words "ritualist" or "liturgical" is not meant to imply that Methodists or Evangelical Germans did not have orders of worship; that antievangelicals were concerned with "right belief" should not obscure the fact that the Presbyterians had several heresy trials in the late nineteenth and early twentieth centuries. Some social historians go too far in saying that the God of the antievangelicals was unfathomable. The meaning of "right action" for the evangelicals is confined to those activities that brought into reality, through voluntaristic or state action, the reform agenda of the Second Great Awakening.

Today, the term "evangelical" is not used in connection with most of the mainstream Protestant denominations. In the early twentieth century, members of many of those denominations thought of themselves as evangelicals because their faith and practice had been influenced by the Second Great Awakening. They continued to hope that state and individual action could together bring about the reign of God on earth. Thousands of congregations were involved in the Anti-Saloon League. The reforms of the Progressive era constituted a large part of the political and social agenda of these Protestants. They were interested in a great deal more than harassing certain immigrant groups or bringing about Prohibition. The reforming and cooperative impulses that propelled the Progressive movement also brought many denominations into the Federal Council of Churches. The benevolent republic that nineteenth-century evangelicals had envisioned seemed on the verge of being realized. Though they could not speak of a Protestant America, it could be stated that progressive Protestantism was setting the nation's agenda in the Progressive era.

Religion and Social Mobility

Social historians have also shown an interest in the question of upward social mobility. Using data from eight rural Illinois townships, Richard Jensen has noted that there was a correlation between pietism and the holding of more rewarding occupations in these rural communities. Two explanations seemed possible to him: either Catholics held the lower slots on the occupational ladder due to discrimination, or Catholics preferred the lower slots and pietists preferred the higher rungs of the ladder. Noting that "there is no evidence of [economic discrimination] on religious grounds," he formulated the question as, "Why did Catholics display little upward mobility?" If we accept the sociological theories of Gerhard Lenski, which in turn were based on the work of Max Weber, it would follow inescapably that Catholics and liturgicals were less favorably inclined toward the capitalist ethic—motivated less toward upward social mobility than were the intellectual children of John Calvin, who had fashioned the religious counterpart to capitalism. Catholics, especially, and other liturgicals seem held back by the burden of some medieval intellectual baggage.

Historian Stephan Thernstrom has provided a detailed quantitative analysis of social mobility in the late nineteenth century and early twentieth century in Boston. He found that Boston Catholics "typically gravitated toward jobs in the lower reaches of the occupational structure." Though as late as the 1920s job notices in the *Boston Transcript* specified Protestants, he ruled out active discrimination as an important factor in accounting for the poor performance of Catholics in climbing the socioeconomic ladder because he assumed that Jews would have suffered similar pressures, yet their mobility record was much better than that of Catholics. He believed that Catholics were held back by their rural origins (mostly in Ireland), the institutional completeness of their communities, and their lack of emphasis on education. Finding cohesion within their own culture, it was enough to achieve some limited status within it rather than in the larger culture. The prospect of obtaining a position on the police force or in some public agency was enough for many. While they did have parochial schools, these institutions may have "muted rather than heightened aspirations." Thernstrom stopped short of endorsing the Weberian explanation that the difficulties Catholics experienced in climbing the occupational ladder stemmed from their religious values. The question of Irish Catholic upward social mobility a century ago is of great interest in light of Andrew Greeley's argument that contemporary Irish Catholics have had considerable success climbing the occupational ladder.

A problem with mobility studies is the difficulty in identifying and measuring active discrimination. Are we to assume that in the absence of quantifiable evidence of economic discrimination, nineteenth-century Catholics did not substantially suffer from it? Similarly, because Jews were able to succeed despite discrimination, is it correct to assume that the Irish probably faced barriers no greater than did the Jews? If we consider prejudice and discrimination within the framework of intergroup conflict theory, a more realistic approach to the problem of discrimination and its relationship to mobility of minority groups may emerge. An important premise is that conflict is directly proportional to the extent to which groups see each other as competitors for resources or threats to their values and ways of life. It would seem that native Protestants would have considered Roman Catholics—especially Irish Catholics—a greater threat than Jews due to their numbers, the fact that they were acquiring some political power, and because the church appeared to be an effective and unified organizational structure. Prominent historian John Higham has noted that nineteenth-century Protestants feared Jews less than they did Catholics. The Irish were subjected to greater abuse than other Catholic immigrant groups because of their involvement in politics and domination of the church hierarchy. After the 1880s, Boston's Yankees were, in the words of Oscar Handlin, "swept away by a fresh wave of hatred against the foreigners who seemed to threaten their very places in society."

The Roosevelt Coalition

American politics passed through another period of realignment in the 1930s, producing the Roosevelt coalition. This was an alliance of labor, intellectuals, southerners, Catholics, Jews, and African Americans. The solid South adhered to the coalition because memories of Republican Reconstruction there made voting Republican appear unthinkable. African Americans left the party of Lincoln because they had suffered most from the Great Depression and had benefited from FDR's New Deal. Blacks and Catholics tended to support the Democratic Party, but those who attended church regularly were even more likely to vote Democratic. After 1960, church attendance did not seem to affect the extent to which Catholics voted Democratic. By the late 1960s, the Roosevelt coalition began to become unraveled, in part because many laborers and Catholics had entered the middle class, moved to the suburbs, and begun to vote like most of their Protestant neighbors. Catholic support for Democratic presidential nominees steadily declined from 1948 to 1984, partly due to the Democrats' positions on cultural questions like abortion, which offended committed Roman Catholics.

Bibliography

Archdeacon, Thomas J. *Becoming American: An Ethnic History.* New York: Free Press, 1983.

Bloom, *The American Religion: The Emergence of the Post-Christian Nation.* New York: Simon and Schuster, 1992.

Carter, Paul A. *The Spiritual Crisis of the Gilded Age.* De Kalb: Northern Illinois University Press, 1971.

Coutts, John. "The Booths' American Mentors." *Christian History* 9 (1990): 21–23.

Craig, Robert H. *Religion and Radical Politics: An Alternative Christian Tradition in the United States.* Philadelphia: Temple University Press, 1992.

Frank, Douglas W. *Less Than Conquerors: How Evangelicals Entered the Twentieth Century.* Grand Rapids: William R. Eerdmans, 1986.

Freedman, Estelle B. "Separatism Revisited: Women's Institutions, Social Reform, and the Career of Miriam Van Waters." In *U.S. History as Women's History,* ed. Linda K. Kerber, Alice Kessler-Harris, and Kathryn Kish Sklar, pp. 170–188. Chapel Hill: University of North Caroline Press, 1995.

Goode, Richard C. "The Godly Insurrection in Limestone County: Social Gospel, Populism, and Southern Culture in the Late Nineteenth Century." *Religion and American Culture* 3 (summer 1993): 155–170.

Greeley, Amdrew M. *The American Catholic: A Social Portrait.* New York: Basic Books, 1977.

Hamm, Thomas. *The Transformation of American Quakerism, Orthodox Friends, 1800–1907.* Bloomington: Indiana University Press, 1962.

Handy, Robert T. *A Christian America.* New York: Oxford University Press, 1971.

———. "Protestant Theological Tensions and Political Styles in the Progressive Period." In *Religion and American Politics,* ed. Mark A. Noll, pp. 281–301. New York: Oxford University Press, 1990.

Harkins, Barry. "Southern Baptists and Northern Evangelicals: Cultural Factors and the Nature of Religious Alliances." *Religion and American Culture* 7 (summer, 1997): 272–298.

Henking, Susan E. "Sociological Christianity and Christian Sociology: The Paradox of Early American Sociology." *Religion and American Culture* 3 (winter 1993): 49–68.

Higham, John. *Strangers in the Land: Patterns of American Nativism, 1860–1925.* Boston: Athenaeum, 1963.

Hofstadter, Richard. *The Age of Reform.* New York: Vintage Books, 1955.

———. *Social Darwinism in American Thought.* Rev. Boston: Beacon Press, 1955.

Hoover, Dwight W. "Middletown: A Case of Religious Development, 1827–1983." *Social Compass* 38 (September 1991): 273–284.

Hunter, James Davidson. "The Evangelical Worldview Since 1890." In *Piety and Politics: Evangelicals and Fundamentalists Confront the World,* ed. Richard John Neuhaus and Michael Cromartie, pp. 19–53. Washington: Ethics and Public Policy Center, 1987.

Hutchinson, William R. *The Modernist Impulse in American Protestantism.* Cambridge: Harvard University Press, 1976.

Jensen, Richard. *The Winning of the Midwest: Social and Political Conflict, 1888–1896.* Chicago: University of Chicago Press, 1971.

Kellstedt, Lyman, and Mark A. Noll. "Religion, Voting for President, and Party Identification, 1948–1984." In *Religion and American Politics,* ed. Mark A. Noll, pp. 355–379. New York: Oxford University Press, 1990.

Kinzer, Donald L. *An Episode in Anti-Catholicism: The American Protective Association.* Seattle: University of Washington Press, 1964.

Kleppner, Paul. *The Cross of Culture: A Social Analysis of Midwestern Politics, 1850–1900.* New York: The Free Press, 1970.

Lenski, Gerhard. *The Religions Factor.* Garden City: Doubleday, 1961.

Leubke, Frederick C. *Immigrants and Politics: The Germans of Nebraska, 1880–1900.* Lincoln: University of Nebraska Press, 1969.

Marsden, George M. "The Evangelical Denomination." In *Piety and Politics,* ed. Richard and John Neuhaus, and Michael Cromartie, pp. 55–68. Washington, DC: Ethics and Public Policy Center, 1987.

———. *The Soul of the American University: From Protestant Establishment to Established Nonbelief.* Modern American Religion, vol. 1. New York: Oxford University Press, 1994.

Marty, Martin E. *Modern American Religion: The Irony of It All, 1893–1919,* vol. 1. Chicago: University of Chicago Press, 1986.

Orsi, Robert Anthony. *The Madonna of 115th Street: Faith and Community in Italian Harlem, 1880–1950.* New Haven: Yale University Press, 1985.

Pollack, Norman. *The Populist Response to Industrial America: Midwestern Political Thought.* Cambridge: Harvard University Press, 1962.

Ribuffo, Leo P. *The Old Christian Right: The Protestant Far Right From the Great Depression to the Cold War.* Philadelphia: Temple University Press, 1983.

Sklar, Kathryn Kish. "Two Political Cultures in the Progressive Era: The National Consumers' League and the American Association for Labor Legislation." In *U.S. History as Women's History,* ed. Linda K. Kerber, Alice Kessler-Harris, and Kathryn Kish Sklar, pp. 36–62. Chapel Hill: University of North Carolina Press, 1995.

Stevenson, Louise. *Scholarly Means to Evangelical Ends: The New Haven Scholars and the Transformation of Higher Learning in America, 1830–1890.* Baltimore: Johns Hopkins University Press, 1986.

Thernstrom, Stephan C. *The Other Bostonians: Poverty and Progress in an American Metropolis, 1880–1970.* Boston: Harvard University Press, 1973.

Ten

Fundamentalists Versus Modernists

In the early twentieth century a great quarrel erupted between Protestant modernists and conservatives. Many of the conservative Protestants were fundamentalists. Although the battle focused on religious matters, much more was involved. At stake was whether to accept urban, cosmopolitan, modern America, or adhere to an earlier version characterized by rural small towns, and Anglo-Saxon hegemony. Over time, it came to involve a debate whether to accept a new morality grounded in majority opinion rather than traditional, absolute theological precepts. These disputes affected politics, and by the late twentieth century they were reflected in the activities of the religious right, a very potent political force.

Modernism is the adaptation of religious concepts to accommodate modern culture; its spirit and positions are diametrically opposed to those of biblical literalists. It involves the acceptance of modern science, especially the theory of natural selection, rather than the biblical account of creation. Modernists interpret Scripture with the help of historical investigative techniques known as higher criticism. Modernists would not accept the virgin birth or the accounts of many miracles; many would not accept the idea that Christ rose from the dead. They would deny the infallibility of Scripture. Modernists assume that God works in history and God's handiwork can be found in progress and human development: Society continues to evolve toward the emergence of the Kingdom of God on earth, but that final stage may not occur in reality.

Fundamentalist Protestantism

By 1919, it was clear that American Protestant Christianity was essentially divided into two camps, modernists and fundamentalists. During the 1890s some conservative Protestant leaders had begun to organize in order to defend orthodoxy against the inroads of the new Christianity. In 1910, conservative Protestants published twelve volumes entitled *The Fundamen-*

tals, which defended orthodoxy and refuted the New Theology. *The Fundamentals* supported belief in the inerrancy of the Bible, the truth of biblical stories, the mission and divinity of Christ, the virgin birth, and millennialism. Fundamentalists vigorously attempted to refute higher criticism. *The Fundamentals* upheld what the authors thought were historical biblical teachings, and worked to expose non-Biblical teachings and attitudes. Above all, fundamentalists were militants: they believed they were locked in a fierce struggle with the forces of evil over the correct meaning of the Bible. Not only was the Bible seen as inerrant, it was scientifically and historically accurate. The formation of the World's Christian Fundamentals Association in the summer of 1919 marked the official beginning of organized fundamentalism.

The stronghold of fundamentalism was the South, but it was also powerful in the Midwest; these areas of fundamentalist strength have been referred to as the Bible Belt. Fundamentalism was strongest in rural areas, but it originated in cities, had urban supporters, appealed to many more than southern populists, and was nationwide in scope. There were ugly disputes between fundamentalists and modernists in some of the large Protestant churches, particularly among Baptists and northern Presbyterians. Although conservatives eventually lost control over many mainline Protestant bodies, many did not become come-outers but remained in their churches to give witness to their convictions.

Fundamentalism was a strong reaction against theological modernism. In this respect it had a clearly definable intellectual core: The fundamentalists employed the works of a group of Presbyterian theologians at Princeton University Divinity School to buttress their positions. However, the Princetonians were defending Old School Presbyterianism, rather than founding fundamentalism. The key Princeton theologians were Charles Hodge and B.B. Warfield, whose writings and teachings defended what had become traditional Protestantism. Charles Hodge argued in *What Is Darwinism?* that natural selection was inconsistent with Christianity. Warfield spent much effort defending biblical inerrancy. Fundamentalists drew heavily upon the writings of the Princeton Calvinists even though the Princetonians did not accept the form of premillennialism that appealed to most fundamentalists.

Many fundamentalists were premillennialists ("premils," in Bible school slang). The premils' thrust was no longer to bring about the Kingdom of God on earth; rejecting postmillennialism, they thought Christ would come before the millennium. Because the world was growing more and more sinful, they could not accept the idea that the millennium would come before the second coming of the Lord. The world was in such a sad condition, they held, that only Christ's second coming would rescue humankind from the abyss of secularism and materialism. Christ's imminent coming made it necessary for his followers to live as though they were facing the last judgment tomorrow. Evangelist Dwight Moody believed that Christ would separate the sheep from the goats when the saints were transported out of the world in rapture, just prior to the Battle of Armageddon. The saints' role was to rescue souls from a hostile, unrepentant world. Their involvement in the affairs of the world was to fight prostitution, drink, and other vices. Through much of the twentieth century, fundamentalists focused on these public questions and otherwise remained aloof from politics. Premillennialism had the effect of excusing adherents from addressing a broader range of issues. Most did not support the Social Gospel.

These premils usually followed the English preacher John Nelson Darby in dividing historical time, including the future, into periods. This interpretation, known as dispensationalism, argues that there are seven time periods, or dispensations. The last dispensation will be marked by the end of the world and the final judgment. This scenario is largely based on the books of Ezekiel, Zechariah, Daniel, and Revelation. (In the contemporary age, this view was popularized in Hal Lindsey's *The Late Great Planet Earth* in 1970.) The most important American to teach dispensationalism was Cyrus Ingerson Scofield, a Kansas lawyer, who in 1909 published the *Scofield Reference Bible,* an annotated Bible that explained scriptures from the perspective of Darbyite dispensationalism. Two million copies of it were sold within a decade.

To dispensationalists, the Battle of Armageddon is to conclude a war that will annihilate one-third of the human race and end with Christ's second coming. God's saints would not be present for the war but would be in rapture with Christ and would return with him. Dispensationalists came to disagree about when Christ takes his people up into the cloud: Would rapture (1 Thessalonians 4:15–17) occur during, before, or after the tribulation? The war was to begin when the Antichrist, Satan's representative, dominated the earth and when gentile armies invaded Palestine, where the world's Jews had regrouped. At the end of the war, the Antichrist would be defeated at Armageddon, and Satan would be placed in bondage. Christ would restore the Kingdom of Israel and reign for a thousand years. Jews would accept Christ as their Messiah. Because Israel would play a central role in the events of the last dispensation, American dispensationalists promoted the creation of a Jewish homeland beginning in the early 1890s, several years before Theodor Herzl, the founder of Zionism, published *The Jewish State.*

Dispensationalists saw the rise of secularism and liberalism, and the deterioration of moral standards, as signs of hope that the second coming was drawing nearer. Bad news for many Christians became good news for dispensationalists. Apostasy in the mainline churches was a clear sign to dispensationalists that the end was at hand. The *Christian Century,* a mainline organ, denounced dispensationalism as a pagan, "neurotic" movement that worked hand in glove with "reactionary," predatory capitalists.

A "Great Renunciation" occurred among dispensationalists from 1900 to 1930. They sharply decreased their support of social reform and private charity, stating that these activities smacked too much of the concerns of the Social Gospelers. They believed that advocates of the Social Gospel had substituted materialism for theological orthodoxy and the primacy of eternal salvation.

At another level, fundamentalism was a sociological phenomenon. It emerged at a time of great social stress when people perceived that the civilization and values that had characterized nineteenth-century America were collapsing and being replaced by the seeming chaos of the twentieth century. It offered people a buffer against the threatening currents of change. Emerging in tandem with it was premillennialism, which helped fundamentalists interpret the changes they were experiencing. Like fundamentalism, millennialism tends to emerge in times of social distress and perceived disaster. Together fundamentalism and premillennialism functioned as a revitalization movement that enabled people to find meaning and develop new ways of thinking and living. For fundamentalism's adherents, religion was not a compartment of life they accessed every Sunday; it was a rich way of life that transcended all and gave them courage and hope.

The Churches in the Twenties

Throughout the 1920s, fundamentalists and conservative Protestant allies waged a losing battle against cultural modernism, materialism, and secular culture. The spirit of the age sometimes distorted Christian teaching and imagery. In *The Man Nobody Knows,* published in 1925, layman Bruce Barton portrayed Christ as a young executive who assembled a remarkable management team. Churchmen complained that some saw God as a grand Rotarian and that religion was seen as just another form of commercialism. There were increasingly numerous ways to occupy one's spare time rather than attending religious services or being involved in church-related activities. Even in rural America, the automobile and radio were forces undermining the influence of Christianity. The enthusiasm that had characterized missionary organizations and Christian benevolence seemed to have diminished. Perhaps this decline was related to the disillusionment of many crusades. After all, World War I was supposed to be a war to end all wars.

The fundamentalist and conservative Protestants found even more wrong with the spirit of the wide-open Roaring Twenties. They insisted on a more demanding code of personal morality than did mainline Protestants. They lost battles on most fronts, but preserved the right to ban the teaching of evolution and the use of certain books in some school districts, usually in the South. Failing by one vote to pass such legislation in Kentucky, they were more successful in Oklahoma, Missouri, Arkansas, North Carolina, and Florida. Unable to pass such legislation in Texas, Governor Miriam ("Ma") Ferguson used her own authority to ban certain biology texts.

An antievolution law was passed in Tennessee in 1925. In Dayton, Tennessee, high school teacher John T. Scopes challenged it by teaching evolution, and was brought to trial. The American Civil Liberties Union offered to defend Scopes, and Clarence Darrow, the nation's most famous trial lawyer, headed his legal team. Former secretary of state William Jennings Bryan led the prosecution. The trial symbolized the clash of modern culture with Victorian nineteenth-century culture and the clash of urban, pluralistic values with rural, conservative Protestant values. H.L. Mencken's columns attacking Bryan were merciless; in one he called the opponent of evolution a "sweating anthropoid." Darrow asked Bryan to take the witness stand as a biblical expert, and proceeded to expose what cosmopolitans thought to be Bryan's ignorance. The "monkey trial" ended with Scopes being found guilty and given a minor fine, a verdict later overturned on a technicality. Still in Dayton five days after the trial, Bryan, "the Great Commoner," died suddenly. He had not been the ignorant, bigoted bumpkin that many suggested, and was neither anti-Semitic nor anti-Catholic. Though a fundamentalist, he had an optimistic view of man's potential and did not speak of human depravity. He opposed Darwinism in large measure because he worried about the influence of social Darwinism; belief in evolution and social Darwinism, he feared, could only give the rich license to do whatever they wished while urging society to ignore the plight of the poor. There is no question that the fundamentalists and conservative Protestants were very strong in the South and had many followers throughout rural America. Bryan saw this dispute as a part of a much larger question—whether schoolrooms would be used for the teaching of materialism and the destruction of religious beliefs.

The Scopes trial has come to be seen as an event marking the defeat of conservative, Protestant values because Bryan and his supporters appeared to be ignorant and intolerant. The election of Franklin D. Roosevelt and the repeal of the Eighteenth Amendment appeared to seal the triumph of secularism and urban culture. In making this appraisal, it is often forgotten that many progressives and mainline Protestants had worked to achieve the ratification of the Prohibition amendment in 1919.

In 1928, Alfred E. Smith, a wet (opponent of Prohibition), urban Catholic Democrat was defeated for the presidency in a campaign in which fundamentalists and many other Protestants fought to save "Anglo-Saxon civilization." Many liberal Protestants, equating Protestantism with democracy, were alarmed by the prospect that a Roman Catholic had been nominated for the presidency. While American Catholics saw religion and politics as separate matters, the Catholic leadership in Rome still thought Catholicism should be the state religion everywhere and that Catholic officeholders were bound to follow the moral guidance of the church. The conservative Protestants would still have opposed Smith had he been a Protestant. Smith was badly defeated, losing even New York and states in the upper South. Nevertheless, the defeat of Smith did not mean that rural, conservative America had won a lasting victory over secularism and the polyglot cities. The Republican grip on the large cities was broken as Smith carried the twelve biggest cities. Southern and eastern Europeans in the cities came to identify with the Democratic Party. With their help, and disappointment with President Herbert Hoover's inability to deal with the Great Depression, Democrat Franklin D. Roosevelt was elected to the presidency in 1932. The Democratic victory marked an increase in the political influence of urban machines and of Catholic and Jewish citizens. Prohibition ended in 1933, but the fundamentalists were able to keep some counties dry.

The end of Prohibition was more than just a defeat for fundamentalists and conservative Protestants; it was a setback for a much larger slice of Protestant America. Fundamentalists and conservative Protestants were often joined by members of the old Protestant middle class, some of whom were theological moderates. They saw Prohibition as a way of defending an older culture that appeared threatened by one less disciplined and responsible. In many ways they were not reactionaries. Many prohibitionists were concerned about the power of the trusts and opposed to child labor, unsafe working conditions, and political corruption. Some were sympathetic to African Americans, Native Americans, and Asian Americans.

Because the defenders of nineteenth-century Protestant values emphasized the development of individual virtues as the foundation of the good society, they stressed self-confidence, personal dignity, character, duty, restraint, self-discipline, and conscience. Their focus was upon what has been called "the bourgeois interior." The waning of Progressivism in the 1920s, the spiritual recession that afflicted churches, and the repeal of Prohibition were evidence that the informal establishment status that Protestantism had come to enjoy was diminishing.

The emerging new society was characterized by cultural pluralism, a less inhibited lifestyle, and the development of a more unsentimental and pragmatic approach to politics. This required the repeal of the Eighteenth Amendment and other mainstays of the old order. Among other repeals were restraints on organized labor and the growth of governmental power. The ideal of a homogeneous, organic society was supplanted by the acceptance of a heterogeneous society characterized by many competing sectors. Government agencies were considered by some to be more capable of providing direction and resolving problems than the church and family—the two key institutions of the pietistic republic of the nineteenth and early twentieth centuries. The moralistic political style of men like Woodrow Wilson and Herbert Hoover seemed anachronistic to many in the 1930s. These distressing developments, often spawned by or associated with the New Deal, made pietists less and less comfortable with the new age. However, not all conservative Protestants opposed the New Deal, and many Protestant theological liberals did oppose it.

Despite serious reversals, fundamentalists and conservative Protestants continued to confront modernism by setting up youth programs and organizations, publishing ventures, mission organizations, educational institutions, and radio (later, television) ministries. To an extent they withdrew from national political debates, but they had not given up or become inactive. Their activities in the 1930s and 1940s prepared them to reenter national political debates by midcentury.

The Old Christian Right

Not all fundamentalists and conservative Protestants abandoned the public arena. Unconvinced that the old, evangelical republic was doomed, some sought to combat these developments and sometimes offered simplistic solutions for the complex problems of the thirties. A few drifted into anti-Semitism and fascism. Among these were Gerald B. Winrod, William Dudley Pelley, and Gerald L.K. Smith. Scholars, noting their fundamentalist or conservative Protestant convictions, have mistakenly assumed that these three spoke for their religious groups. They actually represented a small portion of those Christians swimming against the dominant cultural tide, and their nativist and authoritarian ideologies were not shared by most of their coreligionists.

William Dudley Pelley was a writer and journalist who claimed in 1928 to have had mystical experiences in which he heard voices from the other world. Through "automatic writing" he could describe events and persons far from him. He published a magazine known as *Liberation* (later *New Liberation*), operated Galahad Press, and led Galahad College. He claimed that President Hoover was controlled by followers of the "International Shylock," praised Hitler, and founded the Silver Legion, with himself as "chief," when Hitler became chancellor of Germany. The legionnaires were

Christian fascists who destroyed some property and harassed enemies. Lacking courage, they did not win many street confrontations and avoided starting them. Pelley denied that Jesus was a Jew, saying that Christ was a forerunner of the legion of the Silver Shirts. He relied a great deal on a discredited forgery called the *Protocols of the Elders of Zion*, which suggested there was a long-standing Jewish conspiracy to rule the world and undermine Christian civilization. The nation's main anti-Semite, Pelley also came to dislike African Americans; he claimed that African American men lusted after white women. As chief of the Silver Legion, he wanted to do away with banks, private legal practices, advertising, unions, and money. In their place would be a Christian commonwealth that would employ citizens and would be owned by them. Pelley disbanded the Silver Legion in 1941 and the following year was sent to prison for sedition.

Gerald B. Winrod was a prominent fundamentalist spokesman in the theological and cultural battles of the 1920s. A proponent of "old-fashioned Holy Ghost religion," the Kansas minister spent much of each year on the road barnstorming for fundamentalist causes. In 1925, he established the Defenders of the Christian Faith and edited the monthly *Defender.* In the 1930s, he denounced big government as the first step to collectivism, and charged that Jewish financier Jacob Schiff had financed the Russian Revolution. Winrod also drew upon the *Protocols of the Elders of Zion* and praised Hitler for suppressing Jewish radicals. He distinguished between bad and good Jews, the latter being the vast majority who knew nothing of the nefarious conspiracy. In 1938, he was a serious contender for the Republican nomination for the U.S. Senate in Kansas, but was defeated. During the campaign his criticism of Jews was muted. In 1942 he was indicted for conspiring to bring about insubordination in the U.S. armed forces. Most of his time and energy thereafter was given to his legal problems. Federal prosecutors eventually abandoned his case.

Gerald L.K. Smith was a Disciples of Christ minister who avoided the dispute over creationism and considered accepting some modernist views in the 1920s. While a minister at a Shreveport, Louisiana, church, he became a follower of Governor Huey P. Long, whose Share Our Wealth plan promised every family a homestead and guaranteed income. Smith's involvement in politics led to his forced resignation as pastor in 1934. After Long's murder in 1935, Smith claimed to be his successor, though he was soon removed from the movement's payroll. In 1936, he allied with Father Charles Coughlin and Dr. Francis Townsend, both right-wing populists, in backing William L. Lemke for the presidency. Smith denounced President Roosevelt, unions, and big government, but also called Hitler a "crazy butcher." A talented demagogue, his speeches could move crowds. In 1942, he began publishing a monthly, *Cross and the Flag.* By then he was moving toward fundamentalism but, as a Campbellite, he refrained from embracing that label. His followers became known for anti-Semitism, and he made no effort to correct them. By 1944, he was saying that his greatest enemies were the Jews, who were responsible for the difficulties he encountered in obtaining sites for lectures and meetings.

As presidential candidate for the America First Party in 1944, Smith frequently inquired if the New Deal employed many "Jewish bureaucrats" or if 95 percent of the founders of communism were apostate Jews. In 1946 Smith announced plans to make available *The International Jew,* a collection of Henry Ford's attacks on Jews, and claimed that Jews used Hollywood to turn the nation toward communism. In the 1950s, he worked quietly to help Senator Joseph McCarthy fight to prevent Anna Rosenberg from gaining a top Defense Department job. He praised segregationist governors Orval Faubus of Arkansas and George C. Wallace of Alabama, produced literature for white citizens councils, and called Martin Luther King, Jr., a Marxist.

The nation reacted to these right-wing extremists with a Brown Scare in the late 1930s and 1940s. Many believed that any tactics were justified in silencing these people. Winrod and Pelley were indicted for sedition, though the grounds for the charges were exceedingly weak. In a sense, these pathetic people were victims of the revival of the World War I spirit of 100 percent Americanism, to which they adhered. Activities to silence and disable them would set a precedent for a similar persecution of leftists in the McCarthy era. The thinking of these right-wing extremists would later be accepted by a much larger constituency that included McCarthyites, John Birchers, and other right-wing extremists.

Two important militants who had been involved in conservative politics would be identified with both the old Christian right and the new Christian right. These transitional figures were Billy James Hargis and Carl McIntire. Reverend McIntire identified his cause, the Twentieth Century Reformation, with anticommunism. A bitter critic of the Federal and later National Council of Churches, he often suggested that communists had infiltrated the council, and insisted that God mandated capitalism as the economic system Christians must support. When Senator Joseph McCarthy conducted his witch-hunts in the early 1950s, McIntire helped him identify suspected communists. McIntire operated Beacon Press, a college, a conference center, and a daily radio program. Accompanying him on his Twentieth Century Reformation Hour broadcasts was "Amen Charlie," who voiced his approval of McIntire's excited comments at appropriate times. McIntire also gained notoriety through his association with Reverend Ian Paisley, leader of the violent Protestant extremists in Northern Ireland. Anti-Catholicism was high on his list of priorities. By 1996, his broadcast was carried by only one station, and he was facing financial problems.

Hargis, founder of the Christian Crusade, was a former pastor in Missouri and Oklahoma. Beginning in 1950, he devoted all of his time to anticommunism. He said he would rather be winning souls but God called him to fight communism and modernism. Hargis was a leader in arousing conservative Protestants over the banning of compulsory school prayer. Hargis and McIntire linked the end of prayer in the schools with increased social disorganization, crime, and sexual promiscuity. Hargis sometimes advised congressional conservatives, and McIntire assisted Young Americans for Freedom, a conservative group less extreme than either radio preacher. Hargis's ministry sustained major damage in the 1970s when he was charged with sexual improprieties.

Contemporary Fundamentalism

In the 1970s, some moderate fundamentalists became active in politics and found it necessary to ally with Catholics as well as Mormons and other nonfundamentalists. The decision to work with Catholics represented a fundamental break with tradition since some Conservative Protestants had not yet abandoned anti-Catholicism. Contemporary Southern Baptists have had a dialogue with Roman Catholics, but some still adhere to a fierce anti-Catholicism. The Southern Baptist Convention has continued to oppose diplomatic relations with the Vatican, a position rooted in their historic views concerning church-state relations. Some conservative Protestants have discovered that Roman Catholics share their devotion to traditional morality and opposition to abortion. Among prominent Catholics they have worked with are John (Terry) Dolan, a fund-raiser and organizer, Richard Viguerie, the direct-mail pioneer who was associated with Billy James Hargis, and Phyllis Schlafly, a leading opponent of the Equal Rights Amendment. Though a Roman Catholic, Schlafly is particularly popular among evangelicals because she represents the traditional view that women are responsible for establishing moral standards for the family.

In the 1970s and 1980s, proponents of the Equal Rights Amendment (ERA) were stunned to learn that fundamentalist women opposed it and saw the matter as a religious question. For the proponents, the gender question was a matter of power. For fundamentalist women, it touched a biblically defined definition of their roles and threatened Christian families and the God-ordained headship of husbands. They shared Reverend Jerry Falwell's belief that the women's rights movement rejected "the mandate that 'the husband is the head of the wife, even as Christ is the head of the church.'"

fundamentalist women feared that they would be expected to behave as men and be removed from their God-given place on a pedestal. They agreed with Phyllis Schlafly that the ERA was the "unisex" amendment and an invitation to moral chaos. Their response was an expression of religious and cultural fundamentalism.

In contemporary times, fundamentalist and conservative churches have differentiated themselves from mainline Protestants by their opposition to the ordination of women. Although women's organizations within mainline churches have retained more formal autonomy than those of conservative Protestant women, the women in the latter denominations had more actual authority than their mainline sisters because their churches and organizations were more decentralized. However, clergy in the conservative denominations were inclined to suggest that women were theologically naive and impractical, requiring constant male guidance. In the first half of the twentieth century, both fundamentalists and mainline Protestants have resisted the ordination of women and female pastors. Fundamentalist women have played a larger role in other ministries than have women in mainline denominations. They have benefited from the fundamentalist dislike of centralization and from acceptance of willingness of some women to remain single in service of the Lord. Females were active as fundamentalist missionaries at a time when mainline Protestants were ambivalent about missions. In the years 1920–1950, fundamentalists faced the task of starting from scratch in building denominational infrastructures and needed workers of both sexes. Large numbers of women attended Bible institutes and were active in summer Bible conferences.

Southern Baptists

Fundamentalists were numerous in the Southern Baptist Convention, but did not take control until 1979. Meanwhile, a number of conservative Baptists were so dismayed with moderate domination of SBC agencies and seminaries that they left the denomination and became Independent Baptists.

A conservative resurgence within the Southern Baptist Convention began in the 1970s and resulted in the end of moderate dominance of SBC leadership and agencies. Conservative rebels were reacting against the growth of a bureaucracy and the deprovincialization of the South. The conservatives had not been noted for their support of SBC agencies; they often avoided selecting pastors from the ranks of SBC seminary graduates. They regretted the deterioration of small-town and rural southern culture. Conservatives believed that those who controlled the machinery of the SBC approved and abetted in a process of theological and social liberalization.

Dispensational millennialism was the ideology of many of the conservatives who seized control of the SBC. The stable, rural, southern culture that many had known for so long began to collapse in the middle of the twentieth century. Large amounts of foreign and Yankee money was invested in the South, and industries and cities grew. Blue laws were repealed or ignored, and adherence to temperance declined. Court decisions attacked school segregation, ended school prayer, legalized abortion, and gave women equal employment rights. Southern culture seemed to be facing disaster; amid this great social stress, many embraced dispensational millennialism. It explained why the world around them was deteriorating and promised a new beginning in the apocalypse. Premillennialism also provided its adherents with a sense of belonging to an especially blessed community of believers, whose role it was to prepare for the Lord's coming by restoring the church to its original purity. Through reform, Southern Baptists would strengthen their sense of "chosenness." Members of a revitalized church, they would enjoy a foretaste of the bliss that would characterize the second coming of Christ.

Beginning in the 1970s, conservatives led a grassroots rebellion against bureaucracy and in favor of congregational autonomy. It was to be a struggle between an old southern middle class and a new middle class distinguished by substantial education, support of deprovincialization, and comfortable in urban settings. Conservatives saw SBC seminaries as nurseries of error, though the theology professors were moderates and not death-of-God liberals. The conservative rebels made biblical inerrancy their rallying cry. At issue was control of the SBC agencies, seminaries, and the drafting of doctrinal positions. A basic question was whether the SBC could reach an accommodation with the modern world. Most moderates accepted some form of inerrancy, but now were expected to subscribe to a particular interpretation of Scripture, that of dispensational millennialism. It was this theological position that the conservative leadership, under Wally Amos Criswell and Houston judge Paul Pressler, wished to define as Southern Baptist orthodoxy.

Biblical inerrantists made up a great majority of Southern Baptists, and moderates were clearly a minority relying upon the principle of soul freedom to justify their positions. Speaking at the 1987 convention, Texas evangelist Earnest Eudy argued that the devil was the author of liberal theology: "Satan's goal is to rip the Bible from common Baptist people. He clips the wings of faith with the scissors of reason." Some conservative leaders have called themselves "fundamentalists," and their moderate critics often have called them all fundamentalists. In the South, theological modernism was not present to any substantial degree, and the SBC is not a minority culture.

The SBC's response to the civil rights movement was unsatisfactory to progressives as well as many conservatives. Some conservatives thought that the denomination's support of white supremacy was as important as its emphasis upon evangelism. The Christian Life Commission generated materials designed to help congregations apply biblical principles to race relations, and the Sunday School Board included pictures of African American and white teens together. Emmanuel McCall, an African American, was hired by the SBC Home Missionary Board in 1968 and served as head of the Black Church Extension Division until 1991. The first African American vice president of the SBC was elected in 1974. There are about one thousand all–African American congregations in the denomination. The SBC went on record against lynchings and having clergy preside at Ku Klux Klan funerals. However, Baptist women's organizations were able to do more to attack racism because they enjoyed some financial independence from the SBC. Professor T.B. Maston of Southwestern Baptist Theological Seminary in Fort Worth was an outspoken critic of racism and demolished biblical arguments in favor of segregation. Some of his students also tried to lead the denomination toward a stronger pro–civil rights position. None of the six SBC seminaries had a full-time African American professor until 1991. Some congregations have been integrating, and opponents of segregation have long used denominational publications to criticize segregation.

Not all opponents of segregation have been theological moderates. W.A. Criswell, a leading fundamentalist, said congregations that refused to admit African American members were guilty of "manifest hypocrisy." The national drive for desegregation resulted in the establishment of many Christian schools as all-white bastions, and some congregations built their own restaurants, theaters, jogging tracks, saunas, and basketball courts to cushion their members against contact with nonwhites. Some young moderates were so disappointed with the SBC's response to the civil rights movement that they severed their ties with the church, and some lost their faith.

It has been suggested that the struggle between moderates and fundamentalists within the Southern Baptist Convention involves opinions about integration. When internal warfare in the First Baptist Church of Birmingham resulted in the 1970 secession of its pastor, Dr. J. Herbert Gilmore, Jr., and three hundred of his followers, the issue was whether to admit African Americans to membership, along with the fact that Gilmore was not a fundamentalist. Gilmore claimed his fundamentalist opponents were mainly segregationists. Conservative Baptists, however, have often responded to such claims by indicating that it is a difference in style of worship that separates them from African Americans and that racism is not involved. It would be a mistake to argue that all SBC fundamentalists opposed the civil rights movement. A 1986 survey demonstrated that 53 percent of those who identified themselves as fundamentalists had a positive view of the civil rights movement; 90 percent of moderates thought the movement had positive effects.

The largely conservative Southern Baptist Convention grew to become one of the largest Protestant denominations; by the 1980s, it claimed over 14 million members in congregations nationwide. Probably a majority of SBC members are fundamentalists. Today, there are about twenty Baptist churches with approximately 30 million adherents. The great majority of those people are conservative Protestants.

Disciples of Christ are considered fundamentalists, as are Missouri Synod Lutherans. Independent Presbyterians, such as Reverend Carl McIntire, are also fundamentalists. Other conservative Presbyterians who followed J. Gresham Machen out of the Presbyterian Church in the U.S.A. would soon be known as the Orthodox Presbyterian Church. Orthodox Presbyterians considered themselves Old School Presbyterians and were willing to ally with the fundamentalists against modernism, but insisted that they were not fundamentalists due to their opposition to dispensationalism and Arminianism. George W. Dollar, a fundamentalist scholar, distinguishes between militant fundamentalists and moderate fundamentalists. The militants will not belong to a denomination that includes liberals, and will avoid all fellowship with modernists or liberals; this represents "second-degree separatism." Moderates do not insist on strict separatism. Some fundamentalists have displayed anti-Semitic, anti-Catholic, and anti-Black attitudes.

Holiness Religion

The Holy Ghost Protestants, the holiness and Pentecostal churches, continued to grow, sharing much with the fundamentalists. The fundamentalists refused to include these people in the fundamentalist tent, opposing emphasis on the gifts of the Holy Spirit in the twentieth century. Fundamentalists thought that those who spoke in tongues could be demented. Holy Ghost Protestantism particularly appealed to the poor and marginalized. In the cities it attracted people who had migrated from rural America and felt lost and disoriented. They believed that the Spirit permitted individuals to live wholly without deliberate sin; the individual enjoyed entire sanctification. These people were profoundly dissatisfied with society as it was and found meaning, status, and self-esteem in holiness and Pentecostal religious ideologies and countercultures. Their meetings were somewhat unstructured and frequently marked by spiritual ecstasy, as individuals spontaneously demonstrated in different ways that they felt filled with and guided by the Holy Spirit.

The holiness movement has experienced significant growth since the late nineteenth century, and has been allied with the fundamentalists on many fronts. Most holiness people, as well as the related Pentecostals, were not in the narrowest sense fundamentalists, but areas of agreement were numerous. Their main concern was not the package of historical doctrines the fundamentalists prized; their attention focused upon sanctification by the Holy Spirit and a very strict code of personal morality.

Holy Ghost people advocated the "second blessing" or complete sanctification, which the Methodist Episcopal Church often seemed to slight even though it was taught by John Wesley. In 1835, Phoebe Palmer, wife of a prominent New York physician, began efforts to correct this deficiency. She made lecture tours speaking on this subject, and began her "Tuesday Meetings for the Promotion of Holiness" in New York City. Christian perfectionism and the holiness movement attracted many women who had embraced the idea that they had a special duty to foster morality in their families and communities. A theologian calculated that one woman had as much good influence as seven and a half men!

Holiness people were urged to live simply and be unconcerned about worldly accomplishments and success. Preachers warned against introspection, worry, and nervousness, suggesting that these were symptoms of being self-centered. People were told to surrender their concerns and troubles to Christ and wait to be filled by the Holy Spirit. They were promised a completely new life and eventual victory over sin. They were also being admitted to the exclusive circle of the saved.

Some elements in the Holiness movement emphasized divine healing, a matter that evangelist Charles G. Finney had discussed. By 1900 there were many holiness denominations. The name "Church of God" was used by a number of congregations that were based in the Southeast. A holiness denomination called the Church of God (Anderson, Indiana) was founded in 1881 and has experienced significant growth.

The Church of God (Cleveland, Tennessee)

At a revival meeting in Cherokee, North Carolina, in 1896, the Church of God of nearby Cleveland, Tennessee, was founded when more than a hundred people were able to speak in tongues. First known as the Holiness Church at Camp Creek, it changed its name to the Church of God in 1906. Most original members were poor farmers, formerly Methodists or Baptists. The denomination emerged during a severe economic depression. Many members lived in small cabins in out-of-the-way mountain communities. When the Church of God first spread to urban settings, it used storefront churches and appealed to the poor. At its 1908 conference, the denomination embraced Pentecostalism, emphasizing the importance of receiving the gifts of the Holy Spirit as a means of demonstrating baptism in the Holy Spirit. In 1923 a considerable number of members left the church when it removed its general overseer, A.J. Tomlinson, who was considered to have become too powerful. His followers formed the Church of God of Prophecy, which had 43,441 members by 1969.

Emphasis upon community within the Church of God (headquartered in Cleveland, Tennessee) was reinforced by foot washing and sharing the Lord's Supper. Members were hostile to the materialism of their age and the cold, formal worship of mainline churches. Like most Holy Spirit religions, the Church of God opposed divorce, dancing, immodest dress, church bazaars, church fairs, tobacco use, "necktie socials," most spectator sports, alcohol, and gambling.

Some of these prohibitions reflected the thinking of people who had experienced great economic deprivation. After World War II, many Church of God families moved into the middle class, and the church came to accept most sports and recreational activities as normal parts of life. "Picture shows" were seen as places to view pornography or make love and were condemned, but by the 1930s it was clear that the laity insisted on going to movies. To control the practice many ministers showed acceptable films on church premises. In the 1980s, the church still denounced attendance at movies, but violation of this teaching was considered a minor matter. In the 1950s, many ministers criticized television viewing, but it was not forbidden. The church has consistently criticized the content of most programming. It has never repealed its ban on the use of alcohol. The ban on soft drinks proved unenforceable by the 1930s and was lifted in 1935. The soft drink they opposed most was Coca-Cola, because it contained a very small amount of cocaine until about 1905. By the 1940s most female members defied the ban on wearing jewelry, and in 1958 the general assembly of the church permitted married people to wear wedding rings. Traditionalists were scandalized by this concession.

A few ministers argued that proof of being a true believer was handling poisonous snakes, but many believed that this practice gave the church a poor image. It was condemned in 1928; however, the practice did persist into the 1930s. Snake handling was found in many tiny denominations in Appalachia; sometimes people used the "salvation cocktail," which involved ingesting a small amount of strychnine.

Over the years, the church turned away from pacifism and accepted the doctrine of just wars. Some Church of God and other Pentecostal ministers were jailed for opposing World War I. In World War II, some members enlisted, but most Church of God servicemen were draftees. Since World War II, the Church of God has found it difficult to excommunicate or expel wayward members because so many of its congregants were converts from churches that did not insist that members conform to their teachings.

Women have been accepted as preachers and missionaries from the earliest days of the Church of God, but it refuses to admit them to higher administrative offices. This policy led to a decline in the proportion of females in its ministry from 1913 to 1987. A leader in the effort to win equal rights for women within the Church of God was Emma Sue Webb. She became a pastor in the early 1970s, and found her role limited because of her sex. In 1977, her letter of protest to the general overseer of the church was met by a response justifying policies restricting women. In 1981, she completed a master's thesis entitled "The Limitations on Women Ministers in the Church of God" at the California Graduate School of Theology. Some other Pentecostal denominations place even more restrictions upon the role of women in various ministries.

A number of women have functioned well as pastors in Pentecostal churches in very small towns. They do not challenge the traditional view of women's role in society and may see their own sufferings as divine punishment for Eve's sin. The business meetings of these churches may include only the female pastor and men, or their boards of deacons are composed of men. There is also evidence that women testify at Pentecostal services more loudly and at greater length than do men.

While the quest for sexual equality within the Church of God continues, there has been some improvement in the position of African Americans within it. The national civil rights movement led the church to end segregation in its congregations, and African American leaders have made continual efforts to convince the leadership that more African Americans should hold leadership positions in the denomination. In some other Pentecostal denominations, segregated worship ended in the 1940s.

CMA and the Nazarenes

Another important denomination, the Christian Missionary Alliance, was founded by Albert Benjamin Simpson, a prominent New York Presbyterian clergyman who left his denomination to work in the holiness movement. Simpson advanced a "fourfold gospel" theology, seeing Christ as "Savior, Sanctifier, Healer, and Coming King." Holiness and Pentecostal references to the fourfold or foursquare gospel refer to these four roles. These holiness people were puritanical in their lifestyles, believed in biblical literalism, and adhered to most fundamentalist beliefs. Their services were marked by most or all of the following: highly emotional sermons, healings, trances, visions, singing, dancing, foot washing, speaking in tongues, tithing, adventism, and perfectionism. They also practiced fasting. Holiness people and Pentecostals shared these characteristics, but most Pentecostals believed speaking in tongues was the essential sign that one had received the second blessing, the beginning of sanctification bestowed by the Holy Spirit.

Within the Methodist Episcopal Church, relations between the holiness advocates and their more sedate brethren deteriorated rapidly as people left the church or were expelled. In 1894, the Methodist Episcopal Church, South, disavowed the movement. The former Methodists usually found their way into the Church of the Nazarene, which had been organized by Dr. J.P. Widney and Phineas Bresee in Los Angeles in 1895. Bresee, the key figure, had been a Methodist and was a "come-outer" who called on people to abandon ordinary churches and seek entire sanctification by living to convert and serve the poor. His people were urged to follow a strict puritanical code of morals, later including the avoidance of motion pictures, which were denounced by all fundamentalists and most evangelicals. Some date the founding in 1906, and claim the denomination grew out of a merger that occurred in Pilot Point, Texas, in 1908. It would combine with other groups to become the largest holiness church in 1914. The Church of the Nazarene quickly attracted followers on the West Coast and then spread to the Mississippi Valley. It also absorbed some holiness people in Scotland, becoming an international church.

Holiness People

The Church of the Nazarene first supported postmillennialism, but after a few decades reversed its position and embraced premillennialism. This was a logical development because this and other holiness communities had the greatest appeal to debt-ridden farmers and the poor and working poor of the cities. It is no coincidence that a great growth of holiness Christianity occurred during the panic of 1893, one of the nation's worst depressions.

Economic hardship and unsettled social conditions also attracted the discontented and dispossessed to Pentecostalism, whose appeal to these people would surpass even that of the holiness movement. Pentecostal religion stressed the gifts of the Holy Spirit, particularly speaking in tongues. By 1919, the holiness churches had largely moved out of storefront churches and into middle-class neighborhoods. Reflecting middle-class aspirations, they deemphasized the ecstatic type of religion associated with the Pentecostals and moved toward more "respectable" religion. They still appealed to some of the dispossessed but were changing their focus. The Great Depression that began in 1929 created severe dislocations that led many more to embrace Pentecostalism and, to a lesser extent, holiness religion.

In the years from the 1890s to the 1930s, many of the men who entered these movements had lower social status than their fathers. Most people who embraced the early holiness religion and Pentecostal Christianity detested the socioeconomic system and were angry about their places in society. In their view, society was beyond repair. The presence of monopolies alongside great poverty was a clear sign that end times were near. They looked to the imminent coming of Christ as their deliverance. The belief that Christ was coming soon provided a strong motive for attempting to live holy lives. Premillennialism answered their needs. Postmillennialism, with its promise of gradual change and improvement leading to the coming of Christ, was unrealistic. The Church of the Nazarene found it necessary to reject postmillennialism in favor of premillennialism, and Pentecostals were also premillennialists. Pentecostal worship services were highly emotional affairs, at least as emotional as many meetings during the Second Great Awakening. With some justification, Pentecostals argue that they are returning to an authentic evangelical worship. Emotionalism had been removed from most Protestant revivals when they became highly organized. Revivalists like Dwight Moody made certain that the crowd did not get out of control. Hymns were used to calm crowds and prevent the outbreak of hysteria.

Holiness and Pentecostal religion provided people with self-respect and status as members of Christ's elect. Ecstatic experiences provided an emotional release. For ministers whose careers were blocked in older denominations, it meant freedom to preach what they believed, and possible career advancement. Holiness and Pentecostalism also served as the basis of a coherent subculture for people who clung to the older rural values and lifestyle threatened by industrialization and urbanization.

This subculture upheld a strict moral code and attachment to what has been called "the old-time religion." Its adherents were often inflexible, intolerant, though not condescending, and anti-intellectual. They considered the older and better-established Protestant denominations to be heretical and doing much more harm than good. They detested Catholicism with all the feeling of Reformation-era Protestants. They were suspicious of worldly success and found purpose and meaning through centering their lives in their communities of the Holy Spirit. Their manner was "folksy"; today they enjoy country and western music. In church they preferred to hear banjos, tambourines, guitars, and pianos rather than organs. Clapping and shouting in church seem normal to them and indicate their joy in having heard the good news. Some who adhered to this subculture had migrated to cities in search of work, but they never left their remote rural homes in a spiritual sense.

The Rise of Pentecostalism

A worldwide surge of revivalism occurred in 1904–1906. The American Pentecostal movement largely grew out of the holiness movement and emerged as part of this worldwide surge of revivalism. Many American Pentecostals saw salvation as being represented in three stages: justification, entire sanctification, and baptism of the Holy Spirit. Pentecostals saw baptism of the Holy Spirit as a third blessing, marked by the gifts of the Holy Spirit, particularly speaking in tongues. Other Pentecostals saw entire sanctification and Spirit baptism as separate but possibly contemporaneous events. From time to time, they claimed it might be necessary for the Holy Spirit to provide additional "infillings" of grace. Pentecostals saw the third gift as confirming sanctification but did not insist that possession of the gifts of the Spirit were absolutely necessary for salvation. Holiness people adhere to the Wesleyan approach and reject belief in the third blessing as heretical. There is no one theology common to all Pentecostals. All practice speaking in tongues. The term Pentecostal is applied to all religious bodies that trace their origins to the American phase of this revival. They all accept visions, dancing, fasting, loud singing, and physical gyrations, provided they are "in the Spirit." Few accept fire and snake handling. Healing is common among Pentecostals, and often involves exorcising demons. Their enthusiastic form of worship, visions, trances, and speaking in tongues have been seen as representing primal spirituality or "long-suppressed currents of archetypical human religiousness." Similarly, speaking in tongues can be seen as the prayer of the heart and as "breaking through the limitations of human language" to express deep religious sentiments. What Pentecostals see as religious healing may represent the link between primal spirituality and health or the operation of an inner healing mechanism. Pentecostalism can be seen as an optimistic, expectant, joyful mood. Members believe that the second coming is at hand and that their joyful worship and community is a foretaste of the reign of Christ and heaven. Pentecostals believe that those filled with the Holy Spirit will lead holy lives but are less inclined than holiness people to develop elaborate codes of conduct, placing less emphasis on outward behavior. As some of the Pentecostal groups evolved toward denominational status and greater respectability, their services became more sedate, and speaking in tongues and other ecstatic experiences were reserved for special occasions.

Modern American Pentecostalism began among largely African American prayer gatherings in Los Angeles, but white Pentecostals would soon depart these groups to form their own congregations. The Church of God (headquartered in Cleveland, Tennessee) initially supported biracial worship but called for separate African American and white congregations in the 1920s. The Assemblies of God, the most important Pentecostal denomination, was practically lily-white after 1916, when many African Americans joined nontrinitarians in leaving the denomination. However, many of the white ministers who formed the Assemblies of God had been ordained by Charles Harrison Mason, senior bishop of the Church of God in Christ. Racial friction existed in a number of other Pentecostal bodies. African American churches are not members of the Pentecostal Fellowship of North America or the National Association of Evangelicals. Most white holiness and Pentecostal churches supported racial segregation even more than did the white mainline churches in the South. The white holiness people and Pentecostals argued that it was not the place of the church to make pronouncements on social and political matters. They claimed to be genuine friends of African Americans, but they disapproved of the civil rights movement, often fearing it would lead to racial mixing. Some thought it was an instrument of international communism.

In the 1960s, moderates began to appear within these sects who denounced racial discrimination. In that decade, the Church of God broke new ground for a southern church by fully integrating its African American congregations into its organizational framework. It also took a firm stand against discrimination on the basis of race. Since the early 1950s, the *Pentecostal Herald,* published in Asbury, Kentucky, has spoken out against racism. The Church of God of Prophecy has long practiced religious racial equality, and the small Church of God (Jerusalem Acres) also has a racially integrated organizational structure. Nevertheless, most southern holiness and Pentecostal churches have made less progress than white mainline Protestants in moving toward racial equality. Holiness and Pentecostal congregations are havens for the common people and dispossessed of the South and reflect their fears and their concerns. Those "poor whites" at the very bottom of the white pecking order often are not strongly prejudiced against African Americans and are sometimes sympathetic toward them, holding that African Americans are usually not responsible for the poverty that sometimes afflicts them. As some of these churches evolve toward denominational status and attract more middle-class southerners, they may move more rapidly toward embracing racial equality.

C.H. Mason, a founder of the Church of God in Christ, which is today a large African American denomination, visited the Azusa Street revival in Los Angeles and spread Pentecostalism among his followers. He vividly described his baptism of fire: "When I opened my mouth to say Glory, a flame touched my tongue which ran down to me. My language changed and no word could I speak in my own tongue. Oh! I was filled with the Glory of the Lord."

Opponents of Pentecostalism in Mason's denomination followed C.H. Jones, the other founder, and named themselves the Church of Christ (Holiness), USA, remaining a holiness church. Mason became "General Overseer and chief Apostle" of the Church of God in Christ and held absolute power in doctrinal and organizational matters. Later called senior bishop, Mason traveled widely and proved to be a vigorous leader, providing for ministers to follow migrants to southern cities. A pacifist, he nevertheless supported the sale of Liberty Bonds in World War I and called upon followers to be law-abiding citizens. His pacifism resulted in his being jailed several times, and his activities were carefully monitored by the FBI. Some Pentecostal denominations have had female ministers, but the Church of God in Christ has consistently excluded women from full ministry.

Aimee Semple McPherson, founder of the International Church of the Foursquare Gospel, was an interesting figure in the Pentecostal movement. Her theology centered on Albert Benjamin Simpson's fourfold gospel, portraying the Lord as Savior, Sanctifier, Healer, and Coming King. She was converted by Reverend Robert Semple, her first husband, in Ingersoll, Ontario, in 1907; three years later they went as missionaries to Hong Kong, where he soon died. In 1916–1917, she and her second husband were preaching revivals in the eastern United States. She and Harold Mc Pherson separated in 1918 and were eventually divorced. Aimee McPherson continued preaching successful revivals, and probably was influenced by Maria B. Woodworth, a pastor of an Indianapolis church and prominent Pentecostal revivalist. A Pentecostalist, McPherson insisted that "a church without the Holy Ghost is like an automobile without gasoline."

There were remarkable healings at McPherson's meetings, particularly in the years 1919–1922. The evangelist consistently worked to assure that the healing ministry was subordinated to the main mission of winning souls. She had a gift for playing the piano while full of the Spirit. Her music was considered "wonderful but strange." She built Angelus Temple in Los Angeles and demonstrated there how effectively music and theater could be used in the service of the gospel. This blending of entertainment with worship has been adopted by other Pentecostals and accounts for their phenomenal growth today. She presented 150 different stage productions, including operas. Her complex included a radio station and a Bible college, and the 5,300-seat church foreshadowed today's evangelical megachurches. McPherson's congregation was deeply involved in caring for the poor, particularly during the depression (Figure 10).

McPherson may have been the most prominent woman in recent religious history. Unfortunately, her two divorces, quarrels among members of her family and staff, and a mysterious abduction that many thought was a

Figure 10. Aimee Semple McPherson. Evangelist Aimee Semple McPherson (1890–1944) was a pioneer in the use of theatrical productions for religious purposes. She was resourceful in using modern technology for evangelical purposes, even having radio towers perched on her megachurch. (Courtesy the Library of Congress.)

rendezvous with a lover attracted much attention. At the time of her death in 1944, the denomination had 410 North American churches and 200 missions. Half a century later, there are 25,577 churches in seventy-four lands. She ordained more than seventeen hundred ministers, and the Church of the Foursquare Gospel has about 1.7 million members today. The most successful female Holy Ghost preacher after McPherson was Katharine Kuhlman, who had 750,000 television viewers by the time she died in 1976.

Pentecostalism gives adherents the feeling of possessing real spiritual power. In addition to the power to speak in tongues, there is the added potential for healing and prophecy. Full gospel religion insists that reception of the Holy Spirit will be marked by prophecy, healing, and speaking in tongues. If these elements are not present, the Holy Spirit has not been experienced in fullness.

Traditionally, holiness people and Pentecostals have been suspicious of wealth seeking, but this view has changed in recent years. A number of Pentecostal preachers, particularly some who appear on television, may have accommodated too much with the world. They preach what has been called a Gospel of Prosperity. This view emphasizes that God wants everyone to be happy and enjoy prosperity. God does not send people sickness, suffering, and sorrow. Some seem to have a view of sin similar to that of their liberal opponents: it is reduced to a failure to be true to oneself rather than a willful rejection of the law of God.

Estimates on Pentecostal numbers vary greatly, but it is clear that they are experiencing significant growth in the United States, Latin America, and Africa. Some estimate that as many as one-fifth of American church members today claim to be Pentecostal to one extent or another. A much smaller number claim to have spoken in tongues. The Assemblies of God has many megachurches that, despite their size, provide a warm, welcoming environment where members hear compelling preaching and appealing spiritual music. Other Pentecostal churches are the United Pentecostal Church International, Pentecostal Assemblies of the World, the Apostolic Faith Mission, and the Open Bible Standard churches. Altogether there are more than 150 Pentecostal denominations and sects, with many unaffiliated Pentecostal congregations.

The social, economic, and political changes of the late nineteenth and twentieth centuries literally transformed the nation. The domination of rural and small-town Protestants was ended, and some of their traditional values were threatened. These great changes were accompanied by a widening division between conservative Protestants and those who embraced somewhat more modernized versions of Christianity. The angriest and most doctrinaire of the conservatives were often fundamentalists. Another major phalanx within conservative ranks was the holiness and Pentecostal Protestants. To a considerable extent, their rise also grew out of social and economic changes. By the 1930s, it appeared that most conservative Protestants had withdrawn from the public arena. They were regrouping and building a thriving subculture, and would later reenter public debates more powerful, better organized, and able to strongly influence political developments.

Bibliography

Ammerman, Nancy T. "After the Battles: Organizational Forms." In *Southern Baptists Observed,* ed. Nancy Tatom Ammerman, pp. 301–317. Knoxville: University of Tennessee Press, 1993.

———. "Observing Southern Baptists: An Introduction." In *Southern Baptists Observed,* ed. Nancy Tatom Ammerman, pp. 1–11. Knoxville: University of Tennessee Press, 1993.

Anderson, Robert Maples. *Vision of the Disinherited: The Making of American Pentecostalism.* New York: Oxford University Press, 1979.

Balmer, Randall. *Mine Eyes Have Seen the Glory: A Journey into the Evangelical Subculture in America.* New York: Oxford University Press, 1989.

Billingsley, Lloyd. "Radical Evangelicals and the Politics of Compassion." In *Piety & Politics: Evangelicals and Fundamentalists Confront the World,* ed. Richard John Neuhaus and Michael Cromartie, pp. 203–216. Washington, DC: Ethics and Public Policy Center, 1987.

Blumenthal, Sidney. "The Religious Right and Republicans." In *Piety and Politics,* ed. Richard John Neuhaus and Michael Cromartie, pp. 269–286. Washington, DC: Ethics and Public Policy Center, 1987.

Clabaugh, Gary K. *Thunder on the Right: The Protestant Fundamentalists.* Chicago: Nelson-Hall, 1974.

Clarke, Norman. *Deliver Us from Evil: An Interpretation of American Prohibition.* New York: Norton, 1976.

Cone, James H. *Black Theology and Black Power.* New York: Seabury Press, 1969.

Cox, Harvey. *Fire from Heaven: The Rise of Pentecostal Spirituality and the Reshaping of Religion in the Twenty-first Century.* Reading, MA: Addison-Wesley, 1995.

Crews, Mickey. *The Church of God: A Social History.* Knoxville: University of Tennessee Press, 1988.

Dayton, Donald W. *Theological Roots of Pentecostalism.* Metuchen, NJ: Scarecrow Press, 1987.

DeJong, Mary. "Introduction: Protestantism and Its Discontents in the Eighteenth and Nineteenth Centuries." *Women's Studies* 19 (winter 1991): 99–118.

Epstein, Daniel Mark. *Sister Aimee: The Life of Aimee Semple McPherson.* New York: Harcourt, Brace, Jovanovich, 1993.

Farnsley, Arthur E., II. " 'Judicious Concentration': Decision Making in the Southern Baptist Convention." In *Southern Baptists Observed,* ed. Nancy Tatom Ammerman, pp. 47–70. Knoxville: University of Tennessee Press, 1993.

Finke, Roger, and Rodney Stark. *The Churching of America.* New Brunswick, NJ: Rutgers University Press, 1992.

Glazer, Nathan. "Fundamentalism: A Defensive Offensive." In *Piety and Politics,* ed. Richard John Neuhaus and Michael Cromartie, pp. 245–258. Washington, DC: Ethics and Policy Center, 1987.

Glock, Charles Y., and Rodney Stark. *Christian Beliefs and Anti-Semitism.* New York: Harper Torchbooks, 1966.

Goff, James R., Jr. *Fields White Unto Harvest: Charles F. Parham and the Missionary Origins of Pentecostalism.* Fayetteville: University of Arkansas Press, 1988.

Graebner, Alan. "Birth Control and the Lutherans: The Missouri Synod as a Case Study." In *Women in American Religion,* ed. Janet Wilson James, pp. 229–252. Philadelphia: University of Pennsylvania Press, 1980.

Guth, James L. "Theology and Politics in Southern Baptist Institutions." In *Southern Baptists Observed,* ed. Nancy Tatom Ammerman, pp. 182–200. Knoxville: University of Tennessee Press, 1993.

Hadden, Jeffrey K., and Anson Shupe. "Televangelism in America." *Social Compass* 34 (1): 61–75.

Hamilton, Michael S. "Women, Public Ministry, and American Fundamentalism, 1920–1950." *Religion and American Culture* 3 (summer 1993): 171–196.

Harrell, David Edwin, Jr. *White Sects and Black Men.* Nashville: Vanderbilt University Press, 1971.

Hills, Samuel S. "The Story Behind the Story, Southern Baptists Since World War II." In *Southern Baptists Observed,* ed. Nancy Tatom Ammerman, pp. 30–46. Knoxville: University of Tennessee Press, 1993.

Hollinger, David A., and Charles Capper. *The American Intellectual Tradition.* Volume 2, *1865 to the Present.* New York: Oxford University Press, 1989.

Hutchinson, William R. *The Modernist Impulse in American Protestantism.* Cambridge: Harvard University Press, 1976.

Knight, Walter L. "Race Relations: Changing Patterns and Practices." In *Southern Baptists Observed,* ed. Nancy Tatom Ammerman, pp. 165–181. Knoxville: University of Tennessee Press, 1993.

Lawless, Elaine J. "Not So Different a Story After All: Pentecostal Women in the Pulpit." In *Women's Leadership in Marginal Religions,* ed. Catherine Wessinger, pp. 41–54. Urbana: University of Illinois Press, 1993.

Marsden, George M. *Fundamentalism and American Culture: The Shaping of Twentieth-Century Evangelism, 1870–1925.* New York: Oxford University Press, 1980.

———. *The Soul of the American University: From Protestant Establishment to Established Nonbelief.* New York: Oxford University Press, 1994.

Marty, Martin E. "Fundamentalism as a Social Phenomenon." In *Piety and Politics,* ed. Richard John Neuhaus and Michael Cromartie, pp. 302–320. Washington, DC: Ethics and Public Policy Center, 1987.

———. *Modern American Religion: The Irony of It All.* Chicago: University of Chicago Press, 1986.

———. "The Twentieth Century: Protestants and Others." In *Religion and American Politics,* ed. Mark A. Noll, pp. 322–336. New York: Oxford University Press, 1990.

Matthews, Donald G. " 'Spiritual Warfare': Cultural Fundamentalism and the Equal Rights Amendment." *Religion and American Culture* 3 (summer 1993): 129–154.

McSwain, Larry L. "Swinging Pendulums: Reform, Resistance, and Institutional

Change." In *Southern Baptists Observed,* ed. Nancy Tatom Ammerman, pp. 256–275. Knoxville: University of Tennessee Press, 1993.

Neuhaus, Richard John. "What the Fundamentalists Want." In *Piety and Politics,* ed. Richard John Neuhaus and Michael Cromartie, pp. 3–18. Washington, DC: Ethics and Public Policy Center, 1987.

Norsworthy, David Ray. "Rationalization and Reaction Among Southern Baptists." In *Southern Baptists Observed,* ed. Nancy Tatom Ammerman, pp. 71–97. Knoxville: University of Tennessee Press, 1993.

Numbers, Ronald L. "Creation, Revolution, and Holy Ghost Religion: Holiness and Pentecostal Responses to Darwinism." *Religion and American Culture* 2 (summer 1992): 127–158.

Packard, William *Evangelism in America from Tents to TV.* New York: Paragon House, 1988.

Queen, Edward L. *In the South the Baptists Are the Center of Gravity.* Brooklyn: Carlson, 1991.

Ribuffo, Leo P. *The Old Christian Right: The Protestant Far Right from the Great Depression to the Cold War.* Philadelphia: Temple University Press, 1983.

Riss, Richard M. *A Survey of Twentieth-Century Revival Movements in North America.* Peabody, MA: Hendrickson, 1988.

Rosenberg, Ellen M. *The Southern Baptists.* Knoxville: University of Tennessee Press, 1989.

———. "The Southern Baptist Response to the Newest South." In *Southern Baptists Observed,* ed. Nancy Tatom Ammerman, pp. 144–164. Knoxville: University of Tennessee Press, 1993.

Rudolph, L.C. *Hoosier Faiths: A History of Indiana's Churches and Religious Groups.* Bloomington: Indiana University Press, 1995.

Sandeen, Ernest R. *The Origins of Fundamentalism: Toward A Historical Interpretation.* Philadelphia: Fortress Press, 1968.

Schwartz, Gary. *Sect Ideologies and Social Status.* Chicago: University of Chicago Press, 1970.

Sider, Ronald J. "An Evangelical Theology of Liberation." In *Piety and Politics,* ed. Richard John Neuhaus, and Michael Cromartie, pp. 143–160. Washington: Ethics and Public Policy Center, 1987.

Sobran, Joseph. "Secular Humanism and the American Religion." In *Piety and Politics,* ed. Richard John Neuhaus and Michael Cromartie, pp. 395–410. Washington, DC: Ethics and Public Policy Center, 1987.

Staples, Russell L. "Adventism." In *The Variety of American Evangelicalism,* ed. Donald W. Dayton, and Robert K. Johnson, pp. 57–71. Knoxville: University of Tennessee Press, 1991.

Turner, Helen Lee. "Fundamentalism in the Southern Baptist Convention: The Crystallization of a Millennialist Vision." Ph.D. dissertation, University of Virginia, 1990.

———. "Myths: Stories of This World and the World to Come." In *Southern Baptists Observed,* ed. Nancy Tatom Ammerman, pp. 98–123. Knoxville: University of Tennessee Press, 1993.

Williams, Peter J. *Popular Religion in America: Symbolic Change and the Modernization Process in Historical Perspective.* Urbana: University of Illinois Press, 1989.

Winston, Diane. "The Southern Baptist Story." In *Southern Baptists Observed,* ed. Nancy Tatom Ammerman, pp. 12–29. Knoxville: University of Tennessee Press, 1993.

Eleven

The Contemporary Scene

By the mid–twentieth century, American religions appeared extraordinarily healthy, claiming more members than ever before. Under President Dwight Eisenhower, there were prayers at cabinet meetings, the words "under God" were added to the pledge of allegiance, and the motto "In God We Trust" was placed on all currency. *The Ten Commandments* was a very popular epic film, and a popular song was "Big Fellow in the Sky." Actress and pinup girl Jane Russell acknowledged that she loved God, and added "He's a livin' doll."

Denominational ties were strong, with considerable friction between faith communities. Sometimes social contact between Protestants, Catholics, and Jews was not great, increasing prejudice and suspicion. Separation was more by choice than by neighborhood boundaries. The American population at the end of 1945 included 25 million Roman Catholics, and about 5 million Jews. Protestantism was still dominant in the immediate postwar years. By the 1960s, however, there had been enough growth among non-Protestants and erosion of the long-standing cultural consensus to make it impossible to claim that Protestantism remained the unofficially established religion in the United States. In 1900, pluralism had existed, but on terms satisfactory to Protestants. While there were many religious groups in America, some were at the sociocultural core while others were relegated to the periphery. Six decades later, Protestantism's special status no longer existed. It was only the largest of three religious communities in a thoroughly pluralistic society.

Jewish scholar Will Herberg in 1955 noted that sharp differences between Catholics, Protestants, and Jews were diminishing. Common to all three religions, but standing apart from them, was the religion of the American Way of Life, a civil religion or religion of the republic. Democracy, not the Bible, had become the essential element and might best be called "civil faith." Two years earlier, historian Daniel Boorstin saw a "submersion in a common generalized religion."

Ecumenism

Ecumenism, cooperative efforts of religious groups to respect and understand one another, emerged in the 1960s. Soon they were cooperating on a
number of projects and even Advent and church unity liturgies. Reverend
Eugene Carson Blake, an American Presbyterian leader and head of the
250–member World Council of Churches, believed that the sixties, rather
than the fifties, were the boom times for religion. The quantum growth of
ecumenism in those years made possible what he called the "almost miracu-
lous development of the idea of the unity of the one church of Jesus Christ."
There was diminished sectarian discord. Blake pointed to Dubuque, Iowa,
in the 1950s as a place where there were serious sectarian tensions, but "by
1965, the Lutherans and the Presbyterians and the Roman Catholics were
thick as thieves." To what extent television programming broke down barriers between groups is difficult to judge. The television appearances of
Catholic bishop Fulton J. Sheen, Baptist Billy Graham, and Rabbi Joshua
Liebman contributed to mutual understanding. The portrayals of the lives of
various religious groups in television dramas may have helped dissolve
suspicions and fears. The churches issued joint statements on theology and
fellowship agreement. In 1997 a churchwide assembly of the Evangelical
Lutheran Church in America (ELCA) accepted "full communion" with the
Presbyterian Church (USA), the Reformed Church in America, and the
United Church of Christ. It also accepted a common statement on justification with Roman Catholics that many thought could not be endorsed.

The Second Vatican Council held between 1962 and 1965 was the main
force in ushering in an age of ecumenism. Blake and other Protestant observers were taken completely by surprise: they had not expected the council to initiate liberal reforms. As Roman Catholics prospered and found
more social acceptance, they had largely abandoned what was once a necessary siege mentality. The election of John F. Kennedy to the presidency was
a clear indication that Americans were willing to see Catholics as part of the
American mainstream. The Second Vatican Council, carrying out its reforming and modernizing work, brought dramatic changes to Roman Catholicism. It did much to stimulate ecumenical dialogue, cooperation, and
understanding.

Civil Religion

In the Cold War years, there was great emphasis on American civil religion
as a means of contrasting America's role in the world with that of the Soviet
Union. In the process, many religious and cultural differences were papered

over. In the 1990s, the Cold War was over and it became difficult to refer to an American civil religion or civil faith. Disillusioned intellectuals argued it had never existed and vocal ethnic groups, protesting years of abuse, insisted there never had been one that united the nation. If there ever had been a Judeo-Christian consensus on basic values, it appeared to have evaporated. Conservatives complained that it had become a culture rooted in moral relativism, the idea that there were no absolute truths, and the conviction that any conduct not harmful to others should be tolerated. The dominant culture's ideal of "nonjudgmentalism" is seen by conservatives as an invitation to moral anarchy. Scholars who continued to see civil religion as a useful concept for understanding the past took to referring to it as the nation's legitimizing myth.

Cultural Conflict

By the 1970s, it was clear that there was a growing division between religious conservatives and liberals of all stripes. It was not simply fundamentalist versus modernist, though that chasm remained. The virulent anti-Catholicism and anti-Semitism that sometimes marked American religious history no longer was characteristic of most Protestant conservatives. Conservative evangelical and fundamentalist Protestants were now allied with conservative Roman Catholics in opposition to abortion, the ban on school prayer, illegitimacy, court rulings that facilitated the circulation of pornographic literature and films, and a variety of other issues. The Supreme Court ban on school prayer came in 1963 as the result of a suit filed by the nation's most prominent and outspoken atheist, Madalyn Murray O'Hair. That victory ushered in a period in which there were many other efforts to rigorously enforce the First Amendment to the Constitution. Schools and municipalities invited lawsuits if they permitted Christian themes to creep into their observances of Christmas. Churches that rented space for federal programs such as Head Start were advised to "sanitize" those rooms of religious symbols and materials. School authorities became reluctant to teach about religion even though it had a central role in the development of cultures and civilizations.

Conservative Jews and secularists like Sidney Hook stood with Christian conservatives on many issues, but they did not favor restoration of school and public Christmas observances that emphasized Christian themes. Religious conservatives continued to be disturbed by the great increase in premarital sex and increased acceptance of divorce. Their liberal Christian and Jewish opponents had not approved of these developments, but the conservatives suspected they had only halfheartedly fought these disquieting changes.

Religious liberals were much more likely to be egalitarians and advocate governmental programs to solve social problems. Liberal mainline Protestants could count on liberal Roman Catholic allies on many foreign policy and social justice issues. However, most liberal Roman Catholics would not agree with liberal Protestants, Jews, and humanists that abortion was morally acceptable. Liberal Catholics saw social and moral questions as part of a "seamless garment," a concept developed by the late Joseph Cardinal Bernardin of Chicago. Theirs was a "consistent life ethic," in which they supported the right of the unborn to life but also opposed the death penalty and nuclear arms. They backed social programs designed to uphold the dignity of all people.

Catholics for Choice, a relatively small group of disgruntled Catholics, supported abortion rights. The number of pro-choice Catholics is likely to increase significantly as abortion becomes more acceptable to most Americans and as younger Catholics, strongly influenced by the media and dominant culture, grow up unfamiliar with Thomism, natural law, and their church's teachings. Conservative Jews opposed abortion and shared much of the morality of conservative Christians; Jewish liberals stood with liberal mainline Protestants on abortion, social justice issues, and many foreign policy questions.

Religious conservatives took a tougher position on Cold War issues than did liberals. Among the religious conservatives, there is evidence that theological conservatism was matched by political conservatism. The conservative religious elite successfully brought a large part of their rank-and-file coreligionists with them in embracing political and economic conservatism.

Religious liberals were not completely comfortable with the fact that secular humanists were their allies. On the other hand, the elite in religiously liberal churches appeared to have had little success in convincing their grassroots members to support liberal political positions. Indeed, there was evidence that the Methodists and Presbyterians were moving slightly toward the center in the 1980s. A sharp educational difference existed between religious liberals and religious conservatives, with the liberals much more likely to have had the benefit of higher education. The majority of conservative Catholics and Protestants tended to be found in the lower middle class. Liberal Catholics, Protestants, and Jews as well as allied secular humanists were frequently wealthier and more upwardly mobile than most members of the religious right.

In the 1960s, American culture began to become unglued. The nation's cultural consensus, once based on the heritage of nineteenth-century Protestantism, broke down. Conservative Christians objected to growing divorce rates and the advent of no-fault divorce, birth control, and the "sexual revolution" that made premarital sex and promiscuity acceptable behavior.

Pornography, alcoholism, rising secular humanist influence, the end of organized prayer in the schools, militant feminism and the Equal Rights Amendment, and diminished patriotism were also serious concerns. Alarmed evangelicals agreed with conservative theologian Francis Schaeffer, who held that secular humanism was a religion, "which the government and courts in the United States favor over all others." Schaeffer holds that modern culture, influenced partly by existential thinkers, reflects a contempt for reason and logic. The irrational, he thinks, has been enthroned by modern civilization. Conservative Protestants have been accused of inventing the term secular humanism. In fact, the movement was first named by Jesuit scholar John Courtney Murray, and mainline Protestant writer Martin Marty acknowledged in 1958 that it was the established religion of the public schools. In 1962, liberal Supreme Court justice Hugo Black identified secular humanism as a religion.

The World Council of Churches and the National Council of Churches, which emerged as the successor to the Federal Council of Churches in 1950, came under fire from the many conservatives who were members of their affiliated denominations. These angry conservatives protested the liberal stances of those bodies and attempted to reduce the funds they received from local congregations. Conservatives fought against mergers among Lutheran or Presbyterian denominations, or between Congregationalists and evangelicals. Angry conservatives responded by forming protest groups or creating their own denominations. The reverse occurred in the 1970s when the Association of Evangelical Lutherans was formed by Missouri Synod Lutherans. Moderate Lutherans were displeased when conservatives captured control of the Missouri Synod and pressured liberal professors to abandon their positions.

The seventies were not good years for Christian liberals. Many of them suffered from disillusionment, cynicism, and loss of direction. Beginning in the mid-1960s, many liberal Christian churches began to experience declining attendance, declining growth rates, and falling membership figures. Among mainline Protestants, the Presbyterians and Methodists were hardest hit. On the other hand, conservative Protestant churches experienced substantial gains in membership.

Roman Catholics suffered the most serious declines in attendance and membership. By the 1990s, weekly mass attendance had dropped to 28 percent in many places. Within Catholic ranks, right-wingers began to win a number of victories with the help of sympathetic Vatican officials. These conservative Catholics were convinced that many bishops and theologians had distorted the reforms of Vatican II. A few wished John XXIII had never called the council. Conservatives agreed that the council had resulted in dwindling attendance at mass and sharply declining numbers of sisters, priests, and brothers. Upward social mobility and the end of serious prejudice and discrimination against Roman Catholics may have helped account for poor attendance and fewer vocations. Now respectable and more prosperous, many no longer needed the church as a haven against an unfriendly society. In an increasingly materialistic and sex-saturated age, it was not surprising that far fewer young women and men were willing to serve a church that demanded celibacy and often a frugal lifestyle.

It has been suggested, somewhat unfairly, that the declining influence of Roman Catholicism and mainline Protestantism was due to their efforts to appear relevant to contemporary man; in the process they began to empty their churches and make their approaches to Christianity irrelevant. Some have made the case that decline could be attributed to liberal social policies. There is considerable evidence to indicate that local churches in the 1960s lost members when clergy spoke in favor of desegregation and school busing. Later, clergy in the Pittsburgh area who criticized U.S. Steel for closing mills lost members and often their pastorates.

Conservative Catholics thought their clergy had no business discussing race relations and labor-management matters, and they deplored the involvement of clergy and sisters in antiwar activity as unpatriotic and perhaps aiding godless Communism. The postconciliar years saw a great flowering of Catholic peace and justice activities. In 1971 and 1973 researchers from the Institute of Urban Studies at Notre Dame visited more than eight hundred Catholic social ministries, and their travels did not take them beyond ten states. Priests, nuns, laymen and even several bishops were playing key roles in opposition to the Vietnam War and nuclear weapons, and some served prison sentences as a result of their activities. Daniel and Philip Berrigan, a priest and a former priest, were among the most prominent antiwar figures. Failing to recognize that these activities may have represented living out the gospel to its fullest extent, the conservative Catholics discovered that they had more in common with conservative Protestants than with radical Roman Catholics.

Though there has been a decline in social activism, the National Council of Churches and some of its member denominations have issued challenging statements in favor of economic justice, nuclear disarmament, and other controversial matters. Especially notable were statements issued by the Methodist bishops and the U.S. Conference Council of Catholic Bishops. The national welfare restructuring law of 1996, which stripped many of the poor of public assistance, poses serious problems for these churches. Their social theologies demand that they seek revisions of the so-called welfare reforms. Their individual congregations will have to wrestle with whether their food pantries and distributions of used clothing represent the best they can do for God's poor.

Conservative Protestants saw secular humanism becoming dominant in schools and colleges and advanced by the electronic media. Claims were made that secular humanists were teaching such topics as "values clarification" as a means of leading students to reject values acquired in their homes, and to view all beliefs as mere opinions subject to challenge and abandonment. For a time in the late 1970s, it appeared that Christian schools could be stripped of their tax-free status. In *Roe v. Wade* (1973), the United States Supreme Court made abortion legal in all states by sharply restricting the power of states to regulate the manner in which abortion services were delivered. By 1993, 25 million abortions had been performed since the decision was rendered.

Religious conservatives also objected to what sociologist John Murray Cuddihy called the "religion of civility." Religion had accommodated to secularism and modern culture to the extent that it was considered bad form for any religious group to claim superiority or criticize those with whom they were in disagreement. Like conservative Protestants, many Roman Catholics and Jews were uncomfortable with the religion of civility. However, many mainline Protestants appear to have accepted this concept. By 1993, the religion of civility had progressed to the point that public opinion forced the Westminster Schools of Atlanta, an avowedly Christian institution, to drop its regulation that only Christians be hired as teachers. The end of this requirement was hailed as "an important step for brotherhood in Atlanta."

Conservatives were alarmed by the almost successful litigation on the part of Abortion Rights Mobilization (ARM) to strip the Catholic Church of its tax-exempt status as a chilling example of the agenda of many so-called liberals. At issue was whether a church could address public questions and retain a tax exemption. At one point in the litigation, a federal district judge gave ARM almost unrestricted rights to peruse the financial records of dioceses throughout the nation. Within the circles of the religious left, vilification of Roman Catholicism and conservative Protestantism is reasonably common. Fanaticism, absolutism, and intolerance are not the exclusive possessions of the religious conservatives.

The Evangelicals

The new evangelicals, who formed the National Association of Evangelicals (NAE) in 1942, became a key element in the religious right that was to emerge in the 1970s. These new evangelicals differed from mainline Protestants by insisting upon the infallibility or trustworthiness of Scripture, their crucicentric (cross-centered) theology, and their contention that true believers have experienced conversions. They did not demand belief in inerrancy and total rejection of biblical criticism. It was not necessary for evangelicals to be dispensationalists or premillennialists. They were strongly committed to revivalism and the necessity of individual regeneration. The NAE opposed modernism while being careful to "shun all forms of bigotry, intolerance, misrepresentation, hate, jealousy, false judgment, and hypocrisy." They were activists in their belief that salvation must be reflected by daily works, which include personal piety, philanthropies, and above all efforts to evangelize others. Evangelicals were expected to place some distance between themselves and the world and to live by a strict moral code. They were to pray, meditate, and read Scripture on a daily basis. Their children would regularly go to Christian youth group meetings and church camp as well as attend Sunday school and conservative Christian colleges. The word "evangelical" described most nineteenth-century Protestants and their churches. Their early-twentieth-century successors had often been affected by theological liberalism. For that reason, the word "evangelical" had no clear meaning in the early twentieth century. The new evangelicals have been called the "neoevangelicals" to distinguish them from those of the last century. In a theological sense, the fundamentalists are successors of the nineteenth-century evangelicals, while the twentieth-century mainline Protestants have departed from some of the teachings of their evangelical predecessors.

The National Association of Evangelicals wished to distance itself from the confrontational and theologically extremist image projected by some fundamentalist leaders. Their lobbyists in Washington appeared to be moderate, reasonable people and were successful in persuading government to listen to and take into account evangelical views.

The great majority of the new evangelicals favored conservative political and economic policies, but there were some progressive evangelicals. Most noteworthy among them was the Sojourners Fellowship, led by Jim Wallis, which had a liberal peace and justice agenda. Their opposition to the Vietnam War led to numerous mysterious break-ins at their headquarters.

North Carolina Baptist Billy Graham was moving away from fundamentalism in the 1950s and won respect and attention for evangelical views through his crusades. In 1957, fundamentalists criticized Graham for working with mainline Protestants during his crusade in New York City. Dr. Carl McIntire called him an apostate, and Graham noted that he was opposed by "extreme fundamentalists from the right and extreme liberals from the left." He remained a conservative Protestant, located somewhat right of the Protestant center. Graham proposed that delinquents could benefit from residence in military-type rehabilitation camps and denounced the Yalta agreements. He appeared to support Senator Joseph McCarthy's witch-hunts, occasionally linking liberalism to communism. He was sympathetic to the anti-Catholicism that erupted upon John F. Kennedy's nomination for the presidency. In subsequent years, however, he enjoyed warm relationships with Roman Catholic leaders and even visited the Vatican on several occasions. In 1959, he appeared to endorse Richard M. Nixon for the presidency and called upon evangelicals to become involved in politics. Later, Graham supported Nixon throughout his presidency and appeared as a character witness at the bribery trial of John Connally, Nixon's secretary of the Treasury.

Graham eventually came to function as "the nation's chaplain," having developed close relationships with a number of presidents. In denouncing communism, divorce, sex education in public schools, progressive educational theories, pornography, crime, abortion, and "secular humanism," he spoke for a vast constituency that far exceeded the ranks of evangelicals. Graham welcomed mainline support of his urban crusades and came to value praise from and relationships with Roman Catholic and Jewish leaders. By the early eighties, he seemed to have somewhat reduced his criticism of communism. In 1982, he traveled to the Soviet Union and claimed that the Soviet people enjoyed religious freedom. He preached there and noted that there were churches open.

Billy Graham's success paved the way for the fundamentalist and evangelical reentry into politics in the 1970s. Conservative Protestants' long experience with radio and television ministries was useful preparation for increased political involvement. Fundamentalist and evangelical Protestants dominated religious broadcasting by the late 1960s. By the early 1980s, fundamentalists and evangelicals owned forty television and thirteen hundred radio stations; in 1989, there were 336 television ministries, which usually appeared weekly and were designed to evangelize and attract followers. The ministers and performers were usually telegenic, and their programs were professionally produced and entertaining as well as instructional. Robert Schuller's Hour of Power is considered one of the most effective and well-produced of these programs today. Religious telecasters even provided telephone banks where concerned counselors could advise and pray with viewers. They collected annually about a billion dollars during the early and mid 1980s. President Ronald Reagan thought the National Association of Religious Broadcasters important enough to visit at least four of their conventions.

The secularism and extreme individualism of the contemporary age tended to weaken and deinstitutionalize the family. Evangelicals and religious conservatives made the family a symbol of its hopes and concerns. In period before World War II, the Second Advent had been a source of hope in a hopeless world; now the family also played that role. By the mid-1970s, moreover, many evangelicals found it necessary to admit that there seemed to be too little difference between Christian and non-Christian families. The focus on family values struck a responsive chord in mainstream society. Promise Keepers, an organization encouraging men to be better husbands and fathers, mushroomed in the 1990s. Although feminists identified it with a misogynist plot to subordinate women, most Americans seemed to approve its biracial character and efforts to domesticate men.

The New Religious Right

The "new religious right" and the "new Christian right" became important factors in American politics in the 1970s. The new religious right was an alliance of fundamentalists, evangelicals, Mormons, and conservative Catholics and Jews. It was an unusual grouping, and would have been unimaginable several decades before. The emergence of the new Christian right in the 1970s was in some ways a contradiction of conservative Protestant tradition. The repeal of Prohibition and the ridicule fundamentalists suffered in the 1920s led many to abandon national political life. Reflecting the views of many Americans, H.L. Mencken had continually depicted them as Bible-thumping, intolerant, crude, "boobus Americanus." There was no reason to invite such ridicule, and it seemed that American culture was beyond reform. Moreover, many conservative Protestants were dispensationalists who thought that only the second coming would straighten out America.

Certain that secular humanists had launched an offensive to purge religious elements from American culture, conservative Protestants became convinced that it was necessary to do political battle. Reentering the national political arena was a defensive move. Their belief that values and morality were rooted in transcendent reality was being challenged by secular humanists who established the curriculum in the schools and dominated the media and political parties. The cultural war that characterized much of the 1970s and 1980s can be seen as another phase of the cultural struggle that lent great significance to the Scopes trial in 1925.

Members of the Christian right were not the aggressors in the cultural warfare that characterized recent American political history. Conservative columnist and author George Will argues that they were provoked. Liberalism, he said, "has spawned new 'rights' in the name of which government has been empowered to promote certain values by stipulating behavior." The Christian right had good company in seeing something terribly wrong in America: historian Christopher Lasch saw a culture of narcissism; President Jimmy Carter spoke of a malaise that seemed to have overcome America. Sociologist Daniel Bell traced the trouble to the belief that everyone has basic economic entitlements. Many thought that all moral coherence was gone and that the nation was entering a post-Christian stage.

The Christian right was activist, but its activism was far different from that of the Social Gospelers. Religious conservatives looked to dismantling big government and leaving the slack to voluntary, private charities. Their lukewarm ally President George Bush spoke of "a thousand points of light"—voluntary efforts as the best means of dealing with social problems that government programs did not address. When Jerry Falwell was asked if his conservative organization, the Moral Majority, would address the question of poverty, he replied there would be too many disagreements on how best to help the poor.

A number of factors were to diminish the political effectiveness of the new Christian right. Many evangelical leaders had a very negative view of fundamentalism, even though fundamentalists supplied most of the leadership of the new Christian right. The evangelicals' insistence on being born again and moral absolutes were seen by many Americans as signs of intransigence and bad manners. By exploring the moral dimensions of public questions, conservative Christians were accused of seeking to impose their values upon others and were depicted as fanatics. Many viewed their advocacy regarding matters of morality as a threat to the doctrine of the separation of church and state. Some associated violence against abortion clinics and providers with the entire Christian right. Reverend Jerry Falwell, founder of the Moral Majority, was compared to Ayatollah Khomeini and Adolf Hitler, and many leaders of the Christian right were demonized by the mainstream press. Their efforts to reinforce what they thought were fundamental values flew in the face of a deeply entrenched cultural pluralism that supported tolerance and moral relativism as the highest values.

Scandals associated with the behavior of several well-known evangelists have also damaged the Christian right, even though some of them had only a tenuous connection with it. Jimmy Swaggart, a dramatic orator who strutted, sang, and shouted, was probably the most effective American Pentecostalist. He was certain of his own salvation and that of his followers and assured listeners that Mother Teresa of Calcutta would not enter heaven because she was the wrong kind of Christian. In 1988, disclosure of a sexual scandal in which he was involved with a prostitute made it necessary for him to briefly remove himself from his ministry. In a highly emotional sermon, he admitted his sin. No longer a minister of the Assemblies of God, he subsequently returned to his ministries and weathered a second storm involving his sexual practices. Having survived these crises, he seemed unable to attract the following and contributions he once had.

Swaggart was instrumental in disclosing the extramarital sexual involvements of two other preachers: Jim Bakker and Marvin Gorman. The dispute with Gorman spilled over into the courts, where their wrangling continued for some time. Jim Bakker and his wife, Tammy, had operated a very successful television ministry and a religious theme park complete with lodgings. In 1987, the disclosure of Bakker's sexual involvement with a church secretary and subsequent payment to her of $265,000 in hush money led to disclosure of massive financial irregularities and misuses of funds. The modish evangelist was given a long prison sentence, which was substantially reduced in 1993. Bakker said Swaggart was behind a diabolical plot to take over Bakker's "Praise the Lord Ministry." Swaggart righteously called Bakker "a cancer that needed to be excised from the body of Christ." For a time evangelist Jerry Falwell took over the Bakkers' empire even though he was not a Pentecostal. A little earlier, Oral Roberts, whose City of Faith Hospital and university in Tulsa, Oklahoma, were suffering financial reverses, disclosed that God would "call him home" if $4.5 million were not raised by a certain date. The money appeared and he was not called home! Like other televangelists, Roberts had promised viewers that God would reward them handsomely for their donations, or "love offerings." Roberts was not closely linked to the Christian right, but many made no distinction between televangelists and political preachers of the Christian right.

The religious right has been accused of a desire to censor school reading materials and course contents, particularly in respect to the development of the origins of the universe and life. The conservatives' opposition to abortion is seen as interference with a woman's right to do whatever she pleases with her body and that of the fetus she is carrying. On the other hand, the religious right lodged similar charges against liberal forces. They point out that the *New York Times* never published reviews of Hal Lindsey's *Late Great Planet Earth* or the works of Francis Schaeffer, probably the leading evangelical writer. They also see the use of the Racketeer Influenced and Corrupt Organizations (RICO) Act against antipornography and antiabortion groups as an abuse of the law.

The Religious Right Organizes

Returning to the political arena, evangelicals questioned whether a secular mind-set, reinforced by the media and public education, had created such spiritual and moral ambiguity as to render the nation's political process incapable of dealing with value-laden questions. In 1974 Bill Bright, founder of Campus Crusade for Christ, and Congressman John Conlan developed a strategy to help elect evangelical congressmen. They established

Third Century Publishers to publicize the voting records of congressmen and provide material designed to help evangelicals organize political campaigns. They established the Christian Embassy in Washington, from which Campus Crusaders were to evangelize jurists, congressmen, and bureaucrats. The Embassy board included Norman Vincent Peale, Billy Graham, and W.A. Criswell, a Dallas Baptist who had earlier stated that the election of John F. Kennedy would "spell the death of a free church in a free state."

After the election of 1976, the Christian Embassy ceased to be an important political force. Bill Bright went on to operate Here's America, a program funded by Nelson Bunker Hunt, other wealthy businessmen, and large corporations. It staged a "Washington for Jesus" rally in 1980 and produced the film Jesus for the Campus Crusade. There is no evidence that any of its money was spent on political campaigns. Christian Voice was the first important organization to be part of what the media referred to as the new Christian right. It was a combination of West Coast profamily, antigay, and antipornography organizations. It emerged in the seventies and soon had 150,000 laymen on its mailing list. Of 37,000 ministers on the list, 3,000 were Mormon and Catholic clergy. Evangelist Pat Robertson spoke in favor of Christian Voice on his *700 Club*, aired on one hundred stations of his Christian Broadcasting Network. Christian Voice raised money through mailings, and Jerry Hunsinger, who handled finances for evangelist Robert Schuller and the Moral Majority, managed its money. Christian Voice has a political action committee and remains active in recruiting conservative Christian candidates for office and promoting Christian values in election campaigns.

The most interesting figure in the Christian right was Reverend Jerry Falwell, a fundamentalist who founded the Moral Majority. Falwell, a native of Lynchburg, Virginia, had an engineering school scholarship but chose instead to study for the ministry. At age twenty-three, he established the Thomas Road Baptist Church in Lynchburg, which became one of the nation's largest congregations. His *Old-Time Gospel Hour* telecast reached about 2 million people a week, and took in revenues of $35 million a year. He also operated the Liberty Home Bible Institute, Liberty Baptist Seminary, and Liberty Baptist College, now Liberty University, the nation's largest fundamentalist college. An independent Baptist, he criticized Protestant liberals, Pentecostals, and what he termed "denominational mediocrity."

In the 1960s, Falwell stayed out of politics but defended segregation and criticized Martin Luther King, Jr. Falwell was a consistent superpatriot. He endorsed Gerald Ford for the presidency in 1976 after fellow Baptist Jimmy Carter consented to a *Playboy* interview. That same year he held "Love America" rallies and denounced the Equal Rights Amendment and homosexuality. An effective leader but a poor administrator, Falwell proved unable to handle money well. From the outset, the Moral Majority was in debt.

Over the years, Falwell has made many contradictory utterances and retractions. Once a sharp critic of Pentecostals and liberal Protestants, he came to deny them fellowship, meaning there would be no joint services, but offered them friendship. He described conversations with presidents Gerald Ford and Jimmy Carter that these men denied ever occurred. He has also found it necessary to trim and reverse his position on a number of matters. Falwell appears to accept the fact that premarital sex is common and cannot be reversed.

In recent years, he praised the civil rights movement and publicly regretted his criticisms of Martin Luther King. As head of Liberty University, he has told students they should support creationism but give evolution fair coverage. He recognized that Protestant prayers probably cannot be restored in the public schools and stated he would accept nonsectarian prayers to God. These positions have led fundamentalist hard-liners to denounce him as an apostate and enemy of fundamentalism.

Like many other conservative Protestants in public life, Falwell has had Roman Catholic and Jewish friends and supporters. These relationships could not sit well with some fundamentalist allies and critics. Though many evangelicals also cooperate with Catholics, the National Association of Evangelicals in 1993 unsuccessfully demanded that President Clinton end diplomatic relations with the Vatican. Because they believe that Israel will be the central site of the drama of the second coming, contemporary dispensationalists are its strong supporters. Falwell has claimed, "No anti-Semitic influence is allowed in Moral Majority" emphasizing that many evangelicals "are committed to the Jewish people."

Moral Majority, the best-known organization of the new Christian right, was founded as a nonpartisan, nonsectarian organization in 1979. The group had a southern flavor and was dominated by fundamentalist clergymen. There were four distinct units in the Moral Majority, one of which was a political action committee to raise campaign funds for conservatives. Its executive director was Robert Billings, a founder of the National Christian Action Coalition, who has been credited with persuading the Internal Revenue Service to abandon plans to strip tax exemptions from segregated Christian schools. A graduate of Bob Jones University, Billings had a great interest in fighting state interference with Christian schools. He left Moral Majority in 1980 to work for the presidential campaign of Ronald Reagan.

Tim LaHaye and Greg Dixon were on the original board of directors. LaHaye was an important fundamentalist author who charged that secular humanism was rooted in "amorality, evolution, and atheism." LaHaye was also known for his family life seminars. He founded Christian Heritage College and the San Diego Christian Unified School System. His wife, Beverly, a pro-life activist, works with him in the seminars and founded Concerned Women for America, a 94,000–member prayer chain. LaHaye believed that 275,000 secular humanists and their allies controlled America. This alleged conspiracy involved the Trilateral Commission and could be traced back to the Illuminati of the eighteenth century. Another antigay activist like LaHaye, Greg Dixon organized rallies supporting singer Anita Bryant's campaign against homosexual rights and campaigned for legislation against pornography.

Charles Stanley, an Atlanta Southern Baptist pastor whose televised services have viewers across the nation, was added later to the board, as was Dr. D. James Kennedy, televangelist and pastor of the nation's fastest growing church, the Coral Ridge Presbyterian Church in Fort Lauderdale, Florida. Kennedy once told his television audience that he did not think a saved person ever had a need to be on the welfare rolls.

By June, 1980, the Moral Majority claimed three hundred thousand members, including seventy thousand ministers. At its height, Falwell claimed it had 4 million members. In 1989, he shut down the Moral Majority, stating his wish to return to preaching the gospel. By then, unfavorable media coverage had led many Americans to be wary of the Moral Majority. By abandoning the organization, Falwell liberated himself from its liabilities, and was in a better position to continue to address public questions.

Some conservative Christian clergymen felt uncomfortable about joining either the Christian Voice or the Moral Majority. The Religious Roundtable was created to appeal to these men of the cloth. It attempted to win the support of mainline Methodist, Presbyterian, and Southern Baptist clergy and served as a forum for education and discussion. It held workshops at which clergy learned how to guide their congregations toward backing conservative candidates. Among New Right figures who worked with the Roundtable were Phyllis Schlafly, opponent of the ERA, Howard Phillips, a major conservative writer and founder of the Conservative Caucus, Terry Dolan, organizer and fund-raiser, and Paul Weyrich, head of the Committee for the Survival of a Free Congress and probably the chief New Right strategist. Ed McAteer, a layman and former Colgate-Palmolive sales manager, played the largest role in founding the Roundtable. Ronald Reagan told their Dallas meeting that while they could not give him an endorsement, "I can endorse you."

Many Roundtable members also belonged to the Coalition for the First Amendment, which mustered support for Senator Jesse Helms's bill to restore school prayer. Almost all televangelists were members, including

Oral Roberts and Rex Humbard, who were reluctant to fully enter the political arena. At an August 1980 meeting sponsored by the Roundtable, Bailey Smith, then president of the Southern Baptists, announced that "God Almighty does not hear the prayers of Jews." The furor that ensued made it necessary for Jerry Falwell to reply, "God hears the cry of any sincere person who calls on him."

By the mid-1970s, the nation's leading Pentecostal was Reverend Pat Robertson. A Yale Law School graduate, he was ordained a Baptist minister. Beginning with a small television station in Virginia, he created the Christian Broadcasting Network, which aired his popular talk show the *700 Club*. By the early 1980s, the broadcast received about $2 million in donations each week. In addition to operating the nation's largest religious television network, Robertson would establish his own university and operate a number of for-profit enterprises, among them the sale of vitamins, diamonds, and Sea of Galilee mud masks. In 1985, Robertson and his followers claimed that through their prayers they had protected the East Coast from the full wrath of hurricane Gloria; once, he attempted to restore a dead child to life. Such activities did not win for him the backing of many conservative, noncharismatic fundamentalists. Robertson claimed, "Each year through my 700 Club television program, I see or hear about some fifty thousand people who have received miraculous answers [or cures for illnesses] to prayer most of them instantaneous."

Robertson gave up the ministry to run for president in 1988. Although he failed to win the Republican nomination, he demonstrated skill as an organizer. His method of leading was low-key and well suited to the medium of television. Robertson ceased calling himself a Pentecostal and was deeply involved in the political process in an effort to help set the nation's moral agenda. He frequently brought politics into his television ministry. Like some members of the old Christian right, he appears to understand current events in terms of a conspiracy theory. In *The New World Order,* published in 1991, he argued that President George Bush and other leading politicians were "unknowingly and unwittingly carrying out the mission and mouthing the phrases of a tightly knit cabal whose goal is nothing less than a new order for the human race under the domination of Lucifer and his followers." He believes that a satanic conspiracy against Christian civilization began in Bavaria with the creation of the Order of the Illuminati, ultimately took control of the Freemasons, and included many Jewish bankers. Robertson entertains the idea that the Cold War may have been a hoax designed to increase the U.S. national debt and provide money for profiteers. International financiers, he suggests, may have maneuvered the Bush administration into an unnecessary confrontation with Iraq.

The Christian Coalition, which Robertson founded in 1989, has had some success in attracting Roman Catholic members, and he has claimed, "If the pro-family Roman Catholics and conservative Evangelicals unite together, there is no candidate that we cannot elect anywhere in the nation." In 1993, Robertson allied with Cardinal John O'Connor in New York school board elections, and later was introduced by the cardinal to Pope John Paul II. While Roman Catholics share many of the Christian Coalition's moral values, they approach socioeconomic problems in very different ways, and the prospect of most Catholics supporting the Christian Coalition appears remote.

Religion and Political Battle

As the election of 1980 approached, some in the Christian right thought Ronald Reagan too liberal, and worried that he "was not the best Christian who ever walked the face of the earth." However, there were evangelicals who had supported Reagan for president since 1970. At about that time, a group of evangelical leaders accompanied by crooner Pat Boone visited the California governor. Before leaving they joined hands in prayer. Reverend George Otis was to Reagan's left and felt his hand shaking. Otis felt the "Holy Spirit come upon me," and then said, "If you walk upright before me, you will reside at 1600 Pennsylvania Avenue."

Many leaders of the new Christian right regarded Jimmy Carter as too liberal and barely an evangelical. He did not work to restore school prayer or fight abortion, and he supported homosexual rights and the Equal Rights Amendment. James Robinson of Fort Worth, a noted Southern Baptist, said President Carter "lacked commitment" and did not "understand what it is to have convictions." Moreover, many citizens thought him inept.

In some Democratic areas, the Christian right had to create Republican Party organizations. Members of the Christian right were active in registering voters, and doubtless contributed to Ronald Reagan's victory in 1980. Falwell claimed that the Moral Majority registered between 4 million and 8 million votes. His comment that Reagan was elected in an avalanche of evangelical votes was an understandable exaggeration. The new Christian right probably recruited a substantial number of new voters and persuaded a number of evangelical southern voters to turn away from their habit of voting Democratic.

Evangelicals were instrumental in the failure of Representative John Buchanan of Alabama to win renomination. A conservative and former Baptist minister, first elected to Congress in 1964, he had backed the war in Vietnam and the National Rifle Association; he had also written a voluntary school prayer constitutional amendment. Buchanan was defeated because he was seen as moderate on civil rights and insufficiently opposed to the school prayer ban. The Christian right also claimed credit for the defeat of liberal senators George McGovern of South Dakota, Birch Bayh of Indiana, Warren Magnuson of Washington, and John Culver of Iowa. Neoconservative Norman Podhoretz of *Commentary* attributed Reagan's victory in part to an upsurge of cultural disgust. In 1984, the religious right registered more voters than did Democrat Jesse Jackson. It appeared that the alliance with the hard right paid the Republicans handsome dividends. In addition to supporting Reagan, voters of the Christian right showed a strong tendency to support Republicans for Congress. Billy Graham said he was concerned about the possibility of a "wedding between the religious Fundamentalists and the political right" because "the hard right has no interest in religion except to manipulate it." The nation's unofficial pastor was doubtless correct in his appraisal of the hard right, but most observers would add that the marriage was already consummated.

Under President Reagan, there were some advances for the Christian right. The Justice Department opposed lifting tax-exempt status from Christian schools, and personnel in government-funded medical facilities were forbidden to discuss abortion with clients. Reagan and his successor, George Bush, appointed conservative Supreme Court justices, supported vouchers that parents could spend in private schools, and generally endorsed the religious right's cultural agenda. They were unable to restore public school prayer, and they did little to place an antiabortion amendment in the Constitution. They did not appoint large numbers of evangelicals or fundamentalists to high office. More than a few suspect that their strategy was to verbally endorse the agenda of the religious right while providing it with few concrete accomplishments.

Evangelicals became involved in the operations of the Republican Party and would influence the formulation of party positions on cultural questions. The alliance with the White House of Ronald Reagan and George Bush has given the Christian right a long-sought legitimacy. At the local level, the Moral Majority and Christian right had successes in bringing creationism into some classrooms, in keeping pornographic materials and films out of some communities, in library censorship, in organizing pro-family activities, and in combating efforts to legislate gay rights.

There was much dissatisfaction on the religious right with President George Bush. In the 1992 Republican presidential primaries, conservative columnist Patrick Buchanan ran as spokesman for conservative Christians and garnered more than a third of the fundamentalist and evangelical vote in several states. A Catholic who yearned for the church of Pius XII, Buchanan did not appear to attract a large numbers of Catholic votes. His strident speech at the 1992 Republican National Convention unnerved moderates and may have contributed to Democrat Bill Clinton's election victory. In 1996, Buchanan again unsuccessfully sought the Republican nomination and remained in the race long after it was clear Robert Dole would be the nominee. He was denied high visibility at that year's convention. The Buchanan effort was an attempt to guarantee that the positions of the religious right were respected in the Republican platform.

In the election of 1992, Clinton defeated Bush and independent candidate Ross Perot. Studies indicated that Catholics who attended church regularly were a little more likely to vote for Bush than for Clinton. Evangelical Protestants demonstrated a strong tendency to vote Republican. Those who professed no religious belief were inclined to support Clinton. Several political scientists were prompted by the results of the election to suggest that "evangelicals and committed members of other religious traditions could find themselves united in the Republican Party facing seculars and less committed members in other traditions among the Democrats," although the voting behavior of Jews and African American Christians does not appear to fit this pattern.

In the late eighties and early nineties the cultural and religious liberals had some successes. The election of Bill Clinton placed some of their strongest supporters in positions of power. At the 1992 Democratic National Convention, Pennsylvania governor Robert Casey was denied an opportunity to speak because he was a committed opponent of abortion. In 1996, Casey, then a former governor, was again denied the opportunity to speak at the convention and had to settle for addressing a press conference instead.

One of President Clinton's first actions was to improve the position of homosexuals in the military, and in 1996 he vetoed a bill that would have banned late-term, partial birth abortions. Although he was closely identified with the agenda of the cultural liberals, the president in 1997 instructed the Justice Department to argue before the Supreme Court in support of state laws banning physician-assisted suicides. The Court was unwilling to overturn these laws, and it appears that in the short run political battle over values will not include medically enabled suicides.

The liberal cultural agenda of the Clinton administration reactivated the Christian right. Conservative Christians realized that his administration represents a serious threat to their cultural values. They continued efforts to shape the policies of the Republican Party. By 1993 they had control or significant power in eighteen state parties. Pat Robertson's Christian Coalition was the most effective conservative Christian organization, with an annual budget of about $22 million and many state and local chapters. In order to attract more supporters, the Christian Coalition has broadened its concerns by attacking the 1993 Clinton budget as "the largest tax increase in history" in advertisements aired in eleven states. The ads neglected to point out that most of the Clinton taxes were to be paid by people earning more than $200,000 a year. The followers of Reverend James C. Dobson have also been active in politics, particularly in school board elections. Dobson's radio broadcast was carried by eighteen hundred stations and his magazine *Focus on the Family* and other publications reach about 2 million households. The political activity of the religious right doubtless contributed to the Republican success in winning control of both houses of Congress in 1994, but that success can be also be attributed economic matters and the Democrats' bungled efforts at health care reform. The ability of the Republicans to retain control of Congress in 1996, despite the loss of lackluster presidential candidate Bob Dole, depended upon retaining the support of the religious right, especially in close contests. Dole showed little ability to define his position in moral terms, which may have contributed to the lowest turnout in a presidential election since 1924. Ralph Reed, head of the Christian Coalition, calculated that 29 percent of those who voted were born-again Christians. Their votes, he asserted, prevented the Dole defeat from becoming "a meltdown all the way down the ballot." A gender gap among Christian traditionalists hurt Dole. Traditional evangelical men were 85 percent for Dole compared with 64 percent of evangelical women. The difference between traditional male and female Catholics was 58 percent to 47 percent. A *Los Angeles Times* exit poll indicated that 9 percent of the voters admitted that abortion was the most important issue in casting their votes; Bob Dole got 60 percent of their votes.

Clinton's share of the Hispanic vote increased because the GOP in California took positions unfavorable to resident aliens. The president's increased share of the Catholic vote could suggest that fewer Roman Catholics share the position of the hierarchy on abortion. Some may have backed Clinton because many of his social programs were consistent with Catholic social teaching, but people in the pews seldom have any idea what the popes and bishops have said about socioeconomic questions. Clinton's greatest strength was in the Northeast, where support for abortion and a libertarian cultural agenda is strongest. A case could also be made that Clinton's two victories underscore the declining force of a moralistic backlash in a culture drifting toward a nearly libertarian philosophy of personal morality.

Although traditional Republicans welcome the money and votes of conservative Christians, they frequently do not share their cultural views and are unwilling to surrender control of the party to them. It is unclear how many traditional Christians are sufficiently uncomfortable with libertarian economic policies to refrain from voting Republican. Unbridled capitalism makes greed the ultimate virtue and has destructive human consequences. At the 1996 Republican National Convention, conventional Republicans unsuccessfully attempted to modify the antiabortion platform plank, but it was clear that moderates were rapidly gaining strength and would come to the 2000 convention with greater prospects of influencing the party platform. Nevertheless, the religious right will remain an important element within the Republican coalition and will continue to influence the shaping of party policy.

There is no evidence that the yawning gap separating religious liberals and conservatives will soon be bridged. It involves a cultural war to define what America should be. It is not likely that the religious right's support will grow with the passage of time. Their failure in 1996 to accomplish the reelection of their "poster boy," Senator Larry Pressler of South Dakota, suggests that there are clear limits to the power of the religious right. A number of House candidates who enjoyed the strong backing of the Christian Coalition were defeated, as was a Washington gubernatorial candidate who pledged to appoint only "godly" people to office. Recognizing the judiciary's commitment to abortion rights and growing pro-choice sentiment, some religious right leaders acknowledge that little can be done about abortion. Its importance as an anchor issue for the conservatives is diminished.

On a television talk show in January 1997, Jerry Falwell predicted that "kiddie porn" would be protected under the First Amendment during his lifetime and that of the program host. Falwell has shown other signs of realizing that very little can be done to arrest the spread of what he considers a pagan culture. Religious conservatives revere what they think is eternal and battle a cultural revolution that has succeeded. They live in a society that disdains what is not new and face a culture and technology that prepare the way for almost automatic acceptance of values antithetrial to those they hold dear. It is possible that some conservative Protestants who come to realize this may revert to being aloof from politics and limit their activities to attempting to bring salvation to others on an individual basis. Recognition of limited opportunities for change at the national level could also accelerate the already detectable tendency of religious conservatives to work harder on local rather than national questions.

The Rights of Women and Homosexuals

Battles over rights of women and homosexuals within churches and society have been another dimension of the culture wars in recent years. The revival and massive expansion of the women's rights movement led to demands for sexual equality in the churches. Many churches, such as the

United Church of Christ, the Baptists, the Friends, the Disciples, the Methodists, the Salvation Army, and Pentecostal denominations, had been ordaining women for some time, but there were few female clergy and these did not hold positions of power and influence. Women in larger numbers sought ordination, and there was increased concern that their professional development not be blocked by a glass ceiling. Lutherans and Presbyterians had been ordaining women for more than a decade. Episcopalians debated the matter and began ordaining women in the 1970s; they later would consecrate an African American woman as their first female bishop.

Some Mormon women have argued unsuccessfully for a change in church policy, claiming that if women can become goddesses, they certainly should be eligible for priesthood. They also point to the belief that there is a Heavenly Mother deity as well as a Father God to support their position. This idea is based on the often sung Mormon hymn, "O My Father" by Eliza Snow, a leading figure in the early history of that church.

The Church of Latter-day Saints and the Roman Catholic Church teach that women cannot be ordained as priests. Catholic women demanded ordination, but Rome continues to rule out the possibility of female deacons or priests. Nevertheless, Catholic women have come to occupy important positions in diocesan chanceries and as members of parish ministerial teams. In the eighties and early nineties, the American Catholic bishops failed in repeated attempts to produce a pastoral letter on women. They finally abandoned the effort, with some realizing that any statement endorsing the ban on women clergy could be seen as simply adding insult to injury.

Catholic feminists continue to seek equality and ordination. A number of Christian feminists believe that revelation is continuous to the extent that new wisdom and truth is found through the exploration of feminine nature and thought. This has been criticized as a form of antinomianism, but gnosticism or antinomianism has been a consistent major force in American religious life. During Pope John Paul II's 1979 visit to the United States, Sister Theresa Kane boldly stood before the pontiff and asked that he consider permitting women to exercise all ministries. She spoke for many nuns, laywomen, and men. Many are troubled by the lack of sexual equality in the church.

Some would enter the Women-Church movement, stating that the institutional church had left them. A number privately approach God as mother and demand that the church adopt sexually neutral language in its liturgies. Women with theology degrees often left the church and became Protestant clergy. Some in Women-Church pray and conduct eucharistic liturgies in small groups. Members of Women-Church believe that Christianity is fundamentally sexist and have found it necessary to develop a spirituality that incorporates elements drawn from other religions, as well as ancient goddess worship. They insist that God should not be imaged as a patriarchal male, and they seek to define God as a being with a strong feminine dimension. Members of Women-Church attempt to reclaim some Christian symbols in ways suitable to feminism while abandoning others, and they are strongly anticlerical.

Their position has been called "reconstructive" Christianity, but they are also strongly influenced by the thought of separatist feminists such as Mary Daly of Boston College, who describes herself as post-Christian. At a recent Women-Church gathering, members celebrated Eucharist using apples and with no reference to Jesus Christ. Former Protestant post-Christian thinkers include Carol Christ and Sonia Johnson, a former Mormon.

By 1993, the brochure announcing the third Women-Church convergence in Albuquerque, New Mexico, referred to sacred events rather than liturgy and did not employ the word "Catholic." Though almost forty Catholic groups were represented at the convergence, some wondered if it was losing its Catholic identity. A codirector of the Women's Alliance for Theology defended the group's new direction and said that many question Christocentric theology or are bored by it. Buddhists, Quakers, Jews, Native Americans, and Catholic nuns led the rituals as well as a female African American priest. She had been ordained by former Roman Catholic priest George Stallings, head of Imani Temple in Washington, D.C.

The American Psychiatric Association in 1974 overwhelmingly voted to approve a statement that homosexuality was no longer to be classified as a mental illness. Mainline Protestant churches debated whether active homosexuals should be ordained, and the United Presbyterians decided in 1997 that unmarried candidates for ordination should not be sexually active, which drew criticism from homosexuals and some single, heterosexual clergy. It was not just the liberal Protestants and Roman Catholics who would face the problem of dealing with homosexual clergy. In 1979 Reverend James Tinney, a Pentecostal, announced he that he was gay, and was later excommunicated by the Assemblies of God. Gay people came "out of the closet" and demanded that society accept them on their own terms. They asked that the churches legitimize homosexuality by no longer terming homosexual conduct sinful and by ordaining admittedly practicing homosexuals. Gay-bashing became an openly discussed problem, and an Atlanta church with many gay members was torched following a great deal of vandalism. The appearance of AIDS led to a debate over whether government was doing enough to combat it. AIDS soon spread from gays and intravenous drug users to the general population. While some simply said that AIDS was God's punishment for sin, most churchmen sought ways for their institutions to comfort and care for those afflicted. Though few denominations are now ordaining people who admitted to being sexually active gays, there is some movement in that direction.

The mainstream church that had greatest problems dealing with homosexuality was the Roman Catholic Church. Though some estimated that large numbers of priests are active homosexuals, the church refuses to ordain those who admit to this and continues to consider homosexual acts sinful. To avoid giving the impression that it condoned homosexual activity, bishops decided to no longer permit Dignity, a group of Catholic homosexuals, to hold functions in church-owned buildings. Members of Dignity, yearning for the church to understand and endorse their lifestyles, reacted angrily when rebuffed. In 1989, gays and pro-choice activists demonstrated outside St. Patrick's Cathedral; some entered the church and disrupted the service by shouting, standing on pews, and throwing condoms in the air. A few entered a communion line, received the Eucharist in their hands, and threw it to the floor. Outside, some carried signs reading, "Eternal life to Cardinal John O'Connor NOW."

An organization of Irish gays demanded the right to march in New York's annual St. Patrick's Day Parade, sponsored by a Roman Catholic organization. Their unmet demands received the backing of the mayor and many liberals who denounced Catholic intolerance of homosexuality, overlooking the distinction that conservative Christians draw between homosexual activity and homosexuality.

Movements, Cults, and Non-Western Religion

In the 1960s, some young people rejected the values of Catholics, Protestants, and Jews and turned to Eastern religion, drugs, and cults. This was an effort to replace what they viewed as the discredited values of Western civilization. Some of these movements remained very small, but George Gallup reported in the late seventies that a substantial number of people were involved to some degree in various cults and movements. Not all of them were young people. Some others were "into" various forms of meditation or followed Timothy Leary's advice on using LSD to "get out of your minds and into your senses." Therapies that promised adherents they would learn to "give themselves permission," "free themselves of shoulds," and "go with the flow" flourished among the young, but also had a significant number of older adherents. Theirs was a spiritual quest, often ending in the dead ends of substance addiction and self-indulgence.

Hundreds of thousands practiced yoga and transcendental meditation. Many did so in addition to involvement in more conventional religions. It is difficult to determine if practitioners with no involvement in conventional religion would consider meditation or yoga their religions. There were about 3 million Christian charismatics; these people rejected conventional modes of worship but usually adhered to conventional morality and theology. Several hundred thousand were in the Jesus Movement, but it now appears to be diminishing. Those disillusioned with the counterculture of the 1960s often found refuge there and accepted the movement's authoritarian ways and ultraconservative morality and theology. Some eventually became Jewish Christians, people who insist they are Jews but accept Christ as the Messiah.

It is estimated that there are about one thousand cults active today. The cults usually have in common a charismatic living leader, demands for fanatical loyalty and obedience, recruitment practices of debatable propriety, and insistence that members surrender all assets and raise money for them. In several instances the ultimate test of loyalty and obedience was acceptance of death and suicide. In 1978, nine hundred members of the People's Temple accepted mass suicide in Jonestown, Guyana. Most of them were poor African Americans from San Francisco, initially attracted by leader Jim Jones's mixture of concern for economic and social justice with Pentecostal religion. Prior to the massacre or mass suicide, Jones encountered difficulties with Guyanan and American authorities over violence and threats against opponents and dissenters, reports of sexual abuse of women and children, and evidence that he ordered the murder of a visiting congressman, Leo Ryan. Jones instructed his followers to drink Kool-Aid laced with cyanide; he opted to die of a 38 caliber bullet fired into the head.

Jones originally thought it best to die in a blazing inferno, but it remained for over seventy Branch Davidian followers of David Koresh to die that way in April 1993 at their compound near Waco, Texas. Koresh taught an adventist theology, and was sexually involved with many of the women and girls he led; he aroused the interest of federal authorities by stockpiling arms and weapons.

At Rancho Santa Fe, California, in March 1997, thirty-nine members of the Heaven's Gate cult committed suicide so that God would transport them several days later to a UFO they thought followed in the wake of the Hale-Bopp comet. They believed the spaceship would take them to heavenly bliss on another planet. They were led by Marshall H. Applewhite and Bonnie Lu Trusdale Nettles, who called themselves Bo and Peep, Winnie and Pooh, Chip and Dale, or the Two. Though they claimed to be acquainted in previous lives, they met in their most recent incarnation in a hospital in the early 1970s, where Nettles was a nurse and he, as a heart-blockage patient, had a "near death" experience. Nettles helped him define his mission, traveled with him in seeking followers, and she finally died of cancer. Applewhite referred to himself as "the Present Representation" of the spirit that animated Christ in the New Testament and warned that planet Earth was about to be recycled. He preached celibacy, and he and some of the males in the cult had been castrated; the members dressed to effect a unisex look. These people earned money as computer technicians and used a Web site to spread their views and recruit members. Apparently, each member was given an opportunity to leave rather than commit suicide. Other members of the cult survived elsewhere.

Two of the more notable cults did not begin as religions. Synanon, founded by Chuck Dederich, emerged in California in the 1960s as a community that taught love, peace, healing, and nonviolence. Initially accomplishing positive change in the lives of street people and derelicts, it eventually moved to requiring vasectomies of male members, redefining marriage, gathering weapons, and using force against dissenters and opponents. Dederich intimidated the media by filing suits against the *San Francisco Examiner* and other critics. It may have become a religion to gain First Amendment protection against governmental interference. In 1980, it had few members and was in decline.

Scientology was founded in 1951 by L. Ronald Hubbard as a science somewhat akin to psychology. It is based on the idea that liberating the soul requires locating and healing "engrams," emotional scars from a previous life or one's present life, including the fetal stage. It evolved into a religion and taught that the spirit or "thetan" is immortal and inhabits a succession of human bodies. Scientologists do not remove themselves from society but seek ways to function more efficiently in it. They take courses costing as much as $300 an hour from the Church of Scientology. This movement is probably the most powerful of the cults, even though it has faced litigation for kidnapping, swindling, and breaking into federal offices. Mary Sue Hubbard, the founder's wife, spent several years in prison for obstruction of justice. The Internal Revenue Service spent twenty years scrutinizing the operations of the church, but both sides appear to have arrived at a settlement in 1997.

Both Synanon and Scientology are non-Christian and reflect what is called New Age thought, and have been particularly strong on the West Coast. The Heaven's Gate group is another example of New Age religion. Adherents of New-Age thought seek esoteric knowledge to provide them with a comprehensive explanation of the universe and their place in it. New Age religion is a form of theosophy, which draws on Eastern wisdom, gnosticism, and astrology. Crystals are sometimes used to deepen knowledge, and ancient Celtic wisdom is sought through study of the Druids. New Age includes various forms of goddess worship, which has a growing following in feminist circles and has been welcomed by the Unitarian Universalist Association. New Age thought seeks to liberate the inner self, considered perfect but contaminated by the "lower self" or "outer personality," which is shaped by materialism and modernity.

Some New Age movements attempt to provide followers with the best of both material and spiritual worlds. Werner Erhard's seminars emphasize the importance of positive external achievements while seeking inner enlightenment. A slogan associated with guru Bhagwan Shree Rajneesh proclaims, "Jesus saves, Moses invests, Bhagwan spends." It is thought that fewer than fifty thousand people seriously consider New Age thought to be their religion, though a much greater number have dabbled in it. Some place the number of people who have been exposed to New Age thought between 10 and 12 million. There are about one hundred New Age periodicals, and about $100 million worth of New Age books are sold each year. There are even some New Age radio stations. Some of the young, especially those involved in radical politics, view Christianity and Judaism as the tribal religions of a bankrupt Western civilization; to endorse them is to endorse racism, militarism, imperialism, and capitalism, and anything else is preferable.

At its peak, there were about ten thousand Children of God, who came to believe that former Baptist minister David Berg was the Messiah. By 1974, they claimed to have 120 communes in the United States. Berg took the name Moses Berg, claimed revelations from God, and began writing letters to replace the Bible. Twice, he unsuccessfully predicted the end of the world, but followers continued to collect money and study the gospel of "Mo." Accused in the 1970s of advocating prostitution on the part of female members, incest, opposition to marriage, and irregular financial dealings, Berg began moving his followers to Europe, but his disciples still recruit in the United States, often using aliases such as the Christian Faith Movement.

The Unification Church was founded in 1951 in South Korea by Sun Myung Moon, who claimed to be a messiah. He said that he learned this in a vision in which Christ, the Messiah of the first Advent, spoke to him. Using some elements of Taoism and Buddhism, Moon preached repentance, claiming that he could redeem the world if the church were successful in unifying and governing it. Claiming to be "Lord of the Second Advent," Moon could succeed where Jesus Christ had failed. To accomplish his mission he moved to the United States, where he had forty thousand followers by the early 1980s and church-owned businesses worth about $100 million. Moon spent some time in prison on tax evasion charges. His church does not avoid political involvement, and it owns one of the two major newspapers in Washington, D.C.

Swami Prabhupada was sixty-one years old in 1966 when he came to America and founded the International Society of Krishna Consciousness, also known as Hare Krishna. This meditative religion focuses on the worship of three deities, Brahma, Vishnu, and Shiva. Lord Krishna was the eighth incarnation of Vishnu, and is honored by dancing, chanting, and singing. Worship in these forms, it is claimed, drives ignorance from the human soul. The word "Hare" in Hindu religions means "the energy of God." Followers avoid eating meat, shun luxuries, and practice strict asceticism, usually in monastic communities. Men and women are often segregated, and sex and marriage are not encouraged. The movement supports itself through the sale of flowers, incense, buttons, and literature. Though there could be several thousand members at a given time, tens of thousands of middle-class young people have passed through it. Hindus of all persuasions accounted for three-tenths of a percent of the population in 1990.

Prior drug use often was associated with the decision to join Hare Krishna and other new religions. Through drugs, some felt they had religious experiences, which they sought to revive or continue without drugs in morally conservative movements such as Hare Krishna, the Unification Church, or the Jesus People.

Judeo-Christian dominance was challenged by numerous Muslims and adherents of Eastern religions. About 2 million belonged to Eastern religions, but most of them were immigrants from Asia. It is notable, however, that half the Koreans living in the United States are Presbyterians. Most were Presbyterian before coming here, and some converted after they arrived. Korean Americans have over 1,200 Presbyterian churches, as well as 500 Southern Baptist and 250 United Methodist churches. These Korean Christians work hard, are economically successful, and see their churches as centers of community life. Their Christianity facilitates assimilation. About half of Asian immigrants are Christian; most are Protestant, but Filipinos are predominantly Roman Catholic.

There are many varieties of Buddhism in the United States. Among them are Zen Buddhists from many countries, and the separatist and authoritarian Nichiren Shoshsu Soka Gakkai from Japan, who claim the ability to cure and transform lives, including economically. Entertainer Tina Turner is probably the best-known of its American converts. Many Americans have embraced Zen Buddhism, and today only a fifth of American Zen centers are led by Asians. Allan Watts, a practitioner and advocate of Zen, holds that it has two aspects, "square Zen," or discipline and meditation, and "beat Zen," the sense of total liberation.

Forty-seven organizations were represented at the 1988 American Buddhist Congress in Los Angeles. American Buddhism tends to center on the laity and avoids the traditional emphasis on a hierarchy of monks. It also attempts to meet the concerns of women. There were some sexual and financial scandals in the 1980s. Buddhism appears to be losing many to Christianity, agnosticism, and secular humanism.

There are over four hundred thousand Hindus, who usually worship in their homes rather than in temples. In the 1960s and 1970s, a substantial number of Americans traveled to India in search of inner peace and enlightenment by studying with gurus, such as Bhagwan Shree Rajneesh.

By 1995, it was estimated that there were between 4.6 million and 5 million Muslims in the United States and Canada. There are in excess of a thousand Islamic centers and about half a million mosqued Muslims. The largest numbers of Muslims worship in New York, southern California, Chicago, Washington, and Toronto. Multicultural congregations are to be found in 70 percent of the mosques. The largest groups of Muslims are African Americans or Indo-Pakistanis; Arab Americans are the third largest group. One-fifth of the mosques follow Imam W. Deen Mohammed, who brought the Black Muslims into the orthodox Muslim movement. The Islamic Society of North America claims the adherence of 40 percent of the mosques, and the remaining mosques are unaffiliated.

Most American Muslims belong to the Sunni sect of Islam, but there are numerous followers of the more fundamentalist and often militant Shiite sect. The process of assimilation frequently blurs the distinctions between these sects. The oldest standing mosque in the United States is in Cedar Rapids. Beginning as a community center for Muslims, it became a mosque in 1934 and is known as the Mother Mosque of America. Today members of the Cedar Rapids Islamic community are proud of how well they have assimilated; some have married outside their faith. Muslims, particularly of the first generation, oppose pornography, sex outside the family, and abortion. They adhere to family values that are quite similar to those of conservative Christians and Jews. Like other first-generation parents, they are concerned that their children remain faithful to their religion and its values.

Feminist witchcraft is another recent development. Its adherents reject traditional Judaism and Christianity and claim that women have a higher nature than men. They worship the deity of the earth, the Goddess, whom they sometimes call Sophia. They believe that women participate in her divine nature. One of their most prominent practitioners is Starhawk, who teaches that the Goddess is the source of life and "is nature [and] is flesh." To better get in touch with their natures, some worshipers of the Goddess use Tarot cards and astrology.

Mainline Protestant churches have suffered significant declines in membership and attendance, and a much smaller percentage of Roman Catholics attend mass every Sunday than at the end of World War II. Nevertheless, it is clear that there is no decline in religiosity in the United States as it approaches the twenty-first century. Religiosity is being expressed in the growth of Pentecostal and evangelical bodies and in increased interest in unconventional approaches to spirituality. The great interest in sects, the occult, and unconventional approaches to Christianity suggests that many people find that mainstream religious bodies are not meeting their needs. Nevertheless, there is not enough evidence to suggest that another great religious revival is about to occur.

There has been a sharp decline in a sense of community and an increase in selfish individualism. Individualism has triumphed over the equalitarian ethos, with corrosive privatism and the deterioration of community values. Robert Bellah and his associates have argued in *Habits of the Heart* that the chief ethical rule for many has become radical individualism: the individual should be able to do whatever she or he finds rewarding. The authors believe it is essential to preserve a "morally coherent life" to provide a wholeness that has been lost as a result of specialization and the overdevelopment of individualism.

The serious deterioration of community and excessive emphasis upon individualism probably began with the market revolution in the early nineteenth century; these tendencies were accelerated by subjecting much of life to the demands of the marketplace. The tendencies toward egoism and diminished community are inherent in classical liberal thought; the market revolution unleashed them and accelerated their growth. Bellah and his associates correctly indicate that the resolution of these problems lies in large measure in strengthening the culture's ties to its two taproots, Jeffersonian political thought and the nation's religious heritage. It is argued that devotion to the nation's religious heritage and Jeffersonian egalitarianism can diminish human antagonisms and serve as a basis for community and a sense of mutual responsibility. Without these, there can be no long-term sociopolitical order or economic productivity.

No sharp decline in religiosity appears to be on the horizon. Evangelical and Pentecostal growth are likely to continue. Mainstream religions face the risk of losing more members, but they share a common commitment to working for the establishment of the Kingdom of God on earth. They must now seek a way to accelerate this movement without losing adherents by diluting their message in futile attempts to come to terms with the dominant culture.

Bibliography

Aikman, David. "Rescue to the Christians." *American Spectator* 29 (July 1996): 22.

Bednarowski, Mary Farrell. "Widening the Banks of the Mainstream: Women Constructing Theologies." In *Women's Leadership in Marginal Religions*, ed. Catherine Wessinger, pp. 211–231. Urbana: University of Illinois Press, 1993.

————."Women in Occult America." In *The Occult in America,* ed. Howard Kerr and Charles Crow, pp. 177–195. Urbana: University of Illinois Press, 1986.

Bellah, Robert, Richard Madsen, William M. Sullivan, Ann Swidler, and Steven M. Tipton. *Habits of the Heart: Individualism and Commitment in American Life.* New York: Harper and Row, 1985.

Bloesch, Donald G. *The Future of Evangelical Christianity: A Call for Unity and Diversity.* Colorado Springs: Helmers and Howard, 1988.

Bratt, James D. "A New Narrative for American Religious History?" *Fides et Historia* 23 (fall 1991): 19–30.

Briggs, Kenneth A. *Holy Siege: The Year That Shook Catholic America.* San Francisco: Harper, 1992.

Carroll, Jackson W., Douglas W. Johnson, and Martin Marty. *Religion in America: 1950 to the Present.* New York: Harper and Row, 1979.

Casey, William Van Etten, and Philip Noble, eds. *The Berrigans.* New York: Avon, 1971.

Chittister, Joan. "A Deeper Faith May Shake Church, State." *National Catholic Reporter* (June 28, 1996): 19.

Cohn, Werner. "The Politics of American Jews." In *The Jews: Social Patterns of an American Group,* ed. Lawrence H. Fuchs, pp. 614–626. Glencoe, IL: Free Press, 1960.

Colaianni, James. *The Catholic Left: The Crisis of Radicalism Within the Church.* Philadelphia: Chilton Book Company, 1968.

Cox, Harvey. *The Secular City: Secularization and Urbanization in Theological Perspective.* New York: Macmillan, 1966.

Daly, Mary. *The Church and the Second Sex: With a New Feminist Postchristian Introduction.* New York: Harper, 1975.

Diggins, John Patrick. *The Proud Decades: America in War and Peace, 1941–1960.* New York: Norton, 1988.

Dolan, Jay P. *The American Catholic Experience: A History from Colonial Times to the Present.* Garden City: Doubleday, 1985.

Dolan, Jay P., R. Scott Appleby, Patricia Byrne, and Debra Campbell. *Transforming Parish Ministry: The Changing Roles of Catholic Clergy, Laity, and Women Religious.* New York: Crossroad, 1989.

Elazar, Daniel J. "The Development of the American Synagogue." In *American Synagogue History: A Bibliography and State-of-the-Field Survey,* ed. Alexandra Sheckert Korros and Jonathan D. Sarna, pp. 23–53. New York: Markus Wiener, 1988.

Ellwood, Robert S., Jr. *Alternative Altars: Unconventional and Eastern Spirituality in America.* Chicago: University of Chicago Press, 1979.

Finke, Roger, and Rodney Stark. *The Churching of America, 1776–1990: Winners and Losers in Our Religious Economy.* New Brunswick: Rutgers University Press, 1992.

Gannon, Thomas M., and David F. Schwartz. "Church Finances in Crisis." *Social Compass* 39 (March 1992): 111–120.

Gitlin, Todd. *The Sixties: Years of Hope, Days of Rage.* New York: Bantam Books, 1987.

Gleason, Philip. *Keeping the Faith: American Catholicism, Past and Present.* Notre Dame: University of Notre Dame Press, 1987.

Goldy, Robert G. *The Emergence of Jewish Theology in America*. Bloomington: Indiana University Press, 1990.

Greeley, Andrew M. "The Abortion Debate and the Catholic Subculture." *America* 167 (July 11, 1992): 13–15.

————. *Religious Change in America*. Cambridge: Harvard University Press, 1989.

Green, John, Lyman Kellstadt, James Guth, and Corwin Smidt. "Who Elected Clinton: A Collision of Values." *First Things* 75 (August/September 1997): 35–40.

Handy, Robert T. *A Christian America: Protestant Hopes and Historical Realities*. New York: Oxford University Press, 1984.

Hauerwas, Stanley. *After Christendom? How the Church Is to Behave if Freedom, Justice, and a Christian Nation Are Bad Ideas*. Nashville: Abingdon Press, 1992.

Heelas, Paul. "The New Age in Cultural Context: The Premodern, the Modern, and the Postmodern." *Religion* 23 (April 1993): 103–116.

Herberg, Will. *Protestant-Catholic-Jew: An Essay in American Religious Sociology*. Garden City: Doubleday, 1955.

Hitchcock, James. *Catholicism and Modernity: Confrontation or Capitulation*. New York: Seabury Press, 1979.

Hodgson, Godfrey. *America in Our Time: From World War II to Nixon, What Happened and Why*. New York: Vintage Books, 1976.

Hoge, Dean R. "Why Catholics Drop Out." In *Falling from Faith*, ed. David G. Bromley, pp. 81–99. Newbury Park, CA: Sage, 1988.

Hunter, James Davison. *Culture Wars: The Struggle to Define America*. New York: HarperCollins, 1990.

Jaffe, James. *The American Jews*. New York: Random House, 1968.

Jelsen, Ted G. *The Political Mobilization of Religious Beliefs*. New York: Praeger, 1991.

Johnson, Benton, Dean R. Hoge, and Donald A. Luidens. "Mainline Churches: The Real Reason for Decline." *First Things* 41 (March 1993): 13–25.

Johnson, Haynes. *Sleepwalking Through History: America in the Reagan Years*. New York: Anchor Books, 1991.

Johnson, Joan. *The Cult Movement*. New York: Franklin Watts, 1984.

Joseph, Peter. *Good Times: An Oral History of America in the 1960s*. New York: William Morrow, 1974.

Kelley, Dean. *Why Conservative Churches Are Growing*. New York: Harper and Row, 1972.

Kellstedt, Lyman A., John C. Green, James L. Guth, and Corwin E. Smidt. " 'It's the Culture, Stupid!' 1992 and Our Political Future." *First Things* 42 (April 1994): 28–33.

Kosmin, Barry A., and Seymour P. Lachman. *One Nation Under God: Religion in Contemporary American Society*. New York: Crown Trade Publications, 1993.

Leuchtenburg, William E. *A Troubled Feast: American Society Since 1945*. Boston: Little, Brown, 1983.

Linder, Robert D., and Richard V. Pierand. "Ronald Reagan, Civil Religion, and the New Religious Right in America." *Fides et Historia* 23 (fall 1991): 57–73.

Mannion, M. Francis. "The Church and the Voices of Feminism." *America* 165 (October 5, 1991): 212–216, 228.

Marty, Martin E. *Under God Indivisible, 1941–1960*. Chicago: University of Chicago Press, 1996.

McGreevey, John T. "Racial Justice and the People of God: The Second Vatican Council, the Civil Rights Movement, and American Catholics." *Religion and American Culture* 4 (summer 1994): 221–254.

Moore, R. Laurence. "American Religion as Popular Culture." *Religious Studies Review* 18 (July 1992): 190–195.

Nelson, Lynn D. "Disaffiliation, Desacralization, and Political Views." In *Falling From the Faith,* ed. David G. Bromley, pp. 122–142. Newbury Park, CA: Sage, 1988.

Nelson, Lynn D., and David G. Bromley. "Another Look at Conversion and Defection in Conservative Churches." In *Falling from the Faith,* ed. David G. Bromley, pp. 47–61. Newbury Park, CA: Sage, 1988.

Redmont, Jane. *Generous Lives: American Catholic Women Today.* New York: William Morrow, 1992.

Reuther, Rosemary Radford. "The Women-Church Movement in Contemporary Christianity." In *Women's Leadership in Marginal Religions,* ed. Catherine Wessinger, pp. 196–210. Urbana: University of Illinois Press, 1993.

Ribuffo, Leo P. "God and Contemporary Politics." *Journal of American History* 79 (March 1993): 1515–1533.

Richardson, James T. "New Religious Movements in the United States: A Review." *Social Compass* 30 (1983): 85–110.

Ritchley, A. James. *Religion in American Public Life.* Washington D.C.: Brookings Institution, 1986.

Roche, Douglas J. *The Catholic Revolution.* New York: David McKay Company, 1968.

Rosenberg, Stuart E. *America Is Different.* London: Thomas Nelson and Sons, 1964.

Roszak, Theodore. *The Making of a Counter-Culture: Reflections on the Technocratic Society and Its Youthful Opposition.* Garden City: Doubleday, 1969.

Seidler, John. "Contested Accommodation: The Catholic Church as a Special Case of Social Change." *Social Forces* 64 (June 1986): 847–874.

Shafer, Byron E., ed. *The End of Realignment? Interpreting American Electoral Eras.* Madison: University of Wisconsin Press, 1991.

Sklare, Marshall, and Joseph Greenblum. *Jewish Identity on the Suburban Frontier.* New York: Basic Books, 1967.

Slobin, Mark. *Chosen Voices: The Story of the American Cantorate.* Urbana: University of Illinois Press, 1989.

Weigel, George. *Tranquillitas Ordinis: The Present Failure and Future Promise of American Catholic Thought.* New York: Oxford University Press, 1987.

Wills, Gary. *Bare Ruined Choirs: Doubt, Prophecy, and Radical Religion.* New York: Doubleday, 1972.

————. *Reagan's America: Innocents at Home.* New York: Doubleday, 1987.

————. *Under God: Religion and American Politics.* New York: Simon and Schuster, 1990.

Winkler, Allan M. *Modern America: The United States from World War II to the Present.* New York: Harper and Row, 1985.

Wittner, Laurence S. *Cold War America: From Hiroshima to Watergate.* New York: Praeger, 1974.

Wuthnow, Robert. *The Restructuring of American Thought: Society and Faith Since World War II.* Princeton: Princeton University Press, 1988.

Index

About the Author

Donald C. Swift is a professor of history at Edinboro University of Pennsylvania. His special interests are American religious, cultural, and social history, and he has worked in a number of interdisciplinary situations.